HERESY, MAGIC
EARLY M...

European Culture and Society
General Editor: Jeremy Black

European Culture and Society Series
Series Standing Order
ISBN 0–333–7440–3
(*outside North America only*)

You can receive future titles in this series as they are published by placing a standing order. Please contact your bookseller or, in case of difficulty, write to us at the address below with your name and address, the title of the series and the ISBN quoted above.

Customer Services Department, Macmillan Distribution Ltd
Houndmills, Basingstoke, Hampshire RG21 6XS, England

HERESY, MAGIC, AND WITCHCRAFT IN EARLY MODERN EUROPE

Gary K. Waite

First published 2003 by
PALGRAVE MACMILLAN
Houndmills, Basingstoke, Hampshire RG21 6XS and
175 Fifth Avenue, New York, N.Y. 10010
Companies and representatives throughout the world

PALGRAVE MACMILLAN is the global academic imprint of the Palgrave Macmillan division of St. Martin's Press, LLC and of Palgrave Macmillan Ltd. Macmillan® is a registered trademark in the United States, United Kingdom and other countries. Palgrave is a registered trademark in the European Union and other countries.

ISBN 0–333–75433–6 hardback
ISBN 0–333–75434–4 paperback

This book is printed on paper suitable for recycling and made from fully managed and sustained forest sources.

A catalogue record for this book is available from the British Library.

Library of Congress Cataloging-in-Publication Data
Waite, Gary K., 1955–
Heresy, magic, and witchcraft in early modern Europe / Gary K. Waite.
    p.   cm. — (European culture and society)
    Includes bibliographical references and index.
    ISBN 0–333–75433–6(cloth) — ISBN 0–333–75434–4(pbk.)
    1. Witchcraft—Europe—History. 2. Magic—Europe—History.
    3. Reformation.   I. Title   II. Series.

BF1584.E85W35 2003
133.4′3′094—dc21

                                                                2002044802

10   9   8   7   6   5   4   3   2   1
12   11   10   09   08   07   06   05   04   03

Printed in China

CONTENTS

ACKNOWLEDGEMENTS

I have benefited immensely from the support and advice of many individuals and institutions while researching and composing this book. Although I have been pursuing this subject for many years, the bulk of the writing took place during a sabbatical leave in 2000–2001. The latter portion of this time was spent in the heady climate of Cambridge, U.K., one of the great academic cities in the world. I am deeply grateful to the (then) President, Dame Gillian Beer and the Fellows of Clare Hall for admitting me into their college for the spring and summer of 2001. This provided an opportunity not only to avail myself of the collection and services of one of the great university libraries, but also to receive a unique stimulus to creative thought through the informal interaction with international fellows and graduate students that is the hallmark of Clare Hall. That all members of my family enjoyed their stay as well speaks volumes of the college's friendly and supportive atmosphere. I am thankful also for the generous financial support provided by my home institution, the University of New Brunswick (UNB), especially the History Department, as well as by my in-laws, John and Irene Hayward. Earlier research trips were funded by UNB and by a major research grant from the Social Sciences and Humanities Research Council of Canada (1993–7). Susan Meyer provided helpful research assistance. I am also thankful for the editorial advice and assistance of Terka Acton and Sonya Barker of Palgrave Macmillan, their copyeditor, Tessa Hanford, as well as of the publisher's anonymous reader. It is an honour to be included in Palgrave Macmillan's European Culture and Society series under the editorship of Jeremy Black.

Teaching is an unrivalled path to learning, and I have benefited greatly from teaching the subject matter of this book for many years now at UNB. I am thankful that my students have forced me to probe many questions deeper than I was perhaps inclined to do. I hope that this book will assist all students to continue exploring the power of religious belief, fear of doubt, and irrational suspicion of the "Other", both in the past and in the present.

My greatest debt of gratitude extends to my wife, Katherine Hayward. She has borne a great deal of the family care burden while I pursued the research and writing of this book, and she has remained an unswerving support throughout. She has constantly pressed me to write this book in as interesting and accessible fashion possible, although I am not entirely confident I have reached her standard. To our daughters, Jessica and Eleanor, I give my thanks for their patience with my constant distraction from "real life". It is to Jessica that I dedicate this book as she embarks on the adult adventure.

INTRODUCTION

This book explores the mental terrain of early modern Europe, roughly speaking from 1400 to 1700, a world both comfortably familiar and fantastically strange. If this study highlights the latter, it is only because of the author's belief that it is impossible to comprehend a culture without an appreciation of its darker side. It will therefore take seriously what early modern Europeans believed about the Devil. Even today, belief in this evil persona continues to inspire hostility toward his supposed minions, often leading to allegations of the existence of an organized Satanic ring committing horrific acts of ritual abuse and murder, despite the lack of any supporting forensic evidence.[1] The image of a diabolical conspiracy still possesses latent power to terrorize. In early modern Europe it was central to religious discourse and intellectual debate and ultimately contributed to the seventeenth-century's Scientific Revolution.[2]

Diabolical conspiracy theories laid the foundation for some of the worst judicial persecutions in European history: pogroms against Jews, heresy trials, and the horrendous witch-hunts of the later sixteenth and seventeenth centuries. There is no way to pass off these horrific events as anomalies or as moments of collective psychosis. Instead, they were fully consistent with several basic presuppositions about the workings of the cosmos which, during periods of crisis or religious turmoil, inspired actions of great cruelty.

In this discussion we will explore attitudes toward and prosecution of religious deviance (heresy), magic, and witchcraft from the fifteenth to the seventeenth centuries across Europe, with particular attention to the Reformation and Counter-Reformation era. The study takes seriously the power of religious beliefs to influence behavior, public and private

1

and, conversely, the ways in which political, economic, and social consid-
erations reshaped those ideas. It will examine the reasons for popular
religious dissent, and the means by which church leaders, first Catholic,
then Protestant, sought to counteract doubt, skepticism, heresy, and
popular magical beliefs. In an era when the central identity of both the
individual and society was religious at its core, dissenting from orthodox
teachings on even "minor" theological points was a threat to the officially
sanctioned conception of the cosmos and was readily criminalized. However, doubt is a universal aspect of the human psyche which, when suppressed by those who fear its articulation, often breaks out in the
assertion of irrational beliefs or projection of guilt. Those targeted as
responsible for inspiring such doubt were often attacked as a means of
alleviating the fear of disbelief.

Since in the sixteenth century magic and religion were completely
interwoven, it will be a primary goal of this study to map out some of the
places where these fields intersected. Because of the intense specialization
within the history discipline and the burgeoning number of scholarly
studies on each of these subjects, this study makes no pretense at compre-
hensiveness, but seeks merely to assist students of early modern Europe
to appreciate the dense complexity of life and thought in that period.

Some definitions of terms might be useful. Following the classic study
by Peter Burke we define culture as the complex set of attitudes, beliefs,
and rituals that underpins any society.[3] Of course the way a university-
trained clergyman experienced this shared culture was very different
from that of an urban artisan or rural peasant. For one thing, literacy in
Latin, the *lingua franca* of higher learning and the Church, was the sole
preserve of members of the "higher" culture of clerics, professors, and
aristocracy, although the development and spread of printing presses
and cheap paper helped create a vernacular counterpoint for laypeople.
No longer satisfied with being passive recipients of official religious
culture, literate city dwellers especially insisted on greater control over
their religious experience and were less forgiving of clerical failings.
They expressed such views by their voracious appetite for religious
publications, by creating and joining religious confraternities or brother-
hoods, by writing and performing vernacular religious drama, or by
forming heretical alternatives to the approved Church. They also articu-
lated an intense dissatisfaction with the religious status quo and with an
often poorly informed clerical elite. Such sentiment fed directly into the
Reformation begun by the German monk Martin Luther, but was not
contained by it.

Religion and religious culture therefore feature heavily in this study. Simply put, religion is the attempt of humans to communicate with a higher being and to be subject to its dictates. At times religion included efforts to influence the supernatural world, although there is always a sense that devotees of a god are ultimately at its mercy. Religion is always nonrational, for its tenets cannot be proven by empirical testing and even when such nonrational thought accords fully with what is known empirically about the world, it still might lead to irrational beliefs or actions.[4]

In the Judeo-Christian tradition, the cosmos was ruled by one God (for most Christians one God in three persons – Father, Son, and Holy Spirit) with a supporting cast of semi-divine beings or angels. For Catholic Christians this heavenly domain also included some of the Christian dead who had died as pious heroes or martyrs for the faith. These saints, including the Virgin Mary and the twelve apostles, acted as officially sanctioned mediators between the supernatural and natural worlds. For the mediocre majority the medieval Church created purgatory, a place between heaven and earth where deceased believers were purified of remaining sin. As Jacques Le Goff notes, the natural and supernatural worlds, the past, present, and future, were "conjoined in a seamless fabric."[5]

Most ordinary believers had at best a rudimentary understanding of official church dogma. At this level Gavin Langmuir's distinction between religiosity and religion is particularly helpful: religiosity is the set of beliefs of an individual that help develop and maintain his or her identity and place in the world, while religion is the social codification of those beliefs prescribed by those in authority.[6] There was thus a wide variation in the religiosity of a populace, with those who closely harmonized their "nonrational consciousness and conduct" at the saintly end, and those with little such coherence at the irreligious or indifferent end.[7] Most of those whom the religious authorities identified as heretics were deeply religious, despite the Church's attempts to castigate them as atheists. In medieval Europe, all people, apart from Jews, were by law members of the Roman Catholic Church and depended utterly on its clergy and means of divine grace, the sacraments, for their spiritual life. These sacraments worked *ex opere operato*, by the divine power invested in them, and neither by the recipient's nor the performer's particular religiosity. At birth children were baptized into the Christian fold, and their stages of life marked by five of the other six sacraments: confirmation at the age of accountability (usually by twelve years); confession and penance at least yearly thereafter; participation in the eucharistic Mass which reenacted Christ's sacrifice on the cross; marriage; and at the end of their life, extreme unction, when the dying gave their last confession and received the consecrated bread or Host for the last time. The seventh sacrament, holy orders, was administered only to priests, investing in them the spiritual power to perform the other sacraments and control the eternal destiny of their parishioners.

The Eucharist especially revealed the clergy's power. Taking the bread and wine into his hands, the priest spoke the words of consecration in Latin (a language not understood by most celebrants) and ordinary bread and wine became the true and living body of Christ, God himself. For various reasons the wine was withheld from laypeople. In the thirteenth century the great Dominican theologian Thomas Aquinas (1225–74) provided a learned explanation of this process using the ancient philosopher Aristotle's system of logic. Aristotle believed that every object contained within it its eternal form or essence, so Aquinas argued that when the priest said the words of consecration the inner essence of the bread became the body of Christ while the outer forms – texture, taste, appearance, etc. – remained those of bread. By the late Middle Ages, this transformation of ordinary matter into the divine being had become the object of increasing devotion, and the Host was commonly held aloft on a pole in a glass case called a monstrance and paraded through a community during moments of crisis. Most people could not comprehend Aquinas' explanation of the bread's "transubstantiation", as it was called, hence it became a particular target of skepticism.

At the popular level especially, but not exclusively, the intermingling of religion with magic becomes most obvious. Valerie Flint's definition of magic as "the exercise of a preternatural control over nature by human beings, with the assistance of forces more powerful than they" is a very helpful one in this regard.[8] Even though the early medieval missionaries had demonized the gods of the Celts, Franks, and Saxons, to ease the conversion to Christianity they allowed many pagan practices to be incorporated into popular Catholicism. The result was a fusion of beliefs in which it was no contradiction to use priests or the sacramentals – the blessed objects of Catholic ritual such as holy oil, holy water, or the consecrated Host – in magical efforts to protect or heal.

Those believed to have some control over preternatural power included not only the clergy, but also saints, who left behind their body parts as tangible conduits of divine grace, and informal magical dabblers known as wise women and cunning men who provided their neighbors with medicinal cures, love potions, divinatory services, assistance in finding lost objects, and communication with the dead. Richard Kieckhefer has described magic as a "kind of crossroads" where religion and science, popular and learned forms of culture, and reality and fiction intersected.[9] Standing at this intersection, it was believed, was the Devil, in Christian tradition Lucifer, one of God's leading angels who rebelled against the Creator and was cast out of heaven with his fellow rebels to reside in the earth's atmosphere. Here they plotted their revenge, marking humanity for special attention. The widespread famine, devastating bubonic plague, destructive warfare, and popular uprisings of the fourteenth and fifteenth centuries were therefore seen as Satan's handiwork.

In this era of deep distress, then, the Church saw it absolutely necessary to crack down on all lay challenges to its authority and monopoly over spiritual power. From a sign of weakness requiring mere confession to a priest, the expression of religious doubt became a potential breeding ground for skepticism and heresy. Church leaders therefore developed various means to suppress heterodoxy, most effectively the office of Inquisitor, whose methodology in extracting confessions from supposed heretics was readily copied by secular rulers who likewise saw the danger to civic unity inherent in religious dissent.

While the fifteenth-century Renaissance humanists increased the pressure by attacking Aquinas' philosophical and theological construct as well as popular credulity and superstition, the following century's religious reform movements initiated by the German monk Martin Luther set off a profound period of religious crisis, conflict, and scrutiny of many hitherto unassailable dogmas. As political rulers vied for supremacy, they legislated upon their populace adherence to specific religious affiliations, each with its own catalogue of precisely defined doctrines called confessions, as a means of ensuring total obedience. A few individuals ultimately rejected this confessionalization altogether. Protestants and Catholics found different means to battle against these, the former emphasizing a largely internalized faith with few tangible aids while the latter placed renewed emphasis on the power of the priests and sacraments.

One of the battlegrounds in this confessional conflict was the religious/magical culture of the common people. The assertion that there was a strong correlation between the religious conflict of the Reformation and the rise of witch-hunting was most famously made in 1967 by Hugh Trevor-Roper in his brilliant essay "The European Witch-craze of the Sixteenth and Seventeenth Centuries". Trevor-Roper argued that when Protestant and Catholic leaders met with serious opposition to their efforts to inculcate villagers with correct doctrine, they resorted to the late-medieval device of identifying the dissidents as witches and gaining broad support for their evangelizing campaign among locals who wished to be rid of such evil beings.[10] Trevor-Roper's essay set off a debate that is still raging, although most scholars of witch-hunts now suggest that despite his elegant and compelling arguments, Trevor-Roper's position neglects the fact that pressure for witch persecution arose not from the elite but from the common people who tended to accuse neighbors – mostly correligionists – whom they had long suspected of practicing witchcraft. As Gustav Henningsen asserted in his 1980 study of the Basque witch panic of 1610–14,

> the witch-hunting of the western European villages throughout the sixteenth and seventeenth centuries had very little to do with religious persecution. It was in fact entirely related to the function of witch belief in the social life of the time. That popular and traditional witch-hunting was encouraged by legislation and incited by sermons preached against "limbs of Satan" is quite another matter.[11]

Is there then no basis for postulating a pronounced influence for the Reformation on the rise of witch-hunting? In his groundbreaking study of witch-hunting in southwest Germany, H. C. Erik Midelfort found some validity "in correlating witch hunts with periods of religious conflict and renewal, but the correlation is still incomplete, and the reasons for the beginnings of large-scale witch hunting remain unclear."[12] Jean Delumeau, Robert Muchembled, Brian Levack, Stuart Clark, E. William Monter, and several others have since discovered considerable evidence suggestive of some interrelation between the religious reforms and the witch panic of the later sixteenth century, although there still remains no single, overarching interpretive key to explain the rise of witch-hunting. Instead, a multivalent approach is required, one that takes seriously the various social, economic, legal, political, psychological, biological, and religious factors that combined in particular ways to spark witch-hunting.[13]

The witch-hunts have been the subject of a vast amount of scholarly and nonscholarly attention. For some time the popular view has been dominated by the interpretation of Egyptologist Margaret Murray, who asserted in 1921 that the witch persecution of the sixteenth and seventeenth centuries was the elite's finally successful campaign to eradicate the pre-Christian, fertility religion of the common people. In her treatment, the witch sabbath was merely the demonized version of real gatherings of pagans.[14] The final demolition of Murray's thesis was undertaken in

1975 by Norman Cohn, although it still retains some of its considerable popularity, despite the lack of any clear, supporting evidence.[15] For Cohn, there was no reality behind the sabbath meetings, only the vivid imaginings of Inquisitors and judges.

In recent years, two interpretative schools have dominated the field of witchcraft studies. The first is in many respects a reaction to the posture of Trevor-Roper and his predecessors who made a great deal of the early modern demonological literature and governmental campaigns to enforce religious and moral conformity. Instead of focusing on the ideas about witchcraft, as expressed by the educated classes, scholars began applying the newer approaches of social history in their quest to uncover the beliefs and actions of the ordinary people of Europe. In these works, epitomized in the profoundly influential study of Alan Macfarlane, witchcraft accusations were a product almost entirely of village conflict and communal tensions, and had little to do with elite concerns.[16] The other interpretation arose at about the same time, and concentrated on why women were the overwhelming majority of victims of witch perse-cution. It became all too easy to inflate the number of witch burnings (sometimes as high as nine million) in a polemical effort to adopt the witch persecution as a "woman's holocaust" and to see it as merely the most egregious example of the deleterious effects of misogyny. While it helps to explain why so many of the victims were women, this approach still has difficulty with the 20–25 percent of victims who were men (in a few hunts men were in the majority). It also does not take seriously enough the religious and magical beliefs of the era as precipitating factors in the rise of witch persecution.[17]

This study contributes to the discussion by returning to the question of the Reformation's involvement in the formulation of the concept of the diabolical witch sect. At the same time, it will seek to incorporate the best research from the social history schools in its efforts to evaluate the religious beliefs and fears of both the learned minority and illiterate majority (and those who fell somewhere in between). While acknowledg-ing that misogyny was indeed a factor in why women were more often the victims of witch trials than men, this book does not deal extensively with the gender of accused witches, except to examine the impact of the religious reform of the sixteenth century on attitudes toward women, and point readers to other, reliable works on the subject. Even so, the literature for both the Reformation and the witch-hunts is immense, thus this book will merely highlight some of the points of intersection and direct the reader to the more specialized literature.

As we shall see, in several regions witchcraft trials began just as heresy trials against Protestants and Anabaptists ended, suggesting that heresy and witchcraft trials shared the purpose of "eliminating individuals who were believed to be in league with Satan and corrupting society."[18] While church leaders, both Protestant and Catholic, were determined to suppress religious dissent, this project was massively overshadowed after the middle of the sixteenth century by the fear of a nightmarish conspiracy led by Satan and fulfilled by groups of women and men to whom he had granted magical powers in the hope of overthrowing Christian society. This conspiracy theory had first developed in the fifteenth century, but its proponents had great difficulty in convincing the various authorities of its real danger. The Reformation, especially its more radical manifestations, helped persuade princes and magistrates of the seriousness of Satan's machinations.

The book's first chapter provides a cursory introduction to the mental world of late-medieval Europeans, with special attention to the gradual accretion of conspiratorial theories that led to persecution of Jews, lepers, heretics, magicians, and, in the fifteenth century, witches. By the fourteenth century the Inquisitors appointed by the Pope to investigate heresy complaints were turning their attention to magical beliefs and practices, superimposing what they had learned from their interrogations of heretics onto supposed magicians and devil worshipers. Anxiety about heretical threats and alleged criminal acts of Jews, such as the ritual murder of young Christian boys, also continued to spark violent reaction. Princes learned how to use accusations of heresy and diabolical magic as tools of political propaganda. Fears of diabolical witchcraft spread as a result of clerical propaganda and, in the 1430s, the Council of Basel was a major center for the dissemination of learned demonological notions. The Pope encouraged such preoccupation in part to distract church reformers from clamoring for the decentralization of church authority in favor of conciliar governance. With the publication in 1487 of the *Malleus Maleficarum*, the witch-hunting manual of the German Inquisitor Heinrich Krämer (Institoris), the stereotype of Satan's most frightening allies, female witches, was generally complete. Yet there was, with the exception of individual trials here and there, a lull in witch-hunting. After 1521 printers showed no interest in further reprints of the *Malleus* until the revival of large-scale witch prosecution after 1560.

Chapter 2 will summarize the major developments in the Reformation movements; highlight the widespread preoccupation with the coming apocalyptical judgment; describe the rise of movements for radical reform; and pursue the question of why the authorities came to see these as a diabolical threat worthy of the most vicious repression. Chapter 3 will examine in greater detail the polemical rhetoric used by religious leaders of all camps and discuss the potential impact of such propaganda on the revival of diabolical stereotypes. Some attention will be paid here to the question of why women became a principal target of conspiratorial thinking. Many scholars have pointed to the Reformers' attempts to reinforce patriarchal marriage as one factor. This chapter will also explore how Anabaptism inadvertently contributed to this general targeting of women as witches. The growing fear of "atheism" likewise spurred many leaders to search for a secret or fifth column movement of diabolical agents seeking to sap the inner strength of Christianity through the spread of doubt and skepticism while witches attacked the health of the body politic through evil magic.

Chapter 4 will describe in detail how beliefs about the Devil, magic, and witchcraft were transformed in the Reformations' religious and moral crusading. Here the discussion will engage both the learned debates regarding the Devil, exorcism, and magic and the popular beliefs, practices, and rituals relating to these subjects. Reformers' reactions to the revival of interest in learned forms of magic – the so-called Occult Sciences – will be of major concern. Moreover, the chapter will also describe the "typical" witch trials and demonic possession cases on the eve of the witch-hunts and how these related to the preoccupations of Reformers. Using their tools of propaganda – the sermon, the woodcut image, and the printing press – Reformers generally sought to alter or suppress aspects of "popular culture" viewed as superstitious or pagan. Yet they used some popular beliefs and practices, after properly sanitizing them, to convince the common people about the veracity of the "true faith." Witch trials, exorcisms, and ritual desecration became powerful tools in the Reformation battles.

Following the recent trend in regional analysis of witch-hunting, Chapter 5 will focus particularly on the impact of the religious controversies on local witchcraft beliefs and persecution. The heartland of witch-hunting was also the center of religious conflict and radical dissent. The emphasis in this section will be on exploring the interplay between religious belief and conflict and witch-hunting in the regions most affected by fear of diabolical conspiracies: the Holy Roman Empire, France and Switzerland, and the British Isles.

The book concludes with a similar survey of regions which either suppressed witch-hunting early, such as the Dutch Republic, or which were never captivated by such panics, such as the Mediterranean Inquisitions, or which joined the fray late, notably Scandinavia and Eastern Europe. It postulates a correspondence between the type of religious culture sponsored by the state and the level of witch-hunting in a region. It also pursues the religious factors behind the ending of witch persecution in the phenomenon's heartland. As rulers and citizens developed alternatives to the traditional conception of a unitary religious identity and learned to tolerate the religious "Other", they became less susceptible to heed calls to attack Satan's minions.

1

THE DEVIL, HERESY, AND MAGIC IN THE LATER MIDDLE AGES

To know where a treasure is hidden, first a person must make a general confession of all his sins, under a waxing moon, on a Sunday, when the Sun is in Leo, early in the morning. And when you first arise, sprinkle yourself with holy water, saying the antiphon, *Asperges me, domine, ysopo*, etc., in its entirety. Then go to a crucifix and say before it, *Miserere mei, deus*...in its entirety, gazing constantly at the crucifix, with utter devotion. And when you say these things, then say most devoutly and with contrite heart, "O rabbi, rabbi, my king and my God, and Lord of lords, you who are creator of all things, hear the prayer which I, a wretched and unworthy creature, make,...And I pray you by your kings...that on the following night Haram, a benign spirit, may come to me in my sleep and enkindle my heart and my mind, that I may know how to find a treasure..."

Richard Kieckhefer, ed. *Forbidden Rites: A Necromancer's Manual of the Fifteenth Century* (University Park, PA, 1997), 114.

Let us imagine following this fifteenth-century prescription for treasure hunting. We would need to live in a world wherein religion and magic were intertwined, surrounded by mysterious forces and invisible beings of awesome power that we could command if only we knew how. Our understanding of the universe would have to be very different from today's predominantly scientific depiction of an infinitely large and impersonal vastness of colliding atoms and swirling stellar gasses; instead, it would have to be a small, enclosed cosmos overseen by a divine being which was willing to bend its laws to the benefit of humans. It would be a world

11

wherein some humans, particularly priests, were granted enormous powers by that deity to speak to and for him and even at times to command his angelic assistants.

Early modern people took comfort in this world view, believing that the cosmos had been created primarily for their benefit. Church authorities tried to monopolize preternatural (i.e., "above-natural") power, condemning as heretics those who doubted priestly control over the "other" realm. Religious leaders could hardly contend that popular magical processes were impossible without casting into doubt their own sacramental system which worked by supernatural means that were a clear parallel to the magical. Instead, they asserted that non-approved magic worked by diabolical agency. The Devil was presumed to be behind every non-approved religious activity, sowing among the faithful doubt in the veracity of the Catholic ritual or outright desecration of the same. Papal investigators (Inquisitors) imagined that religious dissidents or heretics secretly worshiped Satan, committed gruesome acts of cannibalistic infanticide, and took pleasure in incestuous orgies. Norman Cohn's argument that these particular charges were largely a figment of clerical imaginations has been supported by every serious investigation into the trial accounts and procedures.[1] At the same time, some elements of what would become the demonic witch stereotype originated from popular beliefs, such as the witches' evil magic and ability to fly or change shapes.[2]

The strength and endurance of this demonic fantasy is remarkable, as is its power to inspire numerous atrocities in the name of the Christian religion. This chapter will set the stage for the larger discussion of diabolical conspiracies in the sixteenth and seventeenth centuries by briefly surveying the mental world of late-medieval people; examining the respective roles of religion and magic in this era; and describing the development of the various late-medieval conspiratorial threats that led to persecution of Jews, lepers, heretics, sorcerers, and witches, all of whom were presumed to be inspired by the Devil.

Late-Medieval Cosmos

Although at night medieval people looked up at the same sky as we do today, they invested it with a different set of meanings. They believed that the universe's creator was benevolent and that he cared deeply about the pinnacle of his creation, humanity. Circling the universe's center on translucent spheres were the sun, moon, and planets, while the stars remained fixed on their own sphere at the cosmos' outer edge. To explain the apparent anomalies in planetary movements medieval scholars postulated that the heavenly bodies traveled through a mysterious fifth element called ether, while everything in the sub-lunar realm (between the moon and the center of the earth) consisted of the primary elements: earth, air, water, and fire. In 1543 Nicholas Copernicus' *On the Movement of the Heavenly Spheres* offered an alternative explanation by suggesting that the sun was the center of the universe. Such an idea would not be taken seriously for nearly another century.

Even though God was believed to reside just outside the celestial spheres, the world was far from benign. It was often capricious and inexplicable, a fact explained as divine punishment for sin. Nothing was morally neutral, and even the qualities of the inanimate elements – hot, cold, moist, and dry – were morally ranked in order of virtue, with hot superior to cold. The universe was similarly arranged hierarchically, with God and pure spirit beings at the top and base matter at the bottom. Humans, who consisted of both material and spiritual components – a soul (and spirit) and body – resided somewhere in the middle.

Like a giant living thing the components of the universe were joined together by a process of influence described as "correspondence." Unlike modern notions of cause and effect, correspondence "worked" on the assumption that humans were a smaller copy, or microcosm, of the larger universe. For every part of the human body there was a matching item in the macrocosmic corpus, while the four elements had their twins in the body's four humors, the basic matter and fluids which were the body's essential building blocks: blood (corresponding to air), phlegm (water), black bile (fire), and yellow bile (earth). Each of these shared the qualities of the corresponding element: blood was hot and moist, phlegm cold and moist, black bile hot and dry, and yellow bile cold and dry. Health was maintained by keeping the proportions among these humors in relative balance. If a patient was feverish and sweaty, he or she would be treated for an excess of corrupted blood by a phlebotomy or bleeding. Although humoral imbalances were internally caused, they could be influenced by the person's diet, state of mind, or stellar and planetary movements. Most learned physicians therefore consulted the stars when preparing their prescriptions. Similarly, herbs that were considered cold or moist were used to cure illnesses caused by an excess of heat or dryness, and so on.

The Occult Sciences and Magic

Both learned and illiterate sought to manipulate the preternatural beings or forces believed to channel the divine power diffused throughout creation. As described by the famous physician and occult scientist Cornelius Agrippa of Nettesheim (1486–1535), stars

> have their own natures, properties and terms upon which one deals with them, and by means of their rays they produce the signs and characters of these even in inferior things, such as elements, stones, plants, and animals and their bodily parts. In consequence, every single thing is allotted some special sign or character which is stamped upon it; and these it gets from the way its constituent parts are arranged in relation to the principles of natural harmony, and also from its own star shedding rays of light upon it.[3]

It was believed possible to capture such rays in their corresponding metals and gems, which could then be used as amulets to supply the human wearer with the planet's unique powers.

While some churchmen condemned predictive astrology as presumptive of God's will, and the brilliant Italian humanist Pico della Mirandola (1463–94) critiqued it for its fatalism and lack of accuracy, astrologers and diviners found ready employ at noble courts where they helped alleviate anxiety about the future and offered a sense of God's proximity and will in the world.[4] The fifteenth century also saw a matching growth of interest in alchemy whose practitioners believed that the seven metals corresponded to the seven planets in a hierarchy with gold and the sun at the top, reflecting the light of heaven itself. Descending from these were the correspondences of silver/moon, mercury/Mercury, iron/Mars, lead/Saturn, tin/Jupiter, and copper/Venus. Alchemists sought to break down the lower metals into their essential elements which then could be recombined into the higher metals, in the process discovering the invisible, spiritual essence permeating the universe. With their ovens and stills they practiced a form of protochemistry, stumbling upon chemical processes that they only vaguely understood. While some alchemists cynically manipulated gullible patrons into funding their projects, such charlatanry should not be taken as the norm. Instead, alchemy required a level of devotion to the task that is exceptional and which would draw devotees well into the eighteenth century.

Inspired by their love of the ancients, some Renaissance humanists sought the spiritual force animating the universe in the writings of the putative ancient Egyptian philosopher Hermes Trismegistus ("Thrice-great Hermes") which purportedly preserved the secret lore of the universe granted Adam by God that had been passed down orally to selected adepts. With such knowledge and ascetic purification they hoped to gain the assistance of the spirits which moved the planets in accordance with the divine will. Until 1614, when Isaac Casaubon discovered that it was a forgery, the *Corpus Hermetica* delighted scholars and occultists alike, helping to inspire a major resurgence of learned magic throughout Europe. Also of interest to Pico and his fellow neo-Platonists was the Jewish Cabala, writings of mystical contemplation on the names and attributes of God as revealed in the Hebrew scriptures. Each letter of the Hebrew alphabet corresponded to a particular divine quality dispersed in creation. For Pico especially, the Cabala provided a unique tool to uncover the essential unity of humanity and of all religions.

The most unorthodox form of occult science was ritual magic which required the precise performances of prayers and rituals to summon and command spirit beings to provide secret knowledge or to perform magical acts. Many ritual magic manuscripts have survived, such as the *Sworn Book of Honorius* or the *ars notoria* which called upon God or angels to provide the wisdom of the cosmos. Ritual magicians contended that since only godly men could command the spirits, the Church's persecution of magicians was misguided. As the fourteenth-century Honorius of Thebes wrote,

> Moved by covetousness and envy under the similitude of truth, these bishops and prelates through demonic instigation spread abroad false and unlikely stories. For it is not possible that a wicked and unclean man could work truly in this Art; for men are not bound unto spirits, but spirits are constrained against their will to answer clean men and fulfill their requests.[5]

Angelic magic may have raised suspicion of unorthodoxy, but there was no doubt about necromancy, which by the fourteenth century had become a major hobby for underemployed clergy or university students. Convinced that since Holy Orders imbued them with spiritual power to exorcise or expel demons from the possessed, clerical necromancers assumed that they could control these malevolent spirits. As seen in their conjurations, it was expected that God would cooperate in such ventures:

> In the name of the Father, and of the Son, and of the Holy Spirit, amen. I conjure you, O elves and all sorts of demons, whether of the day or of the night, by the Father, and the Son, and the Holy Spirit, and the undivided Trinity, and by the intercession of the most blessed and glorious Mary ever Virgin, by the prayers of the prophets, by the merits of the patriarchs, by the supplication of the angels and archangels, by the intercession of the apostles, by the passion of the martyrs, by the faith of the confessors, by the chastity of the virgins, by the intercession of all the saints, and by the Seven Sleepers, whose names are Malchus, Maximianus, Dionysius, John, Constantine, Seraphion, and Martimanus, and by the name of the Lord †A†G†L†A†, which is blessed unto all ages, that you should not harm nor do or inflict anything evil against this servant of God N., whether sleeping or waking. † Christ conquers † Christ reigns † Christ commands † May Christ bless us † [and] defend us from all evil † Amen.[6]

Based on the belief that demons, as fallen angels, maintained their pre-fall intelligence, knowledge, and flying abilities, necromancers hoped to use them to discover secrets, provide magical transport, create fantasies to impress friend and foe, compel love, even to reanimate the dead. Whether from sincere belief or a quest for entertainment, necromancy remained popular, and many unscrupulous practitioners made a good living pretending to call up spirits for naive clients. Their rituals illustrate the permeability of the boundaries between perceived reality and fantasy, between sense and nonsense. They may also have conditioned people to believe more readily the strange stories of magical flight, sabbath banquets, and magical acts arising out of the witchcraft trials. As Kieckhefer reasons, the "playful fantasies of the necromancers, then, became sources for the Boschian nightmares of the witch trials."[7]

Popular Magic

The magic of common people was quite distinct from its learned counterparts, rarely written down but transmitted orally from generation to generation. It was simpler, requiring less by way of preparation and purification, while of extraterrestrial influences, it looked primarily to the moon. It relied little on spirit beings or demons but focused principally on symbolical likeness or opposites. It also had more earth-bound goals than its learned forms: preserving fertility, restoring health, and manipulating human relations within the community.

Even seasonal changes required the repetition of rituals ensuring the return of warm weather and the success of the harvest. The local parish priest was often involved by blessing the objects involved in the ritual.[8] For example, to remedy an infertile field, before sunrise the performer would dig four clumps of earth from the four sides of the afflicted land; sprinkle these with a mixture of holy water, oil, milk, honey, and fragments of trees and herbs, while reciting in Latin the words spoken by God to Adam and Eve: "Be fruitful and multiply, and fill the earth." After further prayer, he was to carry the clods to the church, where the priest would sing four masses over them. Finally, before sunset the clumps were to be returned to the fields, where it was expected they would spread their blessing to the whole field.[9] While such rituals may not have influenced the weather, magical medicine could have had an effect on patients psychosomatically, by manipulating the expectations of patients or victims and thereby relieving or elevating stress levels which could cause the anticipated symptoms.[10] Many potions also required ingesting some curative, poisonous, or hallucinogenic plants. Even so, one of the most popular forms of local magic was the love potion, which in the case of a male victim usually involved the ingestion of such sympathetic ingredients as the menstrual blood of the intended beloved. Such preternatural cures were believed to work mainly through the proper disposition of both healer and patient, not by chemical processes.

The blending of magical and religious notions was clearest in popular conceptions of the sacraments. While theologians understood the Eucharist to be a conduit through which God effused his grace and power to believers, ordinary people regarded the consecrated bread or Host as containing divine power to protect them from harm, even when they had merely seen it elevated in a monstrance.[11] Not surprisingly, many people developed the conviction that consecrated Hosts smuggled out of Mass could be powerful agents in magical activity.

Not only was the universe organic and moralized, it was also gendered. Aristotle, and Aquinas following him, believed that the differences between men and women were built into creation itself so that there were natural roles for men and opposite ones for women; not surprisingly, the male sex was given the positive pole, the female the negative.[12] A curative for a male, dominated as he was by the hot humors, would therefore be distinct from that for a female who was ruled by the lower, cooler humors, even if both suffered from the same ailment. The learned games-playing with polarity became a very useful justification to exclude women from certain occupations or restrict their control over property, while inflation in dowries for both marriage and entry into a convent and shrinking work opportunities added up to a very difficult situation for single women. Despite such gender distinctions, medieval men and women shared an extremely precarious existence, with short life expectancy and frequent ill health. In the fourteenth and fifteenth centuries these difficulties were augmented by frequent crop failure, famine, disease epidemics, especially the bubonic plague, and increasingly destructive warfare.

The psychological impact of such disasters was enormous, spawning extreme group efforts to avert the wrath of God; most famous of these were the flagellants, groups of men who traveled throughout Europe preaching repentance, criticizing the obviously useless clergy, and whipping themselves bloody to appease God. According to the chronicler Guillaume de Nangis, in 1349 masses of flagellants traveled through the Southern Netherlands claiming that their blood had intermingled with Christ's, giving them his power to heal and perform miracles.[13] Hedging their bets, the flagellants also blamed the Jews for incurring God's wrath, the choice being that either God had utterly rejected his Christian people, or he was angry at the presumed blasphemy of nonbelievers. Most Christians chose the latter, in part to help suppress their fear that the first option was the truth.

By 1500 the image of Death had become that of the grim reaper, hunting down the living. In some works, such as the fifteenth-century Flemish comedy, *The Entertainment of the Apple Tree*, Death and the Devil together hunted humans. Here a simple farmer outwitted them both, tricking first Death and then the Devil to climb into his magical apple tree, from which he releases them only after extracting promises for a long and healthy life. Such comedies momentarily alleviated the intense anxiety about the almost instant and horrifying death that the plague raised. That ordinary people took the Devil seriously is seen by their use of his name in magical conjurations. For theologians, demons were as real as angels and saints, while lay people added them to the panoply of other spirit beings inhabiting their forests and meadows: fairies, imps, elves, ghosts, revenants, and wood spirits. James Sharpe finds plenty of evidence in England to suggest that the Devil "was evidently firmly established in the popular consciousness,"[14] while Fernando Cervantes asserts that for both popular and elite cultures, "there is no question that the idea of the devil belongs equally to both cultures and that it cannot be forced exclusively into either of them without gross simplification and impoverishment."[15] Only priests had the requisite authority effectively to counteract the activities of Satan's minions and even they faced a superhuman struggle at times. The sacraments were the principal means of defense for lay people, starting with the rite of baptism which began outside the church doors with the exorcism of the infant, an act nicely portrayed in a sixteenth-century Flemish drama, *The Play of Saint Trudo*, wherein Lucifer and his minions Baalberith and Leviathan are constantly thwarted by priestly power in their efforts to foil God's plans for the future saint, beginning with pedobaptismal exorcism.[16] This drama was part of a longstanding effort to encourage lay people to battle the Devil within themselves as well as without. Fernando Cervantes suggests demons became "instigators of interior desires that individuals could not acknowledge as belonging to themselves."[17] For John Bossy, the contemporaneous replacement of the seven deadly sins with the Decalogue furthermore moved the emphasis on sin from harm against humans to that against God, epitomized as idolatry and blasphemy, and there was no worse form than the worship of demons.[18]

Anti-Judaism

Jews had long been a target of demonization, but were also officially tolerated in the Christian west because they proved an extremely useful, if unwitting, ally in the campaign to expel religious doubt from the hearts of Christian believers. The survival of the Jews was seen as a confirmation of the "Old Testament" background to the Christian faith and allowed for the fulfillment of one of the major signals presaging the return of Christ: the conversion of Jews to Christianity. Moreover, Jews offered preachers a visual aid confirming the gospel accounts of the passion of Christ, helped Christians maintain their self-conception as successors to Judaism as the people of God, and acted as a tangible reminder of God's judgment on those who reject him. Although officially tolerated, Jews lived a tenuous existence within Christendom, non-citizens at the mercy of the Christian majority and authorities. Outside of the Mediterranean region the number of Jews in western Europe was small, concentrated in the major commercial cities of the Holy Roman Empire, France, and England. They possessed no real freedom of religion, although generally they could worship in their own synagogues.

Gavin Langmuir has surveyed the transition in the thirteenth century from Christian anti-Judaism – the expression of religious animosity by Christians against Judaism – to anti-Semitism – the irrational hatred of a category of people called "Jews". Anti-Judaism was based on Christians' need to explain why the vast majority of Jews had not recognized their supposed messiah, Jesus. Christian accusations that the Jews had killed Jesus (deicide), Langmuir suggests, "camouflaged Christian awareness that the continued existence of Jewish disbelief challenged Christian belief" and helped to repress widespread doubts about Jesus' resurrection.[19] At times of intensified religious fervor anti-Judaism could break out in intense violence, yet this was not irrational rage, but an attempt to compel Jews to perform their service of proving the veracity and superiority of Christianity.

As Christian theology became more sophisticated (and for many incomprehensible), Christians turned again to the Jews to help dispel the rising doubt. During Easter, 1144, near Norwich, England, the corpse of a boy, William, was discovered. Six years later, the monk Thomas of Monmouth, who had arrived in the local monastery after the discovery, explained the boy's death as an act of Jews who had crucified him in their hostility to Christ. Many of Monmouth's colleagues were initially skeptical, and no wonder, given the thinness of Thomas' evidence, based on the testimony of a converted Jew that "the Jews, without the shedding of human blood, could neither obtain their freedom, nor could they ever return to their fatherland."[20] Thomas may have been the first to postulate a Jewish conspiracy of ritual murder, but the myth struck a responsive chord among Christians, as seen in its retelling in Gloucester in 1198 where a chronicler admitted to considerable skepticism regarding this story of the unfortunate Harold, who

is said to have been carried away secretly by Jews, in the opinion of many, on Feb.21, and by them hidden till March 16. On that night,... the Jews of all England coming together as if to circumcise a certain boy, pretend deceitfully that they are about to celebrate the feast appointed by law in such case, and deceiving the citizens of Gloucester with that fraud, they tortured the lad placed before them with immense tortures. It is true no Christian was present, or saw or heard the deed, nor have we found that anything was betrayed by any Jew. But a little while after when the whole convent of monks of

Gloucester and almost all the citizens of that city, and innumerable persons coming to the spectacle, saw the wounds of the dead body, scars of fire, the thorns fixed on his head, and the liquid wax poured into the eyes and face, and touched it with the diligent examination of their hands, those tortures were believed or guessed to have been inflicted on him in that manner.[21]

Such stories depicting Jews as ceaseless Christ killers and their victims as miracle performers confirmed beliefs about the death and resurrection of Jesus.

Accusations of ritual murder were followed in the thirteenth century by the equally strange charge of ritual Host desecration. Christians for some time had been expressing serious doubts about the Christian dogma of the real, physical presence of Christ in the Eucharistic bread and wine. The processions, dramas, and supposed miracles of Eucharistic devotion of the Corpus Christi feast helped to dispel such doubt, Miri Ruben contends,

> [v]iewing a Eucharistic miracle could influence understanding of sac-
> ramental claims more than many sermons, and tales abound of shaky
> belief which was strengthened by a vision, such as that told of the
> Patarins of Ferrara who were convinced of the faith when a lamb
> appeared in the host, or that of a northern heretic, Gautier of Flos,
> who saw a baby in the host during a mass celebrated by St John of
> Cantimpré. And it was to counter the nagging questions of doubtful
> believers, as well as of heretics, that miracles were reported, creating
> the setting for the use of *exempla* which retold a miraculous event; the
> story of a woman's pet monkey, for example, which strayed into
> a church and ate the host, and which was consequently burnt by its
> owner who found in its stomach the undamaged sacrament.[23]

By seeking to harm or use consecrated wafers for malicious purposes, evil doers revealed their belief in the real presence and provided proof of the dogma's truth.

While the charge of misuse of Hosts was not restricted to Jews, they became its principal targets, and tales abounded of Jews stabbing conse-crated Hosts which bled in accusation against their attackers. Such stories developed shortly after the Fourth Lateran Council's approval of transubstantiation, a complex explanation of the transformation process of bread into the flesh of Christ which proved a tough sell to those who relied on experience and common sense instead of Aristotelean logic to understand reality. The magical act of bleeding Hosts was a sensory confirmation of transubstantiation, and hence of Christian faith and the priests' spiritual power.

Although many local priests and friars helped spread such hateful beliefs, the papacy sought to keep a lid on anti-Semitic violence, as when in 1272 Pope Gregory X condemned Christian parents who pretended that a child had been abducted so as to extort money from local Jews. He also denounced the illogical belief that Jews, whose scriptures strictly forbade the consumption of any blood, drank the blood of Christian youths.[24] Clearly, then, as doubt about certain Christian teachings increased, so too did anxiety about that doubt.

Doubt and the Rise of Religious Dissent

Medieval Europe was not a good place for the expression of religious dissent. There was a single, overarching ideology explaining life and death, while the Pope, as God's representative on earth, dispensed God's mercy. Lay people were expected to work in the place assigned to them by birth, to be good Christians, attend the sacraments, and live as morally as possible, hoping for eternal rewards that might make the harshness of their earthly existence worthwhile. Those who challenged this model by denying the veracity of the sacraments, saints, and relics, were removing from people's hands their sole means of spiritual protection from the invisible, maleficent forces arrayed against them.

Church leaders called any such variants of Christian teaching heresy. In medieval society, even a simple reinterpretation of an obscure scriptural passage or theological notion could be construed as an attack on the whole faith and world view of believers. Initially lay people reacted to "heretics" with a hostility borne of fear, as when a mob in Soissons in 1114 broke into the prison housing a group of ascetic priests and burned them at the stake.[25] By viewing religious doubts as the malicious product of external threats, the people, according to Langmuir, "attributed cosmic evil to other human beings – heretics, sorcerers, witches, and Jews."[26] In the high Middle Ages there arose several such "heretical" challenges, the most prominent being the Waldensians and Cathars. The Waldensians, founded by a Lyons merchant Peter Valdes (Waldo) who in 1173 gave his property to the poor and embraced a life of apostolic poverty, studied the Bible in the vernacular and preached a simple message of personal religious devotion. When Valdes' bishop steadfastly refused to grant them a preaching license, these "Poor of Lyons" continued their activities regardless, and around the end of the twelfth century the Cistercian monk Alan of Lille expressed his horror that they were allowing women to preach, asserting that Valdes' disciples were really "deceivers" who "seduce the simple folk in various regions of the world, divert them from rather than convert them to the truth." He then comments:

> If it is a dangerous thing for wise and holy men to preach, it is most dangerous for the uneducated who do not know what should be preached; to whom, how, when and where there should be preaching. These persons resist the Apostle [Paul] in that they have women with them and have them preach in the gatherings of the faithful, although the Apostle says in the first Epistle to the Corinthians: "Let women keep silence in the churches, for it is not permitted for them to speak, but to be subject, as also the law saith. But if they would hear anything, let them ask their husbands at home."[27]

As the Church persecuted them, the Waldensians became more radical, eventually rejecting the Catholic Church and its clergy as apostate and corrupt.

For their part the Cathars (the "pure ones") were distinct from Catholic orthodoxy from the start, teaching that only those who had achieved complete purity and separation from all things material could be saved. Espousing the existence of two gods, a good one which created the spiritual realm and an evil one which was responsible for base matter, Cathars believed that the object of the evil god – an extreme version of the Devil – was to imprison good souls in evil bodies. Ultimate deliverance was possible only through the Cathar sacrament called the *consolamentum*, or the baptism in the spirit by the laying on of hands by a Cathar *perfecta*, who lived an extremely ascetic and peripatetic existence. All heretical movements played to the widespread disaffection with the seeming privileges, indolence, and hypocrisy of the Catholic clergy and fed upon the growing wish of urbanites for a more literate religious experience. The Church's efforts to crush Catharism in southern France by the bloody Albigensian crusade of 1209–20 merely drove the heretics underground, and so the papal authorities were compelled to find alternative means to eradicate the threat.

The Inquisition

In 1215 Pope Innocent III called the Fourth Lateran Council to find a better solution. It clarified orthodox beliefs, reasserted the vital role of the priesthood and sacraments, mandated yearly confession and attendance at Mass, ordered priests to keep closer tabs on their parishioners, and stipulated that recalcitrant heretics lose their property. Lay princes, who viewed religious dissent as a threat to the civic order, added mutilation or execution to the designated correction. Without an effective police force, such efforts proved inadequate, until Pope Gregory IX (1227–41) turned to the Franciscans and Dominicans, two recently founded mendicant (traveling) orders of monks which became Europe's greatest preachers, inspiring the dramatic growth of an activist, lay piety in Europe.[28] Gregory used them as the recruiting ground for the Church's new weapon in its war against heresy: the office of Inquisitor against depraved heresy, *inquisitionis haereticis pravitatis*.

In reality the office was little more than a title implying papal authority. Without soldiers or secretaries, Inquisitors relied entirely on the good graces of local rulers. Yet these generally appreciated the Church's help in enforcing religious and civic conformity and in replacing mob action against heretics with a semblance of judicial proceedings. To distinguish truth from falsehood, Inquisitors relied on their experience in hearing confessions and convincing the guilty to repent. There was no need for lawyers or witnesses, only a notary or two to keep detailed records of proceedings and a couple of noble witnesses during sentencing, when the Inquisitor set out the requisite penances for the repentant or handed over the stiff-necked to the secular authorities for harsher treatment. Penance varied from a ten-day diet of bread and water, completion of a pilgrimage, or imprisonment for one year or life.

Even with these weapons, however, Inquisitors complained bitterly about heretics who had learned how to dissimulate or whose silence may have been caused by the Devil. In 1252, Pope Innocent IV's bull *ad extirpanda* gave Inquisitors the right to torture suspects, although only in one session and only in cases of clear suspicion of guilt. As priests were not allowed to shed blood, the application of pain could not cause bleeding, mutilation, or death. By various tools of compression, such as the thumbscrews, or extension, such as the rack or strappado (a simple rope and pulley device which raised suspects off the ground by a rope tied to their wrists bound behind their backs), Inquisitors were now well equipped to restore suspected heretics to the bosom of the Church.

Whatever the legitimacy behind its original motivation, through the course of the thirteenth to fifteenth centuries the office of Inquisitor was readily abused; the increasing practice of trying deceased heretics whose land and possessions were confiscated from their heirs became a major means of funding the tribunals' expensive operations. Thus an individual's beliefs were often of little consequence in determinations, while heresy seemed inheritable. By the early fourteenth century Catharism was a dead letter in Languedoc, and Waldensians widely scattered throughout Europe.[29]

Catharism had been linked with rebellion and, as Malcolm Lambert notes, Cathar belief in a powerful god of evil, "helped to fabricate the image of a heretic as a servant of Satan."[30] The crises of the late Middle Ages led the clergy especially "to consider Christianity as a besieged Jerusalem, assailed by the forces of evil, as Satan and his armies let fly, betokening the end of time." Not only heretics, but increasingly sorcerers and witches "represented the diabolical troops engaged in this dramatic conflict."[31] The image of heretics as vile worshipers of Satan was cemented especially in the work of the infamous Conrad of Marburg who in 1231 was commissioned Inquisitor of Mainz by Pope Gregory IX. Conrad, an experienced crusade preacher, knew how to manipulate the religious enthusiasm of the masses. Like Gregory, Conrad sincerely believed heresy to be part of a grand diabolical conspiracy in which heretics, despite outward appearances of piety, secretly committed the most vile and blasphemous acts imaginable, including worship of the Devil. As another churchman, Guillaume d'Auvergne, bishop of Paris wrote in the 1230s, Lucifer "is permitted ... To appear to his worshippers and adorers in the form of a black cat or a toad and to demand kisses from them; whether as a cat, abominably, under the tail; or as a toad, horribly, on the mouth."[32] Conrad's unorthodox approach was to raise a community's ire against the local demonic threat and direct the flock to round up suspects. All evidence was accepted and suspects given the choice of recanting or facing the flames. Those who maintained their innocence were burned regardless, since they would then receive a martyr's crown. Gregory believed Conrad's reports of a new sect of Luciferans who had made a pact with the Devil, so that when Conrad was assassinated in 1233 by an enraged nobleman, Gregory issued his bull *Vox in Rama* reiterating the supposed activities of the Luciferans and decrying the skepticism of the German bishops.

Some of Conrad's audience applied his conspiratorial notions to others, as on Christmas Day, 1235 in Fulda when the bodies of five boys were found in a burned down mill. With Conrad's words still ringing in their ears, local Christians rounded up the few Jews of the town and accused them of killing the boys to obtain the blood they allegedly needed for their rituals. Had Conrad himself implicated Jews in such noxious acts? We cannot know, but it seems some lay people transposed his notions of a diabolical sect upon the Jews. The German Emperor conducted his own investigation and forbade anyone to accuse Jews of ritual cannibalism. However, not even the Pope's condemnation of the accusations was sufficient to stop the spread of such rumors.[33]

In short time the term Waldensian (Vauderie) became synonymous with worship of the Devil and evil magic. That there were in all likelihood no such organized demonic sects did not stop the authorities from hunting them down and "discovering" proof of their existence largely through intimidation or outright torture. Gregory IX's *Vox in Rama* had formally established, as William Monter puts it, "the notion that religious dissenters – generally Waldensians, who, in fact, led exemplarily plain and sober lives – were really Devil-worshipers who engaged in nocturnal orgies."[34] The approach would be followed frequently in the fourteenth and fifteenth centuries.

Inquisitors and the Mystics

In the thirteenth century groups of devout, unmarried women of the Rhineland cities began living in self-supporting communities which followed the religious vocation without taking the lifelong vows of nuns. These "Beguine" houses were not directly supervised by males, making their inmates susceptible to misogynistic suspicions of clerics who readily imagined the worst of groups of independent women. Many of these Beguines sought through mystical contemplation to communicate directly with God, without the aid of priests, finding inspiration in the loose network of mystics calling themselves the "friends of God." The leading Rhineland mystic, Meister Eckhart (1260–1327), was soon placed under inquisitorial house arrest, although he died of natural causes just prior to sentencing. Many lay mystics were not so fortunate.

Robert Lerner's analysis of the court records relating to the trials of the so-called "Brethren of the Free Spirit" reveals that no such organized, heretical group ever existed. Instead, Inquisitors, trained in the art of making connections between heretical groups and individuals, made much of the idiosyncratic confessions of a few who took their mysticism and anticlericalism to an extreme libertarianism. In 1367, one of these, John Hartmann, confessed during his trial in Erfurt that, "one who is truly free can be subject to no authority because he himself is king and lord of all creatures," and that "just as calves and oxen were created for men to eat, so women were created for the use of the free in spirit," hardly a notion that would be appealing to the Beguines.[35] Yet, in a great leap of logic, the Inquisitors linked the two, suggesting that the few "Free Spirits" that they had caught were merely the tip of the iceberg of an extensive and dangerous heretical sect promoting complete moral license and the eradication of the Church hierarchy. Throughout most of the fourteenth century, particularly the 1360s and 1370s, Beguines were arrested, tried, and punished, many of them facing the fiery death accorded other heretics. The writings of such prominent Beguines as Mechtild van Magdeburg, whose manuscript, "Flowing Light of the Godhead" expressed a deeply sexual conception of the mystical union of the soul with Christ, was used as evidence that the ostensibly pious Beguines were Free Spirits intent on indulging their fleshly urges.[36] Only in the early fifteenth century were Franciscans able to protect the Beguines by making them associated or "tertiary" houses and promising to supervise them. The propaganda and persecution, however, added another layer to the sediment of belief about diabolical heresy, one that increased suspicion of women who expressed a measure of religous independence.

Political Inquistions

Secular rulers very quickly appreciated the effectiveness of crusades and Inquisitions to crush political dissent. The master of secular inquisitorial handiwork was undoubtedly King Philip IV "the Fair" (1268–1314) of France, who used it against Pope Boniface VIII in his efforts to control and tax the French church. Foiled in his plan to bring the elderly pontiff to trial in France, Philip proceeded to try him post mortem, and in 1310/11 the Estates General of France became the first court to convict a suspect of both blasphemous heresy and ritual magic.

Philip had earlier used the inquisition for financial gain. In 1306 he followed his cousin King Edward I of England's example by expelling the Jews from the realm after expropriating their property (unlike England, the Jews were allowed to return to France after payment of a sizeable fee). Unfortunately his financial woes continued, so Philip in

1307 turned his inquisitorial weapon upon the Knights Templar, a wealthy crusading order unfairly blamed for the final defeat of the Crusader States in 1291. According to Philip, the Inquisitor of France had informed him that the Templars were secretly venerating the bust of a mysterious figure, obscurely identified as the demon Beelzebub, and performing sodomy (homosexual sex), renouncing the Christian faith, spitting on the crucifix, and kissing the anus of the order's grand master. On the morning of October 13, 1307, all Templars were arrested, and many tortured, leading to several confessions, including that of grand master James of Molay. The following year Pope Clement V sent his own investigators, before whom many knights reaffirmed their innocence. The Archbishop of Sens, Philip Marigny, ordered over fifty "relapsed heretics" immediately burned at the stake. The Templars fell back in line and the Pope commanded the order's dissolution. For his immense service to the Christian faith, Philip received his share of Templar wealth.

The Leper–Jew Conspiracy of 1321

Confronted by worsening financial straights, Philip V, Philip the Fair's second son, applied his father's methodology to another wealthy target: the leper houses. Mired in a devastating period of famine, epidemics, and increasing social unrest, the French populace was prepared to believe in a conspiracy theory, especially when propagated by royal agents. In 1321 the famous Inquisitor Bernard Gui presented the case against the lepers who, "diseased in body and soul," had sprinkled poisonous powders in the wells to transmit their disease to the healthy and thus take over France. In a clear case of guilt projection, the accusers suspected that this severely disadvantaged group were seeking to exact personal vengeance against those who abhorred them. The first rumors appeared that year in Aquitaine during Easter, always a dangerous season for "outsiders." With the first leper arrests and forced confessions came mob action and in some places inhabited leper houses were burned to the ground. The king issued an edict on June 21, 1321 defining the leper crime as *lése majesté*, a crime against the person of the king, while prosecutors suspected that other masterminds were behind the plot. Since many regarded Jews as inwardly leprous, it is not surprising that lepers began confessing that Jews, in league with Satan and the Muslim sultan of Granada, had bribed them to scatter the alleged poison consisting of

human blood, urine, various herbs, and consecrated Hosts. Throughout
Aquitaine Jews were rounded up and burned, and when the pogroms
reached Paris, the king extorted a fortune of 150,000 livres from the
richest Parisian Jews. However, in 1322 a plot to poison Philip V was
"uncovered" and the Jews expelled from France the following year by
Charles IV who kept their property and the revenues of the leper
houses.

Although the authorities led this notorious assault, lay distrust of Jews
and lepers was ubiquitous, needing only official sanction to turn into
violent action. Resentment against the lepers quickly dissipated, so that
in 1338 Pope Benedict XII declared the Toulouse lepers innocent (as
Jacques Fournier, bishop of Pamiers, this Pope had earlier declared
them guilty). However, suspicion of Jewish poisoning plots simmered,
boiling over in apparently spontaneous massacres of the Jews with the
onset of the plague in 1348/49. The conspiracy theory promoted by
royal agents had evidently taken deep root in popular soil.[37] The Jewish
conspiracy was of course imaginary, but as Gavin Langmuir argues,

> the fear and hatred the image engendered were all too real. Indeed,
> the hatred was peculiarly intense because what these Christians feared
> was buried deep within themselves. They feared and hated their
> own doubts about beliefs basic to their sense of their identity, doubts
> they could neither acknowledge consciously nor eradicate subcon-
> sciously.[38]

When the flagellants realized that their self-mutilation was not diverting
God's wrath, they blamed the immorality of the clergy and the blasphemous presence of the Jews. Local clergy were only too glad to divert
attention to the latter.

Jews and Conversos in Spain

A similar outbreak of anti-Semitic rhetoric and violent action occurred
in Christian Spain where prominent Jews had become indispensable
intermediaries and tax collectors for the Christian rulers. Under the
smooth surface of this multicultural society seethed considerable resentment against these Jewish officials. Some preachers, such as Hernan
Martínez in the 1340s and Ferrant Martínez in the 1380s, further
inflamed this acrimony by preaching fiery sermons during the Christian

holy days characterizing the Jews as Christ killers whose existence was an affront to God. Just before Christmas, 1390, Ferrant Martínez succeeded in closing some of Seville's synagogues, and the following Lent his sermons now included stories that the local Jews were conspiring to crucify innocent Christian boys. Despite the authorities' opposition, on June 9, 1391 a mob sacked the Jewish quarter. The attacks spread quickly to other regions of Spain, and thousands of Jews were killed.

In the face of the violence many Spanish Jews converted rather than commit suicide. Not as conditioned to Christian violence as their coreligionists elsewhere, the Spanish Jewish leaders were so shocked by the violence that, as John Edwards puts it, they succumbed to "a growing belief that God had abandoned the Jews and given his blessing to the Christian Church."[39] Some saw baptism as merely another cultural adaptation, like eating pork or shaving beards, while others expected to return to their Jewish faith once passions calmed. Whatever the motivation, the mass conversions of 1391 brought thousands of former Jews fully into Christian society, allowing many to rise to high positions in government and business, to marry into the landowning class, even to become priests and bishops. The example was set, so that when there was a new outbreak of anti-Jewish hostility in 1415 inflamed by the sermons of the Dominican Vincent Ferrer, thousands more converted.

Unfortunately, converso success inspired jealousy rather than admiration. Suspicions lingered that most conversos were secret Jews intent on infiltrating the government and church so as to overthrow the Christian government, even though many converso descendants were intensely devout Christians. In the middle of the century resentment between old Christians and new Christians broke out in armed conflict. Many conversos left Spain altogether. In 1449 Pope Nicholas V condemned this anti-converso sentiment in his bull *Humani generis inimicus* by asserting that between "those newly converted to the faith, particularly from the Israelite people, and Old Christians, there shall be no distinction in honors, dignities, and offices."[40] His efforts proved fruitless.

In 1478 Spain's most Catholic monarchs Queen Isabella of Castille and King Ferdinand of Aragon responded to mounting pressure from both old and new Christians and began proceedings to establish a permanent office of Inquisition. This they placed under the direct governance of the Suprema, a council of eight royal appointees. The institution succeeded not only in "uncovering" Jewish heresy among Christians, but also in assisting the monarchs' centralization efforts. The extreme measures that the Inquisition would take to purify the realm of supposed

Judaisers is seen in its "pure blood laws" (*limpieza de sangre*) which eased the way for Inquisitors to convict supposed Judaisers by asserting that the sacrament of baptism was unable to purge conversos of their Jewish blood. The theory was simple: if after the application of Christian baptism most conversos and their descendants still remained secret Jews, then the concept of sacramental *ex opere operato* was under threat. A solution to this perceived dilemma was found by postulating demonic and bio-logical factors impeding baptism when administered to Jews. That this notion was outside of Spain a heretical one does not seem to have bothered the first Grand Inquisitor, Tomás de Torquemada (d.1498), who formalized these unusual laws and orchestrated the expulsion of Spain's remaining Jews in 1492. Certainly the *limpieza de sangre* made the Inquis-itors' job easier, for instead of having to extract confessions of heresy from accused Judaisers, they had merely to determine if the percentage of corrupt Jewish blood was more than 1/32, which could reach back as many as three generations, stopping just short of Torquemada's own heritage. Persecution of conversos had little to do with an accused's actual beliefs; when Torquemada tried Juan Arias Dávila, Bishop of Segovia, he ignored the bishop's pleas that he had proven his Christian zeal by vigorously persecuting the Jews of his diocese.[41] In the Inquisition's first decades, thousands of convicted conversos, both living and deceased, were burned and thousands more granted penance. Early on mortality rates of accused conversos hovered around 40 percent, and grand, showpiece executions of dozens or even hundreds of victims, called *autos-da-fé* (acts of faith), brought considerable notoriety to Spain. While after 1540 the death sentence was passed much less frequently, the pure blood laws ensured that no one of Jewish ancestry could hold public office of any kind or inherit land. By this means, the threat to sacramental faith was crushed and doubt dispelled by force.

Joan of Arc

The cynical manipulation of Inquisitions to get rid of political enemies became a frequent enough event by 1400, as evident in the case of the clergy accused in 1406/7 of attempting to assassinate Pope Benedict XIII by magical means, or the trial two years later of the same pontiff by the Council of Pisa for sorcery and divination. Most famous was the trial of Joan of Arc, the young peasant woman of Domrémy who, inspired by the voices of saints and the archangel Michael, led the French army to defeat the English at Orleans, opening the way for the coronation of the dauphin as Charles VII (1422–61). Stories of Joan's supernatural powers abounded, such as the belief that she could fly, which compelled the people of Troyes, Champagne, to open their gates to her.[42] Stinging at their losses to a peasant girl, the English bought her from her Burgundian captors and tried her in 1429 on heresy and sorcery charges before the Bishop of Beauvais, turning her saints' voices into demonic ones and finding proof of her diabolical intent in her insistence on wearing male clothing. In 1431 she was burned at the stake, although like Pope Boniface VIII her reputation was later restored.

Witches: The Devil's Minions *par excellence*

Despite Joan's example, most educated churchmen did not believe the stories of strange processions of women who flew on strange beasts to the wild hunt of the goddess of fertility or the hunt, the German Holda or the Romanized Diana. This moderately skeptical position regarding the efficacy of popular magic was recorded in the ninth-century decretal known as the *Canon episcopi*,

> Bishops and their auxiliaries shall endeavor as far as possible to uproot from parishes all kinds of sorcery and magic, which are pernicious inventions of the Devil. ... Nor should any credence be given to what follows: viz. that certain women, perverted and dedicated to Satan, seduced by diabolical fantasies and deceits, believe and profess that they ride at night-time with Diana, goddess of the pagans, and with Herodias, astride certain beasts, in a company of innumerable other women, traversing immense spaces and obeying Diana's orders like those of a mistress who convokes them on certain nights. ... Great throngs, deceived by this false persuasion, believe in all these lies and thus fall back into pagan error. Therefore priests should preach wherever it may be necessary to point out the falsity of these errors and make it known that such tricks are produced by the Evil One who seduces the mind by vain imaginations. ... So it must be loudly proclaimed that those who believe such things have lost the faith and no longer belong to God, but only to him in whom they believe, that is the Devil.[43]

As this citation shows, most medieval churchmen thought that what such people were experiencing was merely a demonic deception upon gullible imaginations. However, those who believed themselves to perform such magical acts were still viewed as spiritual dangers. In contrast, secular law stipulated the death penalty for all who performed *maleficium*, harmful magic, on their neighbors or communities, regardless of whether or not the Devil was involved. Thirteenth-century scholastics such as Aquinas brought together these two conceptions of witchcraft – spiritual apostasy and secular *maleficium* – into an all-encompassing crime of incredible blasphemy. This assisted judges untrained in the fine art of scholastic theology because they could do away with trying to determine whether the accused's *maleficium* was effective or not and simply condemn all magic as demonic.

The *Canon episcopi* approach was confirmed in 1258 when Pope Alexander IV forbade Inquisitors from investigating cases of divination or sorcery which involved no patently heretical acts, such as praying at the altars of idols, committing sacrifices, or consulting demons.[44] However, Inquisitors continued to press for jurisdiction over magic, justifying their position with the belief that the papacy's foes "were not what they claimed to be, but practiced horrible rites and committed misdeeds without number."[45] Adding sorcery to the alleged crimes of heretics helped Inquisitors win popular and governmental support for their activities, for just about everyone feared *maleficia*.

The real shift in papal policy was made in 1320 by Pope John XXII who was convinced that there had been an attempt on his life by magical poisoning. On his behalf the Cardinal of Santa Sabina announced that "our most holy father and lord, ... fervently desires that the witches, the infectors of God's flock, flee from the midst of the House of God."[46] In 1326 a list of forbidden magical acts that Inquisitors could now investigate included invoking or sacrificing to demons or their images, making a pact with the Devil, and abusing the sacraments of baptism or the Eucharist. Six years later the pope himself proclaimed,

> Grievingly we observe...that many who are Christians in name only...sacrifice to demons, adore them, make or have made images, rings, mirrors...for magic purposes, and bind themselves to demons. They ask and receive responses from them and to fulfill their most depraved lusts ask them for aid...and make a pact with hell.[47]

These condemned acts corresponded to learned necromancy, not to the popular magic of the village witch. Well into the fifteenth century, trials against sorcery focused primarily on courtly necromancers.

The Suppression of Magic

Sorcerers, poisoners, and plotters haunted the halls of most European princely courts. For example, in 1411 Laurens Pignon, the Dominican confessor to the future Philip the Good of Burgundy, composed a little known manuscript entitled the *Traitié contre les devineurs*, or "Tract Against the Diviners," hoping to steer Philip's father, Duke John the Fearless and his court away from the divinatory and magical practices so prevalent in French and Burgundian courts. To do so he affirmed that since demons possessed enormous maliciousness and almost limitless powers, magical heresy caused immense social disruption. Pignon was fighting a losing battle, as the madness of King Charles VI was widely blamed on sorcery and attracted numerous magicians to his court. The political conflict between the houses of Orleans and Burgundy, moreover, had began with the murder of the king's brother at the behest of Duke John the Fearless of Burgundy, who admitted to the crime with the unfortunate excuse that "the devil had driven him" to it. For his part Pignon argued that the civil war had been caused by princely dabbling in the occult and by the general degeneration of the court as a result of such magical activity.[48] Pignon's impression was confirmed by Jean Petit (c.1360–1411), a theologian patronized by Duke John the Fearless for whom Petit composed a justification for John's assassination of Louis, accusing Louis of magically causing the king's madness. Petit's literary opponent, the Monk of St. Denis, denied the charge, contending that Louis had been an inveterate opponent of sorcery, as seen in his support of the trials of several necromancers in the last years of the fourteenth century, including the royal physician Jehan de Bar and the ascetic sorcerer Arnaud Guillaume, both of whom were burned.

News of such courtly sorcery reached the Parlement of Paris by 1390, which decreed that sorcery was now a civil offence worthy of its attention. Almost immediately two cases were brought forward, the first in 1390 involving the jilted lover Marion la Droiturière and a female magician, Margot de la Barre, who specialized in love charms. Under torture the two confessed that when the love magic failed they turned to the Devil, who appeared in a form reminiscent of the costumed demons of mystery plays, and provided the means to impede the former lover's forthcoming marriage. When the betrothed couple fell ill, Marion and Margot were immediately arrested, and after their trial burned at the stake in Paris.[49]

The second case involved a female diviner of Guérart, Jeanne de Brigue, who was arrested for magically assisting an ill innkeeper. Under torture she too confessed to using diabolical assistance, thus the Parlement's jurists assented to her burning, not so much for the magic, but for calling up demons, a form of manifest heresy. Then, in 1398, the University of Paris declared Devil-assisted sorcery to be heretical since it required a pact with the Devil. These cases reveal how learned notions of clerical necromancy were transposed onto incidents of popular magic. Lay magicians may indeed have called upon the Devil for help, imagining him in the form portrayed in popular drama, but it seems more likely that torture and leading questions forced the accused to add demonic elements to their magical rituals.

However, prior to 1420, there exist fewer than one hundred references to trials involving sorcery.[50] Many of these involved individuals accused of performing *maleficia* against the powerful. The accusations against Dame Alice Kytler and her confederates in Kilkenny, Ireland in 1324/25 included *maleficia*, the sectarian organization and apostasy of heresy, and demon worship. Like the Templars' trial, Kytler's demise was politically caused.[51] Invocation of the Devil appeared with increasing frequency, but despite Kytler's example there seemed little real anxiety about a sect of Devil-worshiping, magic-performing heretics. The scattered trials of alleged Luciferans did not generally include charges of sorcery, which remained largely restricted to political enemies or clergy. In no surviving trials prior to the fifteenth century was the full stereotype of the flying, sabbath-attending, cannibalistic witch complete. Even so, the "discovery" of sectarian heretics who worshiped Satan and desecrated Catholic rites helped confirm the veracity of Christian rituals and beliefs.

Waldensians and Witches

While attending the Council of Basel between 1435 and 1437 the Dominican Johann Nider composed a long treatise on sin called the *Formicarius*, recounting an earlier conversation with the Bernese judge Peter von Greyerz (Gruyères) regarding a series of trials in the Upper Simme Valley between 1397 and 1406 against a sect of Devil-worshiping sorcerers who devoured infants and performed *maleficia*. Von Greyerz said they had originated about the year 1375 and while there is no corroborating evidence for such, some Inquisitors working in the Alpine regions during the last quarter of the fourteenth century were claiming that the Devil was instructing his Waldensian disciples in the magical arts. One Inquisitor revealed that some Waldensians "celebrated wild orgies and drank magical liquids provided by a Mistress of Ceremonies," while Wolfgang Behringer has remarked on the close correspondence of Alpine Waldensianism with the earliest known witch trials and how Inquisitors adapted "the popular belief in nocturnal assemblies" to fit their developing conception of the activities of the heretical/witch "syna-gogue."[52]

Despite such blurring of boundaries between theological and magical heresy, it seems that Von Greyerz' trials at Boltigen were the first against a supposed sect of demonic, cannibalistic-infanticide witches. The credu-lous judge justified the use of torture by his fear that the captives could emit incapacitating odors or turn into mice to escape. In their confessions, *maleficia* was front and center, including murder by lightning, magically drowning children, bringing sterility to fields, animals, and women, raising storms, and performing divination. Under torture their leader, a man named Stedelen, provided the how-to details for their malevolent activities, most of which required the assistance of demons.[53]

The roots of this witch-hunt lay in the economic and political conflicts between the new rulers of the region, urban Bern, and the rural society of the Simme Valley, and since the trials were conducted entirely by Bern's secular governor and were opposed by the semi-skeptical local clergy, they were clearly an attempt to establish Bernese jurisdiction over the region. The era's atmosphere of religious confusion bred fears among commoners about the "the doubtful validity of the communion, the concern about the earthly and eternal salvation of every Christian, and the loss of the community of living and dead in heaven and on earth," leading to a "general fear that the world is full of devils."[54]

Fifteenth-century trials

After these trials it appears that church and state authorities became increasingly convinced of a massive diabolical conspiracy combining *maleficia* and Devil worship. The most nightmarish component of this underground witch sect was the ritual murder of infants. In some cases, especially Italy, witches were accused of sucking the blood from infants while they lay in their mother's bed, while in French-speaking Switzerland the accusation involved kidnapping the infants and killing and eating them at the witch synagogues. As Richard Kieckhefer remarks, the myth of blood-sucking witches probably relates to old, commonly held beliefs of vampirism, while the French charges of cannibalistic infanticide paralleled the diabolical conspiracy portrayed by preachers.[55] In both events, the charges that Jews and witches murdered infants fed into parental fears and made prosecution of the foes easier. Moreover, the meetings of *Vauderie* were called synagogues and later sabbaths; both Jews and witches were accused of using poisons to harm their neighbors; both were believed to be in league with the Devil in his assault against Christianity; both were thought to require the blood or bodies of Christian youths for their rituals; both were accused of desecrating the Eucharist in their hostility to the Church. Many Jews possessed reputations as potent magicians, and sometimes charges of ritual murder and sorcery were combined, as seen in a 1407 trial in Frankfurt which involved the purported sale of a child to a Jewish sorcerer.[56] As Jews were expelled from various regions, their supposed diabolical activities were merely transferred onto other suspects.

Even so, trials against alleged witch sects did not begin to escalate until the 1420s, reaching peaks in the 1450s and 1480s, petering out thereafter to the more typical trials against individual witches and sorcerers.[57] Between three and four hundred trials of witchcraft, some involving multiple suspects, are known to have taken place between 1428 and 1500. The heartland of such trials were the Alpine regions of Italy, French-speaking Switzerland, and France. In Switzerland witch-hunting spread from the French- and Italian-speaking regions into the German, where the word *hexerye*, the Swiss-German term for witch that would become the German standard (*hex*), first appeared in Lucerne in 1419, while the first known description in German of a witch-hunt was also from Lucerne (1428).[58] In the 1420s trials of groups of accused increased with regularity, such as the infamous witch-hunts in the secular court of Dauphiné which executed 110 women and 57 men.[59] In the following decade prominent groups of sorcerers were tried in the secular court of London in 1430; in 1430–1 and again in 1439 in Swiss Neuchâtel; in 1433 in Lucerne and Tirol, and elsewhere.

San Bernardino of Siena and the Witches of Italy

Leading the charge against alleged witches in Italy was the Dominican preacher Bernardino of Siena (1380–1444) who, like his contemporary John Capestrano, was also a fervent opponent of religious dissidents, although Bernardino's sermons were much less anti-Semitic than Capestrano's. The common people, who relied almost exclusively on aural means of communication, flocked to hear such preachers in the hopes of receiving means of protection against evil. Thousands listened to Bernardino's long, mesmerizing sermons which profoundly escalated a sense of both personal guilt and anxiety about diabolical enemies. Against the latter Bernardino promoted the veneration of his monogram tablet displaying the holy name of Jesus.

For his efforts Bernardino was accused by other churchmen of encouraging idolatry and magic and spurning devotion for the Eucharist and the crucifix. In the spring of 1426 Pope Martin V summoned him to Rome to stand trial before a phalanx of theologians. On his way he preached in Viterbo, telling his audience that "I am going to Rome to be cremated by fire and you, enjoying peace and tranquillity, will remain behind. They are calling me a heretic and the word circulating in Rome is that I must be burned at the stake."[60] With Capestrano's intervention Bernardino was cleared of the charges, but suspicion lingered until he was completely exonerated in 1432. Having just escaped his own inquisition, Bernardino turned even more vigorously to denouncing other heretics, especially witches and sorcerers whose crimes closely paralleled his own.

Carlo Ginzburg has clearly charted the subtle transformation in Bernardino's views on witchcraft that apparently resulted from his brush with the law.[61] In 1423 Bernardino had declared that old women who believed they flew with the goddess of the hunt and possessed powers to predict misfortunes and help bewitched children, women in labor, and the sick, were actually subjects of the Devil. However, he did not see them as members of a diabolical sect until the summer of 1426 when he began preaching in Rome against a demonic sect of witches. Upon his return to Siena in 1427 he added that it was a sin not to accuse witches: "I don't know how better to tell you: To the fire! To the fire! *Oimmè*! Do you want to know what happened in Rome when I preached there? If I could only make the same thing happen here in Siena! Oh, let's send up to the Lord God some of the same incense right here in Siena!"[62] Whether or not Bernardino was aware that he was projecting onto others the suspicions that had clung to him, his impact was profound. As Franco Mormondo suggests, Bernardino helped "to crystallize and popularize this panic-raising image of the witch as evildoing, heretical, idolatrous 'servant of Satan'" and to convince officials of the necessity of vigorous action against it.[63]

Soon hundreds of denunciations against alleged witches swamped the ecclesiastical authorities, forcing the Pope to restrict proceedings to the most serious cases only. These included the trial of Finicella, about whom Bernardino commented:

> And there was taken among others one who had told and confessed, without being put to torture, that she had killed thirty children or thereabouts, by sucking their blood; and she said that every time she let one of them go free she must sacrifice a limb to the devil,...And furthermore, she confessed, saying that she had killed her own little son, and had made a powder from him, which she gave people to eat in these practices of hers. And because it seemed beyond belief that any creature could have done so many wicked things, they wished to test whether this was indeed true.[64]

By this means Bernardino astutely turned attention away from suspicion of his own heterodox practices toward a more diabolical enemy.

Bernardino's sermons inspired the magistrates of Todi in 1428 to try one of their local and very popular female healers, Matteuccia Francisco. Two years earlier they had adopted Bernardino's anti-sorcery statutes, one of which stipulated "that no one must conjure up devils or carry out or cause to be carried out any spells or acts of witchcraft." At the start of her trial Matteuccia confessed to being a sorcerer and herbal healer with a large and prominent clientele. Suddenly Matteuccia's testimony took a sharp turn as she began confessing to the whole range of diabolical crimes, including the demonic pact, demon-assisted flight, attendance at distant sabbaths moderated by Lucifer, animal metamorphosis, the use of horrific unguents, and killing infants by sucking their blood. Such change, Kieckhefer surmises, was a result of direct judicial coercion or torture. On March 20, wearing a paper hat on her head, she rode a donkey to the public square and was burned at the stake.

Heresy and Conciliarism

Despite Bernardino's rhetoric, by 1400 the real threat of heresy was effectively gone in Italy and severely suppressed elsewhere. Yet Bernardino and his fellow preachers were not really cognizant of this fact, and the heresies of the previous century still lingered in their minds.[65] Such threats helped divert attention away from the very real problems confronting the institutional Church, such as the Papal Schism, increasing anticlerical sentiment, and even outright rebellion. The period between the Council of Constance's ending of the schism in 1418 and the Council of Basel's (1431–47) efforts to replace papal authority with a conciliar administrative system was a particularly tumultuous one. It is no wonder that the Council of Basel's participants raised concerns about the increasing attacks of Satan on Christendom. As part of this information campaign, several more treatises on diabolical witchcraft were composed, including *Ut magorum et maleficiorum errores* by the secular judge of the Dauphiné Claude Tholosan, the anonymous *Errores Gazariorum*, the Lucerne chronicle of Johannes Fründ, and Johann Nider's *Formicarius*.[66] At the Council of Basel in particular delegates "could exchange opinions as if at a European trade fair, they heard not only reports of the trial of Joan of Arc, but also got the first public view of the new image of the witches' sabbath, an idea that had been invented in the region around Lake Geneva."[67] The battle between conciliarists and papal centralists was long and fierce, and Nider's news of a diabolical, magical conspiracy threatening Christendom provided the papacy with a welcome alternative target for clerical attention.

Witch Trials after the Council of Basel

After the Council of Basel the prosecution of groups of witches accelerated throughout much of western Europe, fostered by the agitation of urban preachers.[68] Most trials still involved relatively small groups of defendants, such as a case from the Pays de Vaud in 1448. Beginning with an inquisition against Jaquet Durier, a doctor accused of witchcraft when a functionary for the local châtelaine died under his ministration, the interrogations soon implicated Catherine Quicquat and the miller Pierre Munier. These two seem to have been having an affair, while Quicquat was known to have earlier procured a love potion from an accused witch. The trial against the doctor began with the charge of *maleficia* but moved quickly to implicate him in the diabolical sabbath and cannibalistic infanticide. It was not until Quicquat's interrogation that the sexual and animalistic elements of demonic witchcraft came to the fore, foreshadowing the misogynistic notions of the 1487 *Malleus Maleficarum*. Ironically, even though Munier was the least socially respectable of the accused, he was the only defendant spared torture and a fiery death, thus his confession lacked the diabolical elements of the other two. As the community's miller, Munier was on good relations with the local lords, who may have protected him in this case.[69]

This example reveals how witchcraft accusations could be encouraged by the local authorities as a means of seeking legal redress, in this case a wrongful death, or of getting rid of troublesome residents. At the same time, once initiated, the trial process and the Inquisitor's sermonizing raised popular suspicion toward others in the community. Interpersonal conflicts, suspicion, and jealousy added to sincere fear of *maleficia* or of diabolical heresy to create a ready supply of accusers.

Other cases in the 1450s to 1480s followed a similar pattern. Merely affirming the moderate skepticism of the *Canon episcopi* could be dangerous, as William Adeline, a preacher and former theologian of the University of Paris, discovered. Persistently asserting that the witches' sabbath was fiction, Adeline was degraded from the priesthood and sentenced as a Waldensian witch to life in prison on a diet of bread and water. A signed pact with the Devil committing him to preach against the sabbath's reality was allegedly found on his person, and under torture he confessed to flying to diabolical meetings where he venerated demons and renounced his Christian faith. By this confession Adeline was forced to dispel the doubts he had raised.[70]

The most famous fifteenth-century trial of sectarian witches took place in Arras, northern France, between 1459 and 1462. The charges against the thirty-four accused centered on devil worship and "attendance at the synagogue of the Vaudois." Unusually only one individual was accused of *maleficia*, suggesting that it was clerical pressure and not local fears of witches that had sparked this event. The first accused, a male hermit, confessed under torture that his accomplices included a prostitute and a writer famed for poems honoring the Virgin Mary. Even by the standards of the day the procedures followed by the two Dominican Inquisitors, Jean, Bishop of Beirut, who as suffragan bishop was acting in the Bishop of Arras' absence, and the learned Jacques du Boys, were inexcusable. Several accused were tricked into confessions by insincere promises of leniency, and five were burned at the stake despite never having confessed to the crime. Following Bernardino's model the Inquisitors delivered impassioned sermons on the dangers of the diabolical threat, proclaiming that those who opposed the burnings must themselves be witches.[71] In his report of 1460, an anonymous Inquisitor justified the burnings by describing in grim detail the noxious sabbath activities of the accused and their dangerous opinions about heaven, hell, and the immortality of the soul.[72] News of the Arras trials spread quickly, for in

1460 a messenger was sent from Lille, north of Arras, to discover if there might be Waldensians there as well.[73] Even so, the Arras witch-hunts did not severely infect other territories, especially after the city's merchants began to complain to the Duke of Burgundy about the loss of business (no one seemed willing to risk doing business with possible witches), and after consulting the University of Louvain, Duke Philip the Good ordered a stop to further arrests. Over the complaints of theInquisitors, an appeal of one of the prisoners reached the Parlement of Paris, which ordered the discharge of most of the imprisoned and the recently returned Bishop of Arras formally ended the trials. Du Bois was denounced and seems to have lost his mind, dying a few months later. In a postscript, the Parlement of Paris pardoned all of those condemned and ordered the former prosecutors to fund masses in their honor.[74]

Ulricus Molitor and Heinrich Krämer

Despite this decision, the trials and burnings of sects of witches continued apace.[75] Scholarly interest in the subject remained strong, and a number of handbooks for Inquisitors were composed, including Nicholas Jacquier's *Flagellum Haereticorum Fascinariorum* of the 1450s, and two famous works from the late 1480s, Ulricus Molitor's *De Lamiis* (*The Witches*) of 1489, and the best known Inquisitor's manual of all time, Heinrich Krämer's (Institoris) *Malleus Maleficarum*, or *The Hammer of Witches*, published in 1487. As a means of gauging the range of possible positions we will examine Krämer's pointedly credulous work and Molitor's mildly skeptical treatise.

Although the *Malleus* claims to have been coauthored by the Dominican Inquisitor Jacob Sprenger, Krämer was responsible for most, if not all, of it. Like Bernardino, Krämer's personal motivation for his campaign against witches was vaguely linked with a spot of trouble he experienced with his ecclesiastical superiors. On April 2, 1482, Pope Sixtus IV ordered the Bishop of Augsburg to arrest Krämer and oblige him to return money and silverware that he had allegedly stolen following a sale of indulgences. Before formal condemnation could take place, the Archbishop of Craynensis (Albania) issued a formal call for the reconvening of the Council of Basel as a means of reducing papal authority. Krämer saw his moment, hastily composed a polemical attack upon the Bishop's motives, and was immediately rewarded with the dropping of embezzlement charges.[76] The Pope expected that Krämer would become a fervent opponent of conciliarism, and in October 1483 Sixtus IV commissioned him to combat such errors. The Inquisitor, however, required frequent reminders to return to his anti-conciliarist activities and never fulfilled his pledge to write another treatise on the subject.[77] Instead, he turned to attacking demonic witches. It can be surmised that Krämer, recently released from his own investigation, saw in witchcraft a means to redirect attention from his problems onto a massive threat to Christendom requiring the concerted efforts of all churchmen, conciliarist and papist alike, thereby taking the wind out of the conciliarists' sails.

Krämer, with Sprenger's help, manipulated Pope Innocent VIII into issuing a bull supporting their inquisitorial efforts, the *Summis disiderantes affectibus* of 1484 which offered papal support for the campaign against a vaguely defined diabolical threat. The strength of opposition to their work is evident from Krämer's experience in Innsbruck in 1485 where the Bishop and Archduke of Austria released all of Krämer's fifty suspects. Eric Wilson suggests that Krämer's defeat at Innsbruck colored his composition of the *Malleus*, as he sought to "negate the baleful effects of skeptical clerics" by demonizing magic as a means of maximizing "the potential of the heretical-demonic threat" of *maleficia*.[78] Krämer's reputation as a major hunter of witches was, like the demonic sabbath he pursued, illusory, based more on his baneful treatise than on actual convictions.

Sprenger does not seem to have shared the anti-witch passion of his supposed friend, becoming in fact an implacable enemy of Krämer as a result of the latter's unethical methods of winning scholarly support for his manual among the theologians of the University of Cologne. When only four professors offered qualified support for the text, Krämer, without Sprenger's knowledge, hired a clerical notary to forge a second letter of enthusiastic approval and inserted it into the otherwise legitimate notary instrument issued on May 14, 1487. When the forgery was uncovered, it blackened Krämer's reputation and enraged Sprenger who, as provincial vicar of southern Germany, proceeded to prosecute his colleague for the forgery.[79] Krämer withdrew to the Mosel region where in March of 1488 he further incensed his superiors by approving a community's erection of a counter-magic crucifix. Only in 1491 did he return to his beloved witch persecution when the Nurnberg city council requested his assistance in some trials. Here he composed a treatise counteracting laxity in pursuing witches and rebuking skeptical magistrates.[80] The aldermen refused to allow its publication.

The *Malleus* was intended to assist Inquisitors to extract confessions from accused witches. It irrevocably linked *maleficia* to the Devil's sect, explained why women were so prominent among the accused, and used the "reality" of demonic witchcraft as a proof of the veracity of the Catholic faith. Walter Stephens has shown that Krämer's peculiar obsession with magically induced impotence and theft of penises was rooted in his own need to prove the reality of the sacraments, especially that of marriage. According to Catholic theory, the sacraments worked unfailingly by virtue of the divine power within them (*ex opere operato*). Yet it was self-evident that the sacrament of marriage, which major purpose was to produce children, did not always work as many couples remained childless. By showing that the Devil and his human assistants were impeding the marital act, Krämer believed he had found an acceptable explanation for the sacrament's apparent impotence. He therefore compelled witches to confess in prurient detail to this particular crime, thereby tangibly confirming his faith, just as charges of abusing Hosts confirmed the veracity of the Eucharist.[81]

Above all, Krämer was a vigorous defender of the real presence of Christ in the Host, composing in the early 1490s two treatises on the subject. In one of these, the *Tractatus novus de miraculoso eucariste sacramento* (*New Treatise on the miraculous Sacrament of the Eucharist*), he defended the veneration of a miraculously bleeding Host at an Augsburg shrine against the slanders of a skeptical preacher, threatening all skeptics with excommunication. The second, longer treatise, the *Tractatus varii cum sermonibus plurimus contra quattor errores novissime exortos adversus divinissimum euchariste sacramentum* (*Various treatises with many sermons against four new errors against the divine sacrament of the Eucharist*) appeared in 1494, seeking to inoculate lay people against the growing skepticism toward transubstantiation. Promoting belief in Eucharistic miracles, he fixed "upon the skeptical minds of his listeners a firm belief in both the efficacy of supernatural power in general and in the reality of the threat of demonic magic in particular" and declared that denying the reality of *maleficium* was itself the heresy of unbelief.[82]

Krämer's reputation within the Dominican Order was not fully restored until after Sprenger's death in 1495. Nor did his *magnum opus* have its desired effect. Despite its popularity as a printed manual (at least fourteen editions between 1487 and 1521), it did not spark witch trials throughout Europe, and interest in persecuting witches declined after its original publication. Many church and secular officials preferred the approach of Ulricus Molitor, the jurist of Constance whose 1489 dialogue on female witches reasserted the *Canon episcopi* tradition against the realist camp. In contrast to Krämer, Molitor advocated sending infertile couples to a physician who would undoubtedly discover a natural cause for their affliction. The supposed preternatural abilities of witches to control weather or fly were mere illusions of demons which could not suspend the course of nature. Yet, Molitor also admitted that female sorcerers who worshiped the Devil deserved harsh treatment, not for supposed *maleficia* but because of their apostasy. Molitor too shared Krämer's misogynistic belief that women were incredibly susceptible to the Devil's charms, advising them to remember their baptismal covenant with Christ, resist the Devil, and arm themselves with the sign of the cross.[83] Sprenger had likewise established the cult of the Rosary in Germany as a means of regulating female thought. Many officials clearly preferred Molitor's stance on the subject of witchcraft and disdained the *Malleus* for its advocacy of inquisitorial supremacy over local lords. Instead, civic officials were becoming preoccupied with another sin against God that seemed to be provoking his ire: blasphemy.

The Battle against Blasphemy

Judging from the inquisitorial records of the Low Countries, trials for blasphemy were increasing in the late fifteenth century. Between 1470 and 1517, dozens of individuals were punished for blaspheming the sacrament, denying the virginity of Mary, expressing skepticism about Christ's divinity or resurrection, and desecrating saints' images or sacramentals. Even the eating of meat during Lent was treated harshly as a tangible denial of Christ's crucifixion. While Count John of Nevers was expelled from the Order of the Golden Fleece for his "disbelief," most offenders were ordinary townsmen. Over fifteen men were banned from Ghent between 1478 and 1482 for "swearing horrible and blasphemous oaths against God." At the end of September 1481 the Dominican preacher Jacob Weyts publicly accused the city of harboring heretics, although a chronicler wryly noted that he offered no names. In response, Ghent's magistrates closed the Dominican house until the brothers publicly retracted their offensive remarks.[84]

Civic magistrates, however, did not wish to have their city's reputation besmirched by charges of godlessness, while Inquisitors linked "skeptics" with the largely fictitious "Brothers of the Free Spirit," easing prosecution of individual urbanites who vented anticlerical anger or religious doubt.

Such blasphemy was also tied to sedition, as seen in the case of the five men beheaded in Bruges in 1485 for blasphemy of the "sacrament of the altar" and for their "rebellion against [Emperor] Maximilian and his son Philip [Duke of Burgundy]" who ruled Flanders.[85] Perhaps spurred by this notorious case, on February 19, 1491 Ghent's jurists specified the punishment for a first blasphemy offence as pillorying, the boring of the tongue with a hot iron, and a month's imprisonment on a diet of bread and water.[86] Bruges' council followed suit a month later by stipulating that "no one is from now on in any way to blaspheme the almighty God or his saints, nor to swear any unseemly oaths, upon threat of severe punishment at the discretion of the magistrates by expulsion and other things."[87]

A few years later, in 1495, an official with the court of Brabant, Willem vander Taverijen, composed a treatise on how to deal with heresy, disbelief, blasphemy, sacrilege, and sorcery. While he affirmed that some doubt was merely from individual weakness, the determined expression of such sentiment was heretical. Blasphemy, the "swearing by the head, beard, hair of God, or similar oaths" was worthy of civil punishment because it angered God who countered with "plagues, miserable times from tempests and earthquakes."[88] Sacrilege, which included the desecration or theft of sacred objects, merited punishment in the stocks, while sorcery deserved the torture of red-hot irons. This last crime he defined as "to do any soothsaying or witchcraft under appearance of holiness or religion, or with holy words to hinder someone or to know secret things . . . or to conjure the devil to come." Like blasphemy, sorcery was inviting immediate divine retribution.[89] This Brabant jurist's treatise on crime both confirms John Bossy's theory of the overshadowing of the "Seven Deadly Sins" by the Decalogue in late-medieval religious and legal discourse and reveals how magic and religion remained interwoven in the social fabric. In this context, the spoken word possessed great destructive power, directly through magical conjurations or curses and indirectly by incurring the wrath of God.

Punishment for such crimes was therefore harsh. As a result of her unspecified blasphemy, in 1491 Katheline, widow of Willem sLozen, was stripped naked, placed on a wagon, stroked with a red-hot iron, and taken to the main square where a large piece of her tongue was cut off and thrown into the fire. She was then banned for fifty years from Flanders.[90] A similar edict of expulsion (without the torture) was granted Mathijs van der Eeke merely for covering his eyes with a pair of nutshells when the Holy Sacrament passed by in a procession. Why

Katheline was treated so harshly is difficult to surmise, for even Vander Taverijen had recommended that women and youth be accorded lighter sentences than adult men because of their "frailty of complexion."[91] That she was accorded the hot iron treatment suggests that her blasphemous oath was perceived as a veiled threat of magic.

Such punishments did little to stop blasphemous actions. On July 15, 1506, Jacob de Zomere was banned from Ghent for sticking a knife through a silver crucifix, while Jan Steinic's horribly blasphemous oaths won for him a fifty-year ban the following year. These offences forced the Emperor Maximilian and the Ghent-born Prince Charles, sovereign of the Low Countries, to publish a mandate setting out the punishment for blasphemy: for a first offence, a fine; for a second, a fine and imprisonment; for a third, the boring of the offender's tongue and exile.[92] Charles would reissue and strengthen this mandate twice more, but to no avail. After 1519, Protestant preachers gained a strong foothold in the Low Countries, in part because they were able to feed off this popular substratum of anticlericalism and skepticism toward the preternatural aspects of Catholic belief and practice.

The Possessed Nuns of Le Quesnay

One wonders about the effects of this escalated moral vigilance, of the inflammatory sermons against blasphemy, and promotion of fervent introspection that became the counterpoint to increasing skepticism and doubt. A clue is provided by an extraordinary event around 1491 that shook a convent of Le Quesnay in Cambrai (just east of Arras). Sister Johanna Potiere, one of the mostly aristocratic nuns of this devout Augustinian house, was suddenly and mysteriously overcome with fits that forced her into painful contortions, caused her eyes to bulge out of her head, and to speak horrible blasphemies in a hideous voice, all signs of demonic possession. Quickly the disorder spread through the convent, and three learned clergymen, the deacon Gilles Nettelet and the preachers Nicholas Gonor and Jan Sarrasin were called in to investigate. Their exorcisms led to fascinating discussions with the legion of demons plaguing the women. When asked why they were tormenting these nuns, they replied: "we are perpetually damned for only one transgression, and you Christians commit them infinitely, yet you are always pardoned by grace, by contrition, confession and satisfaction, which we are not allowed." Why, then, the exorcists inquired, do you not afflict soldiers and other dissolute men, instead of these pious women? Because, they answered, the former are already "our friends" and assistants. Approaching the possessed women with the consecrated Host had the desired result, for when confronted by the "true body of Christ," the victims cried out "Jesus" as a sign of their deliverance, while the demons ridiculed Christian devotion to the miraculous without denying the veracity of the real presence. Three long Masses said over a period of three days finally expelled most of the demons, although when the Bishop of Cambrai Henry of Bergen arrived to cleanse and reconsecrate the convent, he had to expel three or four persistent spirits by holy conjurtions and the sign of the cross. An investigation into the cause of the disturbance revealed that prior to the possessions the roughly 45-year-old Potiere had not only committed some unspecified sins, but had composed a "hideous and abominable" work entitled *Mon amoureux* which inflamed diabolical passions. For this she was imprisoned for life, although she died not long after her trial.[93]

By uttering in a horrifically demonic voice the doubts and skepticism being expressed by ordinary people, demoniacs dramatically proclaimed that such skepticism was diabolical. Defenders of sacramental realism cheered when demons confirmed the veracity of the real presence of Christ in the Eucharist and the spiritual power of the clergy. Although it seems unlikely that the original possessions were directly encouraged by the clergy, they were not hesitant to turn these newsworthy events to their own advantage.

Mary of Nijmegen

A late fifteenth-century drama reveals some of the elements of the Devil's conspiracy which by 1500 were known to urbanites. *Mary of Nijmegen* was first printed in prose form in illustrated Dutch and English editions and then dramatized sometime between 1485 and 1510, around the same time as the publication of the *Malleus*.[94] Its story recounts the tale of a young maiden of Guelders, Netherlands, Mariken (Mary), who was sent by her uncle priest to the city of Nijmegen to purchase supplies. Once done, she notices that night was coming and seeks lodging from an aunt who lived in the city. This woman, however, had that day argued so strenuously with several other women over Duke Adolf's imprisonment of his father that they accused her of being a "raging she-devil". She directed this fury at Mariken, accusing her of gross sexual misconduct, finally refusing her request. Disheartened and frightened, the girl collapses next to a hedge, praying for help from either God or the Devil. The latter arrives as a handsome man (albeit with a set of horns on his head), and through his usual means of subterfuge convinces Mariken to make a pact with him in exchange for knowledge of the seven liberal arts – rhetoric, music, logic, grammar, geometry, arithmetic, and alchemy – subjects of learning normally closed to women. She asks to learn necromancy, for her uncle was a practitioner but had refused to show her his magic manual. Naturally the Devil spurns this request, not wanting Mariken to learn how to control him. He also insists she change her name to Emma (Emmeken), as her real name is too reminiscent of the Virgin Mary's, and she promises never to make the sign of the cross. For the next seven years Emma is the demon's mate, amazing people with her knowledge. Then, during a return visit to Nijmegen, she and her demon lover watch a drama entitled the "play of Masscheroen," in which a demon advocate brings Lucifer's case for the souls of men to the court of heaven and is ultimately trounced by God and the Virgin Mary. The play convinces Emma that her soul is in eternal danger, and she seeks release from the pact. In anger, the demon raises her high up in the air and then, to the horror of her watching uncle, drops her to the street below. She survives, recovers from her wounds, and embarks with her uncle on a quest to be restored to the Church, ultimately appealing to the Pope himself. Although horrified at her tale of a seven-year affair with a demon, the Pope admires her penitent spirit, and he commands that for the remainder of her life she wear a set of heavy iron rings as penance. She becomes a nun and for the next several years lives an extremely ascetic life until an angel releases her from the rings, and she dies forgiven two years later.

Clearly Mariken was no simple peasant witch, but a young woman with aspirations of higher learning, indeed a female Faustus. In this play are many of the elements of the demonic witch stereotype that had developed by the late fifteenth century: a pact with Satan, renunciation of Christianity, implied sexual congress with demons, and demonic flight, although this last was not a means of transportation but the result of a demon's pique. However, in several respects Mariken does not fit the stereotype, for she actually receives the promised knowledge, whereas the demonic rewards of ordinary witches vanished once the pact was sealed. Furthermore, Mariken did not carry out acts of *maleficium*, was not part of a Satanic conspiracy, nor did she attend the sabbath and, most importantly of all, she was ultimately forgiven and became a saint. If this play acts in any way as a reflector of the views of the urban playwright, performers, and audience, it appears that necromancy was widely known as a clerical pursuit, that making a pact with Satan was a credible thing, and that the audiences wished for even the most extreme cases of diabolism to be forgivable. Although the play can be read as a warning against women seeking higher education, it can also be seen as a critique of their exclusion from universities which forced some to seek knowledge by forbidden means.

Conclusion

Several points need to be reiterated to bring together this chapter's strands of argument. The early modern cosmos was a living thing that worked by means of moralized correspondences and which provided magic of all sorts with a logically consistent role. The cosmos was also filled with invisible, powerful beings, some of whom, the demons, lived close to humans and received far more attention in art and literature than the angels. Ecclesiastical officials worried about the increased practice of necromancy on the part of the lower clergy, and argued that it was impossible for any human to control demons. These ideas about diabolical magic were transposed by Inquisitors onto the image of a conspiratorial sect of heretics to create the Luciferans, then to transform the Waldensians into witches plotting the destruction of Christendom. The sensational news of each trial spread by word of mouth, by sermon and, by the middle of the fifteenth century, by print.

This cosmos was also highly gendered, and it is not surprising that the ultimate evil, demonic witchcraft, would be associated most strongly with women. The process took about a century, as most of the accused in the early fifteenth-century trials were men, while by the writing of the *Malleus Maleficarum* most suspects were women. Women were generally believed to be weaker in mind and body, and with their cooler humors, more susceptible to diabolical temptation. Despite the Church's assault on necromancers, there remained the assumption that learned clergy could control demons if they followed the rituals to the letter. Women, excluded from higher education and holy orders, could only become the agent of the Devil, whatever rituals they performed. In the harsh economic and social climate of the fifteenth century, moreover, there was an increasing tendency for men to project their own feelings of guilt (for excluding women from universities, skilled vocations, and inheritance or for abusing them in and out of families) or sexual frustration. Celibate clergy were particularly prone to this fear of female sexuality and pollution.[95] By the end of the fifteenth century, the stereotype of a magician had changed from a learned, pious male to that of a sect of vengeful servants of Satan who were mostly old women, seeking power over their lives and neighbors otherwise denied them. Inquisitors and preachers encouraged people to accuse those who fit the stereotype, and with each trial, the stereotype was reinforced.

One of the critical components of the spread of this conspiracy theory was the clerical, and sometimes popular, campaign against skepticism, doubt, and dissidence. Although medieval Europe was a strictly Christian realm, not everyone believed fervently, and there were many expressions of doubt about Christian dogma. As Richard Marius remarks,

> To admit to irreligion or to skepticism was to confess oneself scornful of the common human bonds that defended morality and held chaos at bay. To some extent it was also to scorn one's fellow human beings, for if nearly everyone in a society professes a religion, those who do not profess faith contemn the collective wisdom of the community and inevitably seem a threat – the threat that God or the gods may punish the entire society for the neglect of a few. ... Yet the doubts exist. They exist because the community ardently presses a conformity of faith on everyone; the community does become aware of them; and the religious orders of society in reacting against those doubts push all the harder to make their faith normative and unassailable. The very intensity of this effort to make faith and the culture identical creates in some quarters all the more reaction. ...The late medieval church's response to philosophical skepticism about theology seemed to be an almost subconscious drive to multiply cultic practices that submerged doubt, that made piety so physical, so demanding, that one had no time for reflection and brooding on doubts that reflection might induce.[96]

Efforts to deflect such doubt often took unusual forms, such as charges of Jewish Host desecration, or miracles performed at saints' shrines, or the horrid stories of malevolent witches desecrating Christian holy objects. The battle between zealots and skeptics escalated to a fevered pitch as a result of the sixteenth-century Reformation.

2

THE REFORMATION AND THE END OF THE WORLD

> because of our sins we are in tribulation, for which we must do penance ... for all Christendom is placed in great anxiety, danger and fear on account of the heresies, disunity, dissension, and wars between the Christian princes. ... The Turk, seeing that through the disunity and wars the Christian authorities are weakened, augments himself, so that he quickly deliberates (if God is not merciful to us) to spring upon Christendom from all sides with mighty armies, both at sea and on the land ...
>
> *Een cort begrijp vanden Payse/tusschen den Keyser/den Coninck van Enghelant/ende den Coninck van Vranckerijcke* (Antwerp, n.d. [1544]), iv.

So thought an anonymous Catholic pamphleteer in 1544. By this date the divisions engendered by the various reform movements had left Christian unity an empty shell and had inspired innumerable predictions of apocalyptical punishment, in this citation to be enacted by the Muslim Turks. Such predictions ultimately came to nought, but this was not apparent to people living in one of the most religiously vexing moments in European history. Throughout the sixteenth century the sense of living on the eve of the great tribulation predicted in the book of Revelation remained vivid, inspiring both fear and determination to act. Yet this was not how the century had begun.

By 1500, papal supremacists and Inquisitors had largely managed to suppress both heresy and conciliarism, ameliorating somewhat the profound religious confusion which had driven them to hunt out diabolical sectarian witches. Even Heinrich Krämer saw the writing on the wall, spending the last years of his life (from January 1499 to his death in 1505) battling not witches but Waldensians and radical Huss-ites in Bohemia and Moravia. His major target were the Moravian Brethren who denied the real presence of Christ in the Host, against which he wrote two highly polemical treatises. Although he managed to slip in some of his anti-witchcraft notions in a list of Bohemian errors (identifying opposition to witchcraft trials as a Waldensian heresy), Krämer seems not to have been involved in any further witch trials.[1] Instead, he now argued that the "Bohemian heresy" was a sign of the nearness of the Last Judgment. He was not alone in believing himself to be standing on the edge of the apocalyptical nightmare. The soon eruption of Luther's Reformation movement challenging papal supremacy and Roman Catholic truth escalated this eschatological anticipation to fevered levels, helping to revive the lagging fears of diabolical conspiracies.

The Humanist Challenge

Despite Inquisitors' efforts to distinguish sharply between licit reli-gion and illicit magic, for most people living around 1500, the two realms remained closely interwoven. This situation became a cause of increasing criticism from Renaissance humanists who generally scorned university scholasticism's preoccupation with metaphysics and natural philosophy and promoted the revival of the values of ancient Greece and Rome, although some of these merely replaced Artistolean meta-physics with Platonic mysticism. Others, such as Desiderius Erasmus of Rotterdam, became the sixteenth century's most fervent critic of superstition and popular devotionalism. Erasmus not only mastered the style of Cicero but also was deeply influenced by the spirit of the *Devotio moderna*, a late-medieval movement of reform which highlighted inner devotion to Christ and the sacraments against the crass vener-ation of religious objects. With his *philosophia Christi*, or the philosophy of Christ, Erasmus promoted the personal imitation of Christ and the eloquence of the ancients and satirized both scholasticism and popular devotionalism. In his 1526 dialogue "A Journey for Religion's Sake," two friends, Menedemus and Ogygius, discuss the latter's pilgrimage to several English saints' shrines, especially the Virgin-by-the Sea, wherein was housed a vial of the milk of the Virgin Mary. Menedemus expostulates, "O Mother so like her Son! The son left us so much of his blood on earth; the mother left us so much of her milk. Yet it is hard to believe that the mother of an only child could have had so much milk, even if the baby hadn't had a drop of it." Ogygius explains that they "say the same thing about the Lord's Cross, bits of which are displayed in many places publicly and privately. If all the bits were brought together in one place, they'd be a load for a freighter. And yet the Lord was able to carry the whole cross." When his mate seems skeptical, Ogygius offers the Church's rationale for the existence of multiple copies of a single relic: "After all the Lord is omnipotent and can multiply these things at his will," a response that hardly mollifies Menedemus, who comments, "That's a pious explanation, but I fear that many such things are devised for monetary gain." In the end Menedemus contends that what is most important is to take responsibility for one's own affairs and not to blame saints for misfortune: "Scripture instructs me to look after these things myself. I have never come across a precept telling me to commit them to the saints."[2] Although Erasmus would have preferred worship be concentrated on Christ, he was not averse to the proper veneration of the saints. He wrote in *The Handbook of the Christian Soldier*,

> You venerate the saints, and you take pleasure in touching their relics. But you disregard their greatest legacy, the example of a blameless life. No devotion is more pleasing to Mary than the imitation of Mary's humility. No devotion is more acceptable and proper to the saints than striving to imitate their virtues. ... And although the model of all piety is readily found in Christ, nevertheless, if you take great delight in worshipping Christ in his saints, then make sure you imitate Christ in his saints and in honor of each saint eradicate one vice or strive to attain a particular virtue. If this is the fruit of your devotion, I shall not be averse to these external manifestations.[3]

Erasmus hoped that by providing editions of the original writings of the founders and early fathers of Christianity purified of the medieval scholastic glosses, all of the accumulated misinterpretations keeping people from the *philosophia Christi* would simply fall away and the Church reform itself. His younger admirers clamored more impatiently for such reform and eventually turned to a less diffident champion in the monk and professor Martin Luther.

The Reformation Event: Martin Luther and Indulgences

On October 31, 1517, the Augustinian monk and professor of biblical studies at the University of Wittenberg (Electoral Saxony), Martin Luther (1483–1546), circulated a set of ninety-five theses on the subject of indulgences which he proposed for a scholarly debate. Unexpectedly this academic announcement set off a storm of controversy. Luther's major concern was with the relationship between God and humanity. He was deeply distressed about the discord between his deep religiosity and the laxity of official religion, and sought somehow to bring the two into harmony. He did so by arguing that winning God's pleasure was no human work at all, but a gift given freely by God to the truly penitent. In this scheme, the entire ecclesiastical system of priestly confession and penance would disintegrate. Church leaders could hardly let his opinions go unchallenged.

Despite his bluster and remarkable array of verbal weaponry, Luther was a sensitive man, fearful of the prospect of death and eternal damnation. Throughout his life he remained tormented by personal doubt, attacks which he dubbed the assaults of Satan and against which he recommended direct confrontation by boldly asserting one's Christian faith despite the lurking incertitude, shouting to the Devil "I am a Christian" like a kind of exorcism. He also developed a doctrine of certitude which affirmed that those chosen by God for salvation were given an unshakeable faith and assurance of their election. As a believer's faith increased, Luther asserted, the Devil attacked more viciously, hence escalated bouts of doubt were themselves proof of growing faith. For Luther, the Devil was as real as God, and oftentimes more proximate and tangible than the Creator.

Many of Luther's beliefs were formulated to dispel his lifelong fear of God's displeasure and of death. When as a law student he was caught in a lightning storm in the summer of 1505, Luther was so terrified of death he vowed to become a monk.[4] As an Augustinian monk he tried traditional monastic disciplines – self-denial, lack of sleep or comforts, wearing itchy hair shirts – to assuage his guilty conscience, but nothing helped. He despaired that the saintly panoply was not listening, and began wondering if the Church actually controlled the means of salvation. His thoughts began to coalesce while lecturing at the University, and when in the summer of 1517 he heard that some of his parishioners were purchasing indulgences from itinerant preachers just outside the boundaries of Electoral Saxony (from which they had been forbidden by

Elector Frederick III "the Wise" as a means of protecting his own lucrative relic business) Luther reacted vehemently.

The indulgences were issued by Pope Leo X (1513–21) at the behest of Albrecht of Brandenburg who needed funds to repay the loan incurred to fund his election as Archbishop of Mainz. The Dominican indulgence hawker Johann Tetzel made the extraordinary claim that for some coins these documents could remit sin entirely and spring loved ones out of purgatory. Although Luther's debate on indulgences was never held, the professor sent a copy with a respectful letter to Archbishop-elect Albrecht, informing him of his preachers' misinformation, and circulated the *Ninety-Five Theses* to friends who had them immediately published and disseminated. Tetzel demanded a heresy trial for Luther, but the pontiff did not take the threat seriously, brushing off Luther as a "drunken German" and delaying action because he was trying to woo Frederick the Wise to stand as emperor-elect against King Charles I of Spain. The Pope sent Cardinal Cajetan (1469–1534) to convince Luther to accept papal authority over purgatory, but Luther merely dug in his heels and repudiated the whole doctrine of the treasury of merit and the Pope's power to draw from it.

Luther's papal opponents at first viewed him with some justification as another proponent of conciliarism. In 1518 Luther and one of his Wittenberg colleagues, Andreas Bodenstein, or Karlstadt, faced their most serious opponent, the Ingolstadt theologian Johann Eck, at the disputation in Leipzig. Eck forced Luther into expressing sympathy with Jan Hus and to admitting that he rejected both papal and conciliar authority in religious matters in favor of the authority of the scriptures. Thanks to Frederick, Luther continued to elude the Inquisition and by 1520 had embarked on his prolific propaganda campaign promoting reform. Humanists applauded him as a critic of clerical and scholastic abuses, while German nationalists depicted him as Hercules bashing in the skulls of papal foreigners who were sucking the Germans dry. His key booklets of 1520 and 1521, *To the Christian Nobility of the German Nation*, *The Babylonian Captivity of the Church*, and *The Freedom of a Christian*, called upon lay rulers to inaugurate a variety of reforms of the Church in the face of papal intransigence and popularized the slogan of the priesthood of all believers, that all Christians were ultimately responsible for their own salvation without mediation of a priesthood. He called for the dismantling of the sacramental system, leaving only two sacraments, baptism and the Lord's Supper, the latter to be celebrated in the vernacular and to include communion with both the bread and wine for lay people.

While he maintained that Eucharistic bread and wine became the body and blood of Christ, he rejected any clerical role in this transformation, relying instead on the verbal commitment of Christ at the Last Supper.

Luther furthermore promoted the reading of the scriptures by all believers, translating the Bible from its original Hebrew and Greek into a very powerful German. In every writing and sermon he asserted that salvation was a gift from God received solely by faith and based entirely on divine mercy, without performance of any good works. His famous catchphrases, "priesthood of all believers," and "freedom of a Christian," not to mention his portrayal of the papacy as the Antichrist, made him tremendously popular. When in 1521 he was tried by the newly crowned emperor, Charles V at the imperial meeting or Diet at Worms, Germany, Luther refused to recant any of his writings. Although the emperor had granted him a letter of safe conduct, Luther sensed that his days were numbered. His prince, however, intervened, kidnapping the professor and hiding him at Wartburg castle, thus avoiding a popular uprising. Here Luther translated the Bible and directed the Reformation.

Luther's sophisticated theological ideas were grossly simplified by pamphlet writers and preachers who popularized his catchphrases (today's "soundbites"). As a result, the Reformation movement that he inaugurated quickly spiraled out of his control, a fact which frustrated him, believing as he did that there could be only one true, divinely inspired interpretation of the scriptures. Evidently he did not count on the impatience and militance of much of the German populace, including his Wittenberg colleagues. For while Luther was in hiding, Karlstadt and the young professor of Greek Philip Melanchthon were overseeing the transformation of the religious life of Wittenbergers, following Luther's reform program. At the end of 1521 they believed the populace ready for the conversion of the Mass into the evangelical Lord's Supper. On Christmas Day, Karlstadt appeared before the congregation wearing a plain cleric's robe. When the moment came for the Eucharist, Karlstadt, facing the audience instead of the altar, began speaking the words of the ceremony in German. There was no incense, no elevation of the Host and, perhaps most radical of all, no denial of the consecrated wine to lay people. The tension was palpable as the quasi-magical rite of transubstantiation reinforcing priestly power was replaced by a simple ceremony implying the spiritual equality of all believers.

Karlstadt also preached and wrote against the veneration of saints' images as a form of idolatry. Thus emboldened, crowds of Wittenbergers began removing and sometimes destroying religious images and statuary.

For centuries the devout had venerated the images and relics of saints as direct conduits of divine mercy, but now, suddenly convinced that they had been duped into placing their trust in inanimate objects, they lashed out in ferocious anger, destroying the objects of their previous devotion and implicitly condemning the Catholic clergy who had promoted them. Reformed leaders insisted on the removal of Catholic religious art from churches as part of the refashioning of sacred spaces by eradicating any taint of "priestly magic" and making the word of God the central aspect of worship. The ultimate goal was to create literate congregations which conceived of their faith much more in literary, rather than visual, material, or magical ways.

The violence in Wittenberg was too much for Elector Frederick and Luther therefore returned to Wittenberg in March, 1522 whereupon he immediately condemned radical action and advocated a more leisurely pace of reform which would allow the new ideas to sink into the hearts of all citizens before further external changes be made. Against Karlstadt, Luther asserted that since religious artwork was not explicitly condemned in the scriptures, it was permissible. An enraged Karlstadt denounced Luther as a sellout to the godless authorities and left the city. Impatience for radical transformation mounted, inflamed by Karlstadt and other popular preachers and justified by the almost universal conviction that the end was near.

Luther, the Devil, and the End of the World

Much of what Luther said resonated loudly among the German people. The Reformer's early mental world was shaped within a rural milieu in which, Heiko A. Oberman, has suggested, Luther gained his "respect" for "the at once wondrous and scary world of spirits, Devil, and witch-craft, which the modern mind has come to call superstition."[5] Oberman suggested further that

> Luther's world of thought is wholly distorted and apologetically misconstrued if his conception of the Devil is dismissed as a medieval phenomenon and only his faith in Christ retained as relevant or as the only decisive factor. Christ and the Devil were equally real to him: one was the perpetual intercessor for Christianity, the other a menace to mankind till the end. To argue that Luther never overcame the medieval belief in the Devil says far too little; he even intensified it and

lent to it additional urgency: Christ and Satan wage a cosmic war for mastery over Church and world.[6]

Every believer was intimately and personally involved in this struggle, for the Christian lived on the battleground of the cosmic struggle between God and the Devil which intensified as individuals became more godly. The Devil who constantly harassed Luther was an immensely dangerous opponent who sought to thwart the word of God by dividing the Reformation and making believers doubt their salvation and wallow in uncertainty and fear. To stop these assaults, Lutherans were to announce loudly to Satan, "I have been baptized, I am a Christian."[7] Luther also advocated demeaning the Devil and his agents through the use of crass, even scatological language, hurling verbal excrement at the Devil and his alleged minions, especially Catholics, other disagreeable Reformers, Anabaptists and, most infamously, Jews. Thus Luther's original campaign to eradicate his fear of death was metamorphosed into a battle against death's partner, the Devil.

For Luther, then, anyone who opposed his version of the gospel was a much greater danger to faith than witches. He certainly believed in diabolical witchcraft, and affirmed that witches should indeed be put to death for their apostasy. In 1533 he told this story of his mother's encounter with a local witch:

> Doctor Martinus said a great deal about witchcraft, about asthma and hobgoblins, how once his mother was pestered so terribly by her neighbor, a witch, that she had to be exceedingly friendly and kind to her in order to appease her. The witch had cast a spell over the children so that they screamed as if they were close to death. And when a preacher merely admonished this neighbor in general words, she bewitched him so as to make him die; there was no medicine that could help him. She had taken the soil on which he had walked, thrown it into the water, and bewitched him in this way, for without that soil he could not regain his health.[8]

Such devilish acts, made so much of by Krämer, Luther thought secondary to the diabolical bewitchment of the minds of Christians to follow incorrect interpretations of the Bible.

Not only did Luther struggle daily against Satan, but he lived in the shadow of the apocalypse, believing that he would witness the final cataclysmic battle between the Devil and Christ which would sorely test the faith of believers but ultimately end with Christ's triumph and the judgment of the living and dead. Luther sincerely believed that his rediscovery of the "gospel" would convert the Jews, reveal the Antichrist (as the papacy), and usher in the final judgment. In complete confidence he published in 1523 *That Jesus Christ was born a Jew*, a letter to the Empire's Jews welcoming them with open arms to the new Christian gospel and recommending the end of Christian intolerance against them as a means of encouraging them to fulfill their eschatological mission. He was not alone in such convictions. A confluence of apocalyptical expectations and astrological predictions led many to predict a universal flood and the Last Judgment to arrive in 1524.[9] Events that year seemed to many as a fulfillment of these prophecies.

The Popular Reformation and Revolt

The first quarter of the sixteenth century was a difficult time for most people. The plague continued its regular rounds of town and countryside, while a new deadly disease, syphilis, began its ravages. Military conflicts, especially those between the Habsburg Charles V and the Valois King of France Francis I, caused widespread hardship. In the 1520s and early 1530s a scarcity of food resulted in malnourishment and consumption of tainted foodstuffs, contributing to a general mood of paranoia and fear.[10] On top of these internal crises, Europeans lived under the threat of invasion by the Muslim Turks, a prospect predicted by many preachers as divine punishment for Christendom's tolerance of sin and heresy. Through the 1520s Sultan Suleiman's conquest seemed an eventuality, leading the prominent Lutheran preacher Johannes Brenz to write in 1531 a treatise on "How Preachers and Laymen Should Act When the Turks Conquer Germany."[11] Moreover, news about the strange and frightening peoples of the New World and Far East began to enter the European consciousness, revealing that the world was much larger and less predictable than hitherto believed. The intensifying confusion over religious authority engendered by Luther's break from Rome proved that Europeans were living in the great tribulations predicted by the biblical writers. While Luther and most of his learned colleagues expected that the new kingdom of Christ would take place in the heavenly realm, the common folk, who yearned for justice in the here and now, understandably conceived of Christ's kingdom in more immediate and practical terms.

Thanks to his rural upbringing, Luther knew how to appeal to the populace, and between 1520 and 1525 he unleashed an impressive quantity of vernacular publications which inspired dozens of other preachers, pamphlet writers, and woodcut artists to simplify and propagate Luther's reform message for an uneducated audience. In their works they depicted simple peasants, for decades the subject of ridicule as ignorant beasts, now as the bearers of the gospel. In numerous printed dialogues, Karsthans ("Hans of the Hoe"), a stalwart German peasant armed only with his simple faith in God and knowledge of the scriptures, defeated the scholastic arguments of clerical opponents who sought to suppress reform ideas.[12] These pamphlets fed off the common yearning for a just, Christian world which partially welded together rural and urban commoners, despite the considerable differences in their life experiences. Commoners began more openly to discuss the unfairness of their burdens and possible solutions. Some began to organize, leading ultimately to the greatest populist uprising seen to that day, one that involved some 300,000 commoners. Despite many efforts to exculpate Luther from blame for the German Peasants' War of 1525, there is no doubt that his example of standing bravely against the papal and imperial authorities inspired the common folk to do likewise. His assertion that the Bible was the only religious authority for Christians and his slogans of "the freedom of the Christian" and the "priesthood of all believers" provided commoners with theoretical justification to oppose any lord whose actions could be construed as godless. Popular reform preachers and pamphleteers proved so effective that James M. Stayer has argued that there "is no absolute distinction between Reformation pamphlet literature and Peasants' War programs" and that the sermons and pamphlets "helped to define commoners' notions about divine law."[13]

Peasant protests began innocently enough in the autumn of 1524 on an estate near Schaffhausen when the peasants of the Count of Lupten refused his good lady's command to gather snail-shells–used in the winding of yarn–in the midst of their harvesting efforts. These labor strikes soon spread to the regions around Nuremberg and Lake Constance, while peasants expressed their anticlerical anger by burning their tithe grain in the fields. They also found some allies among commoners in the cities, and a few towns, such as Waldshut, which was engaged in a struggle with the emperor to keep their popular reform preacher, Balthasar Hubmaier, openly sided with the growing peasant forces. Throughout the winter of 1524/25, commoner leaders hammered out a more comprehensive and radical list of demands which proved ultimately destructive of the feudal system. This they justified by appeal to Luther's slogan of "godly law," arguing that the burdens of serfdom were not only unfair but also unscriptural.[14] To this moment the peasants were armed but not seeking violence, a good thing for the princes of the Swabian League who had been totally caught off guard by the rebellion. Instead, the rebels continued to deprive their landlords of their labor as a means of pressuring them to conduct binding negotiations to lighten peasant labor services and payments in kind, to allow them to cut wood, hunt, and fish in the lord's forests and lakes, and to allow a measure of communal self-administration. Some peasant groups also demanded better religious instruction and the right to choose their parish priest.

Feeding off the Reformers' anticlericalism, commoners expressed a special ire for clerical landlords who more than secular landlords insisted on maintaining traditional dues. Leading this charge was Thomas Müntzer, a former associate of Luther who had come to view himself as a divinely appointed agent ushering in the apocalypse. By 1523 totally disenchanted with both the Catholic and Lutheran clergy, Müntzer proclaimed that the common people were the bearers of the new order. In August, 1524, he was given the opportunity to preach before Duke John of Saxony and his son. Explicating Daniel 2, Müntzer encouraged the princes to support his campaign to establish the kingdom of God on earth by helping to destroy the present alliance of secular and spiritual powers and eradicating the godless, those preachers who resisted reform. If they spurned his request, Müntzer warned the princes, God would take government from them and give it to the common people.[15] The duke responded by ordering Müntzer's expulsion from Saxony. In turn, the prophet began urging commoners to resist ungodly authorities, broadening his anticlericalism to include secular princes. Luther joined the fray with a tract entitled "Letter to the Saxon Princes about the Rebellious Spirit," to which Müntzer contributed his "Much Provoked Defense of the Spiritless, Soft-living Flesh at Wittenberg" in which he accused Luther of using his theology as a prop for the existing godless order and announced that "the people will become free, and God alone will be their master." This freedom implied no moral license, for Müntzer expected the peasants to become committed to an intense level of personal devotion to Christ which required bearing the cross of suffering. During spring, 1525, the prophet inspired the rebels of Mühlhausen, Thuringia, to "attack, attack, while the fire is hot! Don't let your sword grow cold or dull. Strike, cling, clang, on Nimrod's anvil and cast his tower to the ground." For, he insisted, "it is not possible so long as they live for you to be free of the fear of men. It is impossible so long as they rule you to speak to you of God. Attack, attack, while it is still day! God goes before you, follow, follow!"[16] God, the preacher insisted, would protect his followers from the weapons of the knights. He was wrong.

In March, 1525 the peasants of Memmingen held a Peasant Parliament to approve a program of twelve articles, a document which while composed by urbanites was printed and widely used by other peasant bands. Whether motivated by only limited demands or by a vision of an egalitarian society ruled solely by the law of God, the rebels were in for a rude awakening. The leader of the Swabian league, Duke Georg Truchsess von Waldburg, was now ready to crush the rebellion. Justification for ruthless action was provided on April 16, 1525 when Jäcklin Rohrbach and other members of the Odenwald peasant band massacred a group of two dozen noblemen at Weinsberg. The "Weinsberg massacre" was widely depicted as a diabolical inversion of the divine social order, leading the parson Johann Herolt to comment: "Then Lucifer and all his angels were let loose; for they raged and stormed no differently than if they were mad and possessed by every devil."[17] The thought that the topsy-turvy world of Carnival might become permanent and commoners become the rulers was a terrifying one to the middle and upper strata of society.

Angered that his earlier plea for compromise had been ignored, at the beginning of May Luther issued his infamous *Against the Robbing and Murdering Hordes of Peasants*, commending the princes to kill the rebels as if they were rabid dogs. The knights needed no such encouragement. At the mere sight of Truchsess' armored knights and foot soldiers, many peasant bands fled without battle, while others were dispersed by insincere promises. In several unevenly matched engagements against battle-hardened soldiers and artillery thousands of peasants, perhaps as many as 100,000, were slain. Müntzer's Thuringian peasant army too was annihilated by the Lutheran Philipp of Hesse and the Catholic Georg of Saxony, while the prophet, found hiding in an attic, was executed. Some peasant bands experienced limited success, such as Michael Gruber's Salzburg army which on June 3 defeated a professional army, and the Tyrolian rebels of Michael Gaismaier which held out into 1526. Gaismaier, who unlike Müntzer tempered his idealism with effective military leadership, also sought the creation of a new Christian, democratic peasant republic but his vision was left unfulfilled as his band dispersed. Gaismaier himself was assassinated in 1532.

Although an unmitigated disaster for the rebels, the Peasants' War forced the princes to ease some of the burdens on their peasants. It also remained a vivid image of the danger of allowing commoners to toy with religious dissent. From that moment on, Catholic churchmen and princes linked Luther with uprising and reform with rebellion, while the peasants themselves now viewed Luther as a traitor. Many gave up hope for change. Those still hoping for religious reform turned to more radical versions, in particular Anabaptism.

Anabaptism

Anabaptism arose out of the same currents of popular reform that had inspired the Peasants' War, and a number of Anabaptist leaders were veterans of the rebellion, including one of Müntzer's disciples, Hans Hut. For his part, Karlstadt, who in 1522 had exchanged his professor's robes for the garb of a simple peasant (after the revolt he returned to his academic calling), continued to write scathing criticisms of Luther's compromising approach, while he condemned the real presence of Christ in the Eucharist and infant baptism as empty ceremonies blocking lay people from genuine contact with the divine. He did not, however, go so far as to advocate adult believers' baptism. Others did, becoming known by their opponents as Anabaptists or "rebaptizers," even though these reformers rejected their first baptism at infancy as an invalid, quasi-magical ceremony with no authentic spiritual effects.

Although the movement would have several distinct origins and branches that differed from each other on many important points, the first known Anabaptist baptisms took place in January 1525 in Zurich, Switzerland, a city where reform was being implemented by the humanistic preacher Ulrich Zwingli. A small group of his supporters, led by Conrad Grebel, became dissatisfied with the slow pace of change and especially with Zwingli's refusal to transform baptism in the same fashion as the Eucharist (like Karlstadt Zwingli rejected the concept of the real presence of Christ in favor of a spiritual interpretation). Zwingli had the ear of the city council which decided that infant baptism should remain. Grebel's group therefore decided to gather at the home of one of their number, Felix Mantz, in order to inaugurate the first believer's baptism. Zwingli accused Grebel of promoting schism, even though, as Stayer reminds us, "the symbolic interpretation of the Lord's Supper advanced by Zwingli was as equally radical a departure from Catholic sacramental theology as was adult believers' baptism."[18]

Forced underground by persecution, the Swiss Brethren (as these Anabaptists called themselves) continued to spread their message of radical reform by word of mouth. In 1529 at the imperial Diet at Speyer, the assembled Catholic and Protestant princes agreed to the emperor's mandate making rebaptism a capital crime. In the course of the next several decades, hundreds of Anabaptists were captured, tried, tortured into providing the names of their cohorts, and horribly executed, usually by burning, beheading or, in a gruesome parody of believer's baptism, drowning. The worst regions of persecution were the Catholic territories, especially the Habsburg Netherlands, which the emperor ruled directly as immediate overlord, and the duchies of the Tyrol and Bavaria, although Zwinglian Zurich and Bern and Lutheran Saxony also used the executioner to enforce correct religious beliefs.[19]

It may be difficult to comprehend how people could put their lives and those of their families at risk for the sake of a theological notion or practice. Yet what motivated both persecutors and persecuted was their sincere belief that this short, earthbound existence was merely a prelude to the eternal kingdom of God. Anabaptism was also viewed as a new form of popular revolt seriously threatening the civic unity of the Empire. The emperor believed that learned reformers and Lutheran princes might be amenable to theological compromise if moderate church reform proceeded, a hope not extinguished until the Regensburg Colloquy of 1541 failed to draft a compromise on the sticky points of priestly powers, transubstantiation, and papal authority. Charles V refused entirely to hold discussions with more radical reformers, such as Zwingli, whose attempts to unite the Swiss Cantons under Protestant leadership led to two bloody wars, during the second of which Zwingli was slain.

Prior to the defeat of the peasants in the summer of 1525, Anabaptism was fast becoming a major force in the communal reform of towns, such as Swiss Hallau, where one source put it "virtually the whole population" underwent adult baptism.[20] In Waldshut, one of the few towns openly to support the rebels, Hubmaier and sixty others were baptized on Easter day, 1525, by Wilhelm Reublin, one of Hallau's Anabaptist preachers. In a short time Hubmaier baptized most of the citizenry and city council of Waldshut, while other Swiss towns, such as Schaffhausen, were moving quickly in similar directions, pressured by the peasant rebels without and their own guilds and journeymen within their walls.

Realizing the fate of its reforms rested squarely on the success of the peasant rebels, Anabaptist Waldshut sent an armed contingent to the Lake Constance army. The defeat of the peasants in mid summer, however, also meant the end of such communal Anabaptism, at least in the Swiss Cantons and southern Germany.[21] Hubmaier fled to Nicholsburg, Moravia, where he oversaw the baptism of that city's lord, Leonhard von Liechtenstein, and of most of its populace, and welcomed the hundreds of Anabaptists fleeing the increasing persecution of the Swiss and German lands.

Not all of these were happy with Hubmaier's communal reformation. Hans Hut, having survived the slaughter of Müntzer's godly band, was baptized in May 1526 and considerably revised his apocalyptical expectations, asserting that members of the elect covenant, marked on the forehead by Hut's peculiar sign of baptism – the invisible mark of Tau (the Greek letter that resembles a cross) – were nonviolently to await Christ's return before joining in the destruction of the godless. In the meantime, they would be protected from angelic destruction by their baptism. Upon their arrival in Nicholsburg Hut and his associates immediately condemned all earthly government as godless, including Hubmaier's, and refused to take up the sword even in a godly cause. Arrested by the Catholic authorities in September, 1527, Hut was horribly tortured and died in a mysterious fire in his prison cell. Not to be cheated of their *auto-da-fé*, the authorities bound his lifeless corpse to the stake and burned him anyway.

Not all Anabaptists gave up militancy as readily as Hut. A plot to capture Erfurt by force fomented by Hans Römer, another of Müntzer's disciples, was discovered by the authorities in 1527. According to one witness, Römer's followers preached that "Whoever will not let himself be baptized again will be consumed by locusts. Müntzer and Pfeiffer [another of Müntzer's associates] were true teachers and were unjustly slain. And all those who had received the sign of baptism again should wait in the hills, for it would rain locusts, and then the world would not last longer than eleven months." Römer himself was not captured until 1534, and in his confession he confirmed the reports of his earlier plans. One of his associates captured in 1528 likewise confessed that "it was their intention, when the disturbance broke out in Erfurt, to strike dead whoever was not [re]baptized or would not accept the sign of baptism. Whoever had more than another should share it with him; whoever refused to do so, should also be struck dead (but they expected that the Lutherans would all join them)."[22] The authorities would find confirmation of Anabaptist sedition, enforced rebaptism, and community of goods, in the Anabaptist kingdom of Münster.

Northern Anabaptism and the End of the World

The vicious Habsburg efforts to crush Anabaptism succeeded in destroying most of the educated leadership of the Swiss and south-German Anabaptist groups, yet many Anabaptists fled to more tolerant regions such as Moravia, or cities such as Strasbourg wherein was found a large Anabaptist community which included several visionary prophets, especially Ursula and Lienhard Jost and Barbara Rebstock. These strongly influenced Melchior Hoffman (1495/1500–43?), a furrier originally from the south-German city of Schwabisch-Hall who, as a lay Lutheran missionary, had won many to reform in northern Germany and Scandinavia, although his increasing obsession with the Last Days and view of himself as the eschatological prophet announcing the return of Christ raised some alarm bells. In his commentary on Daniel 12, Hoffman predicted Christ's return would occur in 1533, an opinion shared by other Lutheran preachers, such as Michael Stifel who was even more precise, setting the date as the morning of October 19.[23] In 1529, with only a few years left before the end, Hoffman visited Strasbourg, where he was deeply moved by the Josts' visions. Once baptized, he pressured the city council to provide a church for the Anabaptists, but since rebaptism was illegal, Hoffman soon found himself with a warrant for his arrest.

In 1530 he escaped to Emden, East Frisia, where he preached to a large number of Netherlandic religious dissenters who had found safe haven from the Habsburg persecution in their homeland. Hoffman personally baptized a few hundred of these during his brief stay in the city and many of them returned to the Netherlands as missionaries, baptizing and establishing Anabaptist communities in several Dutch cities, especially Amsterdam. In 1531, however, several of Hoffman's disciples (covenanters) were executed in The Hague, leading Hoffman to suspend baptisms for two years, after which he expected Christ's return. Persuaded by a supporter's vision that Christ would soon descend to Strasbourg, Hoffman re-entered the city in 1533, hopeful that the messiah himself would release him from jail. It seems that Hoffman remained unrepentant in prison until his death or release in 1543.

In December 1533, the Dutch baker Jan Matthijs ordered an end to Hoffman's suspension of baptism and announced that Christ would return on Easter, 1534. He then dispatched representatives to the West-phalian city of Münster which seemed amenable to Anabaptist reforms. With the help of hundreds of immigrant coreligionists, the Anabaptists of Münster soon won the civic election and took over city government. The prince-bishop of Münster saw this as a usurpation of his authority and began preparations for a siege. In north Germany and the Nether-lands Anabaptism became a mass movement of religious enthusiasm and social unrest, fuelled by eschatological expectations, disgust with the repressive Habsburg persecution, and an intense anticlericalism. In their excitement to be witnesses of Christ's triumphant return, in March, 1534, thousands of Anabaptists sold their possessions and attempted, most unsuccessfully, to reach Münster, the new kingdom of God. Driven by an overwhelming need to purify the city before Christ's arrival, Münster's Anabaptist government declared that all residents had to be baptized or leave, while a community of goods was established to support all of the immigrants.

Things did not go according to plan, however, and on Easter, 1534, Matthijs confidently marched out of the city to face the besiegers, only to be cut to pieces. His successor was an actor, Jan van Leiden, who eventu-ally transformed an Anabaptist magistracy into a Davidic kingdom with himself in the leading role. Justified by the great preponderance of women in the city, the king also mandated polygamy. At the height of the intense siege, news sheets reported horrific acts of cannibalism in the city. They also broadcasted reports of Anabaptist militancy elsewhere, such as the capture in 1535 of a Frisian monastery, Oldeklooster, by 300 Anabaptists under Münsterite leadership. Although retaken by the governor's army a week later, this incident confirmed the authorities' suspicion that Anabaptism would revive the Peasants' War. In May forty Anabaptists captured Amsterdam's city hall, in the process killing a mayor and some of the civic guard, but this uprising too was quickly suppressed. In the end, all attempts to spread Anabaptism by force of arms were put down, as was Münster itself, which fell to the besieging forces at the end of June 1535.

Despite the catastrophic failure of the Anabaptist kingdom, a few Anabaptists remained stubbornly militant, such as the small, roving bands of religious guerillas known as the Batenburgers, followers of the nobleman Jan van Batenburg who enacted vengeance against the authorities by pillage and arson, specializing in the theft of church silverware. After Batenburg's arrest in late 1537, it became known that some of Batenburg's group and other militant Anabaptists were plotting to hire mercenaries to recapture Münster in 1538. Batenburg was executed in early 1538, yet similar groups of religious militants continued to rob and burn in the name of Christ into the 1560s.

Spiritualism and David Joris

Opposing Batenburg within the post-Münster Anabaptist community was a Delft glasspainter called David Joris who, after the fall of Münster, saw himself as Hoffman's successor for the mantle of nonviolent apocalyptical prophet. Although some from both the militant and pacificist wings joined him, most Anabaptist leaders became frustrated with his obtuse spiritualizing interpretation of controversial issues. Despite this, for a few years Joris was the most influential Anabaptist leader in the Low Countries.[24] As apocalyptical expectations remained unfulfilled, Joris became a thorough spiritualist, following the path trodden earlier by Sebastian Franck (1499–1542) who, after a period as a Catholic priest and then Lutheran activist, denounced all confessions and doctrinal squabbling as inimical to true, internal Christian faith. Such spiritualists emphasized the dichotomy between spirit and flesh and relied heavily on an immediate experience with the "inner Word" or voice of the Holy Spirit for religious authority. Thus, the inner significance of religious rites and teachings was far superior to their external forms which caused unnecessary conflict, persecution, and warfare. Some, such as Joris, advocated Nicodemism, attending approved religious ceremonies to conceal one's true beliefs.

Joris' most distinctive idea was his denial of the independent existence of the Devil. For him the Devil originated after the fall of Adam and Eve as the evil nature of humans.[25] This notion provoked considerable alarm among his learned theological opponents, who condemned him as the most diabolical of all Anabaptists and as a promoter of atheism. His unorthodoxy, however, was not limited to demonology, as he became a vigorous promoter of religious toleration, an idea which won him followers from across the social and confessional spectra. His letters and publications were disseminated throughout the Low Countries, Germany, Switzerland, and France, and in an age of increasing religious conflict and bloodshed, such spiritualism influenced many, undercutting the rational for religious warfare. For this reason Joris was regarded by the authorities as a greater threat than Batenburg. Joris escaped the flames only through the devotion of his followers, over a hundred of whom died protecting his whereabouts. For the last dozen years of his life he resided in Basel, Switzerland, as John of Bruges, his true identity a secret until nearly three years after his death in 1556 when a posthumous trial found him guilty of heresy and condemned his corpse to the stake. His death ended neither his influence nor the antagonism of his opponents.

Post-Münster Anabaptism

Joris' approach had been vigorously opposed by Menno Simons (1496–1561), a former Catholic priest of Friesland who, after Joris' move to Antwerp in 1539, began forming the remaining peaceful Anabaptists into a coherent sect known as the Mennonites. Like Joris, Menno lived a peripatetic existence, hounded by the authorities, protected by followers or noble friends, aware that many of his supporters were dying rather than reveal his whereabouts. Throughout his career he distanced his group from the excesses of Münster. His pacifistic fellowships emphasized personal piety and mutual support, membership in which was voluntary and sealed by believers' baptism. Against spiritualists Menno insisted on a visible church, distinct from the world and the apostasy of the mainstream churches, kept pure by banning or shunning any whose sin might corrupt the community. Mennonites not only insisted on nonviolence for the Christian, but also refused to swear an oath of allegiance to the state or participate in civic government. Guided by Menno's vision and writings, northern Anabaptism survived the worst era of religious persecution, emerging after the 1560s as a significant religious minority in the northern Netherlands promoting notions of religious choice and tolerance.

Spurred by both Catholic and Protestant theologians, the princes and magistrates of south Germany and the Swiss Cantons likewise persecuted their Anabaptist dissenters, nearly extinguishing the movement altogether. Those Anabaptists who survived met infrequently and at night in woods and caves, fearful of discovery and arrest. Many fled to more tolerant Moravia joining with the Hutterites who, inspired by the apostolic example of Acts 2:44–45, formed themselves into self-supporting communitarian settlements which at their height in the seventeenth century encompassed thousands of members. Despite their promotion of nonviolence and religious tolerance, suspicion that all Anabaptists were plotting sedition was slow to die.

Women and the Popular Reformation

As if the theological innovations and social rebellion inspired by religious dissent were not problematical enough for mainstream churchmen and princes, the early Reformation also opened up another Pandora's box. Many women, long excluded from religious leadership outside of the confines of a cloister, saw in Luther's "priesthood of all believers" permission to take up the functions of preaching and teaching the gospel previously forbidden them. In his *Babylonian Captivity of the Church* of 1520, Luther had opined, "therefore everyone who knows that he is a Christian should be fully assured that all of us alike are priests, and that we all have the same authority in regard to the word and the sacraments,"[26] rationale enough for some women to start preaching and writing pamphlets on behalf of the Reformation. In 1521 Müntzer's preaching in Zwickau inspired several women to begin preaching. And while women were not prominent leaders during the Peasants' War, there were a few spectacular exceptions, such as Margaret Rennerin, "the Black Hoffmännin," who was something of a Joan of Arc for the perfidious Rohrbach band. According to an official of the city of Heilbronn, Rennerin had "continually and often consoled the band that they [the rebels] should march boldly, [for] she had blessed them so that neither pikestaffs, halberds, nor firearms could harm them."[27] Even though she confessed to participating in the Weinsberg massacre, she was not executed with her male colleagues. In another incident, approximately sixty women plotted on May 5, 1525 to storm a convent in Windsheim, although they were persuaded by the town's magistrates to cancel the assault.[28] Women elsewhere made similar collective protests, such as the group that on September 29, 1522 released the Lutheran Augustinian preacher Hendrik van Zutphen from his imprisonment in St. Michael's Abbey in Antwerp.[29] Here too only three or four of the participants were interrogated, and these were released without punishment. As Natalie Zemon Davis has shown for early modern France, women rebels were typically let off with lesser sentences than their male compatriots because the authorities believed that such female public action was such a reversal of their traditional social/political roles they must have been led astray by men and were not responsible for their actions.[30] However, these same authorities made exceptions in the cases of Anabaptist women and alleged witches.

As reform-minded authorities closed convents, hundreds of nuns were brought out of the forced seclusion within their walls and into society, and not all of them were content to take a back seat to their male cohorts; even Katharina von Bora, the former nun who married Luther, assisted in the management of the Wittenberg Reformation as so much of it was directed from their home. Other nuns, notably the St. Clara convent of Nuremberg led by their learned prioress Charitas Pirckheimer, vigorously resisted the closure of their convents and the ending of their religious vocation.[31] Some Catholic women wrote against the Reformation, such as the famous Antwerp poet Anna Bijns whose poems condemned Luther and other sectarians for deceiving gullible lay people into thinking they could actually interpret the scriptures for themselves. In one refrain she lamented,

> Scriptures are read in the taverns,
> In the one hand the gospel, in the other the stein,
> They are all drunken fools; nevertheless by these
> Are learned preachers ridiculed.[32]

Bijns' efforts were not rewarded, as the Catholic authorities became concerned about activist women, even orthodox ones, and the Council of Trent ordered the enforced claustration of religious women. Many, such as the Ursulines, resisted this order, only strengthening the resolve of male clerics to enforce it.[33] Similarly, after the Peasants' Revolt, Luther and his male colleagues clarified that the office of Protestant preacher was exclusively male. A number of women preachers of Zwickau were exiled in 1529 for their activity, while the council of Memmingen actually passed a law that year forbidding servant women from discussing religion when drawing water from the wells. In 1543 King Henry VIII of England forbade women from reading the Bible, and while his example was not followed elsewhere, most authorities sought to forbid women from discussing scripture.[34]

The rise of Anabaptism, however, gave women another venue to express their leadership aspirations, and they did so in a variety of ways, some as preachers (although here too the male leaders quickly restricted the office of elder or minister to men), others more prominently as prophets, teachers, leaders of house churches and meetings, missionaries, and martyrs. In hundreds of cases, Anabaptist women proved their devotion to their beliefs through separation from families, frightening court interrogations, horrific bouts of torture, and execution. From their prison cells they composed moving letters to family and fellow believers that were later published separately or collectively in Anabaptist martyrologies.

When permitted by the authorities, they would even preach short homilies to audiences attending their execution. According to one Mennonite song about her, Elisabeth Dirksdochter, executed in Leeuwarden in 1549, was asked by the city magistrates about rumors that she was a Mennonite preacher:

> It is said that you deceive many people
> And that you are also a minister,
> So we want you to tell us
> Who have you taught in the past.

She did not deny the charge, but asked them to interrogate her solely about her faith, which she would be happy to explain to them. When she quoted the Bible extensively, her captors expostulated, "the Devil speaks through your mouth." That women could have a knowledge of the Bible confounding the clergy was clear evidence of the Devil's work. In the face of torture, for which she was stripped against her protests, "she kept on invoking God ardently who eased her pain, and she said calmly: 'Go ahead, keep on interrogating me.'" Her experience was not dissimilar to that of accused witches. Elisabeth's intransigence, her seeming imperviousness to pain, and her command of the scriptures, were regarded as contrary to proper womanly conduct, even under these extreme conditions.[35]

Women were also prominent in several of the most infamous cases of Anabaptist radicalism, such as the Strasbourg prophets Ursula Jost and Barbara Rebstock, or the four women who participated with seven male colleagues in the scandalous *naaktlooper* (naked runners) incident in Amsterdam which occurred on February 11, 1535 when the visionary Heynrick Heynricxz commanded his group to burn their clothes and run naked through the streets of the city, crying "woe, woe over the world and the godless" and proclaiming the "naked truth." Puzzled by their behavior, the chief judge, Gerrit van Assendelft, president of the Court of Holland, wondered if they might be possessed:

> It is a strange thing to see these naked people, springing like wild folk. It leads one to think that they are in part possessed by the Devil, although they speak pertinently, with good understanding, and say strange, unheard of things which would take too long to write.[36]

He rejected this diagnosis because the accused seemed to have maintained their faculty of reason. Instead of exorcisms they were treated with flames.

Most infamously, the population of Anabaptist Münster was over-whelmingly female, and the women played critical roles in establishing Anabaptism and defending the kingdom. Inspired by the story of the biblical Judith who raised a Babylonian siege by insinuating herself into the tent of the Babylonian general Holofernes to behead him, the Münsterite woman Hille Feicken on June 16, 1534 snuck out of the besieged city to assassinate Bishop Franz von Waldeck. She was caught and executed before she could fulfill her mission and news of her intentions shocked not only the bishop, but also Jan van Leiden, who became so distressed about such independent female action that shortly thereafter he commanded that every woman be under a male head, resulting in the kingdom's infamous polygamy.[37]

It was not simply the polygamy of Münster that convinced the author-ities that Anabaptism would overturn the institution of marriage, for many Anabaptist leaders permitted a believer to leave an unbelieving spouse and to remarry a believer. This policy was widely feared to give women freedom to break the marriage vow with impunity. Yet, despite their reputation as destructive of gender norms, Anabaptist and Mennonite leaders sought, like their mainstream opponents, to limit the leadership aspirations of their women, eventually restricting official leadership roles to men. Their efforts were not entirely successful, as female vision-aries, martyrs, and house leaders continued to inspire the faithful and frighten the authorities who feared the effects of loosening the strictures of proper female behavior.[38] The parallel between Waldensian women preachers and Anabaptist women activists became a commonplace of Catholic rhetoric.

The Image of Münster and of the "Anabaptist Conspiracy"

The breaking of gender norms, disseminating of wildly heretical notions, and fomenting of sedition became stock charges brought against all Anabaptists, regardless of their real beliefs. Reports from Batenburg's 1537 interrogation that Anabaptists were plotting a new assault on Münster in 1538 so alarmed the authorities that almost everywhere they cracked down on even the peaceable dissenters in their midst. Some of this fear was perhaps reasonable, given the role of radical religious rhetoric in inspiring rebellion, although much of it was clearly irrational as even some preachers and magistrates recognized that most Anabaptists were now utterly opposed to violence. Even tolerant Strasbourg, enduring at that moment another visitation of the plague, uncharacteristically struck out at the Anabaptists in their region.[39] The excessive anti-Anabaptist propaganda promoted by Bishop Von Waldeck continued to haunt civic leaders, keeping alive the fear that tolerating popular heresy would lead to another Münster where societal norms had been turned on their head, a tailormade king, foreigners replaced the stalwart citizenry, private property abolished in favor of community of goods, and the sacrament of marriage obliterated in favor of polygamy. All of these were certainly signs of the Devil's work, as Luther wrote in a forward to a news pamphlet account of Münster from 1535, "the devil himself lived there," recreating the polygamous blasphemy of the Islam world.[40] As Sigrun Haude comments about responses to Münster,

> Anabaptists, together with the Turks, were the great enemies of the sixteenth-century Holy Roman Empire, and "Münster" displayed the worst example of this heretical movement yet. As representations of them in the daily press and in learned writings reveal, the Anabaptists conjured up images of the criminal and the vagabond, the foreigner and the rebel, the devil's handmaiden and the blasphemer, the insurrectionist and the barbarian. A polyphony of fears, some more powerful than others, converged in the Anabaptist.[41]

Anabaptists were also despised by orthodox churchmen for their denial of the real presence of Christ in the Eucharistic elements and their denunciation of the entire sacramental system as priestly magic. Like Karlstadt and Zwingi, Anabaptists transformed the Eucharist into an entirely memorial ceremony using ordinary bread and wine. Their rationale revealed a lay person's commonsense theology, for they could not understand how Christ could be physically present both in heaven and in the bread. For example, during his interrogation before the Amsterdam magistrates on May 12, 1534, the Anabaptist leader Adraien "the one eyed" Pieterszoon confessed that he had told people entering the city's famous shrine, the "Holy Place" which housed an incombustible consecrated Host, that the bread and cheese in his hands were as good as the shrine's Host. He told others to bring "fifty gods" (Hosts) for him to stab and if they bled, he would believe in the sacrament. For him, the Host was merely baked bread and priests could not make gods, for God is in heaven. Those supposed miracles performed by the Host, Adriaen asserted, were merely diabolical imitations.[42] In another, later case from 1557, a Mennonite known as "John the Monk" (Jan de monick) was accused of smearing holy oil on his shoes to show his disdain for this sacramental.[43]

Such examples could be multiplied *ad infinitum* across Europe. Although many Anabaptists experienced ecstatic and visionary incidents, most sought to create a bible-centered faith purified of the taint of magic or superstition. Like Zwinglians and Calvinists (those who followed the French Reformer of Geneva, John Calvin) they desired to cleanse their society of the sinful, superstitious practices that were meriting the wrath of God, such as the idolatrous veneration of saints' images or relics. Anabaptists instead defined the church as the congregation of living believers and rejected completely the concept of sacred places or objects, offering the most radical rejection of the clerical, sacramental church possible in the sixteenth century. They moreover extended their anticlericalism to encompass the new Protestant preachers as well as the Catholic priesthood.

Most radical was their rejection of infant baptism and practice of adult baptism for which the emperor condemned them to death. Both Catholic and Protestant leaders regarded infant baptism as the initiation ceremony bringing children into the Christian community and, for Catholics and Lutherans, as an important weapon to deliver children from the clutches of Satan, hence the rite of exorcism remained important for both of these churches, although Calvinists did away with it as a remnant of papal magic. Many learned polemicists – Catholic, Reformed, and Lutheran – argued that Anabaptist rejection of infant baptism placed children in danger of damnation and led ultimately to social chaos, the two principal goals of the Devil.[44] We shall return to these themes in the next chapters after a quick survey of the developments in the Reformation elsewhere in Europe.

The Reformation in England

Calls for religious reform and social change reached almost all the corners of Europe, including England, although the Reformation here followed a rather different path from the continent. For one thing, while there was considerable popular anticlericalism and appeal for reform, the actual transformation of the church in England was conducted by and for the monarch, King Henry VIII, whose obsession with gaining a male heir led him to seek a divorce from his Habsburg wife, Catherine of Aragon, the aunt of Charles V. With the emperor interceding on

Catherine's behalf, the Pope refused the request and Henry cut off papal control over the English Church. In 1534 the English Parliament proclaimed Henry the head of the Church in England and made it a capital offence to dispute the king's divorce. Henry's chief minister Thomas Cromwell (c.1485–1540) hoped to avoid the religious conflict of the continent by plotting a middle way, a *via media*, between Lutheran and Swiss Reformed variants, although the king, who remained theologically a Catholic, wished for few doctrinal changes and condemned Luther's attacks on the sacramental system. In 1539, responding to the increasing number of Protestants who rejected the real presence in the Eucharist, the king issued the Six Articles which more or less outlawed Protestant ideas entirely. Cromwell became Henry's next scapegoat for his realm's troubles, and was executed without trial in the summer of 1540. For the next two decades there ensued the religious conflict that Henry and Cromwell had sought to avoid, although in the end the Church of England did become that *via media*, a fusion of Catholic and Protestant positions in which most Christians, apart from extreme Calvinists and Catholics, could find a home.

On the ground there was both support for and opposition to the reform initiatives of the crown. Many Lutheran preachers, pamphleteers, and dramatists promoted the Reformation to apparently wide audiences and there seemed an insatiable thirst for printed reform works and vernacular Bibles. Unlike the Pope and emperor who had vainly sought to suppress the publication of vernacular bibles, Henry VIII and Cromwell harnessed the laity's appetite for the scriptures by producing an official English translation. At the same time, the only popular uprising spurred by the Reformation was a reactionary one, as peasants rose up in 1536 to protest the enforced closure of monasteries in a popular movement known as the "Pilgrimage of Grace." In contrast to the peasants of Germany, the English peasants appreciated their monastic landlords who, in contrast to their continental equals, were milder landlords than secular lords. The lack of a major reform-inspired uprising in England speaks volumes of the success of the crown's efforts to control reform sentiment through parliament. At the same time, the crown had no intention of allowing the spread of radical reform ideas, and Anabaptists who had fled continental persecution in the summer of 1535 found themselves in the grips of Henry VIII's much more efficient judicial machinery, leading to the arrest of some twenty-five Anabaptists and the execution of about half of their number.[45] Such measures, however, did little to suppress heterodoxy, and many English were attracted to an increasing number of radical religious groups, such as the spiritualistic Family of Love founded by the Dutch contemporary of David Joris, Hendrick Niclaes. These "Familists", like their later spiritual cousins the Quakers, provoked condemnatory response far out of keeping with their actual numbers or influence.

The Catholic Response

In the face of these challenges to its religious supremacy the papacy did not sit idle. Means were sought to bring dissident princes back into line and to clear up for ordinary believers the prevailing doctrinal confusion. Reform was nothing new to Catholic leaders, who had long been overseeing a wide range of improvements to doctrine and ritual. Many Catholic reformers attempted to use the pressure of the Protestants as a means of compelling the papacy to undertake further reform. Although too late to stop Luther and the rise of the various Reformation movements, in the 1540s the papacy unleashed two major forces that would proceed with the long-desired ecclesiastical changes: the Jesuits and the Council of Trent.

The frustration of orthodox Catholics over the success of the Protestant challenge impelled many men and women to revive Catholic spirituality. The most influential of these was undoubtedly the Spanish soldier, Ignatius Loyola (c.1491–1556), who while recuperating from injuries in 1521 saw visions which led to a deep religious conversion. After a period of intense prayer and asceticism, during which he began composing his famous *Spiritual Exercises*, he embarked first on a pilgrimage to Jerusalem and then pursued studies at several universities in Spain. Suspicion that his mystical experiences were comparable to those of the heretical Alumbrados (an "inner-light" group comparable to the spiritualists) – a target of the Spanish Inquisition – led to investigations of heresy, although these proved unfounded. He then pursued his studies at the University of Paris (1528–35) where he attracted a number of followers with his emphasis on a life of spiritual contemplation combined with rigid self-discipline and vigorous action on behalf of the Church. In 1540 he and his followers were officially approved by Pope Paul III as the Society of Jesus, with an itinerant mission of preaching and teaching of lay people, opposing Protestantism in Europe and exporting Catholicism to the newly "discovered" lands of Japan, China, India, Brazil, and the New World. They established schools, wrote simple catechisms, preached unpretentious sermons, and performed entertaining dramas to get their message across. They also wrote vigorous polemical works against the Protestants, emphasizing the real presence of Christ in the Lord's Supper and papal primacy, among other things. More than any other Counter-Reformation activity, the Jesuit instruction of lay people forced the retreat of Protestantism from southern Germany and helped, with the Spanish and Papal Inquisitions, to drive it out of Spain and Italy.

The Jesuits focused their assault on Protestantism along the very line that divided Calvinists and Anabaptists especially from Catholics: the relationship between the supernatural and natural worlds. For most Protestant leaders, especially Calvinists, God communicated primarily through the written scriptures, although they admitted that natural events were reflections of divine providence. They therefore often interpreted heavenly signs, monstrous births, and natural disasters as messages from God. Generally, however, they did not invest matter with direct supernatural power (as in the Catholic sacramentals) nor did they regard places of worship or particular human beings as essentially sacred by nature. Although God might send a sign in the heavens or an angel to communicate with his children, most Protestant preachers taught that the age of direct miracles had passed and condemned the supernatural workings of Catholic saints, sacraments, and sacramentals as remnants of pagan magic (what their parishioners actually believed is another matter). Against such skepticism the Jesuits became major promoters of Catholic miracles. Their public exorcisms of demoniacs became the most famous expression of this battle between a biblicist religion stripped of most day-to-day supernaturalism and one that provided believers with tangible proof of the divine in their daily lives.

Despite the advances of the Jesuits, reform-minded Catholics waited impatiently for the pope to convene a reform council. Fear of a revival of conciliarism motivated pope after pope to postpone the promised meeting until 1545 in Trent. By this time all attempts to heal the doctrinal split between Catholics and Protestants had failed and most delegates of the Council, which would meet in three major sessions between 1545 and 1563, were content to define controversial doctrines solely to secure Catholicism in Italy, Spain, France, and southern Germany. The result was a strengthening of the authority of the pope and a narrowing of Catholic orthodoxy. Against Luther, the Council: proclaimed church tradition as a parallel authority to scriptures; asserted the importance of traditional acts of penance along with faith in achieving salvation; and defended the special status of ordained priests. It also embarked on a program of improving the educational and moral standards of the clergy with the goal of encouraging better preaching and instruction of lay people.

The Mediterranean Inquisitions and the Suppression of Dissent

Working hand in glove with the new religious orders and the Council of Trent, Inquisitors in Spain and Italy also helped to suppress religious dissent. As we have noted, the Spanish Inquisition had been established specifically to attack supposed Judaisers among the conversos, fueling fears that the New Christians were a Jewish fifth column plotting the overthrow of Spanish Christendom. Between 1485 and 1500, the Spanish Inquisition focused almost exclusively on converso heresy. Thereafter, its attention turned to other crimes, especially ex-Muslim moriscos and, after 1540, to heretics, such as the Alumbrados whose emphasis on the inner reception of the sacraments was seen as a parallel to secret Judaisers. Protestants of all stripes were lumped together by Inquisitors under the name of "Lutherans." By this time the Spanish tribunals had become morals courts and a significant didactic tool in the post-Trent reform movement, while by 1600 their concern had turned to suppressing blasphemy, bigamy, sodomy, sorcery, and witchcraft, although its execution rates were now extremely low; of the 44,674 cases tried by Spanish Inquisitors between 1540 and 1700, only 846 led to executions, a mortality rate of 1.8 percent.[46] It seems that the horrific bloodshed of its first few decades had extinguished the flames of the *autos-da-fé*. It may also be the case that by 1540 the tribunals had so cowered resistance to political and doctrinal orthodoxy that penance alone was sufficient.

In Italy, in 1542 Pope Paul III established the Roman and Venetian Inquisitions as a means of weeding out "Lutheran" heresy from the minds of the faithful and propagating Catholic orthodoxy among the populace at large. In this context "Lutheranism" was a broad term encompassing any form of non-Catholic reform or expression of rigorous anticlericalism, whether or not it was faithful to Luther's actual teachings. These tribunals were modeled along Spanish lines, and they had to follow exacting rules of procedures, such as allowing the defendant rights to a lawyer and to an appeal to a higher court and strictly controlling the use of torture. Since the goal was conversion, those heretics who indicated a desire to be reconciled with the holy mother Church were granted light sentences. Thus, in Italy there was not the vicious and relentless persecution of religious dissenters that characterized the Habsburg Netherlands, for example, where the authorities were much less concerned about persuading heretics to repent than about eradicating all challenges to approved orthodoxy. Even so, by trying thousands of suspected heretics and keeping the diabolical dangers of heresy constantly before the eyes of Italians, these Inquisitions proved remarkably effective in suppressing heterodoxy.

The "Mature Luther" and the Devil

In the face of the increasingly successful Catholic counterattack on the Protestant movements, in the late 1530s and 1540s Luther increasingly depicted Catholicism in repulsive terms. In his 1545 pamphlet, *Against the Papacy at Rome, Founded by the Devil*, Luther commissioned the prominent artist Lucas Cranach to illustrate his accusation that the papacy originated from the union of a she-devil with the Antichrist and to encourage his supporters to show their disdain for papal authority by scatological means. By this time the military conflict between Protestant princes and the Catholic emperor was heating up and Luther feared that an ecumenical council would explicitly condemn his reform. Luther typically cast the theological battle in intensely apocalyptical terms as the Devil's final assault on Christians. He believed that the Devil was marshalling all of his forces together for the final Armageddon, with the pope as the Antichrist, the Turks playing the part of punishing Gog, and the Jews, who steadfastly refused to convert to Luther's gospel, now depicted as a dangerous fifth-column ally of the Turks. His Protestant and Anabaptist opponents he cast as the apocalyptical false prophets and apostles. His verbal attacks became unswervingly vicious; in 1543, hearing reports that Jews were successfully proselytizing in Moravia and Bohemia (there was a new sect of Sabbatarian Christians who worshiped on the Jewish sabbath, Saturday, rather than Sunday), he composed his most infamous work, *On the Jews and their Lies*. In this diatribe he emboldened the authorities to destroy Jewish homes, synagogues, and schools and to steal their money, force them to work in the fields as serfs, or expel them from the Empire.[47] Many of Luther's supporters were deeply embarrassed by these virulent tracts and feared their contribution to the increasing religious intolerance, hatred, and fear of the apocalypse.

Religious Warfare

Frustrated by papal inaction, Emperor Charles V took the lead in restoring Protestant dissidents to Catholicism and, failing that, in eradicating them as a political threat. Because of the political decentralization of the Empire, he was unable to install a Spanish-style Inquisition in the Empire, although on February 28, 1545 he instituted one for the Low Countries where he had greater success in compelling local authorities to arrest religious dissidents. Already several hundred Anabaptists and other heretics had been executed, many burned at the stake. Although not nearly as centralized or effective as the Spanish Inquisition, the establishment of Inquisition tribunals in the Low Countries escalated the persecution there and contributed to the mounting pressure for political resistance that would culminate in the Eighty-Years War against Spanish hegemony.[48]

Unfortunately for him, Charles could not order Inquisitors into the German lands without the agreement of the German princes, many of whom had become Lutherans. In 1529 a number of them, along with magistrates of reforming cities such as Strasbourg, protested the anti-heresy decrees of Diet of Speyer – although many of them approved its anti-Anabaptist mandate – and were thereafter known as Protestants. Two years later they formalized a protective alliance, the Schmalkaldic League. Led by Elector John of Saxony and Landgrave Philipp of Hesse, the Protestant rulers pledged to defend the Reformation, although until 1542 they were hardly a military success. The League's very existence, however, limited the emperor's range of action in suppressing heresy in the Empire. By 1544, thanks to a temporary truce with Francis I and the waning of the threat of Turkish invasion, Charles V was able to turn his attention to the Protestants. Open warfare broke out in June 1546, and although neither side showed military brilliance, the Protestants were too cautious and divided to defeat the emperor's scattered forces, and by November 1548 the League retreated. Charles' terms stripped both Philipp of Hesse and Elector John Frederick of Saxony of their estates. When the Protestant princes defeated him in 1552, the emperor agreed officially to tolerate Lutheranism in the Empire, formalizing this in a treaty signed in Augsburg on September 25, 1555 which stipulated for the first time that an alternative form of Christianity to Catholicism was to be tolerated. This agreement, however, was by no means a declaration of individual religious choice for, based on the principle of *cuius regio eius religio* or "whoever the king, his religion," it decreed that the religion of a prince would be the religion of his territory, and that even with his death his principality was not to switch faiths. Moreover, the tolerance was limited to Lutherans, as neither Calvinists nor Mennonites were included. Although ostensibly signaling the end of religious conflict, the Peace of Augsburg actually became a source of further conflict, as princes broke its provisions by seeking to convert neighboring properties to their own faith and as Calvinist princes sought entry into it. The vicious religious conflict ended only with the signing of the Treaty of Westphalia in 1648.

Henry VIII had managed to steer England relatively calmly through limited reform waters, containing the demands of English Calvinists and suppressing more radical reformers, such as the Anabaptists. His Tudor children, Edward VI (1547–53), who began a more fully Protestant reform of the Church, Mary (1553–8), who sought to restore Catholicism to England and who married the Catholic Philip II of Spain as an ally, and Elizabeth (1558–1603), who returned the realm to a moderate Protestantism which would incorporate some elements of Catholic ritual, were faced with a great deal more dissent than their father. Although the hardline Calvinists remained unhappy with the Anglican compromise, Elizabeth and her Stuart successor, James I, were able to contain much of that dissent by promises of future reforms. This religious disaffection finally joined with the prevalent social and political discontent and gave a special fervor to the military conflict which broke out in 1642 that would ultimately dethrone the king in favor of parliamentary government in the hands of the Puritan Oliver Cromwell.

Across the channel the French religious wars between a zealous Catholicism and an equally fervent and militant Calvinism (Huguenots) kept that country in a state of virtual civil war from roughly 1562 to the signing of the Edict of Nantes in 1598 which granted some measure of tolerance to the Huguenots. A sizeable minority of the populace, especially in the coastal provinces and cities of the south and west, the so-called "Huguenot Crescent" (the earlier heartland of Catharism), had joined Calvin's reform movement. The resulting French wars of religion were immensely bloody as the strident Catholic forces, led by the aristocratic Montmorency and Guise families, fervently opposed any concessions to Calvinism. From 1559, however, the minority Calvinists, who were predominant among the wealthy merchant class, managed to win the support of about one-third of France's nobility, forming an impressive coalition of money and military power. Seeking to avenge the wild iconoclasm of the rank and file Calvinists, in 1560 the troops of Duke

Francis of Guise fell upon a congregation of Calvinists worshiping in Wassey, beginning the decades of vicious conflict. Zealots on both sides refused compromise and rejected the notion that there could be two versions of Christianity within a single realm, both believing the other to be inciting God to wrath. The most infamous act of the war occurred during a period of supposed truce, broken on St. Bartholomew's Day, August 24, 1572, with the slaughter of hundreds of prominent Huguenots gathered in Paris to celebrate the marriage of their champion, Henry of Bourbon, king of Navarre. Weeks of brutal massacres of thousands of Protestants by Catholics in Paris and across France followed, and many Protestants reconverted in the face of this fury. Others held out and withstood bitter sieges, formed armies, sought help from Protestants elsewhere in Europe and survived, although ultimately the Huguenot hope of capturing the crown was dashed. Upon mounting the throne as Henry IV, Henry of Navarre converted to Catholicism in order to restore peace to his realm.

Similar religious warfare erupted in the 1560s in the Low Countries led again by Calvinists. By this time Calvinism had not only penetrated into the Low Countries via the French-speaking or Walloon south, but had become the dominant approach to reform in the cities of Flanders and Brabant as well. Where Lutheranism and Anabaptism failed to reform the region, Calvinism succeeded, but only after a bloody struggle against the Spanish overlords. One of the reasons for its success was the Calvinist reliance on the local community and magistracy for support. As overlord of the Low Countries Philip II (Charles had abdicated in favor of his son in 1555) ordered the Netherlands' governor, Margaret of Parma, to proceed apace with both the Inquisition against heretics and the administrative reforms to reduce the power of local princes and magistrates. Understandably the local aristocracy, led by William of Orange, opposed these changes. Like the religious reformers, they too hated the local Inquisition as a cynical tool of Habsburg centralization and demanded a relaxation of the heresy placards. In October 1565 Philip refused and a number of the local nobility began negotiating with the Calvinist leaders; soon over 350 nobles had signed the "Compromise" committing them to fight against the placards and Inquisition. To many Calvinist preachers it appeared that the Reformation was assured, and in August 1566 Protestant crowds broke into many of the region's major churches and smashed or removed religious paintings, statuary, stained glass, and other sacred objects. This so-called iconoclastic fury was actually the leading edge of a well-orchestrated campaign of religious purification and reform. However, even though Margaret granted concessions to the dissidents, Philip was furious over the desecration of Catholicism and growing strength of heresy. In response he sent an army of occupation under Duke of Alba which arrived in August 1567. The duke established an authoritarian and brutal administration, strengthening the placards and establishing the infamous Council of Troubles which heard over 10,000 heresy cases and executed 1,100 heretics during its existence. In time William of Orange managed to surmount the considerable opposition to rebellion on the part of moderate Catholic princes and magistrates to weld together an army of defense that would eventually battle the Spanish to a standstill along the waterways dividing Zeeland and Holland in the north from Brabant and Flanders in the south. After being restored to William of Orange and Calvinism in 1577, Antwerp fell to besieging forces in 1589, and thousands of its wealthy Calvinist merchants fled north to the newly formed Dutch Republic. The southern provinces were restored to a vigorous, post-Tridentine Catholicism, expelling all traces of heresy and supporting lay Catholics in the north from which, for a time, all priests had been expelled.

The northern rulers immediately ended formal prosecution for heresy and the handing out of death sentences for religious dissent, among the first regions in Europe formally to do so. Interestingly, the rulers of the Dutch Republic did not grant Calvinism the status of a state church, only that of the officially approved church. Those wishing to join the Reformed Church had to undergo a period of examination as to doctrinal orthodoxy and moral fitness before being allowed to partake of communion, a procedure remarkably similar to that of the Mennonite fellowships. Thus, in the Republic membership in the approved church was voluntary and in many regions the Reformed were significantly outnumbered by Catholics and even Mennonites. An informal system of toleration became the order of the day, although there were considerable social and economic advantages to associating with the Reformed, and disadvantages accorded Catholics in particular. However, in this country still struggling to maintain its independence (a struggle that would not end until the signing of the Treaty of Utrecht in 1648), there developed a remarkable religious diversity, as four distinct confessions – Reformed, Catholic, Mennonite, and Lutheran (by far the smallest of the four) – vied for followers.

In this environment, religious competition replaced enforced conformity and people had the opportunity to choose their own faith. Many refused formally to join any church. What these believed is not altogether clear, although the strength of spiritualism here influenced many to depreciate confessional adherence altogether. In the Republic Catholics, Reformed, and Mennonites learned to do business with each other, and while polemicists on all sides tried to reinvigorate religious partisanship, they had little success. Instead, the region became home to religious and intellectual flux and a center for the debate over religious tolerance. At the same time, the tolerant atmosphere fostered dissent within confessions, and the Mennonites especially became infamous for their multiplicity of divisions and sects, ranging from strict followers of Menno to the *Doopsgezinde*, the "Baptist-minded" who were less inclined to develop precise doctrinal statements. Catholic polemicists saw such developments as the natural outcome of the Devil's plans. Those who lived in the Republic obviously thought differently.

Conclusion

In surveying pertinent aspects of the history of the Reformation this chapter has highlighted the widespread preoccupation among members of all confessions and social levels with the nearness of apocalyptical judgment and the need on the part of authorities to persecute dissenters as agents of the Devil's final, apocalyptical assault on Christendom. We have also seen how the authorities regarded the various radical reform groups as diabolical threats to the survival of the social/political order of the day. The Peasants' War, the rise of Anabaptism, the rise of religious conflict and the infamous Münster Anabaptist kingdom, all increased fears of secret diabolical conspiracies that might at any moment break out into open revolt. This anxiety lingered long after the last Anabaptist plot to recapture Münster died with the execution of Batenburg in early 1538. Swiss Brethren and Dutch/North German Mennonites struggled long and hard to prove to the authorities and their neighbors that they were the most peaceable of people and had no plans to overturn the social order. Suspicion, however, remained, nourished by Catholic and Protestant polemicists through the 1540s to 1560s. In the next two chapters we shall examine more carefully the shift in attention during these decades from religious heretics to witches.

3

HERESY, DOUBT, AND DEMONIZING THE "OTHER"

Thus in our day we, too, must labor with the Word of God against the fanatical opinions of the Anabaptists and the Sacramentarians... For we have recalled many whom they had bewitched, and we have set them free from their bewitchment, from which they could never have been untangled by their own powers if they had not been admonished by us and recalled through the Word of God. ... So great is the efficacy of this satanic illusion in those who have been deluded this way that they would boast and swear that they have the most certain truth.

Martin Luther, *LW*, vol. 26, *Lectures on Galatians*, 194–5.

I regard not your swearing, for it is a craft of sorcerers who swear against the truth. But now I see clearly how the souls of our two brothers and sister were murdered and deceived through your magical swearing, that they did not protect themselves against the Devil's cunning, that they did not have the gifts to dispute. ... understand, you noble gentlemen, the misuse and maltreatment of your state or office, which we confess not to be from God but the Devil. For the antichrist has bewitched and blinded your eyes through the cunning of the Devil that you do not perceive yourselves to be what you are.

Hans van Overdamme, Mennonite leader, to his interrogators during his trial in Ghent, 1550, responding to their demands that he swear to tell the truth and lamenting the recantation of three of his colleagues. In S. Cramer ed., *Het Offer des Heeren*, vol. 2, *Bibliotheca Reformatoria Neerlandica* (The Hague, 1904), 110–14.

Whether or not intended by Luther and other Reformers, their movement of religious reform unleashed passions and prejudices which deepened animosities and increased suspicion of "the Other." In the examples cited above, we have first Luther himself comparing Anabaptists to witches and then a Mennonite characterizing his Catholic captors in similar fashion. Both of these comparisons were made prior to the revival of large-scale witch-hunting in Europe. What role did such polemical, demonizing rhetoric play in heightening anxiety about diabolical conspiracies? For a society deeply riven by religious factionalism, calling all citizens to confront the great demonic threat offered a potentially unifying discourse. According to Brian Levack, the Reformations made several contributions to the rise of witch-hunting:

> the demonization of European culture that preceded and accompanied the Reformation, the reliance upon Biblical injunctions against witchcraft (especially Exodus 22:18), the determination of religious reformers to eliminate magic in its various forms, the subjection of the rural masses to a rigorous moral discipline as part of a program of Christianization, and the determination of public authorities to establish a godly state by taking legal action against moral deviants and blasphemers all contributed significantly to the intensification of witch prosecutions in the sixteenth and early seventeenth centuries.[1]

This chapter will examine these factors, concentrating on the perceived need to neutralize the increasing levels of doubt and skepticism which church leaders blamed on their religious opponents, especially Anabaptists and spiritualists.

As we have seen in Chapter 1, Catholic officials prior to the Reformation had become alarmed about the increasing number of cases involving blasphemous denial of the reality of sacramental transformations, applying both rational persuasion and judicial coercion to the problem. They found too that doubt could be dispelled through the empirical proof of miracles or the confessions of Jews, heretics, demoniacs, or witches. Although the sixteenth century is remembered primarily as an age of faith, it was as much an era of heightened doubt, as individuals and groups sought by various means to deal with the conflict between their own subjective religious beliefs and competing official religious cultures.[2] Luther's insistence that the scriptures were the sole religious authority – superior to pope, tradition, and council – was eagerly taken up by lay people, leading to a multiplicity of interpretations and disagreements, and ultimately to a crisis over authentic religious authority that made the religious confusion of the fifteenth-century Papal Schism pale in comparison. This new battle against doubt and disbelief reached fevered levels by mid-century. In a parallel to the earlier Inquisitors' fixation on imaginary "Luciferans" after their successful suppression of Catharism, sixteenth-century authorities become preoccupied with fictional Devil-worshipers after they had virtually suppressed Anabaptism.

The Quest for a Godly Realm

All religious reformers hoped to refashion society into a godly commonwealth. Lutherans looked to their godly princes to legislate ecclesiastical and moral reform, while urban Reformers such as Ulrich Zwingli and John Calvin conceived of the church as virtually coterminous with the civic commune and aimed from the start to involve urban magistrates in the oversight of Christian morality. Calvin, himself an exile from France, developed a theology and church model that were readily transplanted to a variety of locales, from the urban communes of south and western France or the Dutch Republic to the kingdom of Scotland and the American colonies. Sinning Catholics faced the social control force of the confessional and penance system, the threat of excommunication and, in extreme cases, the Inquisitions. Lacking secular power, Mennonites limited themselves to replicating the godly society within their voluntaristic fellowships, and sinners were banned and ostracized by their coreligionists until repentant.

Some scholars have suggested that the witch-hunts were a conscious attempt on the part of religious and secular authorities to enforce the widely desired religious conformity upon the populace. There is some truth to this theory, at least to the extent that the Reformations comprised a grand campaign to improve levels of doctrinal literacy and behavioral conformity among lay people and to suppress deviance of any kind. By sermon, woodcut image, and a flood of printed propaganda, learned Reformers sought to eliminate "superstitious" or pagan elements of lay culture. Pastors were ordered to preach more often, to hold catechism classes and to interrogate their charges about their beliefs and practices. Bishops or their representatives began regular visitations of parishes, interviewing local clergy about the beliefs and practices of their parishioners. The results proved shocking, revealing widespread ignorance, erroneous beliefs, and superstitious practices especially in rural parishes.[3]

Even Mennonites caught the "confessional conformity bug," producing their own lengthy and detailed doctrinal statements which not only distinguished them from the "Devil's church" but led to endless internal wrangling and formation of splinter groups. For all confessions, the religious conflict sensitized leaders to the threat posed by deviance.

How this campaign of religious conformity related to the sudden revival of interest in witch-hunting around 1560 remains, however, unclear. Pressure for the persecution of witches arose first and foremost out of the local community fuelled by the suspicions and conflicts among neighbors, requiring little direct encouragement from the higher authorities. Witch-hunting could hardly have been a cynical maneuver on the part of the authorities to scare the populace into religious and political subservience; on the contrary, many central courts and authorities put the brakes on local witch panics.[4] Even so, by the middle of the sixteenth century the reluctance of local authorities to take seriously Heinrich Krämer's demonic witch conspiracy was breaking down. They therefore became more receptive to the complaints of villagers and townspeople about suspicious neighbors and incorporated these into the preachers' stereotype of demonic heresy. What changed in the minds of church and secular officials? The major event behind this attitudinal shift was the Reformation and the threat to religious, social, and political authority and stability that it posed for both elites and commoners.

While Reformers had succeeded in mobilizing masses of laypeople to condemn the old Catholic hierarchical system, they had no ready-made alternative to put in its stead, nor were they equal to the task of persuading most ordinary believers to make wholesale changes to their beliefs and practices. After the veritable free for all of the "peoples' Reformation" of the 1520s, the authorities sought to contain popular religious sentiment, aided by their preachers and propagandists who railed fervently against heterodoxy, especially the violent kind of the Münsterites or the pernicious notions of spiritualists who seemed to be infiltrating the churches, governments, and homes of the orthodox. With every sign of indifference toward the supposed threat, preachers sermonized even more fervently about the Devil's minions, ultimately convincing many of the existence of a secretive, underground sect of heretics working in league with the Devil to overthrow Christianity on the eve of the apocalypse. If there were real religious heretics in their communities, villagers may have come to see them as no threat at all and disregarded the propaganda against them as governmental meddling. Or they may have transferred the demonizing rhetoric from religious heretics onto those neighbors whom they believed performed *maleficia* against them. Harmful magic was universally feared in early modern society, and when Protestant and Catholic Reformers denounced using village wise women or cunning men to remove magical curses, villagers had little legal recourse to counteract their bewitchment but to take suspected witches to court, an action which the higher authorities made easier by the passage of anti-witchcraft statutes, such as that contained in Charles V's *Carolina* of 1532. The constant fulminating of their preachers about the coming divine retribution for those who tolerated Satan's minions was taken as implicit permission to denounce suspected witches to their local magistrates and lords.

Spiritualism and Religious Tolerance

One of the most popular targets for condemnation by orthodox propagandists were the spiritualists, those religiously devout individuals who depreciated the importance of written scriptures, confessional statements, and disputes over dogma in favor of a religion of the heart. With some justification Catholic theologians blamed Erasmus for inciting such seditious notions and placed his works on the list of books officially forbidden to Catholics.[5] Spiritualism's ethic seems to have best suited the cultural world of the upper classes of town and country, especially merchants, professionals, and the aristocracy. One of the most prominent spiritualists, Caspar von Schwenckfeld, was himself a landed nobleman, while David Joris' supporters included several prominent nobles, especially the wealthy Van Berchem family of Antwerp who moved with him to Basel and financed his religious mission. While in Basel, Joris (as John of Bruges) entered a circle of acquaintances that included the noted French doctor Jean Bauhin (1511–82) and the humanistic anti-dogmatist Sebastian Castellio (1515–63), as well as many other learned aficionados of non-dogmatic spiritualism and religious toleration. When Castellio composed his treatise decrying the 1553 heresy execution in Geneva of the brilliant Spanish physician Michael Servetus (discoverer of the pulmonary passage of the blood), his anthology included excerpts from ancient Church fathers, Erasmus, Luther, Calvin (who had approved of Servetus' execution) and, under a pseudonym, Joris.[6] Hendrik Niclaes' Family of Love embraced a number of prominent families, including the famous Antwerp printer Christoffel Plantijn, while a few of his English adepts served in Queen Elizabeth's court.[7] Although the number of known supporters of such spiritualists was really very small, the orthodox saw their notions as extremely destructive of confessional rigor. Calvin conducted a running battle against such "libertines" whom he believed had infiltrated the Calvinist Church, sapping its resolve to stand openly against Catholic idolatry.

The Netherlands became a prominent home for such spiritualistic notions and the writings of Sebastian Franck, Castellio, Joris, and Niclaes were published and republished there throughout the century. Readers readily disregarded Joris' and Niclaes' narcissistic claims as divine prophets and appreciated their views promoting personal inspiration from the Holy Spirit and an entirely inner religious experience. Spiritualistic individuals could be found in all confessions, especially in the *Doopsgezinde* branch of the Mennonites, and there were a number of Calvinist ministers, such as Herman Herbertsz of Dordrecht and Herbert Duifhuis of Utrecht, who used spiritualism to smooth what they regarded as the harsher edges of Calvinist theology.[8] For Herbertsz these included the uncharit-able belief that the pope was the antichrist when in fact everyone's inner evil desires were an antichrist.

Undoubtedly the most famous Dutch advocate of spiritualism was the writer and playwright Dirck Volkerts Coornhert (1522–90), who in 1572 became secretary of state to William of Orange and who helped influ-ence the prince in the direction of a policy of religious toleration for the young republic. Coornhert was personally acquainted with Niclaes and knew the writings of Joris. Although he rejected the egotistical claims of both prophets, Coornhert followed their critique of theological dogmatism, intolerance, and sectarianism and emphasized that the Devil's true work was to cause people to mistake lies for the truth and fight against each other over doctrinal issues.[9] Another pronounced Dutch spiritualist was Matthias Weyer (Wier), the brother of Johann Weyer, whose acquaint-ance we shall make in the following chapter.

In the Dutch Republic, where stately powers of compulsion were not used to enforce confessional conformity, spiritualistic ideas fused with a merchant's pragmatism to inform the religious attitudes and policies of princes, magistrates, and townsfolk. Here converso and Jewish refugees from Spain via Portugal and antitrinitarian Socinians from Poland joined Calvinists, Mennonites, Catholics, Lutherans, spiritualists, and the uncommitted to help create the most religiously diverse realm in Europe. Amsterdam became a nexus for this intellectual cross-fertilization and a home for leading proponents of religious tolerance, rational skepticism, and empiricism, including Réné Descartes and Benedict Spinoza. In Holland's cities, intellectual nonconformists, including many

of Anabaptist heritage, met regularly to rethink religious and philosophical issues. In the seventeenth century this "Collegiant" movement
paved the way for the rise of rationalism and skepticism in the Dutch
enlightenment.[10]

The Devil and the Antichrist in the Sixteenth Century

For the fervently orthodox, such open spiritualism and skepticism could
be nothing else but the nefarious work of the Devil. Having failed in
his original quest to destroy Catholicism by means of the Reformation
(for Catholic polemicists) or to discredit the Reformation by means of
Anabaptism (for Protestants), Satan had turned to inspiring atheism,
defined as the belief that confessional orthodoxy was just not important.
By deluding people into disbelieving his own existence, Satan made
them easier targets for his evil machinations. In France Catholic demonologists worked hard to convince the moderate majority that Protestantism
was a demonic heresy and that "skepticism and unbelief in demons and
witches" were equivalent to "an attack on the doctrine of the immortality
of the soul" or that "unbelief in demons was the equal of unbelief in
God."[11] While believing that Satan's malicious arsenal still included
demonic magic, demonic possession, open heresy or sedition, emphasis
was increasingly placed on his insidious manipulation of the inner
person by means of false beliefs, doubt, or general disregard for godliness
or scriptural truths. As Erik Midelfort notes for the seventeenth century,
"belief in the powers of the devil was often used as a criterion of sound
religion, since doubt on this point might reveal skepticism, unwillingness
to accept the authority of scripture, or 'atheism.'"[12] Once Satan had
achieved this inner conquest of the human mind, polemicists feared that
the defeat of Christendom through heresy and magic would inevitably
follow. Convincing a sometimes skeptical populace of the reality of the
Satanic threat became a major preoccupation of many Catholic and
Protestant churchmen.

Like Luther, Calvin stressed the supreme danger of Lucifer's spiritual
and mental assaults on people, with little mention of witchcraft. Apart
from the Catholic papacy which he identified as the Antichrist, Calvin's
greatest ire was reserved for the libertines who sought to soften disciplinary
codes or moderate the harshness of double predestination (i.e., that God
has chosen both those who will be damned and those who will be saved),
efforts Calvin feared merely played into papist hands.[13] For example,

before moving to Basel, Castellio had been a teacher in the Genevan Academy until he expressed some doubts about whether the Song of Songs belonged in the canon of scripture, and for this Calvin had his "libertine" colleague fired. In the midst of the battle against the Antichrist there could be no toleration of such doubt, even on relatively minor issues.

The diabolical threat was heightened by the nearly universal belief that Europeans were living on the eve of the return of Christ and the Last Judgment. An example of Catholic propaganda identifying Lutheranism with the Antichrist appeared in an anonymous pamphlet of 1524 which was dedicated to the ruler of Guelders and Groningen, Duke Karl van Egmond (1492–1538), a prominent prosecutor of both Anabaptists and witches in the Northern Netherlands, although his son, Karl van Guelders, the stadholder of Groningen, hindered his campaign against the former. The author of this tract shared Luther's conviction that the end of the world was near, setting February 1524 as the date. The Antichrist was alive now, heralded by the birth of his forerunner, Martin Luther, to a Christian mother and Jewish father (others had it that Luther was born to a Jewish mother and demon father). Luther's heresy was clearing the path for the Antichrist's final assault on Christendom which would be enacted by witches who had made a pact with the Devil and who were already terrifying Eastern Netherlanders by their black magic.[14] In this same year Van Egmont began his great offensive against witchcraft. When after 1530 Melchiorite Anabaptism entered the scene, the duke interpreted them in similar terms, issuing on February 13, 1535 a mandate describing them as a "devilish sect" led by "false diabolical preachers and prophets" who sought to deceive simple people against the holy Christian Church. He hated both heretics and witches, seeing them both as parts of the same diabolical conspiracy auguring the arrival of the Antichrist, and meriting the most severe penalty.

By the 1550s the apocalyptical expectations had been left unfulfilled for all, yet they did not disappear, but returned almost every generation to motivate a new group of believers. After Münster most Anabaptists, who had suffered intensely for their apocalyptical preoccupations, toned down or spiritualized their endtime visions. However, the same cannot be said for Lutherans, as right up to his death in 1546 Luther continued his apocalyptical denunciation of opponents. As Robin Barnes notes, "the decades after Luther's death ... saw the emergence of an increasingly explicit, eclectic, and strident apocalypticism among many Protestants, especially in Germany." Lutheran factional strife, the increasing influence of Calvinism within Germany, and the successful reconquest of southern Germany for Catholicism at the hands of Jesuits, all contributed to a pervasive pessimism among German Protestants who now feared that true religion was in decline, doubt and skepticism on the rise, and the Devil more active than ever before. Signs in society as well as in the sky were interpreted to plot the new date for Christ's return, and 1588 and then c.1600 proved popular choices. The last decades of the sixteenth century, as we shall see in the next chapter, also witnessed a remarkable effort to find magical means to unlock the secrets of creation and of the future, incorporating astrology, alchemy, numerology, and the Cabala within a Christian apocalyptical framework. That the second half of the sixteenth century coincided with the rise of demonic possession and witch-hunting in Germany is extremely suggestive; Barnes for one has raised the "largely unexplored" possible connections between this apocalyptical moment and the rise of witch-hunting, while Andrew Cunningham and Ole Peter Grell have asserted that the witch-hunt "was very much a product of the general apocalyptic mood" of the Reformation era.[15] On this point Stuart Clark too has commented that the "eschatological view that witchcraft flourished because the world was in a state of terminal decline was as common among French Catholic authors...as among the writers of Lutheran Germany and Calvinist England – in this case reflecting the popularity of apocalyptic history in both Reformations."[16]

At moments of crisis the Calvinists could equal Lutherans in denouncing the papacy as the Antichrist. This technique was most prominent in France during the wars of religion (1562 to 1595) when the embattled Huguenots depicted themselves as the children of God fighting to survive the final tribulation of the Antichrist. Even so, there were alternative currents within most confessions that interpreted the apocalypse in very positive, millenarian terms as the creation of a utopian society on earth, while English Puritan writers viewed themselves as the agents of God in the final establishment of England as a "godly republic." Although eschatological predictions were still being made by Catholic writers, Catholic authorities had become wary of the popular penchant for prophecy that had convulsed Italy as well in the 1520s and 1530s, leading to its suppression thereafter.[17] Areas of strong Catholic clerical and inquisitorial presence therefore witnessed a decline in popular apocalypticism; by mid-century they were also relatively mild persecutors of both heresy and witchcraft. Even so, many Jesuits depicted themselves as the prophets of the Last Days ushering in the transformation of the

world, although few went so far as the French spiritualist Guillaume
Postel (1510–81), who was expelled from the order for his unorthodox
belief that a universal language could create a rapprochement between
Christianity and Islam and unite the world. Thereafter his views became
more extreme as he portrayed himself as the firstborn son of the new
restitution, and in 1555 he was judged insane by the Roman Inquisition.
Even so, he had already managed to win many admirers among Catholics,
Protestants, and spiritualists (including Joris and Niclaes), not the least
for his brilliance of mind and breadth of vision.

The Reformation and Anti-Semitism

One of the expected signs heralding the return of Christ was the conversion
of the Jews, but they steadfastly refused to play their role of dispelling
doubt for early modern Christians. They faced increasing levels of intolerance, still plagued by charges of usury, blasphemy, and ritual murder.
However, accusations of Jewish Host desecration seem to have stopped
during the Reformation, as Catholic defenders of the sacrament focused
exclusively on Protestant deniers of the real presence of Christ, especially
Calvinists and Anabaptists.[18] Pressure to convert Jews mounted with the
Reformations' intense eschatological fervor, although some Protestants,
such as the Strasbourg Reformer and Hebrew scholar Wolfgang Capito
and the Nuremberg reformer Andreas Osiander, continued to promote
toleration as a means of bringing about the hoped for conversion of
Jews. When in 1540 the Jews of the Neuburg village of Sappenfeld were
charged with the ritual murder of the boy Michael Pisenharter, Osiander
anonymously composed *Whether it is True and believable that Jews secretly
kill Christian children and use their blood*, a treatise which demolished the
flimsy evidence behind ritual murder charges and provided alternate
explanations for the crimes. For his efforts Osiander was rewarded with
the "most massive and systematic formulation of the blood libel" in
Johannes Eck's *Refutation of a Jewish Booklet*. In this work Eck defended
Christian hatred of Jews by affirming their "murderous nature," their
malicious plots, including the poisoning of wells and their practice of
black magic that added Christian mother's milk to Christian blood as
a salve to wash away the bloodstain imposed on them by God for their
act of deicide. Eck also repeated the myth that Christian blood helped
remove the two tiny fingers that Jewish babies were supposedly born
with on their forehead, an elaboration of the belief that Jews, like the

Devil, had horns. Eck provided what he saw as empirical proof of these beliefs by recounting the recent ritual murder in 1475 of Simon of Trent, as well as similar incidents in Brandenburg in 1510 and Poesing, Hungary in 1529, wherein, as Ronnie Hsia notes, the alleged victims "proved that miracles still happened; they were living relics, embodiments of a salvific source that dispensed grace to their beholders" and dispelled doubt about the truth of Christian dogma about Jesus. When placed on display the victims' corpses, like abused Hosts, bled miraculously. For Eck, Osiander's treatise "undermined the entire theological, or one may say magical, foundations upon which salvific sacrifice and Christian redemption were based."[19] In the end Eck linked Lutherans with Jews, suggesting that the Lutheran denial of transubstantiation was of a piece with the desecration of Hosts committed by Jews. Protestants like Osiander who suggested Jews should be tolerated were immediately scolded as Judaisers. To defend themselves of such charges, many Protestants transferred the accusations to their opponents.

Despite the fact that he too was a target of Eck's polemical ire, Luther in his 1543 tracts *On the Ineffable Name* and *On the Jews and their Lies*, acknowledged ritual murder charges against Jews whom he called "the Devil's children" who used evil magic to destroy Christians. To his wife Katherina von Bora Luther recounted in the same year,

> I became ill on my way just before reaching Eisleben. It was really my own fault. But if you were there, you would have said that it must have been the fault of the Jews or their God. We had to pass through a village before reaching Eisleben which was inhabited by many Jews. Perhaps they were blowing hard at me...and it was done. When I passed through the village, a cold draft came into the wagon and almost froze my head, I swear.[20]

Just as Eck accused Lutherans of being allies of Jews, Luther suggested that the Jewish "superstition" linked them with both Catholics and Turks, all under the Devil's leadership. However, Luther was not as credulous as Eck when it came to the supposed magical acts of Jews, for his primary goal was to attack all manner of religious magic and superstition, although his success in disenchanting Christianity was limited. Luther was sensitive to the fact that Jews accused Catholic Christianity of using word magic, and so he attacked both the Jewish Cabala and Catholic ritual magic. He also suspected that many of his own followers, including many pastors, continued to use magical books, some of which relied on the unpronounceable Hebrew name for God, the Tetragrammaton, for magical efficacy. Hence, Luther's invective against the Jews was as much a condemnation of Christian magical practices as it was of Jewish.[21] In general, Protestants tended to shift attention away from the magical aspects of anti-Judaism such as Host desecration, and were less likely to believe that Jews ritually murdered Christian children, identifying the supposed miracles of the "martyr's corpse" as another form of Catholic magic.

Within the Reformed tradition of Zwingli and Calvin there was expressed much less hostility toward Jews and Judaism and a greater willingness to read Hebrew and Jewish works to assist in the interpretation of the scriptures. There were obvious limitations to this influence, as Michael Servetus discovered to his dismay. Servetus was so deeply influenced by his reading of Jewish theological works that he rejected the Christian doctrine of the trinity, a view for which he was condemned to death in Catholic Vienne. Fleeing incognito, Servetus arrived in 1553 in Geneva, which in general did not execute heretics. His true identity was discovered and he was arrested. Ignoring pleas from many quarters, Calvin supported the Genevan court's sentence of death because Servetus' heresy was so extreme that it threatened all Christians. Possibly too Calvin hoped to counteract the charges of Judaising that had been brought against his movement for its self-conception as the "people of Israel," – with infant baptism as the sign of membership replacing Jewish circumcision – and its condemnation of Jewish ritual murder charges. Although the "disenchanting" effects of Calvin's rejection of the magical aspects of anti-Semitism would become evident only in the long term, in the short term the violent anti-Jewish language that the Reformation engendered and the demonization of opponents actually contributed to demonic and magical beliefs and to suspicion of "the Other", whatever Luther and Calvin's intention may have been.

The extremes to which Protestant polemical writers would go to use Jews as verifiers of the Protestant Christian faith is seen in a pamphlet published in 1601 purporting to recount a story told by Paulus von Eytsen, Lutheran bishop of Schleswig about an incident which occurred when he was a student in Wittenberg. Visiting his parents in Hamburg in the winter of 1542, the future bishop entered a church wherein he witnessed a tall, barefooted man with long hair listening intensely to the sermon and beating his breast each time the name of Jesus was mentioned. Inquiries into his identity led Von Eytsen to a strange discovery: the man was none other than the Jew Asverus who had been an eyewitness to the crucifixion of Jesus in Jerusalem some 1,500 years earlier. His story was an unusual one, to say the least. Like his coreligionists, Asverus had regarded Jesus as a heretic and helped the chief priests to have him crucified. While Jesus was carrying his cross to the place of execution, Asverus held up his young child to see the criminal, but when Jesus got alongside them he said, "I will stop and rest, but you will go." Disturbed by this comment, Asverus returned home, but became so restless he could not remain there, but hastened to the scene of Christ's crucifixion, after which he felt compelled to leave Jerusalem, not returning until long after his family had died. Since then he lived as a wanderer throughout the world, kept alive by God until the Judgment Day as a witness of the reality of Christ's death and of Jewish responsibility for it. According to the pamphlet, Van Eytsen called in the rector of the school of Hamburg to determine Asverus' veracity, and both were amazed by his detailed knowledge of first-century Palestine and his seemingly miraculous facility with a multitude of languages. The pamphlet writer discounted the widely held belief that Asverus' knowledge was provided by a flying spirit which revealed such things to him, pointing to the Jew's intense indignation whenever Christians swore on the cross or wounds of Christ. This myth of the wandering Jew, whether as an individual such as Asverus or as a people, remained popular, and many Protestants, with their strong belief in divine providence, found it conceivable that God might miraculously prolong a human life for this particular purpose. They saw no inherent contradiction between this belief and their denunciation of Catholic belief in Jewish Host desecration.[22]

In the later sixteenth century, then, the negative anti-Semitic polemics won out over Osiander's milder approach and cries for further restrictions on Jewish freedom resounded throughout the Empire, leading to anti-Jewish riots in Braunschweig and elsewhere, while the Strasbourg Reformer Martin Bucer's urging to expel all Jews from Protestant lands fortunately went unheeded. Hsia cites the example of the Lutheran professor at the University of Giessen George Schwarz (1530–1602), who decried the tolerance of some civic officials who were allowing the coexistence of several confessions by comparing such tolerance for Jews, Catholics, Turks, and Anabaptists to ignoring the evil work of witches, blasphemers, and murderers. Hsia concludes that "owing to Luther's powerful legacy and in part to the sharpened polemics among the Christian confessions, hostility to Judaism and Jews became entrenched among the Lutheran clergy during the second half of the sixteenth century."[23]

The Devil in the New World

The European contact with the peoples of the New World and renewed
meetings with the populations of the old, exotic societies of India, Japan,
and China, also increased fears of the Devil and of "the Other". The late-
medieval European world was a very small one, surrounded by hostile
forces and under threat from a resurgent Islam. Christian princes sought
means to bypass Muslim control over the Far East trading routes through
making contact with the mythic king Prester John who supposedly
ruled over a powerful Christian principality somewhere to the east.
Thus the quest to explore the world was part and parcel of the medieval
crusader's mentality to defeat Islam.[24] It took some time for the old
conceptions of the world to adjust to the reality of what the explorers
had stumbled upon. Best-selling travel accounts blending fantastical
fiction with even stranger facts interpreted everything in the New World
as unusual and monstrous. As Fernando Cervantes notes, the power of
these myths over the European imagination meant that Europeans saw
exactly what they expected to see: giants, wild men, cannibals, and cities
paved with gold.[25] After the 1530s, however, as Christian missionaries
sought to convert the New World peoples, a demonological interpretation
was applied to their religious practices. For one early Spanish writer,
Francisco de Aguilar, there was no place like the New World "where the
devil was honored with such reverence," while by mid-century, a "negative,
demonic view of Amerindian cultures had triumphed and its influence
was seen to descend like a thick fog upon every statement officially and
unofficially made on the subject."[26] The Franciscans had managed to baptize
masses of native peoples, an approach that Dominicans complained led
to shallow or insincere converts. In the early 1530s Inquisition tribunals
uncovered evidence confirming such suspicions, leading, as in Europe, to
increased efforts to enforce complete confessional conformity. Pessimism
mounted as it appeared Satan himself was intervening to keep the native
peoples as his idolatrous servants. The discovery in 1562 of widespread
idolatry in Yucatan, Mexico, resulted in mass arrests, torture, and executions comparable to the Spanish Inquisition's earlier assault on Judaising
conversos.[27] The emphasis on witchcraft and pagan ritual as a form of
demonic idolatry, rather than as mere pagan survivals, was a major
factor in this trend as well. The persecution of supposed idolatry in the
New World paralleled remarkably the increasing anxiety over secret
diabolical plots in the Old World, mutually reinforcing or feeding the
anti-Devil frenzy in both locales.

The Devil and Confessional Conflict

The confessional conflict, apocalyptical expectations, fear of Turkish invasion, and the struggle of rulers to gain control over their realms, increased fears of diabolical agents at work within European society. The specific target of suspicion was readily transferable, shifting back and forth from heretic to Jew, to Anabaptist, to New World natives, and ultimately to demonic witches. What may have been passed off as an unfortunate accident increasingly took on eschatological or even demonic significance. For example, on the evening of St. Lawrence Day, 1546, a bolt of lightning ignited the munitions house of Mechelen, Brabant, causing a massive explosion that leveled several buildings and killed hundreds. Similar disasters were often explained as naturally caused in the providence of God. But one reporter noted that in this disaster God was expressing his ire over the sins of Netherlanders who were flirting with various reform movements. On that fateful night, "through the help of the evil enemy [Satan], who always shows his evil," the lightning struck the tower where gunpowder was stored to assist the emperor's battles against the rebellious German princes.[28]

However, another commentator linked this disaster to the Devil's efforts to obstruct the gains made by the Protestant movement and presented it as a warning to the Catholic emperor "to abstain from his unchristian, improper, unfaithful resolutions" which have been given him by the Pope "and the entire spiritless crowd." In this news sheet Charles V's regent, Mary of Hungary, was dressed in apocalyptical attire as the despised Jezebel and the two of them were admonished to stop shedding "the innocent blood, so much of which has been spilt in the Netherlands on account of the gospel."[29] While both writers saw the catastrophe ultimately as an act of God, the Devil played a prominent role for both: for the first as an agent of evil whose indiscriminate, malicious act with the lightning was used by God as a further means to punish sin; for the second as a nasty opponent of true faith whose vicious destruction of a portion of Mechelen inadvertently hindered his own plot to crush the gospel by depriving his agent, Charles V, of his needed gunpowder. Neither tract adequately resolved the question of true responsibility for this disaster, and the second news sheet unintentionally depicted the Devil as a bumbling schemer who could not keep track of all of his plots. In both works the lightning was directed by Satan alone, without the human agency of witches who were elsewhere accused of brewing storms to harm neighbors.[30]

To varying degrees all Protestants condemned Catholic sacramental practice as magical, although the Calvinists and Anabaptists were the most thorough in this regard, while Luther's maintenance of the real presence of Christ in the Eucharist muted his condemnation of priestly magic. Calvinists attacked Catholic sacramentals, priestly power, and exorcism as Catholic magic or hocus pocus. As one anonymous Reformed writer put it in 1556,

> Oh Babylon, Babylon, all the blood of the witnesses of Jesus Christ, from the creation of the world until its end, shall be demanded of you and of your servants, for the sorcerers who conjure demons are more holy than you who are the whorish church. What difference is there between these sorcerers through whom an evil spirit enters into a crystal and from there into their [finger]nail or some into a mirror; but you command Christ to enter into a piece of bread and believe that you could have him as often as you say the words, "this is my body."[31]

Gazing into crystals, a fingernail, or a mirror were all necromantic means of visualizing the summoned spirit. To make such comparisons between sacramental practice and ritual magic was an extreme means of desacralizing and demonizing Catholic sacred objects. In their place Protestant leaders preferred congregational prayer and fasting as a means of assisting those assailed by demons. While most Protestant intellectuals insisted that ghosts were evil spirits, not the souls of the deceased, this merely contributed to the great confusion over the spectrum of supernatural beings on the part of the populace.[32]

The Changing Role of the Dead

As well as seeking to separate the magical from the religious by demonizing the former and purifying the latter, Protestants, especially Calvinists and Mennonites, attempted to redefine the relationship between the living and the dead by closing communication between the two realms. Given the formidable import that the dead had held for the living prior to the Reformation, it is indeed impressive how far Reformers succeeded in this program, in many places weaning people from belief in saints and purgatory, although this was often replaced by reliance on angels or fear of ghosts.[33] The Calvinist assault on old notions about the dead was well orchestrated. In 1565, the year before the iconoclastic fury in the Low

Countries, an anonymous dialogue was published wherein two friends, Pasquillus and Marphorius, discuss the former's trip to hell, in an obvious parody of Dante's *Inferno*. Expressing his astonishment that his colleague was able to be whisked away by an angel to the gates of hell without the traditional ceremonies, Marphorius commented that this was "very different from what I have read in other books, for you have not first killed a ram or a black goat; . . . you have not sought the golden bough, you have not sprinkled yourself with holy water, nor signed yourself with the holy cross, nevertheless you have so quickly gained entry." Bemused, Pasquillus admits that his entry into hell was incredibly easy, as he merely followed the crowds of people, mostly monks, priests, and nuns, filing into it. There was no Purgatory, Pasquillus discovered, for it was a diabolical and papal fiction created by "Hillebrand the sorcerer, that is [Pope] Gregory VII" who was influenced by "the false miracles and visions and deceitfulness of the Devil, transformed into an angel of light."[34] Thus the living should have no further concern about the deceased.

This sharp, theoretical delineation between the dead and the living and between magic and religion was applied to the sacraments as well. In another anonymous dialogue from 1565, a peasant was told by a Reformed pilgrim not to rely on the Catholic priesthood for his salvation. Confronting his priest, the peasant asked if he was "the Antichrist, or must we wait for another?" The priest not only admitted the charge, but revealed also that the Catholic Church had created sacramental baptism so that ordinary believers would be distracted from the clergy's hypocrisy with respect to repentance: "so that we might prove that penance was not necessary, we made baptism so much mightier and stronger, with blessings, with holy water, chrism, incense, bitter salt, so that it would not become vile or stinking," convincing everyone that it was essential for the salvation of children. Similarly, the contrast between Jesus' Lord's Supper and the Catholic Mass could not be clearer, as the priest explained: "Christ held a night meal and we hold a Mass; he spoke to his disciples, we speak to the bread; he said 'this is my body', we say 'therein is his body'; he went from there to his death, we to a well prepared table," and so forth.[35] For this author the Mass was nothing more than veneration of dumb idols.

In this and countless other examples of Calvinist and Mennonite propaganda, the Catholic sacramental system and priestly order were demonized, while in Protestant hands the sacred objects, such as consecrated bread and wine or holy oil and water, or saints' images and relics, became mundane things divested of supernatural power and significance.

How were Catholics to respond to this very effective ritual challenge to their monopoly over divine approval? Rational arguments were so framed as to defuse Protestant criticism, such as those developed by Guillaume du Vair, president of the Parlement of Provence, who suggested that the Devil would not have so attacked the Church's sacraments "if he had not thought that they were truly what we believe them to be, that is to say, the certain effects of the word of God, the treasures of his favors, and the sure signs of the salvation of men." Bishop Friedrich Forner of Bamberg, a zealous proponent of witch-hunting, argued that because Protestants were already apostates from the true religion, the Devil did not bother attacking them. The prevalence of witchcraft among Catholics, another piece of Protestant propaganda, became in the bishop's terms a "most splendid, nay most certain, and infallible sign that the true and saving faith, the true gospel, the true sacraments, the true religion are found among Catholics."[36] Why should the Devil bother with heretics who were already under his spell?

Another approach was to offer empirical evidence of the veracity of the miraculous within the sacramentals, such as the many miracles of incombustible or bleeding Hosts. The power of consecrated wafers, water, salt, oil, incense, and crucifixes, was also proven by their effectiveness in casting out demons from the possessed. The moment that the demon admitted defeat and fled the victim in the face of the priest's power and spiritual equipment was a decisive one in dispelling doubts about sacramental power. In this way exorcisms provided tangible proof of the reality of the Devil, and by contrariety of God, his chosen agents, the priests, and conduits of supernatural power, the sacraments.

With their emphasis on the absolute sovereignty of God, Protestants denied that humans could in any way gain knowledge of or control the supernatural by any means apart from God's own written revelation, while sacred action for Protestants flowed in one direction only. Such a belief should have undercut any place for the magical in religion, but all confessions failed in their goal to separate the two as the magical realm proved remarkably resilient to reform. Protestant laypeople continued to use sacramentals to assist them in their daily existence, while in some respects Reformed leaders created their own magical objects in the printed Bible, hymnals, and prayer books which were occasionally used for healing and protective purposes. Protestants may have condemned using blessed weather bells and Eucharistic processions to divert storms, but in some locales these were merely replaced by the Protestant "hail-sermon." As noted by Robert Scribner, the Protestant version of the old "moralized universe" increased anxiety among the populace who, deprived of the Catholic means of protection, "found themselves prey to anxiety that was hardly allayed by invoking the Protestant doctrine of providence."[37] Every incident of famine, hail storm, war, plague, and the like brought out the moralists' chastisements and inspired further communal and governmental attempts to expunge the offending sin or sinners from the community. Protestant preachers railed ever more fervently against "superstition", heresy, or immorality as the immediate causes of God's retribution. But every catastrophe led more people to return to traditional magical or ritual means of protecting themselves. It became necessary then for Protestant leaders to condemn all such "white magic" as the moral equivalent of the *maleficia* of witches, implicating the practitioner in the forming of a Satanic pact.

Anti-Protestant Propaganda: Diabolical Heretics

As part of their campaign to oppose the incursions of Lutheran and Calvinist reform, zealous Counter-Reformation churchmen, especially the Jesuits, argued that the Catholic Church alone performed true miracles, that the Protestant denial of traditional Catholic rites and beliefs was Satanic, and that Protestants of all stripes, but especially the more radical Calvinists, were agents of the Devil to sow the seeds of doubt, heresy, and atheism, contributing to the alarming increase in demonic witchcraft in Europe. This position could be illustrated by reference to the writings of any number of zealous Catholic polemicists. The case of France presents a very clear example.

According to Jonathan Pearl, the writings of France's demonologists, almost exclusively zealous Catholics, were composed to provide ammunition for the fervent Catholic side in their struggles against both the Protestant minority and the moderate Catholic majority which supported the tradition of royal control over the national church, a position known as Gallicanism. The small but vocal zealot party sought to have the crown eradicate all traces of Protestant heresy from France and to implement the decrees of the Council of Trent in the realm, thereby reasserting papal control over the French Catholic Church. In 1557 it seemed that they would soon have their wish, for King Henry II proclaimed a royal ordinance establishing the Inquisition in France, but it was rescinded the following year and trials against Protestant heretics were more or less ended after 1562.

It was therefore extremely important in this religious–political climate to portray the Protestants in the darkest colors possible and to associate the tolerant position as evil. In this polemical battle, the zealots (later formalized as the Duke of Guises' "Catholic League") decried the Gallicans as the allies of heretics. Zealot demonologists contributed by defining Protestantism as demonic heresy and advocating its complete destruction. Any Catholic official, they announced, who refused to perform his duty of eradicating this diabolical threat to the kingdom was guilty of assisting heresy, atheism, and the Devil. Moderation itself was declared demonic. Unbelief was the greatest threat to civil order and divine pleasure in France, and any signs of skepticism about demonic activity was condemned forcefully as an attack on the doctrine of the immortality of the soul and as atheism. *Politique* judges therefore found themselves condemned as members of "the widespread satanic conspiracy that prevented the rule of godly reformed Tridentine Catholicism in France."[38] After Francis II's death in 1560 the Catholic zealots came to see themselves as "an unjustly spurned minority" frustrated over their inability to influence royal policy. They therefore preached incendiary sermons, marched in long, emotional processions and, as we shall see later, used theatrical exorcisms of demoniacs to extremely good effect. In all of these the message was very clear: the toleration of Protestantism was a diabolical evil that was destroying France.

In France the Jesuits were prominent in this campaign. Particularly influential was one of the first professors of the Jesuit College in Paris, the Spaniard Juan de Maldonado or Maldonat (1534–83). A vigorous opponent of Protestantism, Maldonat lectured Catholics to stand firm against heresy. That his lectures coincided with the second and third wars of religion in France (September 1567 to August 1570) gave his words potentially explosive significance. After another peace was declared in the late summer of 1570, Maldonat returned to Paris and to his lectures after a period of missionizing within the former Protestant stronghold of upper Poitou. After this experience he turned with even greater thoroughness to the subject of demons, strongly linking them to Protestant heresy and arguing that witches always accompany heretics, as in "Bohemia and Germany, [where] the Hussite heresy was accompanied by such a storm of demons that witches were busier than heretics." He claimed that Geneva was now infected by witches who were spreading into France, for "magical arts follow heresy." Pearl's summary of Maldonat's explanation of the process is illuminating: "demons live with heretics; after a violent outburst, heresy degenerates into atheism and magic; the 'curious arts' follow heresy like a plague; demons use heretics to deceive mankind. All this was made possible and worsened through the negligence of unfit or undedicated priests."

The Devil was ably assisted in this process by the curiosity of individuals, for "there is nothing that helps the devil more than curiosity, in which he is well studied. That is why there are more women than men who are witches, since women are more inclined to curiosity." Moreover, denying the reality of demons, or disclaiming the ability of witches to fly with demons to their sabbaths or to make themselves invisible, was akin to atheism. Thanks to their disavowal of transubstantiation, Calvinists were also among such atheists. For this influential Catholic zealot, Protestants were not merely wrong theologically, but were responsible for the rise of both political sedition and dangerous witchcraft. As summarized by Pearl, Maldonat

> labeled the Protestants as heretics and always referred to them as such. Then he argued that in their heresy, they were inspired by and allied to the Devil. He always stressed the intimate connection of witchcraft and heresy, arguing that the Devil made both possible and benefited from the growth. In other words, rather than only saying that witches were heretics, Maldonat inferred strongly that the modern Protestant heretics were witches.[39]

Such demonization of the Protestant opponents, Pearl concludes, was a major factor in the frenzied slaughter by Catholic mobs of Protestants which broke out in Paris on St. Bartholomew's Day, August 24, 1572 and which consumed some 3,000 victims. The stage was set the preceding Advent and Lent by the virulent sermons of mendicant preachers which so stirred up public hatred that it created a climate favorable to violence, although actual massacres could occur only with the tacit approval of the crown and the leadership of local authorities.

The St. Bartholomew's Day massacre in fact followed traditional rites of magical purification performed against the "accursed dead." For example, a Parisian house which had been polluted by Protestant sermons and communion services was torn down by a Catholic mob who, as with former Jewish synagogues, erected a cross over the site; the cadavers of Huguenots were removed from their graves and dragged through the mud, while young children castrated and disemboweled the corpses. These gruesome acts were in some respects a reversal of what the Reformed themselves had performed against the statues of saints during the iconoclastic storms (see Chapter 4 below) and an effort to "reestablish a sacrality that had been violated."[40] The blossoming of a hawthorn bush before a chapel dedicated to the Virgin and miraculous cures performed there helped to confirm for Parisian Catholics that their violent actions had received divine approval and possibly helped alleviate any guilt they may have retained. For the Huguenots, the massacre triggered a great number of conversions as many saw the violence as a sign that God was no longer with them.

Catholic preachers influenced by Maldonat harangued their congregants on the dangers of heresy and the need for its extermination, allowing for the spread of the massacres across France. The famous Flemish Jesuit demonologist, Martin Del Rio (1551–1608), was one of those influenced by Maldonat, and he too argued that "the filth of magic accompanies heresy and follows it like a shadow follows the body" which, he suggested, "is such a clear fact that whomever doubts it doubts the day and makes night out of high noon. The principal heretics have been magicians."[41] In France, the identification of Protestantism with diabolical heresy remained a pronounced one throughout the second half of the sixteenth century.

Anti-Anabaptist Propaganda

Even more than Huguenots, Anabaptists, with their early history of radical nonconformity and insurrection, proved a favorite target for demonizing among both Catholics and Protestants. After the destruction of the Münster kingdom in 1535, Anabaptists offered no serious threat against the social order. Yet, twenty years later the propaganda war against them was intensified, even though fears of Anabaptist insurrection were no longer rational. In contrast to the image portrayed by mainstream polemicists, Anabaptists and spiritualists depreciated fear of the Devil, except to the extent that they linked their persecutors to the Antichrist. They thoroughly stripped away the miraculous and magical from religious practice and their places of worship (where permitted) were devoid of religious imagery (plainer even than the Calvinists) and were designated not as churches but as meeting places. Their ministers were laypeople normally chosen by casting of lots and disallowed from pursuing formal theological or philosophical education so that they would not fall into the trap of clerical pride. They rejected the concept of a sacrament altogether, interpreting the body of Christ present at the Lord's Supper as the gathered group of believers, turning primary attention away from the bread and wine. While their opponents tried to argue that they made believers' baptism into a new idol, Mennonites themselves believed it to be merely a public statement of an individual adult's decision to join the people of God. For them infant baptism – maintained by Calvinists as well as Lutherans and Catholics – implied magical efficacy, as the infant had no control over what was happening to it.

We can explain the ongoing attack on Mennonites by keeping two things in mind. First, for more than three centuries preachers and Inquisitors had been warning the populace about secret, demonic groups that were a major threat to Christian society. After the crushing of the Cathars, Inquisitors began spreading the notion that these demonic heresies had merely gone underground, dissembling and obscuring their true, evil intentions under "feigned" godliness or confessional conformity. In this way the supposed godliness of the small numbers of known Anabaptists could be used instead as evidence that they were the Devil's agents. Second, if the Anabaptist critique was accepted by the authorities, the entire sacramental and theological edifice of the Catholic Church would come crashing down as its miraculous/magical underpinnings were removed. The best way to neutralize Anabaptist skepticism was therefore to demonize the Anabaptists themselves, to compel them to play in the polemical literature, in the court and on the scaffold, the role of secret demonic agent. Most of them, even under severe torture, adamantly refused to perform their appointed parts in this drama, and flung the charge of demonic inspiration back into the faces of their accusers. Many captured Anabaptists and Mennonites were able to dispute the scriptures with their captors as near equals, something that at first caught the authorities off guard. Only diabolical magic, some Inquisitors explained, could have made so many ordinary women and men literate and so confident in the face of the usually terrifying Inquisitor or secular judge. For example, in a series of anti-heresy treatises composed in 1567, the Bishop of Roermonde and Inquisitor of South Holland, William Verlinde (Lindanus), claimed that some Anabaptists had confessed that "as soon as they had given their oath [i.e., joined the Anabaptists], they felt in themselves the singular power of the Devil so that they could begin to read the Scriptures when before they could not read a letter, and once they returned to the Church they could no longer do so."[42] Verlinde moreover accused David Joris of deceiving many people through his denial of the reality of the Devil. According to this learned Inquisitor, Joris' followers had "their origin from a mistaken or straying sorcerer, who around 1545 sowed his malicious teaching from the old cisterns or pools of stinking heresies, reawakening the Sadducee errors of denying angels, devils and baptism, and also the Last Judgement."[43] Joris' reputed miracles, such as transforming water into wine, turning himself invisible to avoid detection, and levitating six or seven feet above the ground, Verlinde explained as acts of evil sorcery. Of course Joris purported to do none of these things.

Anabaptists, Inquisitors and preachers agreed, were the leading edge of Satan's final assault on Christendom to invert the social order. Stuart Clark suggests that the vocabulary of witchcraft was part of a language used to condemn the "properties of a disorderly world," of a world turned upside down.[44] Such language was also used with great abandon to condemn Anabaptists as promoting misrule, as a mirror image of the orderly world. Despite such characterizations, the ideas of this persecuted minority continued to find an audience throughout the century. The authorities soon realized that the campaign to demonize Anabaptists and spiritualists was not working among the populace. In response, some gave up and began tolerating the dissidents, while others became more extreme in their demonizing efforts, but even here the effects were not as intended, as instead of inspiring people to turn in suspected Anabaptist heretics among their neighbors, the polemics heightened fears of other alleged agents of the Devil in their midst.

Another reason for the continued demonization of Anabaptists was the need for Catholic and Protestant clergy to redirect Anabaptist anticlericalism away from themselves back upon the accusers or onto another easily demonized target. From the movement's early days, Anabaptism's leaders had accused the clergy of complete corruption and of practicing sorcery, such as the Hutterites who in 1532 argued that pedobaptism was a "dog's bath" through which "the priest claimed to drive demons out of the pure child while he, himself, is full of demons."[45] In some locales such as western maritime France, anticlerical sentiment included charges that the clergy, whether Catholic or Protestant, used sorcery against their parishioners as a means of maintaining a monopoly over the sacraments.[46] That such charges were widespread is shown by a Catholic catechism published in Freiburg, Germany, wherein the writer denies the belief that the clergy caused hailstorms and suggests that the peasants give up "their dreadful cursing and swearing before blaming such storms on their priests' absence from the parish or for their not properly blessing the weather."[47] Catholics explained Anabaptist obstinacy in not recanting their heresy by reference to diabolical control, and at times turned the tables upon the Anabaptists by using "clerical magic" to compel their confessions; Werner O. Packull cites a case in 1533 from the southern Empire "when the food of eleven prisoners was spiced with holy water and blessed salt in the hope of exorcising the demonic powers believed to hold sway over the prisoners" and in another instance priests were commanded to sprinkle holy water on two recalcitrant women.[48] Torture was more typically applied as a means to loosen the grip Satan had on the accused's tongue, a technique that had been used on both heretics and witches in the late Middle Ages.

The taint of Münster lingered long as propagandists continued to warn their audiences that outwardly peaceable Anabaptists were secretly plotting insurrection. For example, in 1588 the Tyrolian theologian Christoffen Erhard compared the Hutterite Brethren (who practiced community of goods) to the infamous Münsterites and warned the residents of Moravia about the rebellious intentions of the 17,000 Brethren who resided in the region.[49] Many propagandists also linked this supposed renewal of Anabaptist militancy to a larger diabolical conspiracy, one with very clear parallels to the demonic witch stereotype. Persecution of Mennonites and other radical reformers therefore continued apace, and would do so in the southern Netherlands and some parts of the Empire throughout much of the second half of the sixteenth century.

Perhaps of greatest concern to the secular authorities was the connection made by propagandists between Anabaptism and the Peasants' War. As the courtly astrologer Johann Carion put it in his 1543 chronicle, "all heretics are rebels who seek to spread their heresy by force, for their master the Devil is a liar and a murderer."[50] Moreover, many learned polemicists argued that Anabaptist rejection of infant baptism placed children in danger of damnation and led ultimately to social chaos; such could only have arisen, they believed, from the kingdom of hell itself.[51] Protestants saw the rise of Anabaptism as the Devil's means of subverting the Reformers' rediscovery of the gospel. Proof of the diabolical intentions of Anabaptists could be readily found in their habit of meeting at night in dark woods or caves, despite the fact that this procedure had been forced upon them by persecution. Much the same was suspected about the Huguenot preachers in 1550s France who were forced to hold their meetings at unusual times and places, as one pamphleteer put it,

These ministers, who are known as 'beards' or 'uncles', go from one place to another without staying long anywhere; and to console and encourage the unfortunate people, they usually assemble at night, sometimes in a pit or a quarry, for fear of persecution. These clandestine assemblies have given wicked people occasions to vent all kinds of calumny upon them. ... They have had the reputation among common folk of practicing incest, sorcery and enchantment and of being completely devoted to the Devil, meeting in conventicles as much to indulge in lewd behavior and do other execrable things as to conduct their 'Sabbat' (I use their terminology) with the Devil who is present on that occasion.[52]

Many ordinary people too equated refusal to partake of the Eucharist with Anabaptism and magic, all of which were "subversive of the public cult."[53] For the death of such outcasts, no funeral bell was to be rung and no burial was to be conducted in consecrated ground.

Lutherans, Calvinists, and Possessed Infants

The polemical conflict kept the fires of religious hatred and suspicion burning among the various Protestant and Catholic reform currents. Luther's condemnation of Anabaptists as agents of spiritual bewitchment cited at the start of this chapter was enhanced by his successors who were engaged in a struggle to preserve sacramental realism against the desacralizing of Calvinists which Lutherans depicted as leading ultimately to Anabaptism. As Justus Menius, Lutheran preacher at Eisenach put it in 1544, as rejecters of baptism and the Eucharist, Anabaptists were members of the Devil's church, turning people against God and setting them against each other. Children, Menius asserted, must be baptized so that they will be "purified from sin, delivered from eternal death and from the Devil's dominion."[54] Calvinists maintained the importance of infant baptism as a sign of membership in God's covenant, but rejected exorcism as a carry-over of Catholic magic. By the 1550s their position was beginning to influence many Lutheran pastors who were leaving the exorcism rite out of their baptismal services. As Adam Crato, Lutheran pastor in Magdeburg warned, excising exorcism from Luther's baptismal book implied that "Christian children prior to holy baptism are not heathens, nor under the authority of Satan, nor physically nor spiritually possessed." Demons, he cautioned, were everywhere, seeking "to establish their dwelling in the children." For their part, the Calvinist-minded Lutherans accused their orthodox fellows of teaching that a pregnant women

might carry a possessed fetus or "physical devil," a prospect that understandably terrified many Lutheran parents.[55]

The propaganda war of the 1550s and 1560s on the question of
baptismal exorcism was part of a larger Lutheran obsession with all things
diabolical, evidenced in the creation of a new genre of works, the *Devil
books* (*Teufelbücher*), which linked particular vices, such as adultery, to
corresponding demons, which numbered twenty by 1569. Robert W.
Scribner has noted that it seemed "as though the Devil and demonic
spirits had become wilder and more incalculable, attested by the remarkable efflorescence of Protestant demonology, which by the second half of
the sixteenth century attained the level of an obsession."[56] What fuelled
this obsession was the need both to counteract the rising skepticism
toward the demonic realm and to explain the relative failure of the
Reformation to capture the imaginations of most ordinary people. In
a major compendium of Devil books published in 1569 as *Theatre of the
Devils* (*Theatrvm Diabolorum*), the editor, Sigmund Feyerabend, attacked
those doubters who believed and lived as if there was no Devil, propagating the modern proverb: "hell is not as hot as the priests make it and the
Devil is not as black as the artists paint him. ...All that is said and
preached about hell and demons is vain falsehood and a trivial thing to
frighten the people and bring the priests money." Against those who
suggested that the Devil existed solely as the evil thoughts of humans,
Feyerabend pointed to the demons which Jesus had cast out of the
possessed man and into the herd of swine (Matt. 8) and to the fact that
even the pagan philosophers believed in invisible spirits. Like his Catholic
counterparts, Feyerabend took comfort also in the current machinations
of Satan's mob which proved his existence, such as the increasing cases
of physical possession or the rising "war and bloodshed, hunger and
inflation, pestilence and other harmful sicknesses, that here someone has
broken his neck, there an arm or leg which, without fear of contradiction
were caused by the Devil, though allowed by God." As for the relative
ineffectiveness of Luther's gospel, Feyerabend turned to the story of one
of the ancient Church fathers who one day saw a demon with various
flasks and boxes and asked him what he was making with them. The demon
replied that "he had a special salve which he would smear on the eyes
and ears of people so that they could not hear God's word nor perceive
his work and thus be damned, blind and stubborn, in disbelief." Satan
sought to bring discord, both on the world stage, with the Peasants' War
of 1525, the Münsterite kingdom of 1535, and the recent conflict
between Sweden and Denmark, and within marriage by turning love

into hatred and affection into murderous jealousy. Destructive fires, deadly plagues, and personal injuries were all the manifestations of Satan's evil.[57] Just as Heinrich Krämer had turned to diabolical witches to explain infertility within sacramental marriage, this Lutheran writer explained the failure of Luther's gospel to transform human relations within and outside of marriage by recourse to the direct activities of Satan, albeit without the involvement of witches.

As suggested by Feyerabend, there was indeed a dramatic rise in demonic possession cases in Lutheran Germany, some of them quite spectacular events involving large groups of afflicted people. The Lutheran propaganda about exorcism was carried by sermon and pamphlet to the populace at large, many of whom began thinking more intensely about demonic possessions. Pastors used this growing fascination with the diabolical to chastize their flock which they thought were "full of Sadducees, Epicureans, and self-satisfied worldlings, who refused to recognize the reality of the spirit world" while several possessions resulted in "revival sermons and angelic visions."[58] Among the educated classes, Wolfgang Behringer suggests, there arose "a greater willingness...to attribute every conceivable misfortune, not to natural causes, but to the machinations of the Devil" and to heed the "constant clamor for witch-burning from the populace." Many authorities resisted, but most ultimately gave in, such as Duke Wilhelm V of Bavaria who in the 1580s noted that in these "last days" God was punishing his people with the "foul and frightful vice of sorcery and witchcraft."[59] To many the apocalyptical expectation of an increased demonic attack on the church was being fulfilled.

Suppressing Atheists

An example of how the campaign to eradicate alleged skepticism about the spirit world actually elevated fear of demonic activity comes from Strasbourg where since 1525 the city's Reformed preachers had been trying to persuade the Anabaptists to return to the Protestant church. In the 1530s they achieved some success among the Melchiorite Anabaptists by addressing their criticisms about lax disciplinary standards among the Reformed. Even so, the preachers were soon confronted by a new problem in the revival of interest in soothsaying and bewitchment.[60] However, their vigorous efforts to discourage parishioners from seeking out the assistance of magical experts had the unintended effect of stimulating their hearers' interest in the diabolical arts, already raised by rumors of Anabaptist visions and by the artistic renditions of witches by Hans Baldung Grien (1484/85–1545) who resided in Strasbourg.[61] In 1535 the city's preachers asked the city council to extend its disciplinary measures against sectarians and soothsayers into the countryside in an attempt to eradicate superstitious notions. Between 1543 and 1544 these efforts were intensified as part of an investigation into the activity of a popular soothsayer, the priest Ott von Hagenau, whose powers the Reformers ascribed to a pact with Satan. In September 1544 Martin Bucer delivered a sermon on the dangers of soothsaying and Ott was expelled.[62] Over the next decade, the Reformed preachers were also faced with countering Jesuit propaganda promoting Catholic miracles.

Further heightening anxiety about diabolical activity around 1544 was a perceived revival of interest in Anabaptism and spiritualism in the city which "coincided with articles promulgated by Jorists." In their petition for council action of February 1545, the preachers Martin Bucer, Caspar Hedio, and Matthias Zell warned the council of some who "openly maligned Strasbourg's church and religion, some denied the existence of the Devil, and others argued that one should tolerate all citizens whether Jew, Turk or Catholic." In addition, they noted that David Joris was in the area with "a large following who plan to drive out the godless."[63] Joris had in fact just moved to Basel (a mere 70 miles down the Rhine from Strasbourg), while one of his noble patrons, Cornelis van Lier, lord of Berchem, moved in 1545 to Strasbourg. Joris both promoted religious toleration and denied the Devil's independent reality. In the face of this allegedly atheistic threat, the city's preachers preached even more fervently on Satan's existence.

In the 1550s accusations of witchcraft began reaching the ears of Strasbourg's magistrates. In 1556, during an investigation into an Anabaptist gathering, the city council discovered that a Lumpen Barthlin had been attempting to ply his magical talents among some of the religious dissenters, albeit without success. Over the next several decades, prosecution of witchcraft increased in the city, as did publication of works on the subject. Fears about the influence of religious dissenters and of religious skepticism about the Devil helped stoke popular interest in visions, prognostication, and diabolical activity. In preachers' minds the Devil was closely allied to atheism and skepticism, while news of diabolical activity helped counteract popular uncertainty about the spirit world.

The denial of the reality of the Devil also became associated with witchcraft accusations. The Calvinists of Geneva, according to William

Monter, regarded witchcraft as "primarily a theological deviation rather than a magical type of criminal activity."[64] For example, the jurist most prominently involved in sixteenth-century Genevan cases of witchcraft was the French refugee Germain Colladon who advised Geneva's court on 54 witchcraft cases. He depreciated charges of *maleficia* and concentrated instead on answers to the questions, "Does the Devil exist?" and "Do witches exist?" If a suspect gave a negative answer to either of these queries, Colladon assumed his or her guilt, as anyone so "'poorly informed and instructed in the Christian religion' was probably in the Devil's clutches already." Several accused who denied the reality of the Devil were therefore tortured into confessing to witchcraft.[65] (Colladon's test would later be replaced by the more typical search for the Devil's mark.) Thus, news that Joris' followers were disseminating views depreciating the Devil raised debate on the subject and led indirectly to demands for witch prosecution as Reformed preachers sought to reduce popular interest in such pernicious ideas.

Conclusion

The central focus of this chapter has been on how Catholic and Protestant polemics linked religious heresy to a demonic conspiracy. Certainly the rhetoric almost always exceeded actual efforts of suppression, causing the frequent and bitter complaints of zealous theologians. However, throughout the sixteenth century, many thousands of people were imprisoned, tortured, and horribly executed because of the belief that they were a profound threat to the social order and in league with the Devil. What marked the Anabaptists off very clearly from the witches was that Anabaptists actually believed and practiced much of what they confessed to the authorities, while witches were forced into confessing to deeds no human could perform. As we have seen, Inquisitors and theologians had had lots of practice transforming real heretics into imaginary demon worshipers. When real heretics were largely suppressed, the diabolical conspiracy was not dismantled, but merely adjusted to fit other supposed dissidents. The demonizing rhetoric that was casually tossed about in the Reformation era therefore had profound consequences.

In the shift from real Anabaptist heretics to witches, attention turned away from religious dissidents and rebels to unruly women, especially those with reputations for witchcraft, a stereotype enunciated forcefully in Krämer's misogynistic *Malleus Maleficarum* which focused on the dangers of female sexuality and its susceptibility to demonic temptation. Frightened by the sight of women activists, Catholic and Protestant ideologues strengthened the calls for patriarchalism, so that the actions of every woman would be monitored by a male head, ironically the same motivation behind Münsterite polygamy. These theoreticians broadened the image of the potential witch to include any woman who was behaving in any fashion outside the bounds of a properly submissive housewife.[66] By acting as visionaries, prophets and informal house-churches leaders, by divorcing non-Anabaptist husbands, abandoning families, participating in the polygamy and armed defense of Münster and running naked through the streets proclaiming apocalyptical judgment, Anabaptist women gained considerable notoriety as breakers of traditional gender roles and as examples of the effects of loosening the strictures limiting female behavior.[67] Although such male fears of independent female action did not, in and of themselves, create the witch-hunts, they helped focus attention on women as the sex most susceptible to the charms of Satan.

4

THE REFORMATION, MAGIC, AND WITCHCRAFT, 1520–1600

> Moreover, in the year 1568 the Italians and Spaniards going to the Low Countries, carried notes full of spells, which they had been given in order to be safe from all evils. ... In such a case, the Master Sorcerer (who does not deserve to be named [i.e., Cornelius Agrippa]) for the invocation of evil spirits wants one to fast first, and then celebrate Holy Mass. It is not then an easy matter to discover witches, nor to distinguish them from respectable people, and much less now than formerly, although all peoples, and all sects of philosophers have condemned witches. ...
>
> Jean Bodin, writing in 1580 against Johann Weyer, Agrippa's former student. In Randy A. Scott and Jonathan L. Pearl, eds. and trans., *Jean Bodin, On the Demon-Mania of Witches* (Toronto, 1995), 67.

If by the sixteenth century heresy was made an ally of the Devil, then magic became his lover. The era's dramatic increase in anticlericalism, doubt, and skepticism compelled church leaders more strongly to defend their particular beliefs, sometimes by attacking the belief's antithesis as a diabolical inversion of the true faith. As targets Anabaptists and spiritualists worked well for a time but after mid-century there still remained no resolution to the confessional conflicts nor significant decrease in the general populace's attachment to "superstitious" practices. Bombarded by clerical propaganda warning of the various Satanic dangers, lay people seem to have become convinced of a diabolical conspiracy, but reinterpreted it to best suit their daily existence. They therefore began insisting more strenuously that the authorities deal with those neighbors whom they long suspected of performing witchcraft, for this was a demonic danger they could truly comprehend. Initially hesitant to deal with these cases, local authorities were soon convinced, while many clergy quickly depicted demonic witchcraft as the exact mirror image of the true faith, and attacked it with extreme vigor. Whichever confession could prove its power over skepticism and the Devil's realm, was surely the one approved by God.

The process outlined above was only one of many factors involved in the turn from heretic to witch-hunting, which also included a worsening climate in the second half of the sixteenth century, the further central-ization of political and judicial authority on the part of princes, and the deteriorating conditions for women. This chapter will necessarily restrict itself to highlighting some of the major stages in the development of the ultimately fearful stereotype of the demonic witch. These will include: how church leaders demonized first learned magic (the occult sciences) and then popular magic and witchcraft; a description of the typical sixteenth-century trials against witches prior to the major witch panics; and an analysis of the extraordinary cases of demonic possession that proved so useful as religious propaganda. Throughout, we will be concerned about the role of religious faith and conflict in the coalescing of the demonic witch conspiracy by 1560.

The Reformation, Magic, and Science

Undoubtedly the most famous occult philosopher of the early Refor-mation period was the Dutch physician Heinrich Cornelius Agrippa of Nettesheim (1486–1535), author of two apparently contradictory works: *De occulta philosophia* (*The occult philosophy*), published in 1533 although composed in 1510, and *De incertitudine et vanitate scientiarum* (*The uncertainty and vanity of science*), which appeared in 1530. The first book praised the occult sciences and ritual magic, while the second condemned these as vain in comparison with a simple, biblicist faith. After studies at the Universities of Cologne and Paris, Agrippa began lecturing on the Cabala in 1509 at Dôle (during this period he wrote *De occulta philosophia*) and after 1512 at the University of Pavia, Italy, where he may have obtained doctorates in law and medicine. Between 1524 and 1526 he acted as physician to Louise of Savoy, the Queen Mother of

France. From 1532 until just before his death in 1535 he was attached
to the court of the reform-minded Archbishop of Cologne. Agrippa's
reputation as a magus was profound, an early Faust who, if Bodin can be
believed, was responsible for the spread of interest in both natural and
demonic magic. Agrippa's actual beliefs are difficult to assess, although
he clearly belonged to that intriguing group of humanists that included
the Florentine Neoplatonists Marsilio Ficino and Pico della Mirandola
and the German Johannes Reuchlin, who sought through study of ancient
magical texts, such as the Hermetic corpus or the Hebrew Cabala, to
manipulate the secret natural powers within the cosmos and to uncover
the essential religious unity of humankind.

At the same time, Agrippa's humanistic education tended toward
a pessimism with respect to establishing an unassailable philosophical
or scholastic system and a skepticism about "superstitious" practices and
beliefs. Agrippa apparently kept his Neoplatonic mysticism in an unre-
solved tension with his rationalistic skepticism. In this way, he could
condemn Inquisitors who accused poor women of witchcraft while still
maintaining a love affair with occult magic. Each of these intellectual
currents resulted in its own monograph, published in close proximity to
each other, although it was a wise move to publish *De incertitudine* prior
to *De occulta philosophia*, allowing him to use the former to counteract
charges that he was promoting illegal magic in the latter.[1]

For Agrippa, there were three worlds – elemental, celestial, intellectual – each receiving influences from the one above it as the divine
virtues emanated downward as rays. Ceremonial magic (involving the
Cabala) was aimed at influencing the angelic beings of the highest realm,
celestial magic the stars of the middle realm, and natural magic the
elements of the lowest order.[2] Agrippa believed his magic relied entirely
on good angelic beings and the divinely created cosmic forces, such
as planetary rays, and in no way involved the forbidden, dangerous
powers of demons. To him, magic "is a faculty of wonderful power, full
of most high mysteries. It contains the most profound contemplation of
things which are most secret, ... and the knowledge of the whole of
nature. ... This is the most perfect and principal branch of knowledge,
a sacred and more lofty kind of philosophy," requiring an intense education in natural philosophy, mathematics, astrology, and theology.[3]

Agrippa's Cabalistic methodology divided the Hebrew alphabet into
three divisions: twelve simple, seven double, and three "mothers"; the
first corresponded to the signs of the zodiac, the second to the planets,
and the third to three of the four elements (the Hebrews regarded air

as a spirit infusing the other three). While perhaps obscure to the modern reader, for early modern educated people this system of correspondences made sense. For, according to Agrippa, these letters played the role of sacramental vessels containing the essence of the heavenly body, much as the chalice was believed to contain the true blood of Christ. "Accordingly," Agrippa wrote, "the twenty-two letters are the basis of the world and of all the creatures which exist and are named by them."

Similarly, it was widely believed in Agrippa's day that mathematics provided indisputably direct knowledge about the universe; in Agrippa's words, through numbers "we succeed in discovering and understanding everything knowable." Numbers corresponded to cosmic reality; for example, Agrippa believed that the herb cinquefoil could resist poison, expel demons, and help expiation by virtue of its possessing five leaves. One of these taken twice daily in wine could cure a one-day fever, while a similar concoction of three leaves cured tertain fever, and four quartian, and so forth.[4] And of course the numbers corresponded to letters, in both the Hebrew and Latin alphabets, which gave rise to many intriguing interpretations of holy writ and eschatological predictions. Analysis of the sacred scriptures using both Cabala and numerology, moreover, provided the magician with divine clues as to how the virtues of the superior astral body could be drawn into the inferior earthly object.

Like Pico, Agrippa wove together his interest in magic with his non-conventional religious views. Although he believed that the magic he advocated worked "naturally", i.e., by the powers inherent in heavenly and earthly bodies, these powers functioned ultimately at the behest of God who commanded his angels and other invisible divine powers so that all things worked to maintain the divine harmonies. The name of God, especially the ancient Hebrew four-letter Tetragrammaton (IHVH) was likened to the four-letter Latinized name of Jesus, IESV, which was believed to wield ultimate power over creation. Because Jewish Cabalists never used this name, Agrippa believed their efforts were futile. Instead, only the learned, humble, and devout Christian magi who knew how to use the name of IESV, whether spoken verbally in incantations or inscribed on a talisman, could expect the obedience of the angels. For Agrippa, as for most of his Neoplatonic cohorts, religion and magic were inextricably interwoven into a rich fabric of immense color variation but essential unity of design. According to Charles G. Nauert, Jr., Agrippa represented the "Renaissance dream of rediscovering a submerged but divinely ordained wisdom that would both confirm and revivify Christianity" based on the revival of the ancient sources containing portions of the ultimate wisdom originally possessed by Adam.[5] This dream, outlined so eloquently in Pico's *Oration on the Dignity of Man*, posited that, like an alchemist, a truly accomplished Christian philosopher could distil the essential spirit of unity underlying all religions by a comparative reading of surviving sacred writings. Ultimately, the approach immensely irritated orthodox churchmen by promoting tolerance of other religions and challenging clerical monopoly over divine power.

Comparable in many respects to Erasmus' *Praise of Folly*, Agrippa's *De incertitudine et vanitate scientiarum* was a diatribe against all sorts of intellectual activity that advocated reliance on the scriptures and on faith as the sole source for truth. According to George Mora, Agrippa's main message was "the inability of human reason to grasp the essence of the mysterious reality of the world and, consequently, the necessity for anyone involved in the search for the ultimate entities to open his heart to the infinite dimensions of the divine grace."[6] This uneasy alliance between mysticism and skepticism reflected the growing crisis of Renaissance scholarship, one that the religious Reformers sought to resolve by a firm adherence to faith and a rejection of the mystical. In *De incertitudine*, Agrippa recommended that "It is better therefore and more profitable to be Idiotes, and knowe nothinge, to beleve by Faithe and charitee, and to become next unto God, than being lofty & prowde through the subtilties of sciences to fall into the possession of the Serpente."[7] Was Agrippa sincere in this apparent repudiation of his magical writing? That he published his two books almost contemporaneously suggests not. Agrippa realized that the era of general tolerance for the Neoplatonic speculations of mystics such as himself had ended with the Reformation controversy. In an age of increasing intolerance, Nicodemite spiritualism proved attractive, meshing neatly with ritual magicians' obsession with secrecy.[8]

It was in this contradictory realm of magic and skepticism that Agrippa developed his attitude toward witches. Like almost all practitioners of the occult sciences or natural magic, Agrippa sought to dispel assumptions that he relied on demons for the performance of his craft, although his post-mortem reputation as forerunner of Dr. Faustus and rumors that he had kept a black dog as a demonic familiar showed how ineffectual his efforts were. Thus he condemned necromancy and the invocation of demons as horrible abuses of true magic, "entangled in the craftes and errours of the deuils of hell" whose practitioners deserved to be punished with fire.[9] Even so, he was a prominent critic of the methodology of Inquisitors and opposed the prosecution of women for black magic, between 1518 and 1520 intervening successfully on behalf of a poor woman accused of witchcraft in Metz. For Agrippa, only learned men, not ignorant women, had the remotest possibility of summoning demons.

Paracelsus

Renaissance Neoplatonists and occult scientists found themselves in extreme danger of accusations of diabolical agency during the Reformation era. For a time, the activity of Renaissance occultists became more secretive, more apologetic, and more liable to misinterpretation in diabolical terms. Even so, some medical theorists and practitioners, most notably the Swiss physician Theophrastus Bombastus von Hohenheim, known more simply as Paracelsus (1493–1541), were brave enough to challenge accepted authorities such as Galen or Aristotle to forge new approaches to understanding and treating disease. In real terms many of the new cures were hardly improvements on the older medical models, although Paracelsus claimed that his theory of the workings of the human body was more in keeping with both the Bible and the empirical treatment of the ill. He openly boasted that he had discovered many of his treatments from village healers, and wherever he resided, he challenged the local authorities to bring him their toughest medical cases which their physicians could not cure. Even when he succeeded in winning a funded position as a civic physician, his abrasive personality and insistence that the Galenic medicine of the university was utterly useless made far too many enemies, and he had to move on. His curatives, moreover, relied heavily on mercury, the ingestion of which we now know can be damaging, even lethal, although it proved useful in treating syphilis. His theory of human physiology rejected the four humors in favor of a three-fold conception encompassing mercury, salt, and sulfur. Opposing the common belief that health was determined by the stars, Paracelsus argued that illness was caused by the invasion of external agents into the body. His treatments were mostly alchemical, and it is thanks to the publication and dissemination of his medical texts after his death that there was a major revival of alchemical medicine in Europe.

What these later Paracelsian alchemists sought to do was to elevate alchemy, which by the middle of the sixteenth century had a soiled reputation as vaguely linked with heresy or popular magic, into a spiritual quest for human perfection. Practitioners of this higher art, such as the English poet/minister John Donne (1572–1631), the English physician and occult philosopher Robert Fludd (1574–1637), or the Dutch Paracelsian physician and Cabalist Francis Mercury van Helmont (1614–98), insisted that the true objective of the sincere alchemist was to discover the means to convert the human "from a lower to a higher form of existence, from life natural to life spiritual," while Christ's spiritual transformation of the individual corresponded to the action of the alchemist's "philosopher's stone."[10] This alchemical product was believed to provide the spiritual essence of reality and religion, a curative for all illnesses and the means of prolonging life. For example, Fludd suggested that the alchemist's work was intended to transform the practitioner "from an ordinary mortal immersed in the physical world into a superior being fully conscious of the mystery of life and death."[11] Ficino believed that the world spirit that infused creation "was material enough to be consumed, inhaled, or absorbed in various foods, drinks, perfumes, or sounds, each one of which possessed power to ennoble the spirit of a practicing Magus."[12] Even the antitrinitarian heresy of the unfortunate Servetus was linked to his efforts to comprehend how the human's spirit carried the power of life through the body; his studies of the Hebrew conceptions of God, spirit, and air convinced him that human life consisted in the interaction between spirit/air and matter, with the blood carrying the spirit through the lungs.[13]

Although not intended by its leading lights, the Reformation helped shake rigid reliance on traditional authorities in a variety of fields, including natural philosophy (science) and medicine, although in most cases dissidents merely switched allegiance to other ancient authorities. Most importantly, thinkers from a wide range of professions and fields turned their attention to the quandary of religious competition and conflict and to find a solution to religious discordance. Many prominent unconventional medical or "scientific" theorists, such as Paracelsus, Servetus, Johann Weyer, Isaac Newton, and Galilei Galileo, made "scientific discoveries" as part of a religious quest to read the "Book of Nature" as a companion to the Bible and as a means of bringing their empirical study of the human body or the cosmos into harmony with their religious beliefs. How mainstream church and secular leaders responded to these innovations determined to a large extent whether they would be regarded as acceptable or as demonic.

The Reformation and Witchcraft

The Reformation's sense of living on the eve of Christ's return added incredible urgency to the need to eradicate any hint of the diabolical from Christian society. As Andrew Cunningham and Ole Peter Grell have recently suggested, it is "within this eschatological interpretation of a decaying world turned upside down during its Last Days that we should consider the great European witch hunt."[14] In this campaign of cleansing, both ritual and popular magic were depicted as tools of Satan's apocalyptical assault on Christendom, although many learned occultists sought to direct critical attention especially to women practitioners, arguing that their weaker minds made it impossible for them to perform the intricate spells without fatal errors and their perverse wills made them easy prey for Satan. Others, such as Agrippa and his disciple Johann Weyer, suggested that women who believed they had successfully performed magical acts were merely deluded by the Devil, for it was impossible for women to succeed in such endeavors even with Satan's assistance. Diabolical delusion or physical reality: this became the question vigorously debated both within and between learned Protestant and Catholic camps.

Two major positions were maintained with respect to the efficacy of magic. First, the providentialist or moderate skeptic's opinion followed the *Canon episcopi* that the malicious activity of demons was limited to the mental and spiritual spheres. As purely spiritual beings, demons could not directly transgress the laws of nature, but they could cast illusions on an individual's senses to provide a phantasm of magical potency. They could not transform a human into a werewolf or cause witches to fly, but they could delude people into believing they had done so. Only God, providentialists asserted, could mutate creation and perform true miracles. Even so, those who thought they performed maleficent magic against their neighbors were still guilty of blasphemous apostasy and deserved punishment.

The second position was that propagated by "realists" such as Heinrich Krämer: magicians or witches were able, with God's permission and through the agency of powerful demons, to perform the magic ascribed to them. Even though there was considerable disagreement over such details as whether witches could transform themselves into animals or how precisely they could have sexual relations with the spiritual bodies of demons, there was agreement that witches made real, binding pacts with the Devil, flew to their sabbaths where they cavorted together, worshiped and copulated with Satan and his fallen angels, conceived and then murdered unbaptized infants for their magical ointments, and plotted evil magic against others. In this scheme, confessions of accused witches were taken at face value.

Both moderate skeptics and zealous realists therefore believed that the Devil was very real, very powerful, and of malign intent. Both affirmed that Satan sought out human agents to assist him in his campaign of revenge against Christ. Both believed that these diabolical agents needed to be dealt with by stringent means. While moderate skeptics and realists were present in both Protestant and Catholic camps, there was within the Protestant tradition a strong tendency to spiritualize the crime of witchcraft and to depreciate the supposed *maleficia* performed by witches. Thus diabolical and heretical aspects, such as the renunciation of God, despising of the sacraments, and the worship of the Devil at the sabbath, were front and center in their depiction of witchcraft. Wolfgang Behringer suggests that in this spiritualized view, "the witches no longer caused harm through their own powers, or even with the aid of the Devil; rather, they were simply the indirect agents of evil, through their wickedness." Of greatest import was the religious apostasy of those who believed they had made a pact with Satan. As Christoph Mumprecht (1560–1620), an advisor to the Lutheran Count Palatine Philipp Ludwig von Neuburg, wrote,

> when one speaks of witchcraft, one understands by it all kinds of vice that can be imagined, against all the commandments of God, which come together and combine in the same, as idolatry, the most vicious blasphemy, wanton rejection and despising of the word of God, of the holy sacraments, the most wilful denial of God's grace, of the Holy Ghost, *crimen laesae majestatis utriusque*, the cruellest murder, theft, unspeakable immorality, which far exceeds the sin of Sodom...[15]

The debate among Protestants was how to treat such apostates. Most Reformers shied away from capital punishment unless there existed real evidence of harm, but almost all agreed that such blasphemers had to be converted to the true faith or exiled from the community, otherwise God's wrath would come crashing down. During visitations church leaders discovered that the common folk still clung to the preternatural usage of blessed objects, conjurations, and local magical experts for healing, protection, and divination, including Catholic priests, when available. Protestant demonologists therefore directed their energies to changing these popular "superstitious" beliefs, rather than on a frontal assault against the Catholic opponents.[16]

The Lutheran Reformer of the Duchy of Württemberg, Johannes Brenz, was the most famous proponent of the Protestant providentialist position, arguing that misfortune, storms, and famines were God's way of warning Christians to stop sinning. In 1539 the controversy surrounding a damaging hailstorm impelled Brenz to preach against those of his congregants who blamed the storm on witches. Witches who confessed to performing weather magic, he exclaimed, "confused sequence with causal relationship," for the Devil, perceiving that God was about to chastize his people by a storm, prompted his witches to perform their rituals so that he would receive credit and Christians not seek repentance. Godless witches who spurned their baptism and gave themselves over to the Devil deserved to be punished by death, but they could bring neither storms nor pestilence.[17]

Brenz' opinion was comparable to Ulricus Molitor's and proved increasingly influential among Protestants. At the same time, the decrees of the Council of Trent compelled Catholic theologians to define their views in ways clearly distinct from Protestants. Hence, by the 1560s there was considerable pressure for Protestants to line up with proponents of the providentialist position as a means of counteracting the Catholic defense of realism which, as we shall see, included very dramatic displays of Catholic power over demons. By the end of the century the *Canon episcopi* posture was squarely identified by Catholics as indefensibly Protestant, despite its long tradition within the medieval Catholic Church. By the last decade of the sixteenth century it was in fact dangerous for Catholic theologians to espouse it, as Cornelius Loos discovered to his peril when in Trier in 1592/93 he was discovered to have composed a manuscript against the witch-hunts. In an earlier context the opinions of Loos, a vigorous opponent of Protestantism, would not have elicited the violent response that it did, and he was fortunate indeed to escape Trier alive.

Within the Protestant camps there was discord as to the various aspects of the diabolical witch stereotype. But most Protestants, as well as Mennonites, emphasized the inner working of the Devil in the individual's heart and mind, rather than his supposed assault on the human body. Few, however, doubted that with God's permission witches could do some damage, although the emphasis here was on how a spell raised a victim's level of stress to the point of causing a humoral imbalance. In this way the distance between Martin Luther, who suggested that the spiritual bewitchment of heretics was the most deadly form of diabolical assault, and extreme spiritualists such as David Joris, who completely internalized the Devil, was one merely of degree.

Johann Weyer and Jean Bodin

Likewise, the differences between the moderate skeptical and zealous realist positions were not great, as we can see from a quick survey of the two most famous books published in the sixteenth century on the subject of diabolical witchcraft: *The Trickery of Demons* (*De praestigiis daemonum*) of Johann Weyer, published in 1563, and *On the Demon-Mania of Witches* (*De la démonomanie des sorciers*) of Jean Bodin, which appeared in 1580 as a rebuttal of Weyer's tome. Weyer (or Wier) was the court physician of Cleves who opposed the burning of witches. Bodin was the brilliant legal and political theorist whose writings reflected both an unorthodox religious posture and an incredible zeal to persecute witches. Neither of these writers fits neatly into a confessional box, although Weyer has been described as a spiritualistic Lutheran, while Bodin was a very unconventional Catholic. Their books greatly influenced the course of the intellectual debate on witchcraft.

In 1530 the fourteen-year-old Weyer began a five-year apprenticeship with Agrippa, serving his master during the time that Agrippa published his major tomes. Although master and student were very different in personality – Agrippa contentious, Weyer conciliatory – both evidenced a concern for the reform of the church without confessional discord; an appreciation for the sway of emotion over bodily functions; a humanists' critique of scholasticism; and a criticism of Inquisitors. Both found themselves defending women accused of witchcraft.[18] Despite these similarities, Weyer's published views on magic and science diverged from his teacher's and only rarely referred to Agrippa's controversial writings. After leaving Agrippa's employ, Weyer continued his studies in medicine at the University of Paris, although there is no evidence that he completed his doctorate in medicine. After a brief time at the University of Orléans, Weyer returned home to practice. In 1550 he was appointed the court physician of the Duke of Cleves, Jülich, and Berg, a position which he maintained until his death. The relative tolerance of Duke William V who was pursuing an Erasmian-style reform of religious life in the duchy which included reducing superstitious practices and accommodating Protestantism, proved a perfect fit for Weyer's irenic temperament and medical and theological interests. In this atmosphere in 1561 he began composing *De praestigiis* which explained witch confessions as the result of a delusional affliction, caused by the Devil's trickery on the minds of old women already mentally disturbed by a humoral imbalance leading to melancholia. Weyer's immensely popular work went through several editions in several languages, influencing many to dispute witch-hunting, although by the beginning of the seventeenth century "Weyer's arguments were in abeyance and the witchcraft debate in Germany had become essentially legal and jurisprudential in character."[19]

Weyer's major criticism of contemporary demonology was based on his somewhat misogynistic belief that the Devil was too powerful to require the assistance of old women. Diabolical calamity, he contended,

> occurs only because of the demons' own malicious wills and with God's permission, in accordance with His hidden plan, so that these persons might be tested or chastised and corrected. ... This sly old fox needs no one's help, being abundantly capable on his own of mocking men, blinding them mentally and physically, torturing them with unnatural maladies, striking them with ulcers, and disturbing the air in many ways. We read in the *Malleus* that the Devil works evil by himself and does not need the consent of a malicious woman. But he also seeks the ruin of the witch, and therefore he somehow compels her to cooperate. ... Meanwhile, however, certain deluded old women are convinced (and so confess) that crimes of this sort are perpetrated by them, and that these people are severely tormented, world affairs are thwarted, and all kinds of diabolical wonders are brought about.

Despite their sincere belief in their magical powers, witches, Weyer concluded, were merely

> beleaguered by the demon, and their minds so seriously impaired by witchcraft, and their brains – the organs of their thoughts and imaginings – so firmly ensnared by rare and deceptive phantasms and forms because of their unbelief... that they know of nothing else; subjected to torture, they confess to crimes which are purely imaginary on their part, and which truly proceed from Satan, with God's permission.[20]

Thus, demons possessed and harmed humans, but solely with the permission of God who did not allow them to use humans to perform their *maleficia*. Instead, they befuddled the minds of old women suffering from an excess of the melancholic humor to think that they had become the willing slaves of the Devil with enormous magical powers at their command. For this delusion, Weyer prescribed medical and spiritual treatment, not judicial punishment.

Weyer sought to find natural explanations for the many supposedly preternatural events that he himself had witnessed or heard about. For example, to explain demoniacs' vomiting of unnatural objects such as pins, nails, or pacts written in blood on paper or cloth, Weyer referred to his medical examination of individuals who had accidentally swallowed pins or stones to prove that such regurgitation was impossible, hence these demoniacs were frauds. Moreover, the claim that a witch's guilt could be proven by having her speak a blessing over the bewitched was also false, contradicting as it did the well-known medical canon of administering "contraries against contraries" and on Jesus' words in the gospels, "if Satan casts out Satan, he is divided against himself" (Matt.12:26, RSV). There was only one reason why someone afflicted by demonic torment or illness would be healed under these circumstances:

> after the Devil (with God's permission) has tormented these bodies because of the victim's unbelief, he gives way – not under duress but freely and of his own will – in order to confirm the afflicted and the bystanders in their unbelief, and also those who have learned of this strange ailment, and finally the magistrate. I grant that he pretends to be under compulsion, the better to deceive and ensnare, and to make people believe more unhesitatingly that the poor women who recite the words are witches – though they are really innocent.[21]

What better way to entrap people than by giving them the illusion of magical powers?

Weyer's efforts to defend women accused of witchcraft did not immediately put the brakes on the rising tide of witch-hunting, although there developed a school of promoters of his views that became increasingly influential in Protestant circles. However, his views reflected his desire to promote a relative degree of religious toleration. His own confessional position is obscure, although he has been described as an "Erasmian minded Lutheran," and as a Nicodemite spiritualist who had learned from Agrippa how to "to keep his religious views to himself."[22] To support his desire to promote religious tolerance, he quoted Erasmus to the effect that heretics should not be killed, that healing was preferable to harshness, and that a check should be placed on the savagery of Inquisitors.[23] Weyer himself called the persecutors of witches "the special slaves of the Devil; some may call them diviners, but for me they shall stand as the real evildoers."[24] Stuart Clark suggests that "Weyer was inspired to attack the prosecution of witches by precisely those ideals of moderation, even toleration, that the period that experienced it swept away."[25] For example, in the foreword to the second, German edition of *De praestigiis*, Weyer lamented that members of one religion refused to tolerate alternate interpretations, even though there "is no divisiveness in the chief articles of our Christian faith but only in the form or time or some changes of the ceremonies or religion or words or matters that do not touch the saving Articles of the true, established faith."[26] Based on the correspondence from his spiritualistic younger brother, Matthias Wier (1521–60), Johann's religious attitudes emphasized inner faith as opposed to rigid dogmatism. He was also interested in the writings of spiritualists such as Hendrik Niclaes and may have corresponded with David Joris.[27]

Unlike Weyer, Bodin's unconventional religious views – which also leaned toward a spiritualized, universalist church – did not lead him to reject the reality of witch confessions of diabolical activity. Instead, he claimed that his personal involvement in the 1578 trial of the witch Jeanne Harvillier (from Verbery near Compiègne) convinced him to write his book as a means of neutralizing the skepticism that this case and others was arousing within the French intelligentsia. According to Jeanne's confession, her mother had not baptized her as an infant but had instead committed her to the Devil, so that when Jeanne reached the age of twelve, the normal age for sacramental confirmation, her mother presented her to the Devil in the form of a tall, dark man dressed in black with spurs, boots, and sword. From that moment until her arrest at the age of fifty she and the demon were lovers, sometimes holding their trysts in her marriage bed with her husband sleeping next to them; apparently she alone could see this evil angel. Neighbors suspected her of practicing witchcraft, including the poisoning of a man with powders provided by the Devil. After she was convicted, she described how her diabolical consort helped her fly to the witches' assemblies where a great crowd assembled to worship a man in black they called Beelzebub and engage in sexual orgies, after which the "Prince preached to them to trust in him, that he would take revenge on their enemies and that he would make them happy." All the judges in this case advocated the death penalty, although one wished her to receive a merciful death by hanging; he was overruled and she was condemned to be burned alive. It was the relative moderation of the dissenting judge that motivated Bodin to take up quill to eradicate such dangerous skepticism:

> And because there were some who found the case strange and almost unbelievable, I decided to write this treatise . . . to serve as a warning to all those who read it, in order to make it clearly known that there are no crimes which are nearly so vile as this one, or which deserve more serious penalties. Also partly to respond to those who in printed books try to save witches by every means, so that it seems Satan has inspired them and drawn them to his line in order to publish these fine books. One was Pietro d'Abano [a controversial late thirteenth-century professor at the University of Padua who died before an inquisition into his views was complete], a doctor, who tried to teach that there are no spirits; it turned out later that he was one of the greatest witches in Italy.[28]

Another case which Bodin cited was that of the fifteenth-century theologian at the University of Paris, Guillaume de Line (William Adeline), condemned as a witch in December, 1453. He too confessed to attending the witches' sabbath, worshiping the Devil in the shape of a man or goat, and "renouncing all religion." According to Bodin, De Line "was found in possession of a written agreement that he had with Satan, setting out mutual promises, among which the Doctor was obliged to preach publicly that everything people said about witches was only a fable and an impossibility and that one must not believe any of it." The result of the professor's skeptical sermons was of course the multiplication of witches "since the judges gave up their pursuit of witches."[29] Bodin concluded that deniers of the reality of demonic witchcraft must be mad, for "it is hardly less of an impiety to call into doubt the possibility of witches than to call into doubt the existence of God."[30] His opponents on this issue, such as "the Protector of Witches" Weyer, were mad and godless and implicit in the Devil's conspiracy, therefore "one must keep from listening to those who preach that what is said about witches is only an illusion."[31]

While one might gather that Bodin's position accorded fully with the Catholic realist position on witchcraft, such was not the case. At points he acknowledged the validity of some of the Protestants' arguments, such as

Brenz' theory on how the Devil informed his witches of an impending storm to make it appear that they had caused it, suggesting that this was merely one way the Devil worked. Moreover, his solution to the problem of witchcraft deeply disturbed many zealous French Catholics who were engaged in a life and death struggle against Huguenots. Along with advocating the harshest legal measures against witches and blasphemers, Bodin suggested that the best way to prevent witchcraft from arising in the first place was for each father to lead his family in morning and evening prayers, to give thanks to God before meals, "and to give at least one or two hours one day of the week to have the Bible read by the head of the family in the presence of the whole family."[32] And despite the fearmongering that his portrayal of diabolical activity encouraged, Bodin proposed that another remedy was "not to fear Satan at all, nor witches. For there is, perhaps, no greater way to give power to the Devil over oneself than to fear him. . . . Nonetheless, the surest and most effective way of all, is to have faith in God, and to trust in Him like a high and unassailable fortress."[33] Luther could not have said this better, and Weyer concluded his own tome with the following:

> Let us not voluntarily enslave our bodies to Satan and make them his dwelling-place. More than this, by our true faith and the sanctity of our lives let us shut off his every avenue of attacking us, continually imploring the assistance of God's Son with fervent prayer and fortifying ourselves vigilantly . . . with the living word of God and the help of the Holy Spirit, so that even if our sworn enemy boldly attacks us while we are enclosed within these fortifications (as within a solid wall), he will not break through this mighty defense and take us by storm.[34]

To advocate lay reading of the Bible and the repelling of Satan by prayer and faith was, in this era of confessional conflict, identified almost exclusively as a Protestant approach. Thus, despite the enmity between them, Bodin and Weyer were not far apart on the religious solution to the Devil's assaults, but contended primarily on whether or not witches were victims of diabolical illusions, requiring medical treatment and religious instruction, or willing participants in a real, diabolical conspiracy that threatened civic order, punishable by death. The question really was where to draw the line against skepticism. Bodin defended orthodoxy by proving the reality of the demonic realm, a strategy Weyer feared could backfire as more and more diabolical activities were explained as natural events.

The Persecution of Witches during the Early Reformation, 1520–60

Soon Bodin's exotic realm of demonic witches overwhelmed Weyer's cautions, and Europe was gripped in a persecution mania. Prior to this revival of witch-hunting in the 1560s, trials of witches had more or less followed Weyer's models. For example, after the notorious trials of heretical witches in Arras had ended in 1462, there were only scattered trials of magicians before the Netherlandic inquisitorial tribunals, such as the Le Quesnoy possessions of 1491; four "Waldensian" women tried at Bouvignes and Aureloyes between 1510 and 1512; and the trials of Marye de Beauvolz and Pierette Pourreau in Fleurus in 1524 and 1527. These latter two were charged with "Waldensian heresy" because they possessed bad reputations ("vaudoise et femme de très maluaise vie") and had performed harmful magic against their neighbors' animals and infants. Both were eventually tortured into confessing their guilt and burned at the stake.[35] Yet the authorities did not pursue the supposed conspiracy of their "Waldensianism." By this time the authorities had their hands full with a real heretical conspiracy of blasphemous Lutherans.

Martin Luther himself approved of the execution of four witches at Wittenberg in 1541, while just a few years later his major Protestant opponent, John Calvin, was advising the Genevan authorities to "extirpate the race of witches" from its rural hinterland, leading to several trials and three executions, mostly having to do with charges of plague spreading.[36] Preoccupied as they were with the Reformation heresies and conflicts, the authorities showed great reluctance to deal with accusations of witchcraft. Similarly, there was a scarcity of publications of works on the subject (no known printings of the *Malleus Maleficarum* between 1521 and 1569). Yet witchcraft remained of concern within the local community, and people continued by a variety of means to counteract evil magic. It is essential to remember that, as Scribner puts it, "popular magic, sorcery or witchcraft were embedded in the texture of daily life."[37] Most day-to-day witchcraft was rather mundane, such as the cursing of milk so that it curdled or of cream so that it could not be churned into butter; the hexing of various agricultural or artisanal implements; the creation or redirection of storms to destroy crops or cause fires; the effecting of enmity between friends or love between acquaintances; the discovery of stolen objects or of the perpetrator of a nefarious deed; the procurement of abortifacients; or the spread of disease to humans or animals. Until stringent laws were passed forbidding any magical activity, the bewitched found relief through the ministrations of a wise woman or cunning man, or applied pressure on the suspected witch to undo the spell. The Reformation strongly discouraged recourse to these traditional remedies, leading victims to seek legal redress with greater insistence.

In 1536 in Blankenheim, Saxony, the seventy-year-old Else Weissensee was arrested on charges of witchcraft. Through torture and questioning she maintained her innocence and the governor released her, ignoring threats from the commune to bring the case to the Elector of Saxony. At other times the authorities were convinced of an accused's guilt, as in 1529 when a woman called "old Roderin" confessed to a court in Saxony that she had magically stolen milk from her neighbors, an art she had learned from Hans Moller von Dippertswald, who seems to have made a decent living selling magically potent objects such as mandrake roots, thumbs of hanged thieves, or potions against animal pestilence. While Moller was punished only for deceit, his disciple was turned into a diabolical witch, charged also with flying to a witches' sabbath in the form of a cat (that all of her seven "accomplices" were already dead meant that this case did not escalate into a witch-hunt), and burned at the stake. The difference in treatment, as we have seen, was not due solely to her gender, but centered especially on "old Roderin's" bad reputation among her neighbors.

Between 1500 and 1560 there were very few efforts to uncover a large, diabolical conspiracy of witches. Instead, legal proceedings were conducted against individual witches, typically but not exclusively an old woman with a reputation for magic or malicious behavior, and the trial normally ended with non-capital sentences. Some examples from the Netherlands will illustrate these points.

In the northern Netherlands witch-hunting never reached the epidemic proportions of its neighbors to the south and east. The closest that the later Dutch Republic came to a major panic occurred in the eastern province of Groningen where twenty accused witches were executed in 1547 and five more in 1562, both incidents spurred by news of witch trials in the neighboring portions of the western Empire. In the province of Holland, trials of witches started roughly in 1500, although most were restricted to individual witches or their immediate accomplices.

The earliest known cases of sixteenth-century witchcraft trials revolved around mundane accusations of bewitchment of milk, butter churns, and dye pots, actions that impeded individual economic activity. There were a few accusations involving diabolical elements, such as those arising from Schiedam in 1504 wherein some residents complained that they had seen a woman perform a ceremony of bewitchment upon her husband and mother-in-law which involved lit candles and consumption of a "communion" of magically blessed bread and cheese, after which the "Devil had visited her on the second day of Easter."[38]

Around mid-century belief in witchcraft remained strong in this highly urbanized province and, until trials were suppressed around 1610, over 300 individuals claimed to have been bewitched. Many others turned to non-judicial remedies, including consulting counter-magicians. In one case Katharina Galen was accused in 1530 in Haarlem of bewitching a dye tub. Evidence was provided by a priest from Delft, Jan Vos, who was hired by the dyer to identify the culprit. The priest placed some ingredients into a pot over the fire, spoke a conjuration, and waited for the guilty party to begin suffocating. When the dyer rushed to Katharina, whom she obviously suspected, she discovered the woman to be suffering the appropriate distress. Katharina's desperate plea for her accuser to "go home, it will no longer happen" was treated by the city's sheriff as sufficient evidence to proceed to trial, although the magistrates disagreed and released her. Katharina's reputation as a witch, however, endured, so that in 1543 the sheriff compelled her to bless a bewitched woman. She was also supposed to have caused the illness of another woman who refused to work for her, while a cook who declined to roast some wormy mutton for her discovered his property to be similarly crawling with worms. With such evidence, on October 7, 1549 the sheriff arrested Katharina along with some other accused, but she pointed out that the Haarlem magistrates in 1530 had thrown out the original charges because the evidence against her had been procured by illegal means, as the law forbade the use of divination to identify witches. The Court was persuaded and on January 17, 1550, set her free.

In a contemporaneous rural case from Spijkenisse, a 48-year-old peasant woman, Aechtgen Hughendr suddenly developed terrible pain in her legs which became immovably contorted as if tied in a knot. On the advice of her maidservant whose mother had apparently suffered from the same ailment, a flask of Aechtgen's urine was dispatched to a neighboring priest who then referred her to a medical practitioner who diagnosed the cause as excessively cold and impure blood. Suspecting unnatural causation instead, Aechtgen consulted a Mr. Symon of Rotterdam, who confirmed bewitchment and came to Spijkenisse to treat her. His ministrations began with readings from a Latin and Dutch magical text, after which he heated Aechtgen's urine in a never used pot. Since the liquid did not boil over, Symon said that witchcraft was involved, but would only identify the culprit as a "stern whore" who lived nearby. Another priest replayed the urine test, confirmed the diagnosis of witchcraft, but declined to reveal the witch's name because of his religious vows. In May, 1551, the peripatetic soothsayer Dirck Pieterszn of Nijmegen arrived, caught up on all of the local gossip while residing in the village inn, and was taken by the innkeeper to treat Aechtgen. After an eye examination and the usual urine test, he proclaimed the guilty party to be the elderly Anna Jacopsdr and her adult daughter Tryn Pietersdr.

Of the two it was the widowed mother who possessed a bad reputation among her neighbors. When a married couple took her to court for non-payment of debt and for grazing her cattle on their pasture without permission, an enraged Anna placed her fingers on the door of their house and uttered, "if I must swear [my innocence], then you will not live until May." The wife was terrified but her husband seemed unperturbed, saying sarcastically, "well, now I know how long I will live." When he died suddenly, his wife blamed Anna. Aechtgen herself bore a grudge, as ten years earlier her husband had bought from Anna's son a heifer which died shortly after Anna had prophesized that they would profit little from this purchase. Finding herself now under suspicion of *maleficia*, Anna sought to win the other villagers to her side, saying to one "God bless you," believing that a true witch could not express such blessings. During a spinning session, Anna told the other women present that witches have "a little hole in their head, for the Devil cuts their chrism [the holy oil used in baptism] out of them." She then opined that "witchcraft originates from great poverty and that the women who perform witchcraft fornicate with the Devil . . . and that the Devil comes as a young man with a scarlet hat on his head to the women and deceives them." At least this was what her husband had told her about witches elsewhere. Despite her efforts, the village leaders supported the soothsayer and forced Anna and her daughter to read a blessing from a magic book over the suffering Aechtgen, after which they drank three cups of holy water and were kicked out of the house. The next day all three magical performers – Anna, her daughter, and the soothsayer – were arrested. In an unusual twist, the two women were released while Dirck was whipped and exiled from Holland for his forbidden magic.

The vast majority of witch accusations were made against someone possessing a long reputation for witchcraft. In some cases witch accusations were blatant efforts to seek revenge against a political or economic rival, as Marie Holleslootendr, a member of Amsterdam's ruling families, found out. The story began with the failed Anabaptist uprising in 1535 for which the current burgomasters and aldermen, dominated by the Heynen and Boelen families, were blamed for being too soft on the heretics. In this climate, Willem Coeck, who took a ruthless line toward heretics, rose in influence until 1538 when the civic deck was reshuffled in favor of the loyal Bam, Occo, and Buyck families, who pursued a vigorous persecution of Anabaptists, eventually pushing Coeck to the side. Marie Holleslootendr was related to both sides but most prominently to the victors, having married into the Bam family, and her sons won high positions in civic government. Her brother, Jan Ysbrantzn Holleslooten had married a Boelen, hence he and his son-in-law Jan Pieterszn lost political influence.

Pieterszn tried to make the best of a bad situation by converting an oil mill into a brewery, but his beer kept souring, even though that of his next-door neighbor, using the same water and grain, was flourishing. This successful brewer was none other than one of Marie Holleslootendr's sons, Cornelis Jacobszn Bam. At every turn, Pieterszn believed, his aunt was frustrating his ambitions and in July 1547 he hired a 26 year-old soothsayer, Jacob Judoci de Rosa of Kortrijk, to identify the source of bewitchment. De Rosa, a former damask weaver then teacher of French, had learned the craft of curing bewitchment from an Antwerp soothsayer in 1545 and was equipped with the magic book of Cornelius Agrippa and one ascribed to the ancient King Solomon, as well as a magical ring which confined a powerful spirit. With these accoutrements De Rosa and his wife had traveled the Low Countries identifying witches and removing spells until Jan Pieterszn invited De Rosa to Amsterdam. While there, De Rosa gained another client, the ironmonger and magistrate Willem Coeck, who likewise believed his house to be bewitched since his star was waning. Fatefully, De Rosa said that the same woman had bewitched both locales.

Both clients applied considerable pressure on De Rosa to confirm their already held suspicions that the witch was none other than Marie Ysbrant Holleslootendr. De Rosa, sensing the political realities better than his clients, delayed as long as he could; then he publicly identified Marie Holleslootendr as the witch and quickly fled the city. As suspected, the city's sheriff ordered his immediate arrest and when De Rosa was captured in Tiel, Guelders, for another incident of soothsaying, Holleslootendr used her political connections to ensure that he not escape punishment. On July 14, 1548, De Rosa was condemned to a whipping and exile, his books were burned, and his ring melted.

Despite this, he did not retire, appearing in later trial accounts else-where.[39]

In all of these cases, and hundreds of others across Europe, feelings of hostility were readily transformed into suspicions of bewitchment. Many of these early cases were part of larger disputes among neighbors and families, while there was little of the religious conflicts that were raging at the time. There was another form of diabolical activity, however, that would bring the religious battle into the forefront and heighten religious tensions considerably: demonic possession.

Demoniacs and Confessional Conflict

Learned demonological theory distinguished clearly between demoniacs who were involuntarily possessed by an evil spirit and witches who made a pact with the Devil and were his willing accomplices. Demoniacs were therefore treated with exorcisms while alleged witches faced judicial action. Often victims of possession accused someone else of having sent a demon into them, blurring the theoretical line between demoniac and witch. In the 1560s especially, the debate about demonic possession climaxed with a number of prominent possessions that were deeply entangled in the religious conflicts which had helped create the psycho-logical conditions behind such ecstatic behavior and which reshaped the possessions into a spectacular feature of religious propaganda.[40] Even in regions where the Catholic authorities were able to contain the Reformation, as in Italy, there were outbreaks of demonic possession. In one case from Rome in 1554, eighty-two women were so strongly possessed by demons that a French monk's efforts at exorcising them proved fruitless. During one session, the monk demanded that the demons tell him why they had entered these women. According to Jean Bodin, our source for this story, the demons responded that "the Jews had sent them into the bodies of these women (who were mostly Jewesses) angry, they said, at the fact that they had been baptized." He then recorded that Pope Paul IV (1555–9) would have banished the entire Jewish community, which he despised, were it not for a Jesuit's caution that people did not have the power to send demons into others. Paul IV, a former Roman Inquisitor, was a passionate prosecutor of Protestants and enforced the segregation and harsh taxation of Rome's Jews, reversing his predecessor's relative tolerance. This outbreak of demonic possession therefore occurred within a climate of intensified religious conflict and intolerance, against both heretics and Jews. Bodin's purpose in telling this story was to reinforce belief in the reality of the women's symptoms, such as speaking foreign languages, for "atheists" (such as Weyer) who denied that there are devils "cannot claim either that melancholy teaches one to speak Greek, Hebrew, or Latin to a woman who has never learned anything."[41] Undoubtedly the anxiety aroused among the Jews by the new repressive measures was a formative factor behind this collective ecstatic behavior.

The frequency of demonic possessions rose across Europe during the 1550s and 1560s paralleling the escalation of religious polemics and conflict. With its devastating and bloody religious warfare, France was the site of some of the most spectacular exorcisms which assisted the efforts of zealous Catholic propagandists to demonize their religious opponents. The first, and most influential of these public exorcisms began on the afternoon of November 3, 1565, when in a village of Picardy, Nicole Aubrey (Obrey), a young woman of fifteen or sixteen, saw the spirit of her deceased grandfather appear from his grave and enter her, begging her to release him from Purgatory by completing the masses and pilgrimages that he had left undone when he had died suddenly without last rites. The family completed most of these, yet the possession reoccurred, so the local priest was called in. Uncertain of the spirit's true identity, the priest called in a Dominican who declared the spirit to be an "Ange mauvais et Sathanique...un Diable" who, when conjured in the name of Jesus, revealed itself as Beelzebub. A consecrated Host was held up before Nicole's face, causing her to become "hideously horrible to see, frightful to hear [and] incredibly hard and stiff to the touch." Beelzebub accused the audience of various vices and identified the Protestants as his servants. No exorcism seemed to provide permanent relief, so early in the New Year Nicole was sent to Laon.[42] Here the ecclesiastical authorities escorted her each day in a great procession to the cathedral where she was exorcised before a large crowd. Symptoms of demonic possession now included the ability to speak in foreign tongues and superhuman strength, so that one time when the Host was brought to her she broke the hold of several men and leapt high into the air. Each performance ended with a temporary deliverance involving a Eucharistic wafer.

Realizing the threat to their anti-Catholic magic position, the Protestants decried the possession and exorcisms as a hoax and tried to stop them, but the exorcists forced Beelzebub to proclaim even louder that he was the Prince of the Huguenots and to describe how some of his

Protestants had stolen, cut up, boiled, and burned a consecrated Host. According to one witness, the demon seethed, "I with my obstinate Huguenots will do Him [Christ] more evil than the Jews did!"[43] During one exorcism wherein Beelzebub chided his Protestants for keeping themselves covered during the elevation of the Host, "the Catholics and Calvinists looked at each other, both fearing a massacre, and then they all rushed out of the cathedral."[44] Despite the efforts of Protestant leaders to discredit the goings on, some Huguenots were convinced and reconverted. The Huguenot Prince of Condé ordered Nicole imprisoned, but she was released shortly thereafter by the king. Finally, on February 8, 1566, Beelzebub left Nicole's body for the last time in such convincing fashion that one Protestant eyewitness, Florimond de Raemond (a future member of the Parlement of Bordeaux), reconverted, describing the scene in the following fashion:

> Finally Beelzebub, conjured by the presence of the precious body of Jesus Christ [the Host], left and quit his prison [Nicole's body] after having made smoke and caused two claps of thunder, leaving a thick fog that encircled the belltowers of the church, and all those in attendance were delighted at such a great marvel. How long, oh impenitent souls, will you rot in your incredulity and abuse the patience of God?[45]

Very quickly news of this amazing victory of Catholic realists over the Devil, doubters, and Protestants spread throughout Europe, becoming known as the "Miracle of Laon." Sensational pamphlets were published from all quarters, even from the Catholic spiritualist Guillaume de Postel who came to regard the miracle as the herald of the new spiritual age.[46] Most Catholic polemicists used it to condemn religious toleration as a plot of the Devil. The Laon exorcism also seems to have helped spark interest in demonic possessions both in France and elsewhere in Europe, in Germany adding fuel to the fire of the polemical debate over pedobaptismal exorcism that coincided with a noticeable rise of possession cases there.

Even in highly urbanized realms, such as the Netherlands, more than a few Catholic monks and priests supplemented their living by performing exorcisms and various magical services, and there were some Protestant clergy and Mennonite elders who did likewise, although ostensibly as medical practitioners. When the States of Holland complained to the Bishop of Utrecht about ignorant priests who were not distinguishing between the sacraments, which were supposed to work without fail, and the sacramentals and abjurations used in exorcism, which did not possess automatic efficacy, the Bishop claimed he could do little to curb such clerical dabbling in magic.

His response was understandable, for Catholic sacramental thinking ran parallel to magical practice. The booklets of exorcisms composed for priests were in some respects comparable to ritual magic texts. For example, around mid-century some Franciscans near Dordrecht composed a manu-script *Book of Exorcisms* (*Liber exorcismorum*). This collection of abjurations, conjurations, and spells began with the typical means of spiritual prepar-ation for the exorcist, then turned to the blessings or benedictions that the cleric could use to heal eye ailments or the falling sickness, to avert storms, lightning, and hail, to identify thieves, or to lift magical spells and curses. Also described was the technique for the urine test, as were various cures for bewitchment, mostly concoctions of herbs, wine, honey, consecrated incense, and a touch of holy water. As a protective against further assaults, the exorcist was to place around the sufferer's neck a wax *Agnus Dei* (a likeness of Christ as a lamb bearing a cross). Unconventionally, the writer suggested that it "might also be very effective to baptize the patient a second time." To dispel a curse on a butter churn, the priest needed to perform a mass, wash his hands while reciting John 1:1 (a very popular text in Christian magic), utter some special prayers, make the sign of the cross, and finish off with some holy water.[47] Franciscans were clearly viewed as magical experts, for during the 1541 witchcraft trial of Engel Dirksdr, Amsterdam's magistrates and sheriff sought the advice of the local Franciscans as to how to avoid being bewitched by the accused. The Franciscans gave them the name of Brother Gerrit van Zutfen of the Utrecht house, and a city alderman and secretary were sent to consult him. On January 10, 1542, Dirksdr was burned at the stake.[48] Clearly the Catholic Church sought to monopolize control over the supernatural and magical realms, and could not tolerate lay people who sought to use such supernatural power, just as it could not allow them to perform the sacraments or preach.

The Devil in the Images

The Calvinists planned a frontal assault on these monopolistic claims by separating religion entirely from the magical. In the Low Countries they were growing in confidence and in the summer of 1566 targeted church buildings for a great act of cleansing of idolatrous religious images and sacred objects, an act that would prove the utter impotence of the Catholic clergy. For the Catholics, the destruction of such icons was much more than an affront to artistic sensibilities but a direct attack on Christ, Mary, and the saints and a proof of the iconoclasts' nascent atheism. The Calvinist iconoclastic fury was as ritually staged as Catholic exorcisms, and possessed a comparable intent: to prove tangibly that images of saints were inanimate and undeserving of veneration. An anonymous news report of the first wave of iconoclasm in Antwerp in August of 1566 illustrates this point quite clearly. Events began on August 18, 1566 during a feast honoring the Virgin Mary during which her large wooden image, richly decorated as queen of heaven, was carried about in procession. Upon her return to the Our Dear Lady Cathedral, some spectators called out to her, "Mary, Mary, this is your last meal; Mary, Mary, this is your last procession." The next day a group of reform-minded folk entered the church singing Psalms (the only genre of hymn Calvinists permitted). In 1550s' France such "shocking" behavior had led to religious violence, and it did here as well. After warning all citizens to stay indoors, the iconoclasts set to work, pulling down all images from the Cathedral and then moving on to the other churches. The sheriff arrived with some troops, but discovering that the violence was directed "only against the idols" and not people, he decided only to ensure that matters escalate no further. Throughout the night the iconoclasts destroyed all accessible images and windows with incredible speed.

In the morning a great pile of images was collected in the cathedral square. Onto this were thrown vessels containing blessed salt, holy oil, and holy water, as well as the "sacrament houses" containing consecrated Hosts that had not been consumed during Mass. Then, like executioners finishing off the wounded, the iconoclasts moved about the sacred objects stabbing, chopping, and smashing them, so that not a single one was left whole. Not one saint cried out in protest; not a single "sacrament house" oozed blood or water. All were very clearly inanimate, without sentience. Saints' images had hands, but they could not reach out, they had ears but could not hear, feet, but could not run from their enemies. They were dead, and as such, required a burial. On August 22 and 23 they were transported on wagons to the city's mass burial field and buried. In their desecration of consecrated Hosts Calvinists performed the same act attributed to Jews, except in this case the Hosts did not bleed.[49]

Similarly, during the second iconoclastic storm in Amsterdam in September, 1566, after tossing their purloined statues, altarpieces, and pictures on a great heap, participants said of each, "here is such an image which was famed to perform so many miracles," revealing that the material object held no such power at all. Then some of the activists gathered in the Old Church to desecrate sacramental exorcism and baptism, calling out to the priest, "cease with your exorcising of the Devil from the children. You have deceived the world too long with your falsehood. Baptize in the name of Jesus, just as the apostles did."[50] By such means the Calvinists performed a ritual drama of desacralization, attacking both the Catholic realist interpretation of sacramental power and popular usage of it.

A Bewitched Orphanage

In 1566 in Amsterdam the intense religious conflict intersected with fears of witches in a profoundly disturbing fashion. By this year many prominent Amsterdamers who had been excluded from political office were openly supporting the local Calvinist community which on July 8, 1566 began their own preaching and worship services just outside city walls. Rumors of another religious revolt greater than that of 1535 ran through Amsterdam, confirmed when in August and September the Calvinists stormed the city's churches. Such tensions were readily manipulated. Earlier, on January 14, 1566, the city council noted that a large number of inmates of the city's orphanage (thirty in some accounts, seventy in others) were seized by a "special passion" that was drawing large crowds of curious onlookers to the orphanage, hindering the efforts of the institution's administrators to deal with the problem. The city effected to dissipate rumors of demonic activity by isolating the victims and describing their affliction as a miserable mental ailment, but to no avail, as by June the stories of demonic possession were widespread, detailing how the demons forced their victims into horrible contortions, uncontrollable singing, and violent vomiting of pieces of iron, glass, hair, and nails. Efforts at medical treatment and exorcism failed.

Since all of the afflicted orphans were from well-established families and had been apprenticed out to various of the city's craftsmen or shopkeepers, they were not isolated from the political and religious conflicts dividing the commune. When the city council held an emergency meeting to deal with the rising religious tensions, somehow, probably through

family connections, the possessed revealed the magistrates' deliberations even before they had left the city hall. Then, some of the possessed
climbed a church tower to proclaim their denunciation of the person
who had bewitched them all, Jacoba Bam, the daughter of the afore-
mentioned Marie Holleslootendr. The charge was investigated and, not
surprisingly, Jacoba was cleared on July 1. Contemporaries suspected
that the afflicted children had been manipulated by some of the
pro-reform citizens who had been forced to the periphery of political
power.[51] Yet, the original possession of the orphans was most likely
a product of group anxiety related to the scarcity of food in 1565–6 and
the rising religious tensions in the city. Further contributing to this
atmosphere were reports of several recent Amsterdam witch trials,
including the execution of four witches in 1555, the banning of another
in 1560, and, most immediately, the burning of Volckgen Hermansdr
in 1564 for brewing a storm that killed a number of sailors and denying
her baptism and Christendom before the Devil.[52] News of the contemporaneous "Miracle of Laon" may have also provided a model for the
orphans. However, in a reversal of the French case, it was the zealous
Catholic authorities in Amsterdam who were being accused of causing
the affliction, thus they sought to isolate the victims, hush up the rumors,
and dissipate the accompanying tensions. This case provides a rare
example of reform-minded citizens manipulating demonic possessions
against the Catholic hard-liners who held power. Under different political
circumstances, those same rulers would have likely used the demoniacs
to trumpet the power of the Catholic Church over Satan and his minions.

Heresy and Witch-Hunting

In several regions witchcraft trials began at the same time, or shortly
after, heresy trials were ended. This has been shown to be true for parts
of France, Catholic Cologne, and the southern Netherlands.[53] Between
1520 and 1565, several thousand individuals had been executed for
their dissident religious beliefs, some two-thirds of them Anabaptists
who had terrorized the authorities with nightmares of popular revolts
and sedition far out of scale with their actual threat. As William Monter
has noted, it was this fear that finally convinced many rulers to secularize
heresy trials, making it easier to try witches as well.[54]

What escalated local conflicts about the *maleficia* of neighborhood
witches into the infamous witch-hunts was the development of belief

in the diabolical sabbath conspiracy between Satan and his minions. The framework of this conspiracy had arisen first in the fifteenth century within the educated milieu of clerics, jurists, and professors, while anti-Devil preachers and propagandists sought to persuade secular rulers and skeptical bishops to join in the hunt. Although many were convinced, by the start of the Reformation interest in witch-hunting was waning. Then, with the widespread belief that the Reformation heralded the Last Judgment, the impression that Satan was now exerting extraordinary efforts to destroy the church was strengthened, especially as memories lingered of the religiously inspired insurrections of 1525 and 1535. Many lords therefore became more amenable to the clergy's warnings of Satanic activities. While the Catholic authorities were more ruthless in their campaign of eradicating Anabaptists as Satan's minions, many Protestant princes and magistrates joined in as well. After 1560 the supposed witch conspiracy supplanted anxiety about Anabaptists, and the Holy Roman Empire and its neighbors became home to some of the most fearsome examples of what can only be described as persecution mania.

For as long as local authorities were occupied with trying and executing Anabaptists and other religious dissidents, they paid little heed to the pressure of their citizens to bring witches to trial. There were, however, a few regions which remained fixated on the old Waldensian witch threat, and in these there were no Anabaptist hunts. For example, the small Netherlandic duchy of Namur from 1509 until 1646 conducted a series of witch trials in which dozens of alleged "*sorcières et vaudoises*" were executed.[55] Here, unlike many of its neighbors, there were no major Anabaptist hunts. Holland, in contrast, was the location of a vicious judicial attack on Anabaptists, and experienced only modest witch-hunts, forbidding the use of torture and the water test in cases of witchcraft by 1594 and formally suppressing all witch trials by 1614 (the last execution occurred in 1608). Finally, in Flanders, where some of the civic authorities continued to prosecute Anabaptists with great vigor until the early 1590s, witch burning did not generally begin until after the ashes of the last Mennonite had blown away in the wind.[56]

Propagandists and jurists may have clearly distinguished between the heresy of Anabaptism and that of diabolical witches, but in functional terms, both offered leaders with a target for cleansing a community of blasphemy and proving the veracity of the official, orthodox position on God. Some courts learned how to quash blasphemous heresy by cutting their teeth on the Anabaptists, although most Protestant courts condemned recalcitrant Anabaptists to exile rather than death. Once such real heretics were suppressed and still God's wrath prevailed, then attention turned to exposing the secretive, diabolical agents responsible. In this way concern over rebellious Anabaptists and secretly seditious libertines was fused with the older notion of a diabolical sect, leading to mounting pressure to discover and eradicate members of the sabbath conspiracy. As the common people had long wished to get rid of their troublesome witches, they were only too eager to comply.

Inquisitors and Witches in Spain and Italy

Before discussing this turn to witch-hunting, it is necessary here to discuss the Mediterranean states which, in contrast to the northern European states, remained uncaptivated by notions of a diabolical witch conspiracy and which did not generally secularize heresy or witchcraft trials but kept them under inquisitorial jurisdiction. Neither the Italian nor Spanish Inquisitions showed any real interest in prosecuting witches, seriously considering the crime only after 1580. Apart from the Inquisition of the so-called Benandanti of the northeastern Friuli region at the end of the sixteenth and early seventeenth centuries, the Italian tribunals likewise remained hesitant to attack a witch sect.[57] Prior to the witch panic of 1608–12, there were in Spain only a handful of witch trials. Why then was there so little interest in hunting witches in those regions possessing the most effective Inquisitions ever established? The reasons for this anomaly are varied and complex, but before turning to them (in Chapter 6), it is important briefly to examine the handful of early cases.

In 1466 the local authorities of the province of Guipúzcoa, Castile, petitioned King Henry IV for the authority to extirpate the witches who were supposedly harming people and crops. Supporting this clamor was the Navarra canon Martín de Arles who composed a treatise on superstition, later published in 1517, in which he affirmed the Navarra witches' ability to perform *maleficia* with the assistance of the Devil, although he agreed with the *Canon episcopi* that they could not fly. The efforts bore some fruit, as in 1500 a number of residents of the mountainous region of Amboto were accused of worshiping the Devil and practicing magic, while seven years later some thirty women were burned at the stake for witchcraft. In 1527, ten years after the publication of de Arles' work, Spain's most infamous sixteenth-century case of witchcraft began when two prepubescent girls approached the authorities of Pamplona with the disturbing news that they were members of a witch cult but would gladly identify their fellow witch conspirators – by looking at the Devil's mark in their left eyes – in exchange for amnesty. An elaborate procedure was put in place to test their veracity, but independent of each other the girls fingered the same witches from the suspects rounded up by the local authorities. In the end, 150 sorcerers and witches were investigated by Inquisitor Avellaneda who commented that his initial doubts about the verity of the girls' claims of having flown to covens were put to rest when he witnessed one of the accused witches escape from prison with the assistance of a demon. Avellaneda quickly uncovered three distinct covens of over 100 members each and sentenced dozens of the accused. In summarizing the Inquisitor's letter to a Castilian official, Julio Baroja comments,

> The emphasis which Avellaneda ... placed on the evil that was done by large bands and assemblies of sorcerers, together with the fact that the investigations were carried out at a critical historical moment, when Charles I was annexing the kingdom of Navarre, suggests that there may have been some political motives behind what is usually considered to be a religious question. The accused may well have been supporters of the ancient kings of Navarre, that is, *agramonteses*.[58]

The Inquisitor urged the secular authorities to proceed harshly against this conspiratorial threat, and some heeded his advice, with the encouragement of several preachers. In 1530 a General Church Council was held to discuss the matter, and in 1538 further outbreaks of witchcraft in Navarra filled the prisons with accused. In 1555 several towns begged the higher authorities to act against the threat, but the Suprema governing the Inquisition refused, ruling that the accused had been unfairly imprisoned.

Between 1555 and 1558 the civil judges of Ceberio heard a case of witchcraft involving two rival families of the town. Some young girls from each side denounced the other's family as members of a witch coven; the judges saw some merit in one set of accusations and twenty-one members of one family were arrested, interrogated but eventually released with the relatively mild punishment of ordeal by water and whipping. Here the secular judges regarded witchcraft as merely one part of a larger inter-family conflict. In Spain on the whole, however, it was the civil authorities, acting on the rhetoric of local preachers and Inquisitors, who feared demonic witches, whereas the central inquisitorial authorities denounced hasty actions. As was the case in 1527, moreover, suspicion of the existence of witch covens was linked to efforts to resist royal centralization and the resulting propaganda and trials provided means of demonizing those opponents.

In Italy, "Lutheran" heresy and anticlericalism were principally assailed as the sins incurring God's anger, requiring the establishment in 1542 of the Roman and Venetian Inquisitions as means to convert offenders. After the Council of Trent and especially after 1580, the pre-occupation of Inquisitors switched from the pursuit of Protestantism to crimes of sorcery and magic, becoming the object of over 40 percent of inquisitorial activity thereafter.[59] Even so, the focus in the trials was not on *maleficium* but on the so-called white magic of healing, recovering lost treasure, or performing love magic. A large number of defendants in Italian witch trials were ecclesiastics denounced for abusing sacramental paraphernalia and liturgical rites. Formal apostasy to the Devil was only an occasional charge. In these respects, then, Italian Inquisitors and jurists evinced an attitude toward diabolical witchcraft in keeping with that developed by most Protestant demonologists: the real danger to the soul was recourse to magical means of protecting oneself from the vagaries of life which ultimately were in the bailiwick of divine providence.

There were some witch trials in Italy prior to the rise of the Counter Reformation. In 1518 the ecclesiastical authorities of Venice arrested a number of supposed witches, but fairly quickly the republic's patricians stepped in to stop what it perceived to be the excesses of ecclesiastical judges. When in 1534 one of the city's senators announced that he was going to debate the problem of witches, "the whole matter seems to have assumed very little significance in comparison with the more serious threat of Lutheranism."[60] Thus, as in Flanders and the Netherlands, a concerted effort to eradicate witches in Spain and Italy could not take place at the same time as a major assault against religious heretics, however these were defined.

Conclusion

In the Empire there was a shift in perception regarding diabolical heresy between the fall of Münster in 1535 and the revival of witch-hunting in the 1560s–80s. This shift was observed already in the early 1560s by Johann Weyer who attempted to stem the rising tide of witch-hunting which he had hoped had died out with other superstitions. Instead, it had returned, perhaps, he suggested, as a continuation of the blood-thirst that had not been quenched with the persecution of heretics (Protestants and Anabaptists) and which was now attacking old women accused of witchcraft.[61] The process of demonizing the "enemies of God" therefore shifted its focus from heretics to supposed practitioners of magic. The Peasants' War of 1525 and the infamous kingdom of Münster heightened fears of groups plotting insurrection, which became more pronounced in the demonic conspiracy stereotype. Until the 1560s (later in some lands), most courts remained preoccupied with the real heretics who openly confessed their beliefs. However, the rise of Nicodemite spiritualists or libertines raised the specter of Cathar-like dissimulators secretly spreading their noxious views among an ignorant populace. In the last decades of the sixteenth century, courts throughout Europe turned from hunting heretics to attacking this invisible diabolical threat which became increasingly elaborate and fantastical. Behind it all was the need to counteract the expression of skepticism toward the approved understanding of the supernatural realm.

As we shall see, witch-hunting took on a life of its own, with a particu-lar dynamic that varied from place to place. Yet the intensified religious passions and fear of doubt which helped lay the foundations for the diabolical witch stereotype also helped inflame the anti-witch activities of a community, giving justification for both the bewitched to denounce their malefactors to the authorities and for the judges to take such charges seriously. At other times and places, the cooling of these religious passions, especially in regions experimenting with religious toleration, helped extinguish witch panics. This process, however, was extremely complex, and did not always work as expected. In the sixteenth century especially, espousal of tolerance for religious dissent sometimes produced the opposite effect to that intended, as zealots condemned skeptical or libertarian notions as diabolical and destructive of the Christian state. This is precisely what happened with the reception of Johann Weyer's *De praestigiis daemonum*, a work that was extremely modest in its efforts to cool the soaring fear of diabolical witches but which was roundly condemned by Bodin and others as part of Satan's attack on Christendom. For a time, the escalated rhetoric of demonic conspiracies so polemicized the debate about religion and magic that rational and balanced discussion was virtually impossible. The witch-hunts further exacerbated the problem.

5

RELIGIOUS CONFLICT AND THE RISE OF WITCH-HUNTING, 1562–1630

First the Hussites invaded Bohemia, then the Lutherans Germany, and Sprenger and Nider, ... have told us that the Hussites were followed by a great force of workers of maleficent magic, while the Lutherans know what torrents of witches they have poured into the lands of the North, which have become paralysed with fear, as though frozen by Arctic cold. For in these places there is scarcely anything unharmed or free from – I scarcely know what to call them – these animals disguised as humans, these evil spirits. Most of the older ones in the territory of Trier, not only upon the rack but after questioning as well, confessed to the judges that they were first drenched with this disastrous stain when that foul, hellish supporter of Lutheranism, himself well known for magic, Albert of Brandenburg, plundered and ravaged that province with fire and sword. ... Nothing has spread this plague further and more quickly through England, Scotland, France and Belgium than the dread pestilence of Calvinism. ... Now, with this heresy, as in the case of the frenzy of a fever, it has invaded very many people all over the place ...

Martino del Rio, *Disquisitiones Magicae*, as translated by
Maxwell-Stuart, *The Occult in Early Modern Europe*, 165.

An invading force of infiltrators empowered by Satan is a story worthy of a Hollywood blockbuster. Yet it was not fiction but fact in the minds of

151

churchmen such as Del Rio who believed that the Reformation had caused an invasion of demonic spirits. Del Rio's fellow Jesuit Juan de Maldonat neatly explained this coincidence by asserting that as pagan religion was eliminated the Devil found himself cast out of idols but gained a new home in the "divine writings themselves in the minds of heretics." Because error could not long imitate truth, all heresy must "either degenerate into magical arts or into the final extremity of atheism" as heretics "enter upon a close companionship with evil spirits" and learn the diabolical arts. Thus, he contended, as "plague follows famine" so the magical arts, the disease of the soul, follow heresy, while evil spirits use heretics to charm others into error and magic. The neglect of ecclesiastical leaders to teach the faithful, Maldonat admitted, had allowed such ravages, and "what the heretics had made a shell, witches despoil by the art of evil spirits, and what witches leave behind, atheists destroy." Del Rio lamented that while the three unclean spirits which had come "out of the mouth of the dragon" (Rev. 16:13) – Calvinism, Lutheranism, and Anabaptism – were now withering away, "we see various swarms of locust-witches ravaging the whole of the North," while atheists and compromising politicians replicated themselves.[1]

There was, of course, no inherently causal link between such propaganda and the outbreak of a witch persecution, and Del Rio's comments were published after the eruption of a witch panic in the Spanish Netherlands in 1596. Yet, zealots had every reason to dread the susceptibility of a poorly indoctrinated populace to confessional laxity and religious accommodation. Nicolas Rémy, the jurist and witch prosecutor of Lorraine, put this succinctly in 1595 when he observed that the Devil had two routes to tempt humans to abjure their faith and become atheists. The first was through the "light of human reason," resulting in learned heresy and blasphemy, the second through stupidity and poverty, leading to an intense desire for revenge. He added,

> The atheists of the former class are begotten, bred and protected by the freedom which in our time has arisen from the variety and confusion of nations, and it is generally said that their numbers have reached a figure that is not easily creditable. But either because they brood in silence over their blasphemies and, hiding behind the cover of whatever form of religion comes to their hand, escape detection and accusation; or else because they do not, out of zeal for their opinions, collect a following, they are overlooked and are only called – a term of the basest inadequacy in view of the enormity of their

impiety – licentious: in any case no proceedings are taken against them, nor are they held up for a public example.[2]

In this influential jurist's mind, the campaigns against heresy and witchcraft were an interlocked battle against a single, invisible enemy: atheism.

It bears reiterating that the heartland of witch-hunting – the south-western Holy Roman Empire, Switzerland, and France – was also the great center of religious strife. As James Sharpe comments about seventeenth-century England, "the problems caused by the erosion of traditional authority were made heavier, in Puritan East Anglia, by the populace's previous exposure to sermons and other forms of religious consciousness-raising in which the devil and his works figured prominently."[3] By this process of clerical communication learned demonological notions became an integral part of popular culture, interwoven with traditional concepts of religion and magic. Preachers may have interpreted witchcraft in spiritual terms as the ultimate blasphemy against God, but they forgot how readily their unlearned parishioners could "misinterpret" a spiritual truth as applicable to their mundane world. As preachers badgered their flocks to inspect every sinful thought and deed, God's anger remained unabated. Removing the horrible blasphemers believed responsible for divine punishment became a priority, and as real heretical sects had been virtually suppressed (Anabaptists) or driven underground (libertines), attention turned to other demonic candidates.[4] Thus, even if innocent of harming neighbors by *maleficia*, witches were condemned for incurring God's wrath by renouncing their Christian faith.

Ordinary people happily took up the cause of ridding their communities of troublesome witches. On this community level Robin Briggs suggests witch accusations served several functions, such as: drawing communities together to set standards and attack evil; assisting local officials impose tighter moral control on their subjects; increasing the prestige of local clergy, lawyers, and doctors; providing outlets for masculine insecurity, aggression, and a "potent cocktail of forbidden libidinal and social desires"; offering a legal means of counteracting malevolent magic; and supplying booksellers with a ready market for their sensational wares.[5] The publicity surrounding demonic activity also helped fill churches in an era of increasing doubt as to the value of confessional identity.

The discussion in this and the next chapter will pursue regionally the intersections of the campaigns to suppress religious dissent and witchcraft. In general, while popular beliefs about witches varied little across Europe, what determined the extent of judicial action was the acceptance on the part of the clergy, judiciary, and political authorities, of the reality of the diabolical conspiracy idea. Altogether, it is estimated that something in the order of 60,000 to 100,000 witch trials were conducted across Europe, and with an average execution rate of approximately 50 percent, these resulted in anywhere from 30,000 to 60,000 executions.[6] These are considerably greater than the figures for heresy executions, which William Monter has calculated to be in the range of 3,000.[7] Yet if one includes the thousands of Protestants killed by the "Council of Blood" during the Spanish occupation of the Netherlands and during the St. Bartholomew Day's massacres in France, then the differences in scale are not nearly as pronounced. In both heresy and witchcraft persecution, the authorities hoped that such activity would purify their region of godlessness, eradicate religious doubt, and strengthen allegiance to the authority figures. They got more than they expected.

The Holy Roman Empire

On August 3, 1562 in Lutheran Württemberg the hail fell from the clouds onto many of the fields of maturing grain as if heralding the Last Judgment. With an unfavorable dominance of the moon, astrologers had been predicting especially bad times for 1559–62.[8] Coming as it did after several years of crop failure and epidemic disease, the harvest's loss was devastating. The only solution one contemporary reporter could offer was to beg God for enlightenment so that Württembergers would heartily repent and improve their sinful lives.[9] Yet one local lord, Count Ulrich of Helfenstein, was determined to eradicate the specific culprits responsible. His more powerful neighbor Duke Christoph of Württemberg remained uncertain as to the ability of witches to brew up storms, with or without the aid of demons, while many of the local preachers followed Johannes Brenz' reasoning that God alone was responsible for sending storms to punish sin, regardless of the Devil's efforts to steal credit for them.

Unfortunately Brenz' arguments carried little weight with Count Ulrich, who was being pressured by his clergy to adopt the Reformation and by his wife to return the duchy to Catholicism, which he did in 1567. Encouraged by the fervent anti-witch sermons of the Calvinist-oriented

Lutheran superintendent of nearby Esslingen, Thomas Naogeorgus (or Kirchmeyer, 1508–63), Ulrich ordered the arrest of a number of women in Wiesensteig. Esslingen's magistrates saw Naogeorgus' fiery sermonizing about Satan as responsible for the rising terror of demonic witches and on August 18 warned him to stop agitating the citizenry with his notions of a diabolical conspiracy, and eventually fired him. Naogeorgus, long suspected by orthodox Lutheran preachers of harboring heterodox beliefs, may have been attempting to deflect such accusations onto supposed witches, an act similar to that of San Bernardino of Siena. Duke Christoph and the Esslingen magistrates were informed that Ulrich had already ordered the deaths of six witches and that a number of the accused had confessed to seeing some Esslingen citizens (nearly thirty miles away) at the witches' sabbath. In response, the Esslingen authorities arrested three individuals, but ultimately released them. Count Ulrich, however, showed no such leniency, approving the execution of over sixty accused witches, the first large-scale witch panic of the sixteenth century.[10] Immediately preceding this witch persecution was a vigorous campaign of parish visitations searching for remnants of Anabaptist heresy and magical idolatry. Just weeks before Ulrich's actions a large nocturnal meeting of Anabaptists was uncovered in the area, leading to a regional investigation and corresponding spread of rumors. In this way the drive to expunge Anabaptist heresy from the region may have convinced the Count of the reality of diabolical, sabbath conspiracies.[11] According to one contemporary Lutheran chronicler, the *auto-da-fé* of twenty of the accused on December 2, 1562 was the scene of an incredible debate. After the list of their alleged crimes – blaphemy, sorcery, boiling infants to produce their salve, and weather magic – was read out, the sky turned deep red, and an angel of God appeared in the sky, warning the more than 3,000 onlookers to abstain from such godless behavior, else they would face the same severe punishment. The condemned then responded together that "the devil's kingdom is greater than his God's," and the angel vanished in a huff.[12] Whatever happened on that day, there could be no clearer message in our reporter's mind as to the reality of the supernatural realm and the danger of the witch sect.

News of Count Ulrich's supposed witch coven helped foster witch panics throughout the Empire, especially with each new famine, destructive hailstorm, or plague. With each trial, the belief in the diabolical sabbath conspiracy was confirmed, the skeptics denounced, and the reality of the supernatural realm proven. The various principalities of the Holy Roman Empire accounted for a disproportionately high number of major witch panics, and a total of 30,000 to 60,000 trials, with roughly half of these resulting in executions. In 1532, Charles V's *Carolina* had made witchcraft a crime for secular courts, yet this change had little immediate impact as the Empire lacked a centralized judiciary and police force. Besides, until 1555 Charles V and his princes were too preoccupied fighting each other and stamping out Anabaptism to undertake any other campaigns. Thereafter, attention turned increasingly to witchcraft and by the time of Emperor Ferdinand's revised witchcraft statute of 1607, the Empire had gained the dubious distinction as the leader of witch persecution, precisely because of its political weakness and judicial decentralization which allowed local authorities virtual independence in pursuing witches.

In general, with the notable exception of the Duchy of Mecklenburg, the northern and eastern territories were much more restrained than those of the south and west, where most of the infamous witch panics took place. The worst witch-hunts engulfed the southern Catholic prince-bishoprics where the ruling bishops were struggling to shore up Tridentine Catholicism within their small realms against both Protestant incursions from without and confessional indifference and low levels of religiosity within. Behringer estimates that in the first decades of the seventeenth century the two successive bishops of Bamberg oversaw the execution of some 1,500 alleged witches, two Würzburg bishops were responsible for about 1,200 victims, three bishops of Mainz ordered the deaths of 1,800 individuals, and one bishop of Cologne, Archbishop Ferdinand of Bavaria (ruled 1612–50), executed at least 2,000 victims. These figures are staggering for such small territories and illustrate how important the disposition of local authorities was in determining the extent of witch persecution. On the other extreme were the Calvinist rulers of the Palatine of the Rhine who absolutely forbade executions for witchcraft as a means of avoiding the excesses of their neighbors. As Behringer reminds us, other nearby Calvinist territories in the Empire did conduct such trials, hence the distinctiveness of the Palatine was not due to its particular confessional identity.[13]

Yet, the panics in the archbishoprics were very much tied to certain religious attitudes, a point noted by the witch defender Friederich Spee who wrote that the witchcraft persecutions in these territories were "the fatal consequence of Germany's pious zealotry." Although a sense of embattlement by external Protestant forces contributed to a mood of apocalyptical gloom gripping the bishops' courts, the principal concern of Counter-Reformation leaders was to inculcate in their subjects an intense desire to inspect every sinful thought and cast out all diabolical doubt. After describing Archbishop Ferdinand's own daily, excessively ascetic efforts to repulse Satanic temptation, Behringer concludes that one "need not be a strict Freudian to understand how this accentuated consciousness of one's sinfulness might arouse self-deprecation, neurosis and projection complexes."[14] Hence, what spurred a desire to hunt the Devil's minions on a major scale was not so much the battle between one confession and another, but the struggle to instill in one's less zealous coreligionists a passion for the true faith which would eradicate personal doubt.

The witch panics of the Franconian prince-bishoprics

Although the most common or ordinary trials for witchcraft arose from within the face-to-face communities of rural villages, the major witch panics were often urban enterprises, in large part because it was in the towns where the major courts were located. In the urban milieu, denunciations moved quickly from the stereotypical rural crone to urbanites. For example, during the 1580s and 1590s, the citizens of Trier participated in a terrifying witch panic wherein over 300 accused witches named about 1,500 different accomplices, many of these encompassing middling to upper class townspeople. It was here in 1593 that the Dutch priest Cornelius Loos (1546–c.1597) was accused of complicity with the Devil for having composed a manuscript, *De vera et falsa magica* (*The true and false magic*) rebutting the reality of preternatural witch activities.

Loos' treatment was part of the Archbishop Johann VII von Schönenberg's (r. 1581–99) campaign to expunge the diabolical danger. He was encouraged in this godly work by his assistant bishop Peter Binsfeld's *Tractatus de Confessionibus Maleficorum et Sagarum* (*Treatise on the Confession of Witches and Sorcerers*) which, after its publication in 1589, became the major witch-hunting manual in the German lands. Binsfeld affirmed that witches dangerously profaned the sacraments, brought down the wrath of God upon the land, and destroyed harvests and caused famine. Magistrates must uncover every member of this demonic conspiracy and compel them by torture to confess their hidden evil. Lax magistrates themselves merited God's anger, he warned.[15]

Just three years after Binsfeld's book, part of Loos' skeptical tome was printed in Cologne and it appears that the Binsfeld party pressured the Trier court to prosecute the Dutchman in order to win an inter-Catholic scholarly argument over the true nature of demonic heresy. Loos survived only by recanting; hundreds of others were not so fortunate. Once the *autos-da-fé* had ended, two of the twenty-two villages around Trier were left with only two inhabitants apiece.[16] In the prince-bishopric of Würzburg, Bishop Julius Echter von Mespelbrunn accused Protestants of witchcraft as part of his campaign to return his realm to Catholicism, but this sort of crude confessional manipulation of witchcraft denunciations was rare.[17] What was far more prevalent was the use of such charges to warn the populace away from heresy and superstition in general and reinforce the veracity of their ruler's faith.

The dynamics of witch-hunting can be illustrated also by the case of Ellwangen, where a trial against an elderly woman in 1611 snowballed into a panic. This quite small Catholic territory, ruled by a secularized monastery, had already executed dozens of alleged witches in 1528 and 1588–9. In 1611 it experienced a witch-hunt on an altogether unheard of scale. As in Württemburg in 1562, a number of damaging hailstorms, mysterious livestock deaths, and an outbreak of plague preceded the event; and while Midelfort admits we really do not know why the hunts began, his comment that 1611 "also brought the first Jesuits to Ellwangen," is instructive in the light of our discussion here. Certainly not all Jesuits promoted witch-hunting, and one of its greatest opponents was the Jesuit confessor Friederich Spee, who in 1631 published anonymously his condemnation of the witch-hunting procedures (the *Cautio criminalis*). However, Jesuits generally pushed for a harder, Tridentine line against reform incursions.[18] Whatever their role here, on April 7, 1611 the elderly Barbara Rüfin, wife of Casper Rüf from the village of Rindelbach, was arrested and brought into Ellwangen on suspicion of witchcraft, a charge which revolved around her supposedly desecrating the consecrated Host and a general reputation for witchcraft. Apparently she found no support in her husband who regarded her as a witch, nor her son who charged her with attempted poisoning. Several sessions over three days of being stretched on the rack loosened her tongue and she confessed to desecrating the Host, making a pact and having sex with the Devil, and performing *maleficia* on her family and neighbors. As was typical in such cases, once the torture was ended she denied everything, but was compelled to return to her confession after further painful persuasion. On May 16, she was beheaded and burned. But this cleansing of the community merely whetted the judges' appetite to exterminate a suspected sect of witches in their community. With mounting frequency, denunciations flowed into the court from concerned neighbors and interrogators became more efficient in evaluating the accusations, finding the Devil's mark on the accused, and extracting the required confessions. By the end of the year residents of the town had been witness to over 100 executions in seventeen separate *autos-da-fé*, and a further 140 or more in an equal number of burnings the following year. Details of witch activities from one case were pursued in subsequent interrogations and a list of thirty questions was prepared for each accused, helping to explain the consistency among confessions. These included the standard test of having the accused recite the Lord's Prayer, Ave Maria, Apostles Creed, and Ten Commandments, followed by interrogations into how the defendant was seduced into the Devil's service, what sex with him was like (not allowing that there might have been none), and who were the accused's associates. The resulting picture of witchcraft centered on the renunciation of God, the Church, and baptism, submission to diabolical sacraments, desecration of eucharistic Hosts, and the grisly use of infant corpses in the witches' ointment.

In 1613 the local Jesuit teacher Father Johann Finck noted that over 300 accused had been executed, including one of his own pupils, commenting "I do not see where this case will lead and what end it will have, for this evil has so taken over, and like the plague has infected so many, that if the magistrates continue to exercise their office, in a few years the city will be in miserable ruins." He did not have long to wait, for in June of 1615 charges of performing black masses and baptizing infants in the name of the Devil resulted in the trial of three priests who prior to sentencing were degraded from holy orders by having the chrism on their right hand, tonsure, and forehead literally cut out and having the wounds rubbed with salt and vinegar. In the resulting hysterical atmosphere several individuals voluntarily confessed, including a sixteen-year-old woman described by Father Finck: "God has comforted us especially through a girl of 16, who last month was executed with six others. She could no longer endure the persecutions of the devil and placed herself voluntarily in custody. With tears she explained that she would rather bear death and the stake than put up with the tyranny of the devil any longer. Standing, she received the death blow."[19] Apart from clearing her conscience of guilt, her expiatory confession implicated over thirty-four others. Another voluntary confession was provided in 1611 by a seven-year-old girl named Margaretha who confessed to riding to the witches' sabbath and to all manner of ungodly dealings with the Devil. At first the magistrates blamed her fall into the Devil's clutches on her having been ineffectively baptized by a Lutheran, so the Jesuits taught her Catholic dogma and applied the rituals the Lutherans had excluded from her baptism, such as exorcism. Yet, four years later she continued to boast of her magical abilities. Unfortunately we do not know her ultimate fate.

Even those higher up on the social ladder were implicated. Magdelena, the wife of the chapter scribe Georg Weixler, was imprisoned and abused by the jailer who was eventually arrested and executed for his crimes, but this did not stop her own execution. Prior to her death she wrote her husband, "I know that my innocence will come to light, even if I do not live to see it. I would not be concerned that I must die, if it were not for my poor children; but if it must be so, may God give me the grace that I may endure it with patience."[20] An Ellwangen judge who publicly defended his wife was himself executed in November, 1611. The magistrates energetically defended the proceedings in "the kind of passionate self-defense that springs from glimmers of self-doubt," as Midelfort suggests.[21] The trials petered out when it had become clear by 1618 that many potential merchants and students were avoiding Ellwangen because of its reputation as a center for witchcraft.

The paranoia suffered by residents of a city in the midst of a witch panic was comparable to the mass hysteria engendered by a plague epidemic, although the former died out when the community could no longer bear the economic and social costs of the trials of dozens or hundreds of its citizens, or when members of the aristocracy found themselves implicated. Even then, some of the political elite were executed before the fires were extinguished, as a past-mayor of Bamberg, Johannes Junius, discovered in 1628. Bamberg's witch panic was like Ellwangen's approved by the prince-bishop, and led to the deaths of at least 300 judicial victims. As the accused struggled in the interrogation room to come up with credible names of fellow sabbath conspirators, the social status of the implicated rose. On June 28, 1628 Junius protested his innocence and challenged the court to bring forward a single witness who had seen him at the witches' meetings. Dr. Georg Adam Haan, a former council colleague of Junius, accordingly denounced him to his face. Still the 55-year-old Junius denied the charges. He was put to the thumbscrews, then the leg-screws, both of which were ineffective as Junius continued to assert that "he has never denied God his savior nor suffered himself to be otherwise baptized." At this point the official record and Junius' own account of the proceedings diverge, for the former stated that Junius felt no pain during his torture, while Junius himself described the experience as horrifically painful, leaving him unable to use his hands for a month. As witches were believed to be protected by their demons during torture, the court officials carefully noted any variation in Junius' reactions during these sessions, so if his screams were muted they could record the effect as painless, thus explaining his reticence to confess and justifying continued pressure. He was accordingly stripped and searched for the Devil's mark, which was found in a clover-leaf shaped birthmark and pricked three times, an action which produced neither pain nor blood (not unlike the proper application of a hypodermic needle). This was evidence sufficient to proceed to the infamous strappado, and according to Junius' account they raised and dropped him eight separate times, an experience which caused him "terrible agony." At the end of this horrible day, June 30, the executioner told him, "Sir, I beg you, for God's sake confess something, whether it be true or not. Invent something, for you cannot endure the torture which you will be put to; and, even if you bear it all, yet you will not escape, not even if you were an earl." Even with this advice, his Christian piety and fear of lying to God made him hesitate, until, in hopes of later confessing to a priest, he confessed on July 5. His tale is familiar: after losing a lawsuit and a considerable sum of money, he sat despondently in his garden when a lovely woman "like a grass-maid" appeared and enticed him into sexual improprieties. She then turned into Beelzebub and threatened to kill him unless he renounced God and underwent a diabolical baptism. He confessed also to the usual sabbath activities, desecrating Hosts, and poisoning his horse with diabolical powders which were intended for his children.

Junius' letter, smuggled out of prison with the assistance of the jailer on July 24, provided his daughter with his motives to confessing. It begins,

> many hundred thousand good-nights, dearly beloved daughter Veronica. Innocent have I come into prison, innocent have I been tortured, innocent must I die. For whoever comes into the witch prison must become a witch or be tortured until he invents something out of his head and – God pity him – bethinks him of something.

He assures Veronica that torture alone compelled him to give a certain number of names of accomplices from specified city neighborhoods. And, when his interrogators were dissatisfied with his confession of acts of *maleficia* and were about to raise him again on the strappado, he admitted to desecrating "a sacred wafer ... When I had said this, they left me in peace."[22] In the German prince-bishopric panics, the most important service that accused witches could perform was to confirm the reality of the sacraments. In this example, Junius' prosecutors were satisfied with his required confession of *maleficia* only when he admitted to Host desecration, a position that Bishop Friedrich Forner of Bamberg helped foster with his belief that witches abused all seven sacraments. He also countered Protestant propaganda by asserting that witch sabbaths were more prevalent in Catholics territories because, as Stuart Clark summarizes him, "the devil could only gain true apostates from the true faith; Protestants were already in this state and represented no gain. Catholic witchcraft was, thus, a 'most splendid, nay most certain, and infallible sign that the true and saving faith, the true gospel, the true sacraments, the true religion are found among Catholics'."[23]

Bavaria – panic and restraint

Some parts of Germany, such as Bavaria and the Lower Rhineland, had relatively few witch scares, although just about every area participated in the major panics of the late 1580s and early 1590s. The Duchy of Bavaria, Wolfgang Behringer estimates, experienced approximately 4,000 trials and anywhere from 1,000 to 1,500 executions, both fairly moderate figures for a territory of this size, compared to the confessionally mixed territories of the German southwest where over 3,000 witches were executed between 1561 and 1670. A high proportion of Bavaria's witch trials occurred during the 1590 persecution, an event which made an increasing number of Protestant preachers and princes and the Catholic rulers of Bavaria wary of the extreme social damage that witch trials incurred. By 1600, moreover, many Protestant theologians identified intense witch-hunting with Catholicism, while the scholars of Bavaria were divided between a zealous witch-hunting and a moderately skeptical party, the latter winning the ear of the rulers.[24]

The northern empire

As in the south, there was considerable variation in the level of witch persecution in the northern German principalities, although most regions were caught up to some extent in the major panics around 1590 and between 1627 and 1631, with the Duchy of Westphalia and the Archbishopric of Cologne leading the way. Until 1627, however, the core region of the principality of Cologne had escaped major witch panics, but in that year the authorities conducted an extermination program against witchcraft that Gerhard Schormann has compared with Jewish pogroms. Both, he notes, were depicted medically as the surgical removal of a corrupt organ from the body of Christendom so as to preserve the whole from the spread of infection, and both were conducted by the central authorities. The witch persecution was led by Prince Ferdinand von Wittelsbach (r. 1612–50). His struggle to maintain Catholicism in a principality surrounded by Lutheran and Calvinist princes helped convince Von Wittelsbach in the late 1620s to unleash his full territorial machinery to enact a "final solution" to the witch question and preserve the health of his realm.[25]

Similarly, the small County of Lippe, now part of Northern Rhine-Westphalia, belonged to the heartland of witch-hunting, experiencing peaks in persecution around the same time as other German regions; the worst panic in the Lippe town of Lemgo occurred in 1628 when over eighty people were executed. Similarly, neighboring Osnabrück executed close to 300 accused witches between 1561 and 1639, more than half in the panics of 1583 and the 1630s, while Minden killed 138. Until 1600 Lippe was like the Franken territories, a small, Catholic region with larger Lutheran neighbors, while Lemgo was Lutheran. After 1600, Lippe turned Calvinist, while Lemgo remained Lutheran. One of the earliest known trials in Lemgo was conducted in 1566 against a male sorcerer, Johan Büchsenschütz, who was accused of using a crystal ball, blessing sorcery books, and selling spells and talismans. Despite being tortured, however, the accused denied that his magic was diabolical, but was "under the appearance of the Word of God." Büchsenschütz's very Lutheran appeal to the Word of God in a Lutheran city within a Catholic county may therefore have complicated matters for Lemgo's magistrates, who burned his books but not his person.[26] With its small, decentralized state and legal system, Lippe possessed all of the elements required for major German witch panics, including a confessional struggle that created an atmosphere of uncertainty and mistrust.

Swiss Confederacy

In the various cantons that together formed the Swiss Confederacy, the witch-hunts were also quite intense, with about 10,000 trials and high execution rates.[27] The Reformation divided the Confederacy between six Protestant and seven Catholic cantons, leading to open warfare in the

1530s and continued polemical conflict thereafter. As each canton was judicially autonomous there was considerable variation across the various regions: the Pays de Vaud, the French-speaking Calvinist dependency of Bern, was one of the worst regions, killing more than 90 percent of the over 2,000 accused brought before its courts, while Calvinist Geneva had a relatively mild record of witch prosecution, conducting 479 known trials and executing 132 of the accused (27.7 percent). However, eighty-four of these victims were caught up in the *engraisseur* or plague-spreader panics of 1545, 1567–8, 1571, and 1615, when outbreaks of the plague led to a frenzied search for those responsible. Many of these accused were compelled to admit to membership in a Satanic conspiracy, but the central accusation was the smearing of plague essence on door handles, a clear parallel to the charges brought earlier against lepers and Jews starting in the 1320s. Geneva executed only about 17 percent of its "regular" witches, although many others were banished.[28]

Geneva's moderation, outside of plague epidemics, was not based on a purely confessional distinction, as William Monter notes, for other Swiss Protestant authorities were as enthusiastic witch persecutors as their Catholic neighbors.[29] Even during the *engraisseur* panics the vast majority of Geneva's accused witches were women, showing that Reformed regions were as likely as Catholic territories to identify poisoning and witchcraft as a female crime. Calvin strongly promoted the submissiveness of women within patriarchal marriage, and most of the *engraisseurs* were older women (in the Geneva panic of 1571 only nine of ninety-nine accused were men, while in other years the rate of female accused in Geneva hovered around 76 percent).[30] Like most church and state leaders, Calvinists sought to control or contain female behavior and to strengthen the authority of males within the family as a microcosm of the centralizing power of princes. What mattered then, was not so much the particular confessional identity of a region, but a combination of factors which included: an especially intense, gloomy form of religiosity among its elites; an accompanying fear of unruly female behavior; a continued concern about the incursions of heterodoxy; and an apparent rise in blasphemy, skepticism, and doubt among the populace.

Monter's study of Jura witch-hunting reveals also the prevalence of demonic possession cases, not merely as a clerical tool of religious propaganda, but more essentially as an element of popular witchcraft beliefs. In the Franche-Comté, a French-speaking region technically under Charles V's Burgundian jurisdiction but which had its own parlement, demonic possession was part of the ordinary witchcraft of peasants. Initially jurists, such as Henri Boguet, Grand-Judge of Abbey of St. Claude and writer of the demonological work *Discours des Sorciers* of 1602, did not know how to treat such demoniacs and their denunciation of witches. Boguet's first witch case in 1598 involved an eight-year-old girl, Loyse Maillat, who on June 5, 1598 was suddenly "struck helpless in all her limbs." No cure could be found, so on July 19 her parents took her to church to be exorcized. While there, it was discovered that she was possessed by five demons named Wolf, Cat, Dog, Jolly, and Griffon (names that would spring readily to a child's mind). When the priest asked the girl who had cast the spell on her, she pointed to one of the spectators, Françoise Secretain, an old woman who the night before the fits started had requested a night's lodging of Loyse's mother, who initially refused because her husband was away but finally succumbed to François' pleas. While the mother was momentarily absent the visitor supposedly compelled the girl to eat a piece of bread "resembling dung." The next day Loyse was possessed, and only the fervent prayers of her parents could expel the demons which, in the form of red or black fist-sized balls, danced around the fire before vanishing, leaving the girl to recover.

In court Boguet forced François to confess to the accusations, despite the fact that

> To look at her, you would have thought she was the best woman in the world; for she was always talking of God, of the Virgin Mary, and of the Holy Saints of Paradise, and she had in her hand a long rosary which she pretended to say without interruption. But the truth is that the Cross of this rosary was defective, and it will be seen that this fact furnished evidence against her.[31]

Once the determination of guilt was made, a process of rationalization was required to explain away the accused's supposed piety and turn her saintly behavior into demonic. After being stripped and searched for the Devil's mark, she confessed to bewitching Loyse, to having given herself to the Devil in the shape of a large, black man, and to having flown on a white staff to the witches' sabbath where she and other witches danced and beat water to produce hail. She confessed also to murdering another victim by means of poisoned bread and to killing cattle with the touch of her hand or a wand. According to his own account Boguet had struggled hard whether to accept the girl's testimony, for in capital crimes proofs needed to be clearer than daylight. However, the girl "never wavered" and her parents corroborated her story; moreover, as witchcraft was usually committed in secret, "it did not call for such positive proof as would be required in the case of any other crime." From the moment he made this decision, the die was cast, and he noted that Loyse's confession led him to the discovery of "countless" other witches. Subsequent trials provided further evidence of the veracity of his unusual decision to accept a mere child's evidence and helped quash any residual uncertainties he may have harbored. As with Heinrich Krämer, this inner battle against doubt made Boguet an even more ardent hunter of witches than usual: of thirty-five that he himself tried between 1598 and 1609, he condemned twenty-eight to death (eight were burned alive) while four more died in prison.[32] In 1611 he requested his printers to stop reissuing his demonological treatise, because, Monter suggests, he was hoping to be selected to sit on the local parlement which had just overturned some of his sentences for witchcraft.

Boguet found further examples of witchcraft-induced possession both in the writings of other demonologists, such as Bodin, and in his own courtroom (one involved a twelve-year-old boy who had denounced his father) to dispute Johann Weyer's skepticism on the matter. Boguet's examples suggest that it was popularly believed that a witch could send demons into a victim through enchanted food, usually an apple in what Boguet took to be a demonic replay of the temptation of Eve and which warned against the mortal sin of gluttony. That Boguet thought such cases arose from peasant culture is evident from his comment that

> Every day in our own town we continually meet with large numbers of persons who, for the most part, impute their possession to certain Vaudois or sorcerers. The truth is confessed by the devils themselves, being wrung from them by the might and virtue of exorcism, and of the glorious body of St. Claude . . . his body may be seen laid out whole upon the altar of the church in the eternal triumph of countless miracles which are performed upon those who resort to him; and demoniacs especially are every moment being healed by his prayers and intercessions.[33]

In Burgundy, demonic possession was a common form of bewitchment for which many of the afflicted sought out the miraculous cure of a saint's relics; Monter has found further "evidence from other parts of Franche-Comté [that] confirms the impression that here demonic possession was built into the base of popular witchcraft."[34]

By the early 1600s in urban Geneva causing diabolical possession had become the single most common act of *maleficia*, while many of the more traditional features of witchcraft, such as making hail or the sabbath, virtually vanished. There had been several earlier cases of possession, such as that of a man who in1578 was handed a three-day sentence for taking his diabolically possessed eight-year-old daughter to a Catholic priest for an exorcism, or the 1587 trial of a widow accused of putting nine devils into a child, although she too was treated mildly. But in 1607 the attitude of the Genevan authorities changed when they were con-fronted with a case of mass possession of several women and children, seventeen of whom were quarantined while the city's pastors prayed for them. Here the Reformed pastors were concerned not only about the disturbances the demoniacs caused during Communion services, but also about the propagandistic points the Catholics would score if the Genevans could not cure the afflicted in a Protestant fashion. Soon the demoniacs were accusing others of bewitching them and turned to the courts for a solution (it was at this time that the Genevans began searching diligently for the Devil's mark), although most of the convicted were expelled rather than executed.

For his part, Boguet, like so many other witch-hunters, projected his inner conflict over the reality of witch and demoniac confessions onto the screen of the battle against religious doubt. As one scholar put it, for fervent Catholics such as Boguet "the saint, the sorcerer, and the possessed were the elementary figures in a militant theatre which... dramatized the Tridentine liturgy and dogma" and which provided a symbolic representation of the battle against Protestant heresy.[35] After estimating the number of witches in France alone to be at least 450,000, Boguet continued,

> for if we but look around among own neighbors, we shall find them all infested with this miserable and damnable vermin. Germany is almost entirely occupied with building fires for them. Switzerland has been compelled to wipe out many of her villages on their account. Travelers in Lorraine may see thousands and thousands of the stakes to which witches are bound. We in Burgundy are no more exempt than other lands; for in many parts of our country we see that the execution of witches is a common occurrence.

Witches by the thousands, he affirmed, were everywhere, "multiplying upon the earth even as worms in a garden." For magistrates to ignore this immense threat was a clear act of disobedience to God, for God has "sometimes brought them [cities and villages] to utter ruin for the same crime of witchcraft." His own battle against doubt he externalized in the following form:

> I know that there have before this been those who have not been able to believe that what is said of witches is true; but in these present days they are beginning to believe it, owing to a special grace of God, who has opened their eyes, which had been blinded by Satan that by this means he might, as he has done, increase his kingdom. These men, I say, are now busy in hunting down witches, so that not long ago they caused some to be put to death. And I take this as a sign that in a short time Satan and all his subjects will be overcome, and witches will no longer boast that they are able to make war upon a King...

He expressed "astonishment" that "there should still be found to-day people who do not believe that there are witches. For my part I suspect that the truth is that such people really believe in their hearts, but will not admit it." As a means of further expelling such insidious doubt from his own mind, he condemned all skeptics as members "of the witches' party," an incrimination which he thought explained why so many witches escaped the death penalty.[36] Boguet, who set aside judicial caution by accepting a child's fantasies of diabolical magic, spent the next several years defending that decision to himself and others and vindicating the reality of all manner of supernatural manifestations against even mild skepticism.

The Spanish Netherlands

Emperor Charles V may have had great difficulty in coordinating a judicial assault against blasphemy in the largely decentralized Empire, but he had much greater control over his Habsburg and Burgundian inheritances. Here, as in Spain, he and his son Philip II passed laws against heresy and witchcraft with some expectation that they would be heeded, establishing inquisitorial tribunals when local courts proved recalcitrant. However, his Netherlandic domains rebelled against such measures, and it took Spain's great military might to return the southern territories to fealty to the crown and Catholicism. The northern provinces ceded, forming the Dutch Republic which developed such an unusual attitude toward persecution of both religious dissent and witchcraft that we will reserve its discussion to the next chapter. In contrast, the Spanish Netherlands were not allowed to tolerate religious dissidents who faced continued horrible persecution. The only permitted religion was post-Tridentine Catholicism, and great efforts were made by Inquisitors, secular priests, and Jesuits thoroughly to inculcate proper Catholic attitudes within each citizen. Even so, the Habsburg authorities faced great difficulties in this campaign, for the various reform groups had made significant inroads within the populace, while the Calvinists of the Dutch Republic and north and western France provided a potent source of Reformed propaganda.

Here too there were several waves of witch-hunting. For example, in the Duchy of Luxembourg witch persecutions occurred in the periods 1580–1600 and 1615–30, consuming over 350 condemned. Namur, which unlike most regions had continued a fifteenth-century style hunt for demonic Vauderie into the sixteenth century, executed some 200 alleged witches between 1509 and 1646. The highly urbanized province of Flanders tried over 600 and executed over 200 supposed witches between the late fifteenth century and the 1690s, the bulk of these falling into the last decade of the sixteenth and the first of the seventeenth century. The peak year was 1596, just four years after Philip II's new legislation transferring jurisdiction for the crime of witchcraft from ecclesiastical to secular courts.

The new law was merely one of several contributing factors in the rise of witch-hunting in the southern Netherlands; as elsewhere, individuals with reputations for witchcraft and soothsayers who unhexed the bewitched were the usual victims. In 1545 Charles V had introduced a quasi-Spanish Inquisition to the Low Countries which, by his abdication in 1555, had virtually suppressed Anabaptism. Yet demonizing rhetoric escalated. In this climate, many Flemish Inquisitors and magistrates became convinced of the diabolical conspiracy of witches. For example, in Laarne on September 11, 1607 a judge convicted Paesschyne Neyts, wife of Pieter Tweecruys, of, among other things, "abandoning God almighty your lord and creator, and clinging to the Devil of hell, enemy of the human race, to whom you have opened yourself over some years in the form of a calf." Two years later a nearly identical accusation was brought against a sixty-year-old widow of Nazareth named Janne Slaenders who, "for about the last thirty years has abandoned God of heaven," clinging instead to "the enemy of hell," attending with some other women the "dance in Gansbrouck on Eecke near Landuijt," where

sat "the enemy in the form of a goat" the hind foot of which each partici-
pant kissed. Although acts of *maleficia* remained an element of all of
these later cases, they were merely aspects of the more serious diabolical
apostasy. Neyts, for example, was convicted also of receiving a poisoned
apple from the Devil and giving it to her daughter's employer, Janneken
Scheers, who accordingly died in misery. The account then returns to
the more sensational elements, for Neyts apparently also confessed that
when her husband was absent from home performing his military service
for the city of Oostende, in her despair and loneliness she accepted the
sexual advances of the Devil, still in a calf's shape, at which time he marked
her on the hip.[37]

Such descriptions of diabolical Flemish witches were replicated in the
courts of the province dozens of times after 1590, yet they were a clear
contrast to the descriptions of witches in the Dutch Republic, where the
presumed *maleficia* remained the principal charge. The statistical difference is striking: the southern provinces executed over 900 witches, while
the northern region killed about 160.[38] An important difference, as we
have already suggested, was the propaganda of zealous Catholic anti-
heresy and witchcraft activists who were sponsored by the Spanish
authorities as the leading edge of the recatholicization of the southern
provinces. The transition from heresy to witch-hunting was often an
abrupt one, and the faggots piled beneath accused witches were ignited
only after the heresy fires had grown cold. After the victory over the
Reformed in Antwerp and the flight of thousands of Calvinists from that
city in 1585, the battle against heresy moved from one conducted against
an external, easily demonized enemy – Calvinists and Mennonites – to the
less visible but even more dangerous threats of neighbors thought to be
secret demonic agents. In some cities where religious dissidents had
been heavily persecuted, such as Kortrijk and Antwerp, the magistrates
seem to have become disgusted with the process of burning people as
a means of averting divine wrath, turning instead to some measure of
religious compromise and resisting the efforts of Counter-Reformation
churchmen to promote severe witch persecution.[39] In others, the civic
leaders moved almost seamlessly from one form of persecution to the
other. While zealous propagandists frequently expressed disappointment
with the state's efforts to eradicate heterodox notions and enforce Catholic
dogma and practice, their efforts were partially effective in stirring up
concern about supposed diabolical conspiracies. In Spanish-controlled
regions such as the Franche-Comté, Lorraine and the southern Netherlands, Spanish royal agents successfully encouraged witch prosecution.

Undoubtedly witch panics required little in the way of propaganda to leap across political boundaries to engulf citizens and rulers in a swirl of denunciations, trials, and executions. They could, however, spread farther and faster when encouraged by authorities, as seems to have happened across much of Europe in the 1590s, partly as a result of a growing conviction in the reality of a demonic witch sect, and partly as a vaguely defined means of eradicating false belief within a populace in the era of confessionalization.

France and Lorraine

Although in the fifteenth century France had led the way in witch-hunting, in the sixteenth and seventeenth centuries witch persecution here was no more intense than in England; the maximum number of victims for the period between 1560 and 1670 was a few thousand, a figure which reveals considerable moderation in the judicial treatment of witches and a general lack of the kind of panics that gripped many regions bordering on the country. Alfred Soman has shown that even though it approved slightly more than 100 lower court capital sentences, the Parlement of Paris acted as a major brake on witch trials, overturning more than 1,100 other cases. Even so, there were in France several infamous incidents of demonic possession leading to witch trials, and even though these did not lead to mass trials, the publicity and panic that they engendered brought the subject of the diabolical into public discourse. Moreover, as Erik Midelfort has noted for the German lands, ordinary people had great difficulty in distinguishing between "the supposedly clear categories of witchcraft and possession."[40] Demoniacs not only denounced witches but also inspired imitation. Ultimately, however, these infamous instances of demonic possession served the cause of skeptics rather than of the defenders of supernatural reality, and on the whole contributed to the discrediting of witch-hunting. A discussion of them will therefore be reserved for our final chapter. More typical witch-hunting in France was centered on the eastern, north-eastern, and extreme southwestern portions of the realm, regions too of strong Huguenot presence.

As elsewhere, France had its share of learned promoters of witch persecution, including legal experts such as Jean Bodin whose rebuttal of Weyer's skeptical tome in 1580 was the first major demonological book in French. This was followed in the last decade of the century by the treatises of Nicholas Rémy, a judge of Lorraine who oversaw several hundred witch trials himself, and Boguet. Despite the considerable opposition that they faced from more moderate learned fellows, their demonological efforts seem to have contributed to the increasing pace of trials after 1580. For one thing, as jurists and legal experts, they shared numerous anecdotes drawn from their own courtroom experiences which may have influenced local court officials more readily than mere theoretical musings. Structurally, their treatises followed the model set by earlier writers on the subject by organizing their material thematically around the various demonological aspects, each of which was proven by recourse to both the writings of the ancients and church fathers and "real" confessions provided by "actual" witches. It still proved difficult to oppose the authority of the ancients and the scriptures even when apparently contrary to empirical evidence. Likewise, the courtroom was a daunting place for ordinary folk, and it is amazing that so many illiterate women protested their innocence on witchcraft charges for so long given the weight of literate, male, legal authority that was confronting them.

Rémy's treatise, *Demonolatry*, provides a sufficient example of this process. Claiming to have presided over 900 death sentences over his fifteen-year career as Lorraine judge, he asserted his

> head was entirely filled with considerations of the monstrous assem-
> blies of the witches, who were very frequently among those who came
> up before me for trial, with thoughts of their banquetings, dancings,
> charms and spells, their journeyings through the air, the horrid
> practices of their carnal relations with the Demon, their frequent
> transmutation into other shapes and form (for so it seemed), and all
> the crimes and blasphemies with which it is well known that their lives
> are polluted and utterly defiled.[41]

Rémy's declaration that he had become convinced of the reality of a dia-
bolical sabbath conspiracy as a result of hearing witch confessions cannot be taken at face value, for these were the product of considerable judicial pressure. It is much more plausible that after hearing his initial cases Rémy turned to the writings of learned demonologists for the theoretical superstructure upon which to arrange the strange accusations he was hearing. As he compelled his defendants to conform to this intellectual construct, he found further evidence of the reality of his religious beliefs. He concluded his treatise by declaring,

I shall not fear to proclaim freely and openly my opinion of them [i.e., witches], and to do all in my power to bring the very truth to light: namely, that their lives are so notoriously befouled and polluted by so many blasphemies, sorceries, prodigious lusts and flagrant crimes, that I have no hesitation in saying that they are justly to be subjected to every torture and put to death in the flames; both that they may expiate their crimes with a fitting punishment, and that its very awfulness may serve as an example and a warning to others.[42]

Composing his treatise after his retirement, Rémy seems to have used such categorical assertions to suppress the moments of doubt about his bloody activity that he surely endured.

England and Scotland

Ever since the pioneering works of Keith Thomas on magic and witch-craft in England and Alan Macfarlane's on the witch-hunts in Essex, the focus on witchcraft has been on the local social relations and popular belief systems which lay behind specific accusations of witchcraft. A typical scenario portrayed an elderly or middle-aged woman suddenly down on her luck and forced to beg from her neighbors. When refused by some yeomen farmer or his servants, she might mutter a curse, so that when a sudden, inexplicable ailment befell the farmer's family or livestock, suspicion, fueled by guilt over the lack of charity, fell upon the woman, who may already have possessed a reputation for harmful magic.[43] The psychological process of guilt projection and accusation was a common-place elsewhere in Europe.

More recently, James Sharpe has counted a total of 474 accused witches (nearly 90 percent of them women) brought before the home circuit assizes. Fewer than forty trials immediately followed the passage of Elizabeth I's witchcraft statute of 1563, although that decade witnessed the publication of the first polemical tracts and news sheets on the subject. Thereafter assize trials jumped dramatically to over 100 cases each decade until 1600, dropping to twenty or fewer in the 1620s and 1630s. It seemed that serious witch persecution was dying out as it had in England's major economic competitor, the Dutch Republic.

Such was not to be the case, for in the 1640s, as England was plunged into a Civil War between Oliver Cromwell's Parliamentarians and the Royalists, a major witch panic erupted in Puritan Essex and spreading from there to neighboring counties. Altogether, Essex, with over 470 indictments, accounted for nearly twice as many cases as the other four major regions of witch persecution put together. Since several of these counties were undergoing similar socio-economic pressures to Essex, Sharpe suggests that its exceptional witch persecution record might be explained by the nature of elite politics within the county which were intimately intertwined with religious conflicts. For example, the first person to have been executed for witchcraft under the new witchcraft statute of 1563 was Elizabeth Lowys, whose persecution was nourished by Thomas Coles, an archdeacon of Essex and a returned Marian exile. Many of the Protestant divines who faced persecution under Queen Mary understandably saw the religious struggle against both Catholicism and skepticism in the light of the apocalyptical battle. Sharpe points out the high correlation between levels of heresy and witch burnings in Essex, and notes that

> In one case where it is possible to grasp the mechanics whereby heretics were brought before the authorities, arising from Great Bentley, it is possible to see elements of community dismay and neighbours informing on each other, admittedly co-ordinated by the local clergy-man, which look very similar to the background to many witchcraft cases. And, interestingly if ironically given his earlier adherence to the Protestant cause, one of the Justices of the Peace who played a leading role in processing the accusations against these heretics was Lord Darcy of Chiche, kinsman of that Brian Darcy who, as landlord and Justice of the peace, managed to orchestrate a local witch-craze in Essex in 1582. Going back to the political and religious situation in Essex in the early years of Elizabeth might well offer evidence of a context in which the actions and attitudes of members of the local religious and secular elites helped construct a tradition of witch-hunting within the country.[44]

A few examples from Essex and elsewhere will illustrate some intersections between fervently held religious beliefs and conflict and concerns over demonic witchcraft.

Persecution of leading Protestants was a hallmark of Queen Mary's reign, as was the suppression of Catholicism under Queen Elizabeth I. Even after the establishment of the Church of England in the reign of Elizabeth, there were many malcontents who, demanding a more thorough church reform, eventually separated from it, leading to a proliferation of sects which Puritan ministers regarded as a form of diabolical blasphemy nearly as bad as the prospect of the restoration of Catholic "papalism", the great Antichrist for most Calvinist divines. Efforts to restore Catholicism were also linked with Philip II's efforts to assert his claim to the English throne as Queen Mary I's consort, and proof of this threat was found in the Spanish Armada of 1588 which was destroyed by a storm, an event interpreted by the English as a sign of God's blessing upon their Protestant nation. Puritan ministers were fighting a three-front war against a resurgent Catholicism, a variety of home-brewed religious dissent groups, and what they saw as entrenched religious indifference on the part of many parishioners. Puritan writings therefore reveal an intense sense of embattlement, of assault by invisible, demonic forces. Armed only with the word of God and prayer, Puritans propagated a defense strategy based on the imprinting of sound doctrine and proper Christian virtues upon the psychology of individuals, shaping and directing their attitudes and decisions. Only if morality, sobriety, prayer, and humble devotion to God's will became every English person's second nature, could they resist the twin dangers of Catholic invasion and heresy. Despite their vigorous efforts, the Protestant preachers soon discovered that many of their flock remained obstinately fond of the old "superstitions" or utterly indifferent to the task. In witchcraft the divines found an ally in this battle.

In sermons and writings Protestant preachers attempted to discredit Catholicism by associating it with magic. One of the earliest writings on the subject was Francis Coxe's *A short treatise declaringe the detestable wickednesse of magicall sciences*, published in 1561. Coxe, a reformed necromancer, argued that permitting the magical arts in England was an act of treason against both the prince and God. Like those opposing the decriminalization of marijuana today, Coxe suggested that not even relatively benign magical crafts such as astrology could be tolerated, for these were merely Satanic snares to entrap people into the "hard" forms of magic such as necromancy. He claimed that necromancy was prevalent mostly among the Catholic clergy and that a new statute was needed to dissuade others from embarking on this diabolical path which was turning Christians into infidels and "the temple of ye holy Ghoste into a synagoge of Sathan." Although in times past fear of the "godly" law against magic had deterred many from such wicked practices, the law "for lacke of execution hath lyen a slepe."[45]

Coxe's opinions were shared by many Protestant pamphleteers, such as the author of one of the earliest English witch pamphlets,

The Examination of John Walsh of 1566, which asserted that the accused, John Walsh, had learned his sorcery from a Marian priest, and that invoking his spirits required a book of sorcery, magical circles, candles of virgin wax, and waxen images of the intended victim, accoutrements indeed of clerical necromancy. Walsh's case, along with that of a priest's concubine who confessed to having learned sorcery from her paramour, revealed the "fruites of Papistes and papistrye" as an increase in super-stitious practices. The author also lists several popes, most notably Alexander VI, who had gained their throne by diabolical means and used necromancy against their foes.[46] Coincidentally, Walsh's trial occurred on August 22, 1566, just a few days after the start of the iconoclastic fury in the Low Countries, and was another part of the Calvinist assault on Catholic ritual.

Coxe's comments also pointed to a lacunae in English law. The creation of Henry VIII's 1542 witchcraft statute was possibly linked to lingering concerns over the trial of Anne Boleyn, who, among her many alleged treasons, had been charged with witchcraft, while the discovery of a waxen image of Prince Edward with pins stuck in it may also have incited the monarch to suppress magic. However, the young Edward VI (1547–53) began his own reform of England's laws by repealing many of his father's statutes, but died before he could replace them. Mary Tudor (1553–8) was simply too busy to turn to the project. Hence, between 1547 and 1563 witchcraft was not a secular crime in England, although it remained a subject for the realm's ecclesiastical courts; Coxe's treatise was therefore part of a broader campaign encouraging Elizabeth to fill this legal void.[47] Why Elizabeth took up the matter is not clear, although Keith Thomas suggests that it "may have been precipitated by political conspiracies in which magic was employed against the reigning monarch,"[48] while Deborah Willis sees it as part of the Queen's efforts to distinguish herself from her Catholic predecessor and to keep at bay both the Catholic holdovers and the ardent Protestant Reformers, many of whom had just returned from their exile on the continent imbued with an even greater zeal to eradicate Catholic remnants.[49] An apparently sudden increase in 1559–60 of witchcraft cases brought before the ecclesiastical court of Canterbury also raised concern.[50]

The last revision of the witchcraft statute occurred under the watch-ful eye of King James I, whose own concern about magical plots against the crown had earlier led him when king of Scotland to participate in several trials in the early 1590s and to publish his own demonological treatise, the *Daemonologie*, in 1597. Yet, and despite his evident involvement in creating the 1604 witchcraft statute, once monarch of England James placed a restraining hand on witchcraft persecution, largely because he defined the crime as treason against the crown, noticing little to disturb him in most of the cases he witnessed in the early seventeenth century.[51] English law, moreover, required royal permission to proceed to judicial torture, while trials were heard by juries which looked for sound evidence. Based on these legal constraints and the lack, until the 1640s, of widespread concern about a diabolical witch sect, it is apparent why the hunts here were considerably more moderate than elsewhere.

Prior to the Civil War there were a few witch panics, especially in the 1580s and 1640s in Essex, coinciding with moments of vigorous Puritan activity. Macfarlane's analysis of the trials, however, revealed no apparent link between the two events, as many Puritan preachers remained disdainful of the popular fear of witchcraft and very few actually took part as witnesses in trials against witches. Instead, some, such as George Gifford (c. 1548–1620) publicly condemned blaming disasters on old women when such came directly from God as a punishment of the victim's own sin, not that of his or her neighbor.[52] Although Gifford's published works on witches were, by the standards of his day, moderate and intended to stop indiscriminate prosecution of witches, his writings about Catholics and Protestant sectarians were far from that. As preacher in Maldon, Essex, Gifford published a number of attacks against both Roman Catholicism (by far his greatest enemy) and Protestant dissidents such as the Separatists (Brownists), Family of Love, and other promoters of "atheism." His famous treatises on the Devil and witchcraft therefore need to be read in the context of his whole literary corpus.

Undoubtedly Gifford's most ambitious project was his series of fifty sermons on the book of Revelation, a large tome of over 450 pages published in 1596. This was not the first time that his congregation had endured a lengthy discourse on the apocalyptical visions of St. John; in the first sermon he half apologized to them for expounding again on this subject. For Gifford this prophetic section of the Christian scriptures was being fulfilled in his own day as the Protestant forces of Christ battled against the antichristian papacy. Assisting the apocalyptical beast were newly arisen "filthy monsters": Anabaptists, Libertines, Familists, and other secret agents of Satan working from within the godly commonwealth to spread license and atheism now that his open allies, the papacy, were hindered by English law. For Gifford and other Puritan preachers,

Catholic sacramental practice and veneration of the saints were forms of demon worship which gave credence to the superstitious and magical beliefs of the "vulgar sort." The gravest danger to the English common-wealth was therefore not the *maleficia* of witches but moral laxity and doubt in the providence of God, sins which would lead the realm back into the arms of the papal whore of Babylon. He wrote,

> For what can bee more bitter then in steede of a liuely feeling through faith, that wee are reconciled to God through the bloud of his sonne, and insteed of the spirit of adoption by which we are sanctified, which beareth witnes to our spirits that we are the children of God, to haue the doubts and tortues of conscience, which I say doe follow of super-stious and corrupt doctrine? The assurance of faith, or full perswasion of the remission of sinnes, is condemned of the papists as high presumption: and to bee in doubt is deemed great humilitie.[53]

The inner turmoil of Puritans over whether or not they were members of the elect is a well-known topos in religious psychology, as believers frantically searched for signs indicating they were members of that exclusive club and grieved over every sinful thought that might indicate their exclusion.[54] One has to wonder about the effects that Gifford's intense hatred of Catholicism, obsession with the Devil, and constant harping on the signs heralding Christ's return had on the minds of his congregation. Writing about the possession case of Helen Fairfax in 1621, James Sharpe comments about the possible role played by the sermonizing of a local vicar who like Gifford was an experienced anti-popery controversialist:

> One can safely surmise that attentive listeners to his sermons would have had their sensibilities alerted to the wiles of the Antichrist. Similarly, the images of God which Helen recounted give us insights into how a young Puritan woman might see her creator, while it seems likely that the monster dripping with blood which she saw owed not a little to the Book of Revelation.[55]

Gifford was therefore not alone in planting such images of the Devil and Catholics in the minds of parishioners. As the Puritan bishop of Salisbury John Jewel wrote in a letter to the famous Italian Reformer Peter Martyr Vermigli in 1559,

It is incredible how great a crop and forest of superstitions has sprung up in the darkness of the Marian time. Everywhere we found relics of the saints, nails by which foolish persons imagined that Christ had been crucified, and I know not what fragments of the holy cross. The number of sorceresses and witches had increased immensely everywhere.[56]

Shortly afterward Jewel gave a sermon before Queen Elizabeth, warning her about witches and sorcerers who "within these few last years are marvellously increased within your grace's realm. . . . Your grace's subjects pine away even unto the death, their colour fadeth, their flesh rotteth, their senses are bereft."[57] Jewel and his cohorts fervently longed for a witchcraft statute that would eradicate malicious magic and suppress the remnants of Catholic superstition. Their zealous sermons on this matter may have had some undesirable side effects. For the Puritans of New England, Richard Godbeer notes, those

> who used countermagic assumed that suffering was the result of affliction by outside forces and could be removed through magical ritual. Ministers insisted that the sources of sin and suffering were internal, as were the means for resisting them. Yet at the same time they maintained a tradition of externalizing evil and so inadvertently promoted recourse to countermagic. Clerical statements about Satan's role in the generation of human sin and suffering could result in the very abdication of responsibility ministers claimed to abhor.[58]

In other words, while Gifford intended his writings and sermons to end both white magic and witch accusations, his apocalyptical demonizing of his religious opponents and endless harping on the need for all believers to inspect and take responsibility for the demon-inspired sin within them may have had the opposite effect. Moreover, as in Germany where clerical visitations helped increase fear of heresy and witchcraft among parishioners, several English bishops ordered their clergy to beat the bushes of their parishes for any signs of superstitious practices, helping in fact to draw attention to the subject. In 1576 the Archbishop of Canterbury, Edmund Grindal, instructed his clerics to inquire "whether there be any among you that use sorcery or witchcraft, or that be suspected of the same, and whether any use any charmes or unlawful prayers, or invocations in Latin, or otherwise . . . and whether any do resort to any such for help or counsel, and what be there names."[59]

Demonic possession and witchcraft

In England witchcraft accusations often originated from victims of demonic possession, a phenomenon very much linked to confessional conflict. One of the earliest such incidents reveals this quite well. In September 1584 the Jesuit priest William Westen and eleven other Catholic priests illegally conducted in Denham a series of well-attended exorcisms of six demoniacs which apparently convinced hundreds of Protestants to reconvert to Catholicism. They also helped introduce "Continental" notions of demonology into the popular consciousness of Englanders.[60] As in France, these English exorcisms were intended as proof that the Catholic priests alone had power over the Devil. The demoniacs cooperated sensationally with their priestly exorcists, confirming the power of the consecrated Host and the relics of recent English martyrs while, in their demonic voices, identifying the Protestants and Queen Elizabeth as Beelzebub's allies. Such cooperation was the product of both religious zeal and the unorthodox techniques of the exorcists, which included binding the afflicted to chairs and forcing them to inhale noxious fumes and swallow some foul drink. Elizabeth's principal minister, Francis Walsingham (c. 1530–90), allowed these scandalous events to take place until he had collected enough evidence to pounce on all of the leaders of the infamous Babington plot, who aimed to assassinate the Queen, restore Catholicism to the realm, and open the door to a Spanish invasion. Among the exorcists was one of the plot's leaders, John Ballard, while one of the possessed was William Morwood, servant of the central plotter, Anthony Babington. Westen himself probably knew of the conspiracy, but the evidence against him was insufficient to proceed to his execution, although he was imprisoned for ten years.[61]

Neither the publicity of the exorcisms nor Westen's influence ended with the Babington affair. Along with his demonological notions Westen had brought to England's Catholic priests an extreme Counter-Reformation asceticism. Many resisted, forming an anti-Jesuit Catholic party which preferred to negotiate with the crown for a means to stay both Catholic and loyalist. Discussions culminated in November 1602 with a promise from Bishop Bancroft that all Catholic priests who swore allegiance to the Queen would be treated mildly. For his efforts, Bancroft was accused by the Puritans in Parliament of high treason for negotiating with Catholics. To dispel Puritan charges of incipient Catholicism and hostility to Puritanism (he had overseen the condemnation of the Puritan "dispossessor" John Darrell three years before), Bancroft began an examination into the Denham exorcisms, a published account of which kindled the fires of debate about the Devil's assaults on England through treasonous plots, demonic possession, and witchcraft (one of the demoniacs had accused a witch of causing the bewitchments).[62]

One pamphlet recounting how a possession led to a witch trial provides a number of important clues as to both the ongoing confessional disputes and Puritan religious attitudes and psychological states. The pamphleteer's propagandistic goal was to rally parishioners to daily vigilance against the Devil, for the book of Revelation prophesized "that the devil hath great wrath, knowing that he hath but a short time," a prediction that was now fulfilled in the "outragious fury that Sathan useth in raising persecution against Gods Saints, by his mischieuous instruments, & corrupting mens minds by his wicked suggestions, but also in tyrannizing, according to his limited power ouer them by torments." The most important sign of the soon coming of judgment was "the cooling of Charity, [and] quenching of the Spirit" which the author believed characterized his own day. The story of the "pittifull vexing of this poore distressed child" revealed that Christians could withstand the Devil, if only they availed themselves of the proper weapons.

This account of the trial in 1596 of Alice Gooderidge of Stapenhill before the Derby Assizes began with the demonic possession in Burton-upon-Trent of thirteen-year-old Thomas Darling. For our pamphleteer it offered rebuttal to "both the peeuish opinion, that there are no wiches, and the Popish assertion that only their priests can dispossesse," for a Puritan minister, John Darrell, was instrumental in releasing the boy from his torment. The long story began innocently enough on February 27, 1596 when Darling returned home ill from a trip to the woods, being overcome by "sore fits" in which he shouted "Looke where greene Angels stand in the window, and not long after would often complaine, that a green Cat troubled him." A physician found no sign of disease, even though he "doubted that the Childe was bewitched." In between fits the boy seemed fine, mature beyond his years, showing "the frutes of his education, which was religious and godly." In fact, he hoped to become a preacher, "to thunder out the threatenings of Gods word, against sinne and all abhominations, wherewith these dayes doo abound."

Whatever their cause, the convulsive and hallucinatory fits increased in extremity over the following weeks, marked by superhuman strength and unusual contortions. Moments of calm were filled with prayers and scripture readings, particularly from John 1 (commonly used in countermagic), although these often caused new fits, proving that his body was inhabited by demons who found the word of God repulsive. When suspicion of bewitchment was expressed, Darling finally told his story of how, when wandering in the woods, he had stumbled upon a little old woman whom he remembered had earlier begged at their door. As he walked by her in the copse, he passed wind, a rude act which the woman took as intentional. In anger she spoke the rhyme "Gyp with a mischiefe, and fart with a bell: I wil goe to heauen, and thou shalt goe to hell" and stooped to the ground for some mysterious purpose. Immediately suspicion alighted on Alice Gooderidge, the daughter of "the witch of Stapenhill" and a reputed practitioner of "diuellisch practises."

As the fits continued into Easter, the boy's relatives sent for Gooderidge; when she appeared before Darling, "he fell sodainly into a maruellous sore fit." Gooderidge denied any knowledge of the boy, but some of the bystanders persuaded Darling to perform the scratch test, after which the accused told the boy "take blood enough child, God helpe thee," a blessing which Darling interpreted as an effort at countermagic, for he said "praye for thy selfe, thy prayer can do mee no good." The pamphleteer displayed his Puritan disgust with such forms of soothsaying to "discry a witch" as lacking both natural cause and scriptural warrant, thus they too were "amongst the witchcrafts, whereof there bee great store used in our Land, to the great dishonor of God." A more orthodox test was applied by compelling her to repeat the Lord's Prayer and Creed, which she failed by skipping over key phrases such as "lead us not into temptation."

Moved to tears by Darling's descriptions of terrifying visions of a monstrous green cat with eyes of fire, the bystanders "thought it good that the Witch were brought before a Justice." Thus the nearly 60-year-old Gooderidge and her "witch" mother Elizabeth Wright were taken to the Justice of the Peace. Gooderidge confessed to having cursed the boy, but explained that she had thought him to be another youth who had broken her basket of eggs. The Justice of the Peace tested the boy by having him read from John 1, which resulted in another fit. Thus the judge ordered the accused to face their accuser, but Wright's mere glance caused the boy further quaking which ended only with her withdrawal. These tests justified the search for the witch's mark (the extra nipple used to feed a demonic familiar), which was found on Elizabeth, although on Alice only a fresh wound was discovered which was assumed to be her effort to remove evidence. Gooderidge was therefore committed to the Derby gaol.

Darling played the role of Puritan demoniac with aplomb, dramatically reenacting Christ's resistance to Satan's temptations, crying out "Doost thou say thou art my god, and that I am thy sonne?: Auoyde Sathan, there is no God saue the Lord of hosts," and "And dost thou say, that if I wil not worship thee, thou wilt torment me three times more; if thou torment me three hundred times, yet canst thou not touch my soule." When the demon was pressed for the witch's identity, Darling voiced the Devil's reply, "thy Mistris hath giuen thee a drop of her bloud to thy dinner, and that therefore thou wilt tel no tales of her?" At least one acquaintance remained unconvinced, grilling the boy with critical queries and telling him to stop the pretense. Upset, Darling confronted him, saying,

> you bade me I should not dissemble, saying that there was no witches: also you asked of me if I thought there were a god? God blesse me from such comforters: I pray you al pray for me that the Lord would deliuer mee from this temptation: at which wordes speaking hee was ouerthrowne into a cruell fit; which beeing ended, that man which thought there was no witches departed.

By implication such skepticism toward the reality of the boy's bewitchment was diabolically inspired.

Confronted again by Darling's convulsions, Gooderidge admitted "that she indeed did vex the childe, but if they would forgiue her, it should cease." In early May, after a soothsayer applied upon her a mild form of torture (heating a pair of new shoes on her feet until they tightened painfully, a procedure our pamphleteer thought ridiculous), she finally confessed: "I met the boy in the wood, the first saterday in Lent, and passing by me, he called me witch of Stapen hil: vnto whom I said, Euery boy doth call me witch, but did I euer make thy arse to itch?" Later she added that when she had stooped to the ground "the Diuell appeared to me in likenesse of a little partie-colored dog red and white, and I called him Minn. Seeing that euerie boy calleth mee witch, therefore goe thy waies and torment this boy in euerie part of his bodie at thine owne pleasure . . ." After these words Darling's fearsome cat became a dog.

Meanwhile, the boy was visited by more godly ministers, one of whom was a Mr. Hildersham of Ashby de la Zouch who tested the boy's faith, concluding,

> howsoeuer the Papists boasted much of the power their priests had to cast out diuells, and the simple euerie where noted it as a great

discredit to the Ministers of the Gospel, that they do want this power, yet did he professe there was no such gift in them, that thogh the Lord oft in these daies, by the praiers of the faithful casts out diuels, yet could he not assure them to cure him. To holde this faith of myracles to remaine still in the church, is an opinion dangerous.

Hildersham's advice was not long maintained, for close on his heels came one John Darrell, a Puritan divine whose career with helping possessed teenagers had begun in 1586. Against his many detractors and skeptics, Darrell assured Darling that his demonic possession was real, and that he must vigorously resist Satan, for to fail was a sin. He gave the boy and his guardians a book called *The Enemy of Securitie,* told them what to expect next and to pray and fast. Although Darrell soon left the scene to avoid charges of seeking "vainglory," Darling followed the preacher's script and as the bystanders sang Psalms and prayed, the boy's visions now alternated between sightings of Christ and the apostles and terrifying visions of drunkards, swearers, and filthy talkers being punished in hell and of apocalyptical scenes of the Last Judgment. Finally the demons admitted defeat, saying, "we cannot preuayle, let vs goe out of him, and enter into some of these heere." The alarmed viewers were saved by their pious activities and the demons departed, shouting "Wee cannot preuaile, for they will not be holpen with Witches. Brother Radulhus we cannot preuaile: let vs goe to our mistres and torment her, I haue had a draught of her blood to day." The boy recovered while the witch was overcome with a sudden attack of "the Ague," dying before sentencing.[63]

This was, however, not to be the end of the matter for the other protagonists; when Darrell faced his own trial for fraud, Darling and his Bible-reading friend Jesse Bee were summoned to testify. Under pressure Darling confessed to counterfeiting his possession, although he retracted this once released. For his part Bee continued to believe in Darling's heavenly speeches (Darrell now admitted that they may have been the work of Satan) although he commented that Darling had caused some of his fits during the Bible-reading sessions so that "when the word of God was read, those who were present might thereby the better bee brought to thinke that the devil could not abide it, & so have a more due and godly regard afterwardes for it."[64] At least for the next few years, Darling remained a convinced Puritan, in 1602 suffering a whipping and mutilation of his ears for his zeal. Although Darrell's opponents concluded Darling's fits were fraudulent, it must be remembered that the discredited exorcist had entered Darling's story late in the day. It seems fairest to explain Darling's ecstatic behavior as a result of unconscious psychological forces of repression and projection that afflicted many of the hyper-godly.

Doubting one's election was a frequent subject of Calvinist sermons, tracts, and individual counseling. For example, the 1585 tract *A Godly and comfortable treatise* could have provided a script for Darling's behavior. For those godly periodically vexed by doubt, the author reassured that thoughts of despair were from the Devil, against whom one must not dispute, for he is far too subtle an opponent, but merely "saye shortlye vnto him: away Sathan with sorrow, it is written, Thou shalt not tempt the Lord thy God."[65] Darling's victory over Satan affirmed for his anxious audience the veracity of the Protestant portrayal of the spirit realm. Darrell was not without defenders, one of whom interpreted his persecution as part of the battle against "Papistes and Atheistes." While most Calvinists were skeptical about exorcisms, our writer argued that it was blasphemy to deny the ability of the godly minister to cast out demons "at the prayer and fasting of his holy people." This divine power, he asserted, was distinct from the "false miracles" of the "Romish Synagogue" which "draw foolish people to their vaine superstition." In contrast, Darrell's "dispossessions" had inspired a religious revival which Satan opposed by discrediting Darrell's ministry by having the "Papists" deny that there is "any such power to be in our Church;" inspiring atheists to "scorne whatsoever tendeth to prove that there is a God or a Divel;" and, most grievously, egging on their own clergy to deny Darrell a fair hearing and spread rumors that Darrell had "cast out Divells by witchcraft or coniuration." Behind this trial lay the question of the existence of the spiritual realm and of God himself. The author concluded:

> Because Atheists abound in these dayes and witchcraft is called into question. Which error is confirmed by denying disposession & both these errors confirm Atheists mightily. For thus will they gather if 11. possessed (at sundry times & in sundry places) were all counterfeits, why should we thinke there is any possession at all? If neither possession, nor witchcraft, ... why should we thinke that there are Divells? If no Divells, no God."[66]

The justices were not convinced and, as James Sharpe notes, the publicity of this case "served to discredit exorcism in the Church of England."[67]

As the Puritan ministers became increasingly frustrated with the slow pace of reform on the part of Elizabeth I's government, they turned to strengthening the devotion of their flocks, untainted by doubt in their divine mission. By the 1590s many of them were convinced that the Reformation was an utter failure.[68] Some were led into separatism, while others, such as Gifford, continued to fight for the erasing of blasphemy from the entire realm. This frustration becomes evident in pamphlets describing witch trials, such as *A Detection of damnable driftes, practiced by three Witches arraigned at Chelmisforde in Essex* of 1579, which warned against being lulled into a false sense of security by the limited Reformation undertaken by Elizabeth. Instead, believers must beware the "Ambushementes of Sathan" who draws the simple into silly witchcraft, and plots treason against her majesty with those in high positions. The solution was for everyone to "stop by all possible meanes" any incidents of witchcraft in their neighborhoods and through prayer and "assured faithe in the merites of Christ Jesus shield thy self."[69]

In another pamphlet describing the trial of four accused witches from Windsor, the author opined that

> among the punishmentes whiche the Lorde GOD hath laied vpon vs, for the manifest impietie and carelesse contempt of his woorde, aboundyng in these our desperate daies, the swarmes of Witches, and Inchaunters are not the laste nor the leaste. For that old Serpent Sathan, suffred to be the scourage for our sinns, hath of late yeares, greately multiplyed the broude of them, and muche encreased their malice.

Such diabolical magic was a canker upon the body politic, he suggested, one that many lower justices too readily winked at. Though without the Devil witches could do no magic, still by the law of God and of this land they were to be executed as traitors to her highness and realm.[70] And in another trial account from 1589, from Chelmsford, Essex, the author used the story as a lesson for readers to "with-draw our filthy affections and naughty dispositions," to curb the "desire of our diuelish appetites." The testimony of the elderly widow Joan Cunny added weight to this homily, for she had confessed that her familiar spirits had been unable to harm some men, including the local parson, because they "had at their comming a strong faith in God, and had inuocated and called vpon him, that they could doo them no harme." A daily, practiced piety was the best defense against the spite of witches.[71]

For both Protestant and Catholic tellers of these possession stories, the intended goal was to frighten the faithful away from ungodly living and heretical notions and toward full conformity to official orthodoxy, indeed, an eradication of religious doubt. Specific charges against witches, however, arose usually not from the elites but from neighbors deeply fearful of the power of suspected witches. As Protestants sought to replace magical remedies with prayer and bold assertions of faith, many ordinary folk took offenders to the courts where it was widely believed God provided special protective power to the judge and court officials against the machinations of both the alleged witch and the Devil. Thomas Cooper, a prominent vicar and author of *The Mystery of Witchcraft*, wrote that the power of witches was restrained by divine providence and the magistrate's authority. "For though, if a priuate person detain them, they may either hurt or escape, yet if once the magistrate hath arrested them, Satans power ceaseth." Cooper's long treatise illustrates also how witchcraft and possession cases could be used in the battle against doubt. Cooper's 1617 work sought to uncover the "seuerall Stratagems of Sathan, ensnaring the poore Soule by this desperate practize of annoying the bodie: with the seuerall Vses thereof to the Church of Christ. Very necessary for the redeeming of these Atheisticall and secure times." Like a talisman, *The Mystery of Witchcraft* was to act as "a preseruatiue against the secret Atheisme that fretteth like a Gangrene," threatening to sap the life out of religion.[72] That virtually no one explicitly rejected the existence of God did not matter, for those who disputed the reality of specters or demonic possession, for example, were in Cooper's mind incipient atheists, upon whom could be projected one's own doubts, making a physical enemy of an inner state.

Scotland

As the witch-hunts of the Scottish lowlands were promoted by secular and church authorities they were quite intense. After the legal implementation of the Reformation in 1560, the Protestant clergy became important governmental assistants to local lords. They significantly raised the standard for lay participation in religion and their sermons, preached before captive parish audiences, proved powerful forms of indoctrination on several fronts.[73] In the minds of the Scottish King James VI and his Protestant divines, the witch was a monstrous criminal who had committed the ultimate treason by rejecting God and entering into a compact with the Devil, hence charges of *maleficia* played second fiddle to the diabolical and heretical elements. Prior to the 1563 law condemning the practice of magic and transferring jurisdiction for witch-hunting from ecclesiastical to secular courts, witch trials were rare, although three witches were burned in St. Andrews in 1542. The new statute did not immediately precipitate witch persecutions, as over the next few decades the Reformed clergy and General Assembly were preoccupied with the campaign to make the crown give the Kirk sessions greater power to deal with "heresies, blasphemie, witchcraft, and violation of the Sabbath day."[74] Instead, Scottish witch-hunting occurred between 1590 and 1662, with national hunts in 1590–1 (those overseen by James VI), 1597 (the year of James I's *Daemonologie*), 1629–30, 1649, and 1661–2. Altogether Christina Larner estimates over 1,000 executions, many of these during brief, terrifying witch panics reminiscent of the German model, such as that of the small county of East Lothian in 1649 which led to the burning of over 200 accused.

The first major Scottish witch trial was that conducted in 1591 in North Berwick under the command of James VI who was investigating a treasonous plot to sink his flotilla by storm as it sailed from Denmark. This case began when David Seaton, a deputy bailiff of Tranent, suspected his maid Geillis Duncane of practicing evil magic because she had developed a reputation as a successful healer. By application of crude torture Seaton forced her to confess and provide the names of several other alleged witches, including the elderly Agnes Sampson, an Edinburgh woman called Agnes Thompson, the skipper Robert Grierson, and a schoolteacher named Doctor Fian (John Cuningham). Some of these confessed to bewitching the former Earl of Angus whose mortal ailment had confounded his physicians. Soon news of the case reached the King, and he decided to attend further deliberations personally. Before his majesty Sampson and Thompson described diabolical sabbath meetings of more than 200 participants wherein the Devil proclaimed his utter hatred of James VI and commanded his minions to do away with him. James was apparently incredulous, but when Sampson took him aside and divulged to him the words that he had spoken to his Queen Anne on their wedding night in Norway, he was convinced. Sampson then provided the recipe for the magical poison she had prepared for the king and described how the witches had stirred up a peculiar wind that divided the King's ship from the flotilla, although the plot ultimately failed because his faith "preuayled aboue their ententions."[75]

Convinced of the threat against his person, James VI composed his own demonological treatise and exerted royal pressure to eradicate the threat, leading to an indiscriminate witch-hunt in 1597 which surpassed accusations of royal treason and ultimately required the King's intervention to stop the denunciation of the innocent. Thereafter, witchcraft remained an important tool in the power struggle between ecclesiastical and secular authorities, while the Calvinist clergy, knowing full well the King's personal interest in witchcraft, sought to placate James by pursuing action against witches. This seems to have been the principal motivation behind the witch-hunt in Aberdeenshire in 1596–7.[76] Thus, while they did not normally promote witch-hunting, Scottish ministers and elders assisted in interrogations and, as members of the General Assembly, they applied constant pressure on the government to construct a godly state by eradicating superstition and witchcraft. Later witch-hunts, such as the 1649 panic, which accounted for several hundred more trials, mostly in East Lothian and Berwickshire, were part of a crusade to depict the government as a "covenanted" state which could claim direction from God as readily as the clergy.[77] A period of relative calm during the interregnum was inspired by Oliver Cromwell's justices who were more skeptical about witchcraft accusations and forbade the use of torture. However, with the Restoration, witch-hunts were revived in 1661–2, leading to over 600 trials and about 300 deaths. Once again, concern over the mechanics of the witch panic led the Privy Council to enact new legislation making such chain reaction witch-hunts virtually impossible and to try witch-hunters and "prickers" for fraud.

Thus in Scotland trials against witches became part of a larger dispute between a newly Protestantized church and state representatives over who controlled morality, whereas in England the clergy were never as powerful a force as their Scottish brethren. In both regions, however, the preaching and propagandizing of clergy, especially of the Calvinist variety, were important factors in the development of a particularly guilt-laden attitude among lay people, an attitude which in some cases resulted in sudden outbreaks of demonic possession or witch denunciations. In neither realm, however, were these unusual incidents the expressed wish of the preachers, although some of them quickly found ways to manipulate such preternatural behavior to their confessional advantage.

Ireland

On the other hand, trials were rare in Ireland, even after the Irish Parliament passed its own witchcraft statute in 1586. One trial involved a Protestant minister John Aston charged with using magic to discover the whereabouts of treasure. In a more typical case from 1661 a Florence Newton was charged with witchcraft. As the "Witch of Youghal" this woman already possessed a reputation for witchcraft, so that when she was refused charity at the home of John Pyne, it is natural that she would be accused of magically causing the fits of one of his servants, Mary Longdon. However, even at this late date, Newton was not compelled to confess to diabolical activities or involvement in a conspiracy, and no hunt ensued.[78] Although belief in witchcraft was promoted by Protestant settlers and missionaries in the second half of the seventeenth century, Ireland remained almost entirely Catholic and its extremely popular fairies were not successfully converted to witches until the nineteenth century. A major reason for this, one which we will explore in the next chapter, was the fact that Ireland remained relatively unmoved by the confessional conflicts or campaigns to inculcate proper religiosity that were the hallmark of its neighbors, England and Scotland, or that would later convulse it.[79]

Conclusion

We shall turn to other regions of witch persecution in the next chapter when we discuss the "periphery" of witch-hunting – the Mediterranean regions, Scandinavia, and Eastern Europe – which either started witch-hunting late or were not seriously caught up in such activity to begin with. That chapter will also discuss the effects of changes within the religious and political sphere on the decline of witch-hunting. Before embarking on that enterprise, it will be useful to summarize a few of the major points made in this chapter on the intersections between the Reformations and the sudden revival of witch-hunting.

What lay behind the origins of witch-hunting (as opposed to magic or witchcraft which were endemic features of the European landscape) was the need to defend particular religious beliefs against both heretical challenges, such as Anabaptism, and inner doubt. As the Jews before them, alleged witches and demoniacs provided tangible proof of the reality of the Christian supernatural realm. And while many ordinary peasant denouncers of local witches were not deeply concerned about the diabolical conspiracy, their social betters and religious leaders clearly were. Atheism was a term freely tossed about in the religious propaganda, yet most of those accused of this blasphemy were, in fact, deeply religious individuals who condemned the political interlinking of church and state so important to both popular religion and the authorities. The cross-confessional belief in the nearness of the apocalypse added urgency to the campaign to establish a purified and firm faith, one that necessitated the demonization and eradication of "peasant superstitions." As we shall see next, the witch persecution too increased skepticism, leading many authorities to suppress it at about the same time that they gave up efforts to enforce confessional conformity.

6

RELIGIOUS PLURALISM AND THE END OF THE WITCH-HUNTS

It is strange to see the madness of the people, that will ask the devil who sent him. And then he telleth who is his dame [i.e., the witch], and to how many she hath sent him, and how many he hath killed. If it were the Devil indeed, would they believe him? Is it not his desire to bring innocent persons into danger? ... it is no godly zeal but furious rage, wherewith the common sort are carried against witches. Moreover there be none more extreme haters of witches, than such as be infected with a kind of witchcraft themselves: for what are they but witches ... which have their night spell, and so many charms & devices to avoid the dangers of witchcraft, or to unwitch? None are more furious against witches than these, & such as of all others are ye readiest to run for help unto the devil: therefore I may boldly affirm, that it is of a mad rage, and not of a good zeal that the most are carried withall against witches.

> George Gifford, *A Discourse of the Subtill Practises of Devilles by Vvitches and Sorcerers*. (London, 1587), G4v and I1v [spelling modernized].

George Gifford was no religious skeptic but a devout Puritan preacher who decried the "vulgar" fear of witches and called for judicial caution. Yet, his fiery sermons raised the dreadful specter of a demonic plot between the Antichrist – the papacy – and his apocalyptical beastly assistants – Protestant dissidents, especially Familists and Baptists. Did he thereby restrain or encourage fear of demonic witchcraft? Where belief in a diabolical conspiracy embraced both populace and rulers, judicial action against Satan's presumed minions was the result. There were a variety of factors determining the extent of witch-hunting in a particular territory, including the relative independence of local courts, the use of torture, the prevalence of communal tensions, and the anxiety produced by plagues or climatic, social, and economic crises. The goal in this chapter is more narrowly to evaluate the religious aspects behind the absence or ending of witch-hunting. Beginning with the Dutch Republic, where trials against both heresy and witchcraft were suppressed remarkably early, the discussion will move to areas under the jurisdiction of the Mediterranean Inquisitions (Italy, Spain, and Portugal) where suppression of heresy remained a priority but where there was no corresponding transition to witch-hunting; and then to regions where witch-hunting arrived late, such as Scandinavia and Eastern Europe. It will finally examine the role of religion in the eventual stifling of witch-hunts in the Empire, France and England.

This deliberation follows Stuart Clark's suggestion that one reason "for the decline of witchcraft prosecutions and of witchcraft beliefs in general was the coming of a religious pluralism that permitted the members of all types of churches to coexist and spelt the end of the confessional state."[1] Using the typology developed by the eminent sociologist Ernst Troeltsch, Clark defines a "church" type as universal, compulsory, and conservative, reinforcing the secular order's hierarchies, while sects were selective, voluntary, aimed at personal perfection, and condemnatory of the secular realm. A state church viewed witchcraft as "a serious counter-institutional competitor" for the fidelity of its members, the witch as a rival to the official priesthood, and the witches' sabbath as the diabolical reverse of the approved liturgy. In contrast, for sectarians, the state church was part of the secular world and its devils were of no concern. Most sectarians – Anabaptists, spiritualists, Familists, and Quakers – identified the Devil with their persecutors or spiritualized him altogether, in the process suppressing fear of witchcraft among their members.

In broad terms, Clark's typology helps predict the level of witch-hunting in a particular region. First, where a church-type model was enforced upon the populace by the authorities, there was a concomitant suppression of religious deviance and of skepticism toward the official dogma. The propaganda accompanying this campaign dehumanized and demonized the religious "Other" to make the populace less sympathetic to the subversive notions of dissidents. The resulting climate of suspicion was amenable to witch-hunting, as local officials and ordinary folk were commanded to look out for heretical and diabolical activity in their vicinity.

Such was the case for the centers of major witch-hunting, such as the Empire, Switzerland, or Scotland. Second, in territories where a church type was followed but with some informal accommodation for "quiet" religious dissidents, as in England, there was a lower level of witch-hunting, but even here tensions produced by the polemical warfare among Puritans, sectarians, and Catholics helped foster some localized witch panics.

Third, in those areas where there was no significant religious competition to the state church, or where there were present effective tools to keep such in check, or where a large segment of the population willingly adopted the official ideology, there was little need to encourage massive witch-hunting. This was the case in the regions under the jurisdiction of the Spanish, Portuguese, Roman, and Venetian Inquisitions. And finally, where the authorities adopted a sect model for religious affiliation, not enforcing membership in a state church and allowing a degree of religious pluralism, there was little desire to hunt witches; this was the situation in many parts of Eastern Europe until the middle of the seventeenth century (when the "church-type" model became predominant) and in the Dutch Republic.

The Dutch Republic

For those scholars who use a social crisis model to explain witchcraft panics, the Dutch Republic remains an enigma. It endured many of the same climatic, economic, and political crises as regions with major witch panics, and for the eighty years between the start of its war of independence against Spain in 1568 and the final victory in 1648, the United Provinces of the Dutch Republic was an embattled realm, one that, during the pauses in the conflict, should have seen at least a few witch panics on a scale similar to its southern neighbor, the Spanish Netherlands. Prior to the revolt, both the northern and southern provinces of the Low Countries had conducted one of the worst heresy persecutions outside of Spain. Yet it appears that the elites who led the Dutch Republic did not suffer from the particular religious mindset amenable to persecution mania, unlike their Catholic opponents. Instead, once embarked on their war with Spain, the Dutch authorities showed little desire to allow or encourage persecution of heretics of any kind. For one thing, they had aligned themselves with the Calvinists who, the object of vicious persecution themselves, preferred persuasion rather than the stake to achieve a unitary Calvinist realm. The lack of publication of demonological works throughout the sixteenth century, moreover, strongly suggests little market for such literature.[2] After a quick summary of witch-hunting in the Republic's most populace province, Holland, we will consider the factors behind the country's distinctiveness.

A total of 193 adults, mostly women, were formally accused of witch-craft in Holland, thirty-three to thirty-five of whom were executed (a relatively low execution rate of 18 percent overall). The peak periods of persecution occurred around 1540, 1564, 1585, and 1591. The last three periods can be linked to economic difficulties, as the year 1564 marked the beginning of the economic conflict between England and the Low Countries and the blocking by Denmark of the Sound, the major conduit for Amsterdam trade. Most of the witches tried in 1564 were from regions heavily dependent upon such international trade, although Hans de Waardt notes that it was "probably more the feeling that prosperity was suddenly and unexpectedly in grave danger that stirred up fear of witchcraft and not so much the actual economic depression."[3] In the latter two peaks, 1585 and 1591, Spanish ships made fishing the North Sea a virtual impossibility and most of these trials were conducted in fishing towns, while many of the prosecuted women were accused of causing shipwrecks. Even so, the number of executions was extremely small and to describe even the worst year of witch persecution in Holland as a panic is misleading.

The Republic's ongoing war against Spanish hegemony has been depicted as a reason for its lack of interest in hunting witches. However, the magistrates of the Spanish Netherlands showed no comparable reluctance to hunt witches during the civil war. A more likely reason for the Republic's distinctiveness in this regard was its booming economy. Its peasants resembled self-conscious entrepreneurs producing for the world market while urbanites possessed a remarkable range of social and economic mobility; both were less susceptible to fear diabolical conspiracies. The lack of a strong, central authority in Holland after 1581 also allowed this tolerance to win the upper hand and be enshrined in the law and governance of the realm.[4]

After seeking advice from the professors of the University of Leiden, in 1593/94 Holland's central court forbade the use of torture and the water test in witchcraft cases, making conviction extremely difficult. The last person to be executed in Holland for the crime of witchcraft was a woman burned in 1608 (the first in fourteen years), while the last formal indictment led to an acquittal in 1614; through the course of its "Golden Age", the province suppressed all further trials against withcraft.

Compared to its immediate neighbors to the south and east, these are extraordinarily early dates for the legal squelching of witch trials. Even in the "heartland" of witchcraft persecution in the northern Netherlands, the province of Groningen, its two major "panics" took place quite early, in 1547 (twenty executions) and 1562 (five). The relative disinterest in witch persecution was certainly not from a sudden disbelief in the reality of witchcraft or a lack of desire of commoners to oppose *maleficia*, for belief in witchcraft, soothsaying, and other forms of popular magic remained important aspects of "popular" culture well into the nineteenth century.[5] There was therefore something quite distinctive about Dutch culture that made skepticism toward diabolical conspiracies a stronger force than elsewhere. What most distinguished its religious life from that of the south was the remarkable informal tolerance that developed in the former as compared to the uniform and aggressive Tridentine Catholicism promoted by the Spanish rulers of the latter. In the Dutch Republic the members of the States General decided against giving Calvinism the powers of a state church, although they did grant it privileged status as the only officially approved confession. Adherents of the others – Lutheran, Mennonite, and Catholic – were informally permitted to continue their own forms of worship, although for a time all unconverted Catholic priests were expelled from the realm, and other restrictions were placed, in ascending order, on Lutheran, Mennonite, and Catholic worship which had to be contained within sanctuaries hidden from street view (however, the rise to power in 1619 of the ardent Calvinist Prince Mauritz led to the temporary exile of the dissident Arminians). In other words, the authorities did not engage in a concerted effort to enforce a unitary faith upon its citizens or to expel all forms of doubt or heterodoxy, despite the pressure of individual zealous Calvinist pastors for them to do so. Instead, the Reformed Church remained a voluntary society, and in many regions attracted only a minority of citizens as members, while the government continued on its path of religious accommodation for the sake of good business. For the Catholic priest Cornelius Loos, this apparent victory of heresy and of religious toleration was the real enemy, not some imaginary sect of witches.

Here too spiritualism, with its depreciation of confessional conformity and promotion of religious tolerance, was quite strong and the Republic developed the dubious reputation as a comfortable home for a wide range of foreign unorthodox groups, such as the Polish Socinians who rejected the doctrine of the trinity, English Separatists, and conversos and Jews from Portugal and Spain. Mennonites soon found themselves struggling with how to retain their self-image as God's martyred elect in a non-persecuting realm in which many of their number were prospering. Even prior to the Reformation, Dutch theologians, strongly influenced by Erasmian humanism, had shown a pronounced reluctance to adopt the sacramental and diabolical realism of a Heinrich Krämer, although Hans de Waardt finds little evidence of a dominant skepticism among Netherlandic jurists until the generation of those born around 1600.[6] Moreover, prior to the 1560s the authorities conducted several vicious judicial campaigns against Anabaptists, although most of these occurred in the aftermath of Anabaptist militancy or were pressed upon local authorities by the Habsburg government. As the citizenry learned to tolerate the religious "Others" in their midst, they were less threatened by the expression of dissident religious notions.

A public controversy over exorcism in Utrecht in the 1590s nicely illustrates the points raised here about the distinctiveness of Dutch religious attitudes. Like most of the Republic's cities, Utrecht (formerly the region's ecclesiastical capital) was a religiously diverse community with large Calvinist and Catholic, and smaller Lutheran and Mennonite congregations, as well as a significant group of spiritualists or libertines who often blended in with the other confessions.[7] Since public Catholic worship was not yet permitted, staged exorcisms proving the supernatural superiority of Catholic priests were not possible. Yet Catholic exorcists still quietly performed their ministry and many ordinary Protestants, now disallowed the use of countermagic to cure bewitchment, often availed themselves of priestly services, much to the chagrin of Reformed preachers who had considerable difficulty in offering their flocks effective alternative defenses against Satanic assault.

The debate in Utrecht began with the possession of a velour maker, David Wardavoir, reported in 1595 by a Calvinist pamphleteer who refuted Catholic rumors that Wardavoir had been cured by the exorcism of Catholic priests, for he was instead "delivered not through conjurations, as is the usage among the exorcists, but by God's grace through a constant faith."[8] However, after 1599 such propaganda was neutralized when an unusual Reformed minister, Johannes Bergerus, arrived in the city. A former Bavarian Franciscan and then Lutheran pastor, Bergerus had already been forced out of several Reformed parishes in rural Groningen for a variety of offences. Bergerus sought to fill the void for Protestant exorcists, although his techniques were unorthodox even by Catholic standards. For example, one of his bewitchment remedies said to take "thrice-three teeth of a dead-man's head, pulverize them and make a fumigation from them, and vomit; take the witch's excrement and put it in one of your shoes and put it [i.e. that shoe] on the other, wrong foot." Given that Reformed individuals plagued by witchcraft were supposed to take the "religious high ground" by "an enlightened dependence upon God's grace alone," it is easy to see how Bergerus attracted a large clientele among the less certain of Utrecht's Protestant population.[9]

In response, in 1603 several of his ministerial colleagues, led by Johannes Lindenius and Johannes Gerobulus, publicly denounced the exorcist and his demoniacs as frauds. However, two of the latter, the sisters-in-law Mayken Huberts and Clara Gelaudens, whose afflictions had begun some time earlier and who as demoniacs were currently recipients of civic alms, rushed to Gerobulus' home and threw themselves at its door. They then moved their anti-skeptic campaign to the main city square, drawing large crowds with their loud shouting. Even when thrown into jail, the two women's voices attracted the curious around the prison's windows. The sheriff released the women into their husbands' custody, but the latter, poor textile workers, took the unusual step of filing a lawsuit against Lindenius for blasphemy and slander for denying their wives' possession. The council, sensing the large support for the plaintiffs, acted circumspectly by putting the demoniacs to the typical tests of possession. When Mayken's demon refused to translate some Latin, the court proceeded with its efforts to determine if the women were frauds, mad, true demoniacs, or witches. In the end, despite compelling evidence of fraud, the court merely ordered the husbands to keep their wives out of public view, otherwise they would be cast into the madhouse. The most important goal of the magistrates was to dissipate the dangerous tensions that had arisen in the city. The case reveals the widespread belief in demonic possession, the difficulty that "skeptics" faced in counteracting such sentiment, and the opportunity that possession offered even poor women to defy learned ministers, for the voice of the demoniac was that of a powerful, if malevolent, male spirit.

The skeptical tradition and Balthasar Bekker

Elsewhere, such defiance toward leading ecclesiastical figures might have led to trials and executions. By adopting a voluntaristic church model, the Republic shied away from state persecution of heterodoxy. Thus the notions of radical reformers, such as Mennonites and spiritualists, were allowed to intermingle with the region's mainstream religious discourse, influencing many who did not regard themselves as dissidents. One such idea was the spiritualization of the Devil, equating him essentially with inner sinful desires. Even some of the Reformed clergy were infected with this idea, such as Hubert Duifhuis (c.1517–81) of Utrecht and Herman Herberts (1540–1607) of Dordrecht and Gouda, the latter of whom was investigated as an adept of Joris and who had published a controversial tract identifying each person's evil thoughts, not the Pope, as the Antichrist.[10] For such spiritualistic-minded individuals, "there is no mightier witchcraft in the human than the ensnared holiness that he received in the flesh [i.e., preoccupation with religious ceremonies]" as the spiritualist Hendrik Jansen Barrefelt put it around 1580.[11] Undoubtedly the most influential Dutch spiritualist of the century was Dirk Volkerts Coornhert (1522–90), who in 1572 became secretary of state to Prince William of Orange, encouraging him to adopt a policy of religious toleration for the young Republic. Coornhert, a Catholic with spiritualistic tendencies, was an acquaintance of Hendrick Niclaes and knew the writings of Joris. Although he rejected the narcissistic claims of both prophets, Coornhert followed their condemnation of theological dogmatism, intolerance, and sectarianism. Like them he restricted the Devil's work to the mind where he caused people to fixate on doctrinal precision instead of brotherly love.[12]

As witch prosecutions rose across Europe, a number of Dutch Mennonites wrote works on the subject, all opting for an extremely limited role for the Devil that largely undercut belief in demonic witchcraft. For example, in 1638 Jan Jansz Deutel, a Mennonite printer of Hoorn, emphasized the impotence of the Devil and chastized people for ascribing powers to him that belonged only to God. Marijke Gijswijt-Hofstra suggests that Deutel's position was "positively revolutionary," for his "denial of the power of the devil was in complete contrast to the ruling theological opinions."[13] Mennonites opposed the witch persecutions for another very practical reason: they themselves had been the target of a vicious demonization campaign that had led to torture and execution of hundreds. Such sentiment was expressed in 1659 by the Mennonite cloth merchant Abraham Palingh (c.1588–1682), who implored the magistrates of his city, Haarlem, not to prosecute old women maliciously accused of witchcraft, suggesting instead that they be treated in Haarlem's hospital. He condemned the persecution zeal of both Catholics and Lutherans and ridiculed their fear of witchcraft, which was a mere deception of the Devil.[14]

Such radical notions were kept alive in the Dutch Republic also in the salon-like gatherings of undogmatic advocates of religious exploration and toleration known as the Collegiants, which included a variety of confessional adherents, from Socinian to Mennonite to Reformed. In the course of their discussions, the Collegiants eventually shed the eschato-logical and theological notions of their predecessors and became advocates of rationalism, skepticism, and broad-based religious freedom. They also came to deny the intervention in the human realm of both evil spirits and angels.[15] Among those influenced by these ideas was the learned Reformed preacher of Amsterdam, Balthasar Bekker (1634–97), who in 1693 published his famous book, *The Bewitched World*, arguing that the Devil possessed no physical reality but was merely a symbol of evil within humans, while a few years earlier he had translated an English witch trial pamphlet, using it to expose the absurd nature of the charges. Despite the strength of the spiritualizing currents that we have been describing, Bekker's opinions ignited a storm of controversy that in the end cost him his job.[16] His opponents sought to discredit him by associating his beliefs with the views of: Joris; Thomas Hobbes (1588–1679), who fashioned a thoroughly materialistic conception of the universe; Benedict Spinoza (1632–77), who suggested that knowledge gained from religious sources was uncertain compared to that of the natural order; and Socinians. They were also deeply disturbed by Bekker's championing of Descartes' Cartesianism, which many feared would leave God out of the scientific picture entirely.[17]

Collegiantism and Cartesianism were not the only routes to depreciating the Devil's agency in human affairs. Another was Neoplatonic mysticism. Pico della Mirandola's efforts to construct a complete harmonization of human religion did not die out with him. Instead, it was revived later in the sixteenth century in the wake of the posthumous publication of the medical and religious writings of Paracelsus. Central to Paracelsus' writings was alchemy, which later adepts combined with their reading of the Jewish Cabala to discover the essential unifying principle of all know-ledge, natural and religious. This search for perfection culminated in the person of the Dutch Paracelsian physician and Cabalist Francis Mercury van Helmont (1614–98), whose writings promoted both religious toler-ation and scientific empiricism.[18] Unconventional religious exploration and alchemy were no strangers to scientific empiricism; Isaac Newton, founder of the law of gravity, was also an alchemist and biblical scholar who metamorphosed the Devil into human evil desires.[19] What united these disparate groups and individuals, from Joris to the Collegiants to

Bekker and Van Helmont, however, was a passion to promote religious tolerance. The Dutch Republic's environment provided fertile soil for such ideas to flourish.

Witchcraft and the Mediterranean Inquisitions: Italy and Spain

The Inquisitions of Rome, Venice, Spain, and Portugal were also remarkably restrained when it came to persecuting witches. Some of the earliest witch trials had occurred in Italy, strongly encouraged by preachers such as Bernardino of Siena and by local efforts at communal moral cleansing. Yet witch trials here peaked by 1550 and were concentrated thereafter in northern Italy, such as those in the Friuli against the Benandanti. In this case, Inquisitors were shocked by popular belief in a cult of "good men" who periodically left their bodies to defend the crops against evil sorcerers. Over years of interrogations, Inquisitors transformed the Benandanti from the good men into conventional witches.[20]

For the first several decades of their existence the Inquisitions of Rome and Venice were preoccupied with the Protestant threat, while Spain's tribunals remained fixated on the converso problem. Until the 1580s, 80 percent of cases brought before the Venetian Inquisition involved Protestants of some type (including a few dozen Anabaptists), while in the southern, Spanish-ruled regions of Italy, more defendants were accused of harboring Islamic beliefs than Protestant. As for persecution of Jews or Judaisers, only the Holy Office of Sicily – which was reorganized by Spanish authorities in 1537 – persecuted Jews to any significant extent, and even here interest waned after 1560. After 1580, by which time Protestantism had been suppressed, Inquisitors broadened their scope of activities as they sought to remold popular religiosity and shore up Tridentine Catholicism. Attention accordingly shifted to eradicating popular "superstition," blasphemy, and irreligious behavior, and illicit magic replaced Protestantism as the single greatest charge brought before most Italian tribunals.[21] Even so, Inquisitors developed the reputation of being soft on the crime, for in their efforts to suppress magical superstition among the populace they showed little concern about witchcraft per se or about a supposed pact with the Devil. Instead, they applied the same rules in trying witches that they had used with Protestants, aiming for reconversion and rewarding the contrite with penance instead of death. Only the recalcitrant and repeat offenders were treated harshly.[22] Thus, while Italian Inquisitors heard many illicit magic cases, they executed very few. Instead, they used the trials as tools to bring the populace's beliefs and practices into harmony with Tridentine Catholicism. Illicit magic was therefore regarded as a crime equal to blasphemy and heresy, and the diabolical sabbath conspiracy was practically ignored.

The Compendium Maleficarum of Francesco Guazzo

This mildness on the part of Inquisitors was certainly not from a lack of local demonologists promoting witch-hunting, such as the Milanese monk Francesco Maria Guazzo whose *Compendium Maleficarum* was published in 1608. Like most such works, Guazzo's was highly derivative, borrowing heavily from the treatises of Krämer, Molitor, and more recently Rémy and Del Rio, although a series of woodcut drawings detailing each of the horrific acts of the sabbath was new. Ironically, Guazzo composed his treatise between 1605 and 1608 at the court of Duke John William of Cleves and Jülich, the very place where Johann Weyer had earlier written his skeptical tome. Circumstances had radically changed in the duchy, as the current duke had ended the irenical atmosphere of Weyer's day, committing himself to a fervent Tridentine Catholicism and to the eradication of witches, actions rewarded in 1596 with a dedication in Franz Agricola's anti-Weyer treatise on witchcraft, *Von Zauberen, Zauberinnen und Hexen* (*On Sorcerers, Sorceresses and Witches*). Guazzo was summoned by the duke who feared he had been bewitched by an old man who had committed suicide in prison rather than face the stake.

Guazzo's treatise unintentionally provides evidence of the strength of the skeptical tradition in his homeland. His purpose was "that men, considering the cunning of witches, might study to live piously and devoutly in the Lord." Fear of diabolical witchcraft thus served a positive religious function by driving people to the true faith, even though the Devil's assaults on firm believers could be as dangerous as his blatant attacks on the weak:

When he sees men of weak and timid mind, he takes them by storm: when he finds them dauntless and firm, he becomes as it were a cunning fox to deceive them: for he has a thousand means of hurting us, and he uses countless methods, superstitions and curious arts, to seduce men's minds from God and lead them to his own follies; and all these he wondrously performs by means of illusions and witchcraft.[23]

In other words, the Devil tempted the simple minded with crass witchcraft, but for the learned he used subtler tools, such as Protestantism or skepticism, to mislead believers. Even though the Devil was regarded as the father of lies, when he spoke out supporting Catholicism against Protestantism, Guazzo accepted his words as fact. For example, he recorded that the demon expelled in 1566 from Nicole Aubrey, the famed demoniac of Laon, "in the hearing of all mocked at the Calvinists, crying out that he had nothing to fear from them since they were his friends and allies."[24] When Luther died in 1546 at Eisleben, Guazzo added, "the demons flew to his funeral from those who were possessed." Moreover, he affirmed the physical reality of all sabbath activities, including flight, infanticide, and sexual intercourse with demons, aligning the spiritual interpretation with "the followers of Luther and Melancthon" who alleged that "witches went to their Sabbaths in imagination only, and that there was some diabolical illusion in the matter, alleging that their bodies had often been found lying at home in their beds and had never moved from them." Guazzo's rebuttal postulated that the Devil actually deceived spouses by placing a false body in the bed in lieu of the real partner, who was busy attending the sabbath.[25] A realist interpretation, he asserted, was now generally held by the theologians and jurists of Italy, Spain, and Catholic Germany. And while Guazzo did not explicitly identify diabolical witchcraft as a Protestant doing, he described the witches' desecration of Catholic sacraments in terms that could just as readily have applied to the iconoclastic Reformers. At their infamous meetings witches make vows never to adore the Eucharist and

> that they will both in word and deed heap continual insults and revilings upon the Blessed Virgin Mary and the other Saints; that they will trample upon and defile and break all the Relics and the images of the Saints; that they will abstain from using the sign of the Cross, Holy Water, blessed salt and bread and other things consecrated by the Church; that they will never make full confession of their sins to a priest; that they will maintain an obstinate silence concerning their bargain with the devil.[26]

A near century of anti-Anabaptist propaganda also had its effect, as Guazzo made diabolical rebaptism a prominent feature of the witches' sabbath, depicting it in a way strikingly similar to images of Mennonite baptismal ceremonies.

Like Krämer, Guazzo strongly defended sacramental realism and power, going beyond most other Catholic demonologists by asserting that the Devil could truly enrich his subjects and that witches, with God's permission, could actually control weather. For Guazzo, the Devil's inversionary scheme extended to the sacramental concept of *ex opere operato*, so that if a witch's magic proved ineffectual because God had protected an intended victim, then the witch had to turn the evil magic upon him or herself, for "the devil will not endure that the injunctions he has laid upon them should all come to nothing. And she to whom the fateful lot falls has to suffer the evil for them all." This supposedly happened to Catherine Praevotte of Freising whose efforts to poison a neighbor's daughter were repulsed by the prayers of the intended victim's mother. Satan therefore commanded Praevotte to poison her own infant. In this way Guazzo explained why some witch hexes proved impotent and provided, in a diabolical mirror image, a tangible confirmation of sacramental realism.

Mere expression of skepticism toward the witches' sabbath was a major sin:

> they who assert that all this is not true, but only a dream or an illusion, certainly sin in the lack of true reverence to our Mother the Church. For the Catholic Church punishes no crime that is not evident and manifest, and counts no one a heretic unless he has been caught in patent heresy. Now for many years the Church has counted witches as heretics and has ordered that they be punished by the Inquisitors... Therefore either the Church is in error, or they who maintain this belief.[27]

Like so many of his colleagues, Guazzo drew his line defending his belief system on the shifting sands of demonic witchcraft, arguing that to dispute one aspect of the witches' sabbath was to doubt all. Guazzo's extremely defensive tone reveals the strength of opposition within the Italian intelligentsia and Church hierarchy to his ultra-realist position.

Italian Inquisitions and witchcraft

However, many local Italian judges were like Guazzo extremely unhappy about the laxity of the Roman Inquisition toward witch persecution, and they began applying considerable pressure to be given jurisdiction for the crime. On November 28, 1619 this conflict climaxed with the execution, over the protests of the Roman Holy Office, of two alleged witches by the Milan court. Hoping to repulse charges of leniency, on March 20, 1623 Pope Gregory XV issued the Bull *Omnipotentis Dei*, officially decreeing the death sentence for even first offenders convicted of having apostatized to the Devil and killed others by *maleficia*. However, to ease the Bull's severity, prominent members of the Roman Holy Office composed and circulated some guidelines for Inquisitors as to the treatment of accused witches. These reveal considerable affinity with the writings of Catholic moderates, such as the Jesuit Adam Tanner's *Disputationes Theologicae* of 1617 which rejected the evidence of accused witches against their supposed coconspirators. In May, 1624 a senior member of the Holy Office sent a copy of the guidelines to a provincial official, advising that

> The question of witchcraft has always been considered fallacious and uncertain here, as it is, in fact; and, often, even experienced and knowledgeable persons have exceeded proper bounds, and quickly encountered difficulties, which occasioned errors prejudicial to the Holy Office, to inquisitors, and also to those instituting trials, since it is a crime difficult to verify, and in which a great role is played by the frivolity and flightiness of women, and the treachery of the Devil who is the teacher and father of lies. Therefore, in regard to what your lordship writes about the witches, I must tell you, by order of my most illustrious colleagues, that you and the father inquisitor should take careful note of the enclosed Instructions, which I send to you.[28]

While these comments about the testimony of women were hardly laudatory, they were at least more consistent than those held by Heinrich Krämer and Jacob Sprenger who believed much the same about the reliability of women's evidence but who still took seriously the testimony of female witches supposedly in league with the Devil. In any event, throughout the seventeenth century Italian Inquisitors dealt with thousands of cases of illicit magic, but passed virtually no death sentences for the crime; there was no transition here from trials against real heretics to a campaign against a diabolical witch conspiracy.

The Spanish Inquisition and witchcraft

In broad terms the situation was comparable in Spain where attention remained concentrated for some time on the presumed Judaising of conversos, thanks largely to the influx of Portuguese conversos in the second decade of the seventeenth century and revival of fears of widespread Judaising. Even so, the severity of the persecution rose and fell with the level of perceived threat and supply of suspects. Until the 1540s, Spanish Inquisitors fiercely attacked the conversos, thanks to the fanaticism of individual Inquisitors and the pressure of Old Christians to suppress the alleged New Christian plot against the Christian state. Moreover, southern Spain, formerly under Islamic rule, proved infertile ground for belief in diabolical witchcraft, in part because the Devil was of much less significance in Muslim and Hebrew thinking. For example, in 1526 a number of Inquisitors, theologians, and lawyers met in Granada to discuss the interrogations of accused witches in Navarre. The meeting resolved "that the existence of a sect of witches was still to be regarded as a dubious matter about which the judges could easily be deceived."[29]

By the 1540s the centers of presumed Spanish crypto-Judaism had been destroyed and the supply of ready suspects dried up. Not willing to close shop altogether, the Inquisitors, like their Italian counterparts, turned to other forms of "religious" offences, especially "Lutherans" – anyone expressing vaguely Protestant ideas. Execution rates, however, plummeted. Between 1540 and 1614, Judaisers made up only 5.9 percent of the 29,584 accused brought before all Spanish Inquisition courts, while the Suprema now began rectifying the excesses of local tribunals, frequently overturning local death sentences.[30] Only 2 percent of all cases prior to 1615 involved illicit magic. In fact, apart from the Alpine region of Italy, the Mediterranean Inquisitions accounted for no more than a few hundred witch executions among the thousands of trials against illicit magic.

Similarly, the Portuguese Inquisition, established in 1547, almost exclusively investigated Judaisers. Up to 1580, its three tribunals at Lisbon, Coimbra, and Evora conducted thirty-four *autos-da-fé* which proclaimed almost 2,000 sentences, over 200 of them capital ones, although not all were carried out. By 1580, Stephen Haliczer notes, a violent anti-Semitism had overwhelmed most of the clergy and populace, leading to an even worse wave of persecution between 1581 and 1600, climaxing with some fifty *autos-da-fé* that penanced nearly 3,000 convicted and condemned 220 to death. The decades of the 1620s and 1630s witnessed the worst Judaiser persecution, with nearly 5,000 punished and 230 executed (of over 390 death sentences). Many Portuguese Jews and conversos fled their homeland to southwestern France, the Papal States, Amsterdam, the Turkish lands and, interestingly enough, Spain, drawn by the new moderation of the Spanish Inquisition. This sudden influx of New Christians into Spain revived persecution of conversos there, who between 1615 and 1700 accounted for more than 20 percent of the Inquisition's over 15,000 cases.[31] In this climate, efforts to demonize magical offences were considered an inefficacious distraction.

The few witch panics in the Mediterranean region were imports from northern lands. Leading Inquisitors shared Cornelius Loos' perspective that the real danger to the Church was theological heresy, not the fantastical and largely imaginary acts of witches. In Italy, humanists ridiculed the Dominican defense of realism, lumping together scholastic demonology and popular superstition, a criticism that led central Inquisitors to shy away from openly espousing credulous views on demonic agency. Central Holy Offices mandated rigorous controls over the trials of accused witches, demanding concrete proof of guilt prior to sentencing and strictly limiting the use of torture. How these cautions worked is seen clearly in the famous witch panic of Logroño.

The Basque witch panic of 1608–12

Gustav Henningsen's richly detailed study of the internal struggle among the three members of Logroño's inquisitorial tribunal illustrates the determinative role played by leading individuals in inspiring a witch panic. Driven by religious zeal and a personal need to justify their initial credulity in a complaint of bewitchment, they incorporated belief in demonic witchcraft into the very core of their faith. The case began in December 1608 when Maria de Ximildegui, a young woman originally from the Basque village of Zugarramurdi (across the Pyrenees from France), returned home after a stay in the Pays de Labourd village of Ciboure. Her time in France corresponded with the beginnings of a witch panic there which had been encouraged by the local ruler, the Spaniard Tristan de Gamboa d'Alsatte, lord of Urtubie, who had written to King Henry IV of France "that the number of sorcerers had increased so alarmingly during the previous four years that no corner of the region was free of them."[32] In response, the crown sent to the region the French judge Pierre de Lancre, who by the end of 1609 had tried dozens and burned at least eleven witches, including three priests. Three years later he published his own treatise on the subject (the *Tableau de l'inconstance des mauvais anges et demons*) in which he refers to about three dozen children who had testified to being involuntarily carried to witches' sabbaths.

Upon her return to Zugarramurdi, Maria de Ximildegui began describing her involvement in a witch sect and how during the summer of 1608 she had repented and been reconciled to holy mother Church. Claiming to have attended a sabbath in Zugarramurdi itself, she provided the names of some of her new neighbors as fellow witches, including María de Jureteguía who initially denied the charge until it became clear her accuser's detailed testimony had convinced family and friends. She then confessed to a priest, blaming her aunt for having initiated her into the sect as a girl. Paranoia soon gripped the village as residents feared an attack by the remaining witches. The others accused by Maria de Ximildegui quickly confessed, and the priest decided that confessional absolution and neighborly reconciliation would sufficiently restore village harmony.

But news of these events reached the Logroño Inquisitors who deemed the reconciliations inadequate. Investigators were sent, reports prepared, and the decision made to conduct a formal Inquisition. Initially only two of the requisite three Inquisitors were available, the monk Dr. Alonso Becerra Holguin and the recently appointed priest Juan de Valle Alvarado; the third position was not filled until June 20, 1609, when the priest and canon Alonso de Salazar Frías (c.1564–1635) arrived. By this time Becerra and Valle had already found precedents in the Inquisitorial archives and were convinced by their interrogations of four suspects of the reality of the threat. The Suprema, however, remained skeptical, demanding precise, eye-witness details of the witches' sabbath and physical evidence, such as witches' salves and powders. Becere and Valle instead concentrated on extracting further confessions in a process of imprisonment and interrogation that Henningsen compares to brainwashing. The Inquisitors were amazed by the detail and consistency of the suspects' stories and seemed blithely unaware of the psychological impact of their detailed questioning and of the richness of storytelling in an oral culture.

Only after convincing themselves of the veracity of the threat did the Inquisitors send one of their number on a search for corroborating evidence. At each village the Inquisitor promulgated the Edict of Faith detailing all forms of heresy – from Judaising to Protestantism to popular skepticism and magical superstition – and commanded all residents to attend church on the following Sunday. At that time they would hear the Edict and a sermon detailing the dangers of the Devil's doings and participate in a High Mass, after which they would all confirm their faith in the Catholic Church and pledge to assist the Holy Office in uncovering heretics. Informants and repentant heretics were granted a week's grace and promised gentle treatment. The following Sunday the excommunication was promulgated against all unconfessed heretics while the faithful were sprinkled with holy water to protect them from demons. When the first results proved meager, Valle convinced himself that this was the result of the Devil's control over his human agents, not evidence of the falsity of the accusations. Alibis were broken by recourse to the "counterfeit-body" theorem whereby the Devil appeared publicly as one of his witches so as to provide him or her with an alibi. Given such logic it is hardly surprising that Valle's evidence confirmed the reality of the witch sect. While at Urdax he also communicated with the witch judges from across the French border and agreed to hunt down all of the French witches who had fled to Spain.

Concerned about Valle's procedures, the bishop of Pamplona, Antonio Venegas de Figueroa, decided upon the unusual step of conducting his own visitation which persuaded him that the whole affair was a matter of self-delusion or deceit. In response, Valle compelled the local priests and friars to preach vigorously about the dangerous sect of witches, leading the skeptical bishop to conclude that "if the people had not known previously what an *aquelarre* [witch sabbath] was, they soon got to know about it now."[33] Some preachers participated enthusiastically for obvious personal reasons, such as Lorenzo de Hualde, the rector of Vera whom the residents resented because he was a Frenchman appointed by the Lord of Urtubie. Hualde had assisted this lord in his French witch-hunts, hence, the bishop claimed, the priest was blatantly using witchcraft accusations to get even with his detractors. His dubious technique of extracting confessions from children and adults by keeping them confined for over forty days in the church rectory and regularly interrogating them proved effective. To the confessing children he gave talismans with the names of Jesus and Mary inscribed upon them. His opponents in the village who denied the reality of the witch sect he excoriated as suspected witches.

All of this evidence was forwarded to the Logroño Tribunal and to the Suprema, and an *auto-da-fé* was organized for October 1610, even though outbreaks of a strange disease in the prison had decimated the list of suspects, something that Inquisitors Becera and Salazar put down to the Devil's work. Even so, the bodies of five of the deceased were burned along with several living accused, while some others were granted penance. The grand event was witnessed by a massive crowd of some 30,000 spectators, many of whom arrived skeptical but left convinced: one witness reported that "Having listened to so many ghastly monstrosities for the space of two whole days ... we all returned to our several homes, crossing ourselves the while." Another commented, "May God in His mercy assist us to stamp out this devilish and pernicious sect which is so alarmingly widespread."[34] King Philip III ordered a preaching crusade throughout the afflicted region and soon thousands, many of them children, were coming forward with evidence against their neighbors or themselves.

However, cracks in Inquisitorial solidarity were forming. Although he seems initially to have concurred with his colleagues, Salazar began to insist on stronger evidence before assenting to death sentences, and such dissent meant referral to the Suprema. Arguments amongst the three Inquisitors increased, and Salazar embarked on his own visitation. Unlike Valle's tour, Salazar's followed the Suprema's instructions to the letter. Searching for solid evidence of a witch sect, Salazar found only credulous acceptance of the fantasies of children, gross abuse of legal procedure, and the effects of personal ambition. After examining thousands of confessions and accusations, Salazar concurred with the skeptical bishop of Pamplona. Back in Logroño, Salazar's two colleagues, who had staked their careers on the reality of the witch sect, were compelled to expend every bit of energy defending their original decisions. The preaching campaign of the friars had also convinced parents that their children were in danger of abduction by witches, and the pressure for immediate and extreme action against the accused rose to a fevered pitch. Skeptics were decried as tools of the Devil, and there was no space for reasoned debate. Despite this, Salazar calmly reinterrogated witnesses and accused alike and discovered the proffered witch ointments to have been fake. After eight months on the road, he presented his report to the Suprema that there was no solid evidence for any of the accusations, concluding

> I have not found a single proof nor even the slightest indication from which to infer that one act of witchcraft has actually taken place... Rather I have found what I had already begun to suspect in these cases before my experiences during the visitation; that the testimony of accomplices alone – even if they had not been submitted to violence

and compulsion – without further support from external facts substantiated by persons who are not witches is insufficient to warrant even an arrest.[35]

The nearly 2,000 accused were eventually cleared, and the Suprema adopted more rigorous regulations on the conduct of heresy trials that effectively ended witch panics.

The reasons why some individuals became fervent proponents and others critical skeptics of a demonic witch conspiracy resided within the particular psyche. Yet, one thing is clear: when prominent individuals realized that their personal integrity and world view had become intertwined with their decision to believe in a witch sect, they had no choice but to fight with everything in their power to defend this religious construct. Even though many of the skeptics, Salazar included, had originally concurred with the witch trials, they had not made that fateful decision to invest their personal honor in such sentiment and were able to maintain an admirable level of objectivity when evaluating the evidence. It helped too that unlike so many witch persecutors, Salazar was no philosophical realist.

Despite the differences in typology of victims between the Spanish and Italian Inquisitions (Judaisers for one, Protestants for the other),both reached their peak of activity after 1580, with a sharp decline around 1615. This period coincided with both the first major apex of witch-hunting in northern Europe and with the major push within post-Tridentine Catholicism to instill the new, narrower definition of Catholicism within the minds of all believers. Despite this campaign, the skeptical tradition in Spanish and Italian intellectual circles, the ongoing concern with Judaisers, and the insistence on strict procedural rules for the Inquisitions resulted in a nearly insurmountable inertia for zealous witch-hunters to overcome. Its reputation notwithstanding, after 1540 the Inquisition became a remarkably lenient court for the repentant, certainly in comparison with the bloodbaths of many secular courts which cared little about repentance and conversion.[36]

The "Periphery": Scandinavia and Eastern Europe

The principalities outside the witch-hunting "heartland", Scandinavia and Eastern Europe, were among the last European regions to be Christianized. In Scandinavia, pre-Christian magical and fertility practices coexisted with Catholic Christianity much more obviously than elsewhere in the west, and already in the thirteenth and fourteenth centuries Scandinavian law was condemning alleged witches to death, while witchcraft was associated with heresy and both with the idolatrous worship of Satan.[37] In the sixteenth century, the Protestant clergy urged the authorities to press the campaign to the limits, now with the purpose of eradicating remnants of both Catholicism and "pagan idolatry". Despite this clerical pressure, the various territories that made up Scandinavia were more restrained in witch-hunting than the German Empire, although with something around 5,000 executions, it was hardly a region of moderation. Here most of the major panics did not take place until the middle of the seventeenth century, and it was not until these trials that the full, diabolical conception of witchcraft was accepted. A major reason for this relative restraint was, as in France, the moderating influence of the central courts and their insistence on proper jurisprudence.

However, the first chain-reaction witch-hunt was quite early, in the 1540s in Denmark when the Lutheran Bishop Peder Palladius strongly urged the prosecution of witches as a means of purifying the realm of residual Catholicism on the eve of the return of Christ. The hunt claimed over fifty victims, many of whom had manifested Catholic tendencies. However, the government soon put in place regulations forbidding the use of torture and reliance upon the denunciations of convicted witches, and requiring automatic appeals of death sentences to a central court, squelching further panics. In Norway, governed by Denmark and under the same legal strictures, the diabolical conception of the witch never superceded that of the more traditional maleficent witch, thus witch-hunts were restrained. One of the region's early trials, however, illustrates again how the religious controversies contributed to the start of witch-hunting. In the 1570s Anna Pedersdotter Absalon, the wife of the Lutheran minister Absalon Pedersen Beyer, was tried for witchcraft in an evident effort to stop Beyer's iconoclastic efforts by attacking his wife. In this case Anna was cleared, but after his death she was tried and executed in 1590 for *maleficia* and of turning her servant into a horse and riding her to the sabbath.[38]

Swedish authorities showed little inclination to indulge in witch trials until the second half of the seventeenth century, although there were clusters of cases in the crucial years between 1590 and 1610. The major peak for both northern and southern Sweden occurred quite late, in the 1660s, with the notorious Blåkulla panic of the north when large numbers of children confessed to having been abducted by alleged witches and taken forcibly to the witches' sabbath. At least 240 accused were burned at the stake in the state's efforts to protect its children from such malicious harm. In the south, the major witch-hunts occurred even later, from 1669 to 1672, although here the trials only occasionally hinged on the accusations of children, concentrating instead on *maleficia*. By this time the belief that witches consorted with demons at the sabbath had been "firmly implanted in the popular imagination."[39] Routine application of the dunking test and of judicial torture made confessions and denunciations of others a matter of course, and the trials quickly spun out of control. Here too there were a large number of those claiming to have been possessed by demons, although the courts distinguished between "true" demoniacs and those "who had betrayed the baptismal sacrament by turning their bodies into an abode for demons" but who had not yet become full apostates. Swedish soldiers returning from the German battlefields after the end of the Thirty Years War in 1648 may have contributed to this spread of demonological notions into Scandinavia.

In Finland and Estonia, the rise of witch-hunting in the seventeenth century was very much related to Swedish influence. Both had fallen under the orbit of Sweden by the early seventeenth century and the Swedish ecclesiastical officials overseeing the Lutheranization of the dependent states frequently preached vigorous sermons against Catholic and pagan idolatry. For example, in the 1640s the Swedish Lutheran Bishop Isaac Rothovius embarked on a crusade against Catholic and Calvinist ideas as well as residual pagan superstition which he described as sorcery. He began the cleansing of the Turku Academy of such errors, a work that was followed up in the 1660s by one of that university's graduates, the judge Nils Psilander, who overlaid learned demonological theory upon the popular beliefs of the Finnish people. The result was a chain-reaction hunt that barely escaped escalating into a panic, thanks mainly to skeptical juries.[40] In Livonia, the situation was quite similar, as the Swedish Lutheran Superintendent Hermann Samson (r.1622–43) inaugurated an anti-witch campaign by printing a series of sermons on the subject in 1626 and by overseeing a series of clerical visitations during which he and his officials encountered evidence of the shocking survival of paganism. What most concerned these ministers was the possibility that such pagan idolatry would leave the populace open to a return to Catholicism. In 1637 the Livonian Consistory was commanded to discover "whether the peasants still organized idol-worship and . . . assembled on hillocks or in valleys, near chapels or chapel ruins, to worship idols and sacrifice," and it seems that the clergy found plenty of confirmation among parishioners. A major visitation throughout southern Estonia in 1667–8 revealed that almost every parish reported examples of such perfidious activity, leading to "the first massive offensive against the traditional religion of Estonia – and with the imposition of serfdom."[41] Here then was one region where the demonization of religious unorthodoxy led very directly to witch trials, although it must be remembered that Estonia was exceptional in this regard, and the witch trials themselves were relatively restrained.

Eastern Europe

Like Scandinavia, major witch-hunting was a latecomer to the eastern European principalities, not dying out there until the middle of the eighteenth century. The reasons for this "delay" in witch persecution are multivalent, yet the religious/political dimension is prominent. Levack explains Poland's belatedness in hunting witches as a result of a series of devastating wars around the mid-seventeenth century that distracted the legal authorities from prosecution of magic. Moreover, until 1648 the Catholic rulers of Poland officially tolerated Protestants and conducted no major heresy or witch persecutions. However, after 1648 a new militant Catholicism came to the fore, leading to increased restrictions against Protestants and promotion of an uncompromising Catholicism for the populace. Although Levack notes that religious intolerance did not necessarily lead to witch burning, he finds the correspondence of the two in Poland as too significant as to be mere coincidence. He suggests that "the burning of witches was one of the means by which an intolerant Catholic majority expressed its will to impose religious uniformity on a country which, even in the late seventeenth and early eighteenth centuries, remained religiously pluralistic."[42] In other words, until the middle of the seventeenth century the Polish authorities followed a model of informal confessional coexistence comparable to that pioneered by the notables of the Dutch Republic, although in Poland this approach was only provisional and not a permanent part of the population's religiosity. Consequently, until the middle of the seventeenth century, there was no government-supported effort to spread fear of a demonic conspiracy.

The large-scale witch persecution in seventeenth-century Silesia, the Germanized western portion of Poland, showed signs of having been stage managed as an instrument of princely authority, particularly in the duchies of Troppau and Jägerndorf ruled by Karl von Liechtenstein and his son Karl Eusebius, who oversaw several witch-hunts as part of their recatholicization efforts.[43] Despite the skepticism of many clerics, the populace and the state both found the burning of witches advantageous. Prior to the confessional campaign, in fact, it was not witches who were persecuted during incidents of bad harvests and plague, but the so-called "grave diggers" (*Totengräbern*) who were accused of digging up and eating corpses during famines and spreading disease by magical means. Clerical visitations brought such unorthodox folk beliefs and practices to the attention of the authorities.

Inspired by the infamy of the *Totengräbern* and witch persecutions, there was in the seventeenth and eighteenth centuries a rise in belief in revenantism, the notion that the dead could rise from their graves to kill or harass the living. In parts of Eastern Europe revenants or vampires became the favorite target of blame for devastating plagues. Grieving survivors disinterred the remains of the first person to die unexpectedly and inspected it for signs that he or she was a member of the "living dead." If the corpse had not decayed as anticipated, showing instead signs of suppleness, fresh blood on the lips, or growing nails and hair, then gruesome preternatural countermeasures were taken to kill the revenant, usually by driving a stake through its heart. An early case of revenantism occurred in Silesia in 1591 when a shoemaker who had committed suicide on the eve of a plague outbreak was believed to be terrorizing his neighbors. Those attending the disinterment were shocked to find his body in good condition and they proceeded to stake it, during which the corpse bled copiously and groaned (actions that pathologists can now readily explain). If such action against the original vampire did not end further deaths, then villagers proceeded to the bodies of the revenant's victims in the assumption that they too had become vampires.[44]

In a moment we shall see how the vampire epidemic helped end witch-hunting across the Austrio-Hungarian empire. We must return to the larger pattern of persecution in Silesia. As elsewhere, the Jews had been the traditional scapegoat for all manner of disasters, especially the disappearance or murder of children and the spread of plague. Also, in 1315 a group of Waldensian heretics were accused of performing perverse rituals of child murder and magic during secret meetings. In 1455 the anti-Semitic friar John of Capistrano preached through the realm, leading to the expulsion of the Jews. By this time, there was much talk of Jewish sorcerers and even of a Jewish "witch sabbath" that, unlike its Christian counterpart, was entirely male. In the sixteenth century, judicial attention turned to trying shepherd sorcerers, the *Totengräbern*, Jews, witches, and vampires, so that by the end of the century there was a confusing blend of notions arising out of the trials of these disparate groups.[45] Between 1676 and 1725 such beliefs were applied to alleged witches, several thousand of whom were condemned, despite the Catholic bishop's efforts to wrest control over such cases away from the municipal courts which abused proper judicial procedure with great abandon.

Hungary, Poland's southern neighbor, took even longer to adopt the demonological theory that was required to escalate a trial against a single maleficent witch into a hunt for members of a demonic sect. As in Poland, ideas of diabolical witch activity were spread among Hungarian villagers by resident German and Austrian troops. However, it was not until after the expulsion of Turkish soldiers in 1690 and a period of civil war that the Hungarian courts turned with any seriousness to the problem of witch-craft, leading to several waves of panic between 1710 and 1750 which saw at least 100 trials each decade.[46] Other eastern regions, especially those more distant from German influence, were less preoccupied with the issue, and while there were trials or the odd panic in such territories as Transylvania, Wallachia, and Moldavia, demonological ideas were less prominent in the Slavic regions dominated by the Eastern Orthodox Church. These areas were, until the second half of the seventeenth century, also relatively free from campaigns to drive out heterodoxy and to compel a unitary set of beliefs or a confession upon the minds of the general populace. When such efforts to ensure religious conformity were pursued by the authorities, there was a corresponding rise in witch-hunting.

One of the great ironies of the witch-hunts was the fact that while they were encouraged by some elites as a means of developing confessional uniformity and suppressing religious doubt, in the end, the process of prosecuting witches itself raised more doubts about the supernatural realm than it resolved. When witch trials or demoniacs were discredited, so too were many of the ideological elements that underpinned them. Many theologians and pastors feared that tolerating skepticism toward the demonic would lead to the spread of doubts about God himself. When increasing legal, medical, and theological evidence discredited the methods used to extract witch confessions, the whole demonic construct came under fire. What allowed the authorities in every region to turn back from their persecution of diabolical witchcraft was first and foremost the calming of confessional conflict and the cooling of religious passion.

France: The Embarrassment of Demoniacs

Despite the remarkable publicity surrounding the possession and exorcism of Nicole Aubrey in Laon in 1566, there was a lull in such phenomena in France until the exorcisms of four individuals in Soissons in 1582. There was no corresponding calm in the conflict between hardline Catholics and Huguenots, which broke out in another vicious civic war shortly after the "Miracle of Laon." In Soissons, the staged exorcisms were witnessed by thousands who were proffered evidence of the real presence of Christ in the sacramental wafer and its power over the demonic realm. One contemporary pamphleteer, Charles Blendec, hoped that his publication would convert Huguenots and "Aristoteleans and atheists, quite numerous nowadays, who do not believe in devils."[47] Demons afflicting the possessed obliged the exorcists by praising the Huguenots and admitting that God had allowed their activity for his own glory and to the confusion of the heretics. However, despite the efforts of Blendec, the Soissons exorcisms received relatively little publicity, in part because the tests put to the demoniacs by some Franciscans – sprinkling the possessed with ordinary water but pretending it to be blessed – had ambiguous results. The following year the local authorities issued a warning against naive acceptance of possession claims, insisting that physicians be consulted before an exorcist. Not everyone took this advice seriously, as the case of Marthe Brossier of Romorantin reveals.

Early in 1598 Marthe Brossier began screaming in church that one of her neighbors, Anne Chevreau, had bewitched her, causing her to be possessed by a demon. Brossier's motivations for this seemingly unexpected action were complex, but revolve around the inability of her father, Jacques, to provide her with a dowry, either for marriage or entrance into a convent (Marthe, already twenty-five, had two older unmarried sisters). Marthe was therefore facing very bleak prospects for her life. In late 1597 she cut off her hair, donned male attire, and ran away from home. She was found and returned, but her family's shame was considerable, as was the fear that her cross-dressing might elicit suspicion that she was a witch, as it had with Joan of Arc. Just a year or two earlier, in fact, three women of Romorantin had been tried and executed on charges of witchcraft which including causing others to be demonically possessed. Her father pressed the case against Anne, whose family had shunned a marriage arrangement with Marthe's oldest sister, and the unfortunate woman was arrested, jailed, and interrogated. However, the local judges decided to wait until Marthe's possession was declared authentic. To this end, Jacques called upon the local curé, who declared her a demoniac and began exorcizing her. Even so, there remained many skeptics and Anne composed her own perceptive commentary on the affair. To her, Marthe was not so much a fraud but a weak-minded woman troubled by depression and fantasies. For the sake of family honor Marthe's father had to prove her possessions to be true. He therefore took her on a travelling exorcism show, looking for the moment when an exorcism would provide definitive proof of Marthe's claims. In the process she learned a great deal from individual exorcists and from her copy of a book about the "Miracle of Laon." Formal certification of her possession, however, proved elusive, and when the bishop of Angers put Marthe to the requisite tests, he found her wanting and told her to go home and stop playing tricks. She ignored his advice and continued to Paris, arriving there in early March 1599, just days after the Parlement of Paris formally signed off on the Edict of Nantes.

Knowing that the ecclesiastical authorities of the city might be resistant to allowing public exorcisms during this delicate moment of religious peace, she and her father went immediately to the monastery of the Capuchins, who had no such reservations. Instead, these monks exploited Marthe's exorcisms as a weapon against the Edict's tolerance toward Protestants, whom Marthe's demon, Beelzebub, claimed as his allies. By the end of the month the whole city was in uproar and the city's bishop, fearing a revival of the religious bloodshed, sent a team of theologians and physicians to examine her. Their diagnosis suggested fraud. With his hard-won religious peace at stake, Henry IV ordered Marthe's arrest. The Capuchins protested, claiming that the government's action was instigated by the heretics. On May 24, the king ordered Brossier and her father to return home and desist from further incendiary behavior. This they did, and it is likely that the case against Anne Chevreau collapsed. However, faced now with even greater disgrace as a fraudulent demoniac, Marthe returned to her devilish activities, and a local anti-Huguenot prior took her to Italy for an audience with the Pope. Under pressure from the French crown, the prior returned home without fulfilling his mission, leaving behind Marthe, who found herself an object of ridicule in Italy where anti-Huguenot rhetoric was of little effect. She was last seen in 1604 being exorcized in Milan.[48]

Was Brossier merely a pawn in the hands of hardline Catholic priests infuriated by tolerance toward Huguenots? Certainly her behavior was exploited by them, but she seems to have been a quasi-independent instigator of events. Like Brossier, many women discovered possession to be a socially sanctioned means of expressing their deep frustration with the restrictions which family and society placed upon them. The famous case of the deeply religious Elizabeth de Ranfaing of Lorraine who began her career as a demoniac in 1620 after her parents had married her to a much older and abusive soldier is quite illustrative of this process.[49] Many demoniacs were also deeply disturbed by the leniency granted to the Protestants, although many became little more than pawns in the religious controversies. Even so, the public exorcisms provided these laywomen with a great deal of public attention and a sense of personal fulfillment. The fact that most of the possessed were laywomen, however, made Catholic leaders uncomfortable, since women were increasingly being restricted to the private sphere and it was thought highly unlikely that God would allow them such a public voice in religious affairs. Nuns, possessing as they did a formally approved religious vocation, took up the cause. In the most famous of these cases – those at Aix-en-Provence (1611), Loudun (1634), and Louvais (1633–44) – entire convents became possessed and a local priest condemned for bewitchment. For brevity's sake we will discuss only the first two of these.

It is not difficult to find a psychological explanation for the strange fits of Madeleine Demandols de La Palud, which quickly spread to many of her sisters at the Ursuline convent of Aix-en-Provence. While a student at the Ursuline school in Aix, Madeleine suffered from depression that was relieved by returning home and confessing frequently to her parish priest Louis Gaufridy. Rumors began circulating that the long, private meetings involved more than confessional counseling, and her parents were undoubtedly happy when she entered the local Ursuline convent. However, in the religiously intense confines of this cloistered monastery where the nuns were expected to be models of Tridentine Catholic purity, she began telling scandalous stories about her meetings with the priest. She was quickly transferred to Aix, but at Christmas 1609, she began to experience uncontrollable fits and to see demons. The convent's spiritual advisor, the Jesuit Jean-Baptiste Romillon – a former Huguenot who had become an ardent campaigner against clerical immorality – immediately diagnosed her as possessed, although his exorcisms failed. He pursued her accusations against Gaufridy, who denied any impropriety. As a result of Romillon's questioning of the other nuns, many of them too began to share Madeleine's obsession with Gaufridy and to convulse uncontrollably. Romillon took Madeleine and another afflicted nun, Louise Capeau, to the Inquisitor Sébastien Michäelis who, at a popular saint's shrine near Avignon, turned the sisters' private fantasies into a grand piece of anti-Huguenot theatre. The demons remained and Michäelis in February 1611 convinced the Parlement of Paris to begin proceedings against Gaufridy. The trial was a spectacular one, what with the demoniacs' frequent courtroom fits and Gaufridy's firm denials. Once the Devil's mark was found on his body, Gaufridy finally confessed to being the "Prince of the Synagogue" and to having mistreated the sacraments, giving Hosts which he had consecrated at the diabolical sabbath to dogs. He was horribly tortured and executed. Suddenly, Madeleine was freed of her demons, although Louise's continued for another year until another accused witch was burned.[50] A visiting nun from Lille who witnessed some of the exorcisms helped spread the possession phenomenon to her own convent, while Michäelis wrote and published his widely disseminated account of the affair, translated as *The Admirable Historie of the Possession and Conversion of a Penitent woman, Seduced by a Magician that made her to become a Witch* (London, 1613). Apart from spreading the fame of this case, Michäelis wrote his massive tome to counteract skeptics who questioned whether "a woman should speake and preach in the Church, since that Saint Paul forbiddeth a woman to speake there" and whether to believe "all that the Deuill saith."

The exorcisms overseen by Michäelis made preachers of demons. Against the heretical incursions, Louise Capeau's demon confirmed central Catholic doctrines such as Purgatory, the immaculate conception, the sacraments, and the real presence of Christ in the consecrated Host. In December 1610, the demon Verin announced through Louise Capeau that "the houre of that great day of Iudgement is at hand, for Antichrist is borne and brought forth some moneths past by a Iewish woman. God will rase out Magick & al Magicians, and witches shall returne home vnto him," major signs of the coming seven years of tribulation heralding the end of the world.[51] While theologians debated the murky issue of whether or not demons could ever be expected to tell the truth, many laypeople were convinced, escalating religious passions and apocalyptical fears. Similarly, one of the possessed Brigidine nuns of Lille in the 1620s admitted that she spoke about the Antichrist "because a certain very famous preacher of the Company of Jesus

preached to us on an occasion that the Antichrist was already born."
In the light of these peculiar events, one Catholic polemicist, Jean le
Normant (who in 1611 himself had been possessed), advised King
Louis XIII that he should personally submit to exorcism and once
freed of any demonic interference, oversee the exorcism of the whole
kingdom.[52]

The most famous case of a possessed convent was that of the Ursuline
house of Loudun, which was an even more explicit manipulation of
a witch trial to dispose of a political enemy, this time the Jesuit Urbain
Grandier. In the dispute between Cardinal Richelieu and the town's
governor Jean d'Armagnac over royal plans to destroy the city's fortifica-
tions, Grandier sided with the latter party. He also made enemies of
a prominent citizen, Philippe Trincant, by making his daughter pregnant.
Trincant's revenge started with the testimony of some of his associates
that Grandier was living a lecherous life, rumors that quickly reached
even the cloistered Ursulines. An enraged Grandier denied all and
sought legal redress, but even though he won formal retractions, these
only made Trincant more resolved to destroy him. Trincant's opportunity
came in September 1632 when Sister Joan and several other nuns began
experiencing convulsions which their family members could explain
only as bewitchment. While modern psychology might diagnose their
affliction as a neurosis brought on by fear of the plague, intense religious
introspection, and sexual repression, the nuns behaved as expected within
a seventeenth-century religious context. The exorcists, intentionally or
not, helped plant the idea that Grandier was the one responsible, and
Trincant and his allies pushed for a trial. The exorcisms and stage-managed
trial scandalized the nation as Joan's recantation of her accusations
fell on deaf ears and Grandier was burned regardless of his refusal to
admit guilt through bloodcurdling torture.[53] The Huguenots exploited
the trial's obvious abuses and pronounced all Catholic exorcisms as
fraudulent, a position that called into question the whole intellectual
construct of demonic witchcraft. Long before Louis XIV in 1682 formally
ended witch persecutions in France, the central court and royal authorities were habitually overturning death sentences pased by local courts.

German Witch-Hunts and Friedrich Spee

Even during a German witch panic local officials could become convinced
that the judicial procedures, especially use of torture, were creating, rather

than uncovering, a witch sect. Protestations of innocence even by prominent individuals such as the Ellwangen judge Michael Dier (Dirren), burned in 1611 for contesting his wife's execution, were not immediately effective in forcing a reevaluation of witch-hunting, as Ellwangen's panic continued until 1618.[54] While mass panics may have eroded confidence in the legal process and raised fears about the survival of the community, this form of incertitude was often temporary, as some regions had multiple scares. Moreover, the judicial burning of thousands of people by 1590 made it extremely difficult for many to admit that their authorities had made such a grievous error.[55]

By 1600 Protestants were identifying the hardline, fanatical position against witches as a Catholic preoccupation that had arisen out of the "idolatries" of the papacy, and they tended to discredit the fantastical aspects of the witch stereotype in favor of a purely spiritual crime of diabolical illusion. This helped relieve, but not eliminate, pressure for witch persecutions in many Protestant realms. To distinguish their position more sharply from the Protestant, many Catholic theologians and jurists continued to promote the full witch stereotype and witch persecution became something of a hallmark of Catholicism.[56] Thus, uncovering and destroying a sect of witches who practiced an inversion of the Catholic religion remained an important weapon in the Catholic polemical arsenal against doubters.

Catholic skeptics, however, did not give up their fight against witchcraft belief. Although harboring its share of demonologists, the Jesuit Order also led the way in the skeptical camp as well, most notably in the writings of Adam Tanner and Friedrich Spee von Langenfelds. Both gave voice to growing concerns about the social effects of witch-hunting, while Tanner reconciled opposition to witch persecution with Catholic theology, a not inconsiderable task given the confessional importance of witchcraft persecution for Catholicism after 1600.[57] For several years Spee acted as a confessor to imprisoned witches, becoming convinced that while witchcraft might be real, the vast majority of those whose confessions he heard were innocents forced by torture into confessing their guilt. He put his critical opinions to print in 1631 in his anonymous *Cautio criminalis seu de processibus contra sagas liber*, a work of considerable influence. This focus on judicial abuses was perhaps the best way for Catholic intellectuals to attack witch persecution without risking charges of supporting Protestant heresy. Although major climatic catastrophes in the second half of the seventeenth century inspired sporadic witch trials across the

German Empire, by the end of the century Protestant rulers had abandoned them while most Catholic courts were acting with greater circumspection.

England and Religious Compromise

In the second half of the seventeenth century England's rulers too turned firmly away from promoting or permitting witch persecution, and for many of the same reasons as their Dutch and German contemporaries. Since the supposed *maleficia* performed by witches was most commonly associated with rural life, such as the bewitching of livestock, crops or milk, the increasing urbanization of England helped lower concern with traditional witchcraft, although other forms of magic, such as divination or love magic, remained a part of daily life in cities as well as the country.[58]

Like the Netherlands, England also had its share of skeptics, most famously the country gentleman and Justice of the Peace Reginald Scot (c.1538–99), whose book, *Discoverie of Witchcraft*, appeared in 1584. Expressing disgust at what he saw during some witchcraft trials, Scot tried to remove the theological and juridical support for such prosecution. Both common sense and the scriptures argued against the reality of many of the diabolical deeds ascribed to witches, and to prosecute women especially for these was a horrible injustice. In fact, those who deserved judicial punishment were the "witchmongers" and promoters of fantastical opinions. Scot went even further in his critique, asserting that as a purely spiritual being the Devil possessed no corporeal nature, for "diuels are spirits, and no bodies. For spirits and bodies are by antithesis opposed one to another: so as a bodie is no spirit, nor a spirit a bodie. And that the diuell, ... is a creature made by God, and that for vengeance ... and of himselfe naught." Biblical terms describing Satan as physically real were merely metaphors for this spirit of evil.[59] The deeds attributed to diabolical witches were impossible, for a spiritual being could have no physical involvement with humans, apart from inwardly tempting them. As Keith Thomas notes, Scot's position that "Satan was merely a symbol of man's evil temptations, incapable of corporeal existence," undercut the rationale for prosecution of diabolical witchcraft.[60] It is also interesting that like Johann Weyer, Scot was in touch with spiritualists, in his case members of the Family of Love.[61] Even if a minority position among England's intelligentsia, Scot's perspective was common enough.

Debate over the genuine problems confronting judges and jurors in proving witchcraft accusations was also becoming a factor in the dismissal of charges. Robert Filmer's *An Advertisement to the Jury-men of England, Touching Witches* of 1653 did not reject the reality of witchcraft per se, but highlighted the difficulties in determining guilt on the basis of demonological theory, especially since convictions necessarily rested on the intellectual construct of the demonic pact and on the dubious procedure of compelling witches to testify against alleged coconspirators. Attacking the demonological treatises of Del Rio and especially William Perkins, Filmer sought to ridicule judicial reliance on the notion of a pact. For example, if the centerpiece of the demonic pact was the renunciation of Christian baptism and faith, Filmer contended that

> it will follow that none can be Witches but such as have first beene Christians, nay and *Roman Catholiques, if Delrio* say true, for who else can renounce the patronage of the Virgin Mary? And what shall be said then of all those Idolatrous Nations of Lapland, Finland, and of divers parts of Africa, and many other Heathenish Nations which our Travailers report to be full of Witches.[62]

Not an argument likely to break down the bastion of a century's worth of demonological theory and witch persecution, perhaps, but one indicative of a more cautious attitude among the judicial elite of England. Filmer's pamphlet was only part of a major debate over the judicial role of spectral evidence, such as the bewitched who in court suddenly "saw" the ghost of the accused or a demon, or who experienced fits when the accused was brought into court. Judges increasingly insisted on more earthbound proof. After the Restoration of the monarchy in 1660, the rift between the culture of the elites and that of the commoners widened, leading the intelligentsia to associate witchcraft beliefs and pressure to prosecute witches with the vulgar superstitions of the masses.[63]

The Restoration, however, did not end religious and political turmoil, and every theological dispute added strain to the government's efforts to maintain political equilibrium. Several leading intellectuals, such as Henry More and Joseph Glanvill (1636–80) vigorously defended the reality of witchcraft as part of an effort to hold back the tide of Deism (which emphasized the non-miraculous and predictable nature of creation and which depreciated religious enthusiasm, confessional rigor, and reliance on revelation), fearing that denial of witchcraft would ultimately expel the Devil, then God himself, from the cosmos.[64] Despite their efforts, many learned clergy agreed that the age of miracles had passed. Most of their parishioners disagreed, judging from their consumption of the flood of printed prodigy and miracle literature in the 1640s and 1650s.[65]

The rise of party politics soon swallowed up witchcraft as a tool in the ideological and political debates. During the Civil War, the English were forced to rethink their conception of religious and secular authority and governance, and many Puritan leaders viewed the real threat to civil order as coming from tolerance of religious plurality. The populace still longed for the traditional, divinely ordained political and social order, but that order was passing away. The witchcraze launched in the 1640s by the infamous witch-finder general Matthew Hopkins helped skeptics associate witchcraft prosecution with disorder and fanaticism. After the Restoration, promotion of witch-hunting became identified as a strictly nonconformist occupation. Since the learned Anglican clergy already linked nonconformism with subversion and disloyalty to the crown, attacking sectarians necessarily involved discrediting fear of witchcraft. Like the continental Anabaptists in the previous century, English sectarians were readily demonized; because they too rejected infant baptism for believers' baptism, English Baptists shared the Anabaptist fate of being likened to demonic witches who had similarly renounced their original baptism.

It was the Quakers, however, who were victimized the most in this polemical shift. As described by Peter Elmer, the obscure appearance of the Quaker movement around the same time as the Civil War suggested to many who opposed its individualistic and anti-authoritarian bent that it was ultimately subversive of the political order. Protestant polemicists saw it as part of the same diabolical Jesuit plot to subvert the true faith that had hindered Cromwell's godly work. Conspiratorial notions of Quakers arose just as interest in persecution of witches was on the decline, and Quakers became in Elmer's phrase "surrogate witches." Like witches, Quakers confirmed the official ideology by acting as a demonic mirror image. All political factions, from high Anglican to Puritans to nonconformists, co-opted the language of witchcraft in their party polemics, and it soon lost its power to inspire dread. Even the Quakers became widely tolerated as eccentrics.[66] By the early eighteenth century the force of diabolical rhetoric had lost much of its edge, "as the memory of the religious upheavals of the 1650s receded, the devil became marginalized."[67]

Despite these developments, witchcraft latently retained some of its force, requiring only a new political or social crisis to spark renewed cries for a witch-hunt. Hope for a return to a non-party, unitary Christian government lingered, and some thought to whip up enthusiasm for this nostalgic notion by reviving fear of its ungodly opposite: the diabolical witch, symbol of ultimate disorder and depravity. By the 1720s, however, most political leaders had accepted the permanence of party factionalism, and witchcraft lost its motivational potency. As there developed a consensus on the issue of religious pluralism, witchcraft was shunted to the sidelines; in the same parliamentary session as the repeal of James I's witchcraft statute in 1736 was a bill to provide relief for Quakers from mandatory tithe payments, a position rejected by the hardline Tories.[68]

Witchcraft's last political stronghold, Ian Bostridge has shown, was in the struggle of Scottish politicians and churchmen to oppose complete English dominance of their society. For many Scots the Devil's minions were the English who had stopped prosecuting witches. The anti-repeal cause was taken up in Parliament by Lord James Erskine, whose passionate speech on the abiding importance of demonological theory for sound governance was greeted with laughter. At the heart of Erskine's opposition, however, was the battle over Scottish rights, defined in this case as the rights of the Scottish Calvinist Kirk to maintain jurisdictional control over all ecclesiastical and moral offences. The opponents of repeal lost their case and the new law, which was extended to Scotland, outlawed accusing others of witchcraft or pretending to possess magical powers. One of the three main sponsors of the repeal bill, moreover, was John Conduit, Isaac Newton's nephew and his successor as master of the mint. Newton had entrusted his unpublished papers to Conduit, who may have been influenced by his uncle's unorthodox belief that the Devil was merely a symbol of individual evil.[69] By repealing the witchcraft statute, Parliament was effectively removing the Devil from the legal realm, symbolizing the increasingly secular nature of England's government, and highlighting its turn away from state-sponsored efforts to compel doctrinal uniformity.

The Embarrassing Case of the Hungarian Vampires

The suppression of witchcraft persecution by the state could follow the gradual model of Germany or England, or it could ensue from a sudden, and largely unexpected, act of a monarch. The latter was the case for the

Austria-Hungarian Empire ruled by the enlightened Empress Maria Theresa. As we have noted, the peak of witch persecution in Hungary was quite late, the first major panic occurring not until the 1720s and 1730s, and a second wave beginning in 1755. In 1756 Maria Theresa suddenly ordered all lower court rulings against alleged witches to be passed on to her court of appeals, which overturned nearly all death sentences. She then issued a new decree, entitled the "Imperial and royal law for uprooting superstition and for the rational judgment of magical and sorcery crimes," which made further prosecution of witchcraft virtually impossible. The second wave of witch panics in Hungary was immediately squelched, despite the protests of local court officials about this royal infringement on their jurisdiction. What inspired this sudden *volte face* on the part of the Empress? The answer is to be found in the rise of a parallel, if more exotic, supernatural phenomenon to witchcraft: vampirism.

By the middle of the eighteenth century the fear of and fascination with vampires had reached epidemic proportions. With every plague outbreak in and around Hungary, corpses of suspected revenants were disinterred and re-dispatched in a grisly manner. The recently deceased had become the ideal scapegoat for personal and communal disasters, replacing the heretic, leper, Jew, and witch as the ultimate "Other" whose mere presence in the community was spreading death. Belief in revenantism was constructed upon the intellectual foundation that supported Christian teaching about the incorruptible bodies of saints and the resurrection of the dead, while by disinterring and burning long-deceased heretics, the Church had provided the model for disposing of the threat. Thus, local clergy tolerated popular action against revenants as a way of diverting skepticism toward Christian dogma of life after death.

The Empress and her court, however, found the Europe-wide publicity about Hungarian vampires deeply embarrassing. Official investigations began in 1755 with the disinterment of the corpse of Rosina Polakin in Hermersdorf, near the Silesian and Moravian borders. As expected, Rosina's remains appeared fresh and undecayed, and her family was forced to drag it outside consecrated ground and have it beheaded and burned. When Maria Theresa heard of this macabre affair, she immediately sent two of her court doctors to investigate. After receiving their lurid report, she consulted with her principal court physician, the Dutchman Gerard van Swieten, who agreed with his colleagues that the Empress should immediately abolish such superstitious behavior. In

March she issued a decree forbidding action against *magia posthuma*, while Van Swieten published a learned treatise on the subject, explaining how each of the supposedly preternatural signs of vampirism could be medically accounted for. As Maria Theresa's scholars turned their energy to explaining this new sensation, they applied their conclusions to the older but still terrifying phenomenon of witchcraft. Very quickly witchcraft, magic, and vampirisim were linked as vulgar and offensive superstitions, entirely unbefitting the realm of an enlightened monarch. The law of 1756 put the matter in this fashion: "It is well known, what an unbearable extent has been lately reached by the craze concerning sorcery and witchcraft. Its foundations were laid by the inclination of the idiotic and vulgar crowd toward superstition."[70] Maria Theresa's actions did not, of course, immediately end belief in witchcraft nor fear of revenants. But they did bring an end to both panics. For his part, Van Swieten had studied medicine at the University of Leiden under the renowned professor of medicine Herman Boerhave (1668–1738) who had made no secret of his distaste for charlatans who pretended to be practioners of magic. From Erasmus, to Joris, to Weyer, and Van Swieten, the skeptical currents flowing through Dutch culture trickled far across Europe.

7

CONCLUSION

The goal of this book has been to show how the changes within the early modern religious climate intersected with the discourse of magic and witchcraft. The cosmos of early modern Europeans was an organic, interconnected thing, the parts of which interacted by a process of influence called correspondence. In this environment, magic was merely a means by which humans sought to manipulate creation's hidden forces and invisible beings. Some of these beings were believed by the Church to be malign, although it was its own clergy which became the major practitioners of angelic or demonic magic. Church authorities became deeply concerned about clerical necromancy and, through a process of transference, added diabolical magic to the supposed crimes of heretics and Jews.

Religious dissidents, such as the Waldensians and Cathars, had proven a serious challenge to Church authority, for in those regions where they were popular, they convinced many laypeople that alternate beliefs were not a threat to communal survival. Doubt as to the veracity of Church-approved dogma increased, and the Pope developed the ultimate weapon to deal with this, the office of Inquisitor. By its process, accused heretics were compelled to recant their evil errors and to acknowledge that they had been misled by the Devil. The recalcitrant were handed over to the secular ruler for punishment, and the horrible *autos-da-fé* became an effective means of moral persuasion.

Similarly, Jews proved a useful, if unwitting, tool in the drive by church leaders and ordinary parishioners alike to eradicate doubt. Already associated with Satan by virtue of their refusal to convert to Christianity, they became frequent targets of ritual murder accusations and Host desecration charges. These helped prove the veracity of Christian teaching about Christ's death and resurrection and his miraculous appearance in the consecrated bread. In times of hardship, such as famines or outbreaks of epidemic disease, Christians turned against the increasingly isolated Jewish communities with a vengeance, and bloody pogroms became the rule. Some authorities, such as the kings of France, cynically manipulated popular distrust of Jews (and lepers) by elaborating and disseminating conspiracy theories as a means to enrich themselves or rid themselves of political foes. In Spain, thousands of Jews converted rather than face the flames, leaving that region with a singular problem of how to incorporate these conversos into Christian society. Suspicion that the New Christians were still practicing Judaism in secret and hatching plots against the Christian governments led ultimately to the creation of the Spanish Inquisition and to the elaboration of the bizarre pure blood laws.

In all of these repressive actions, the Church and state sought means to maintain control over the beliefs of the common people, an increasingly difficult task thanks to rising levels of literacy and increasing anticlerical sentiment. Several infamous attempts at magical murder of popes and princes by clerical necromancers likewise gave Church leaders the motivation they needed to begin demonizing ritual magic. By the fifteenth century, the theory that sectarian witches were plotting the destruction of Christendom with the aid of the Devil was widespread, thanks largely to preachers seeking to counteract anticlerical sentiment (or, in the case of Bernardino of Siena, to divert attention away from his own heresy). It was further reinforced by the sensational news of trials of groups of witches. The diabolical conspiracy also diverted attention away from the conciliarist threat to papal authority onto an even more frightening target.

As inquisitorial concern shifted from the magic of learned clerics (who were presumed able to control demons by virtue of their supernatural power) to popular, demonic heresy, the gender of most accused changed from male to female, a fact illustrated with the publication of the infamous *Malleus Maleficarum* in 1487. By the end of the century, the demonic conspiracy was more or less complete, and many churchmen were promoting the eradication of this sect of malicious, magic performing, heretical witches who had made a pact with the evil one. Yet, as Heinrich Krämer discovered to his chagrin, many authorities were not so easily persuaded, and the number of trials was in decline by 1500.

By this time there was also a pronounced sense of the nearness of apocalyptical judgment and an expectation of an escalated assault on humanity by the Devil's agents. Martin Luther used this fear to promote his agenda for reforming the Church, which quickly gained immense popular support. Many people, however, wanted to move further and faster than Luther, and in the early 1520s the "Reformation" was already extremely diverse, with various groups of laypeople and clergy trying to take reform in an assortment of directions. Several infamous episodes arising from popular discontent, such as the Peasants' War, Anabaptism, and the Münster Anabaptist kingdom, heightened anxiety about secret diabolical conspiracies that might at any moment break out into open revolt. Even though later Anabaptists and Mennonites sought to convince the authorities of their peaceable intent, suspicion lingered, fed by Catholic and Protestant polemicists. During the "early" period of the Reformation, say up to the Peace of Augsburg of 1555, the authorities had their hands full with religious dissidents of many stripes, and major witch-hunting virtually disappeared from across Europe. However, during the 1540s to 1560s, the countless sermons and pamphlets warning the populace of the Devil's evil plots and the nearness of the Antichrist's arrival had worked their magic, reviving fear of diabolical conspiracies.

Although the demonizing rhetoric was always greater than actual efforts of suppression, during the sixteenth century thousands of individuals were arrested, tortured, and executed because they were perceived to be a profound, diabolical threat to the social order. Until the 1560s and 1570s, the judicial slaughter targeted religious dissidents, particularly Anabaptists in the Empire, Anabaptists and Calvinists in the Low Countries, and Calvinists in France. Starting in the 1560s, judicial persecution of a sect of witches was revived, and once again the beliefs about religious dissidents were transposed onto the imaginary sect of witches. Among these was the belief that Anabaptism had unleashed unruly women from male control. Inspired also by reformers' calls for increased patriarchalism, the old stereotype of female witches found a second wind.

In the 1560s, Johann Weyer observed that there was an apparently sudden, widespread revival of witch-hunting, something that he decried as a continuation of the bloodthirst that had not been quenched with the execution of religious dissidents. Until this time, most courts were too preoccupied with real heretics who openly confessed their beliefs. However, the rise of Nicodemite spiritualists or libertines raised the specter of a fifth column of dissimulators secretly spreading their harmful views among an ignorant populace. In the last decades of the sixteenth century, courts began attacking this invisible diabolical threat in earnest. Behind all of this persecution lay the need to neutralize the expression of doubt and skepticism toward officially approved beliefs. The intensified religious passions and fear of doubt helped inflame the anti-witch activities of a community, justifying neighborly denunciations and serious judicial action. Those who expressed notions of religious tolerance or skepticism toward diabolical conspiracies were increasingly condemned as atheists or as demon-inspired themselves. Jean Bodin's vicious rejoinder to Weyer's tome is merely one example of this trend.

What lay behind the origins of witch-hunting (as opposed to magic which was an ancient and endemic aspect of European culture) was the need to defend particular religious beliefs against both heresy and inner doubt. Alleged witches and demoniacs provided tangible proof of the reality of the Christian supernatural realm, just as heretics and Jews had done earlier. The widespread belief in the nearness of the apocalypse intensified the drive to purify society and establish or reinforce a uniform and unchallenged belief system. To do so required the demonization and eradication of anything that could be construed as offensive to God, especially since storms, famines, plague outbreaks, and religious conflict seemed on the rise, indicating divine displeasure. Starting in 1562 in Wiesensteig, Württemberg, local authorities began taking seriously their subjects' denunciations of neighbors whom they suspected of causing destructive hailstorms, livestock deaths, or human disease. And while there were a handful of opponents of such scapegoating, during the decades around 1600 just about every government permitted or encouraged at least one major witch persecution.

In general, the heartland of witch-hunting proved also to be the center of religious conflict and heresy persecution: the Holy Roman Empire, the Swiss Cantons, France, and the Southern Netherlands (as well as Puritan Essex in England and Scotland). In all of these major episodes of witch persecution, the religious dimension was prominent, and not just in the terrifying panics encouraged by the Franconian archbishops. After decades of confessional conflict and propaganda, many people were utterly confused as to which confession was divinely approved. In a few places, particularly the Dutch Republic, confessional competition was allowed to blossom, and many citizens were permitted to comparison shop, as it were. In this environment, some people refused to join any church. Such a relaxed attitude toward confessional conformity significantly reduced concern about diabolical conspiracies or a witch sect, even though belief in magic continued just about everywhere. In some regions, such as Poland, authorities moved in the opposite direction, from religious tolerance to enforced confessional conformity, and witch-hunting increased correspondingly. In the Mediterranean regions, where both heresy and witchcraft remained for the most part in the jurisdiction of the Inquisitions, witch persecution proved an anomaly, in large measure due to the Inquisition's success in removing all challenges to orthodoxy. In the end, many authorities suppressed witch trials at about the same time that they gave up efforts to enforce confessional conformity.

The trials and executions of alleged witches and the dramatic exorcisms of the possessed were for a time remarkably effective in reaffirming belief in the "other world." At the same time, closer examination of these unusual and frightening events soon caused many intellectuals and jurists to dispute their intellectual underpinnings and to force reconsideration of the proceedings. While this led proponents of exorcisms or of witch persecution to fight harder against this new tide of doubt, the ultimate result was a mounting sense of unease with notions of diabolical plots. In other words, the very tools that proponents of witch-hunting promoted as means of eradicating doubt in themselves became the motor propelling skepticism. Moreover, in many places the authorities and populace both learned how to adjust to a measure of confessional coexistence and religious tolerance, while the presence of some religious disagreement, confusion, and doubt became a matter of course rather than a threat to the survival of the state.

Unfortunately, belief in diabolical conspiracies has not died out completely, nor has the magical universe disappeared entirely, as the recent revival of interest in occult sciences, earth magic, and "new age" religions shows. Since the end of the seventeenth century, old prejudices and conspiratorial beliefs have surfaced often enough in times of hardship or rapid transformation to work their old damage to groups and individuals perceived as in league with the forces of evil. "Witch-hunting" has become a remarkably flexible term to describe any form of persecution against groups or individuals, and comparisons between the early modern witch-hunts and contemporary persecutions, such as the American Senate's anti-Communist hearings of the 1950s, have become commonplace.[1] Less well known is how Heinrich Himmler, head of Hitler's infamous SS, established in 1935 a special SS unit of historians – the H[exen]-Sonderauftrag – to ferret out every archival reference to a witch trial, and their prodigious efforts uncovered some 30,000 cases. Himmler's rationale for this unusual activity was two-fold: first, to support his anti-Church (especially anti-Catholic) propaganda by placing responsibility for the infamous witch-hunts in the lap of the Church; and second, to find evidence of pre-Christian, Germanic paganism that was suppressed by the witch persecution.[2] Most recently, the witch-hunts have been portrayed by some feminists as a "Holocaust against women" which, as a comparison with the horrific Nazi destruction of European Jews, implies that the witch-hunts were a highly organized campaign against an identifiable group that consumed women in the millions. As we have seen, such was not the case.

Real witch-hunting still goes on, especially in certain parts of rural South Africa where concern about witchcraft has arisen dramatically in recent decades, leading to several hundred lynchings. In these cases, as in the early modern European trials, fear of the magic, malice, and conspiratorial goals of supposed witches, heightened by the tensions produced by local social conflicts, provide the major reasons behind the murders. Like the earlier European witch persecution, organized public witch-hunts have become a common means in South Africa to deal with communal misfortune. They have also become tools in recent power struggles within the African National Congress.[3]

Elsewhere, the methods to quell dissidents and skeptics developed by early modern proponents of heresy and witch-hunting have proven readily adaptable. Recent efforts of fundamentalist religious leaders to battle against the seemingly insurmountable drift to disbelief and skepticism have led to a renewed interest in the Devil. Once again, this mythical, frightening figure is being used to prove the existence of God and the supernatural realm. By suggesting the existence of a pernicious, highly organized, secretive, and immensely dangerous Satanic cult whose members have infiltrated the highest levels of society, some Christian leaders have been able to capitalize on the fear aroused to restore a measure of credibility to their apparently out-of-date notions. Serious investigation of many cases of supposed conspiratorial Satanic abuse of children has time and again proven most charges to be groundless, although the reputation of many an accused has been irrevocably damaged in the process. While this has had the general effect of discrediting such "moral panics", believers in conspiracy merely point to the judicial investigations as in themselves proof that the Devil has his talons hooked deeply into the higher reaches of government. In the context of early modern societies with unitary and state-mandated ideologies, such beliefs led to vicious persecution. Even in our multi-cultural and religiously diverse environment, however, the right confluence of crises and widespread anxieties could broaden the appeal of the fearmongering of a minority fringe.

NOTES

Introduction

1. See James T. Richardson, Joel Best, and David G. Bromley, eds., *The Satanism Scare* (New York, 1991).
2. Stuart Clark, *Thinking with Demons: The Idea of Witchcraft in Early Modern Europe* (Oxford, 1997).
3. Peter Burke, *Popular Culture in Early Modern Europe* (New York, 1978).
4. Here I follow Gavin Langmuir, *History, Religion, and Antisemitism* (Berkeley, 1990), esp. 143–57.
5. Jacques Le Goff, *The Birth of Purgatory*, trans. Arthur Goldhammer (Chicago, 1984), 209.
6. Langmuir, *History, Religion, and Antisemitism*, esp. 136 and 160.
7. Ibid., 172.
8. Valerie I. J. Flint, *The Rise of Magic in Early Medieval Europe* (Princeton, NJ, 1991), 3.
9. Richard Kieckhefer, *Magic in the Middle Ages* (Cambridge, 1989), 1.
10. Hugh R. Trevor-Roper, *The European Witch-Craze of the Sixteenth and Seventeenth Centuries* (Harmondsworth, 1969).
11. Gustav Henningsen, *The Witches' Advocate: Basque Witchcraft & the Spanish Inquisition* (Reno, 1980), 18.
12. H. C. Erik Midelfort, *Witch Hunting in Southwestern Germany, 1562–1684: The Social and Intellectual Foundations* (Stanford, 1972), 6.
13. See esp. Robin Briggs, "'Many reasons why': witchcraft and the problem of multiple explanation," in *Witchcraft in Early Modern Europe: Studies in Culture and Belief*, eds. Jonathan Barry, Marianne Hester, and Gareth Roberts (Cambridge, 1996), 49–63.
14. Margaret A. Murray, *The Witch-Cult in Western Europe* (Oxford, 1921).
15. Norman Cohn, *Europe's Inner Demons* (London, 1975).
16. Alan Macfarlane, *Witchcraft in Tudor and Stuart England: A Regional and Comparative Study*, 2nd ed. with introduction by James Sharpe (London, 1999).
17. See Anne Llewellyn Barstow, *Witchcraze: A New History of the European Witch Hunts* (New York, 1994), and Robin Briggs' rebuttal in *Witches and Neighbors* (New York, 1996).
18. Brian P. Levack, *The Witch-Hunt in Early Modern Europe*, 2nd ed. (London & New York 1995), 120.

The Devil, Heresy, and Magic in the Later Middle Ages

1. Cohn, *Europe's Inner Demons*.
2. Carlo Ginzburg, *Ecstasies. Deciphering the Witches' Sabbath* (New York, 1991).
3. Agrippa, *De Occulta Philosophia*, book 1, chapter 33, in P. G. Maxwell-Stuart, ed., *The Occult in Early Modern Europe: A Documentary History* (Basingstoke, 1999), 71.
4. J. R. Veenstra, *Magic and Divination at the Courts of Burgundy and France. Text and Context of Laurens Pignon's* Contre les Devineurs *(1411)* (Leiden, 1998), 134–5.
5. As cited in Robert Mathiesen, "A Thirteenth-Century Ritual to Attain the Beatific Vision from the *Sworn Book* of Honorius of Thebes," in *Conjuring Spirits: Texts and Traditions of Medieval Ritual Magic*, ed. Claire Fanger (University Park, PA, 1998), 143–62, here 148.
6. Kieckhefer, *Magic in the Middle Ages*, 73.
7. Richard Kieckhefer, *Forbidden Rites: A Necromancer's Manual of the Fifteenth Century* (University Park, PA, 1997), 64.
8. Flint, *The Rise of Magic in Early Medieval Europe*.
9. Kieckhefer, *Magic in the Middle Ages*, 58–9.
10. Edward Bever, "Witchcraft Fears and Psychosocial Factors in Disease," *Journal of Interdisciplinary History* 30(2000), 573–90.
11. Miri Rubin, *Corpus Christi: The Eucharist in Late Medieval Culture* (Cambridge, 1991).
12. Susan Stuard, "The Dominion of Gender: Women's Fortunes in the High Middle Ages," in *Becoming Visible: Women in European History*, eds. Renate Bridenthal, Claudia Koonz, and Susan Stuard, 2nd ed. (Boston, 1987), 153–74.
13. Paul Fredericq, ed., *Corpus documentorum Inquisitionis haereticae pravitatis Neerlandicae*, 3 (Gent and Gravenhage, 1906), 17. Hereafter, Fredericq, *Corpus*.
14. James Sharpe, *Instruments of Darkness: Witchcraft in England, 1550–1750* (London, 1996), 75.
15. Fernando Cervantes, *The Devil in the New World: The Impact of Diabolism in New Spain* (New Haven and London, 1994), 3.
16. "Tspel van Sinte Trudo," in G. Kalff, *Trou Moet Blycken. Toneelstukken der zestiende eeuw* (Groningen, 1889), 89, line 192.
17. Cervantes, *The Devil in the New World*, 20; See also Cohn, *Europe's Inner Demons*, 73.
18. John Bossy, *Christianity in the West 1400–1700* (Oxford, 1985), 35–8, 138–9; "Moral Arithmetic: Seven Sins into Ten Commandments," in Edmund Leites, ed., *Conscience and Casuistry in Early Modern Europe* (Cambridge, 1988), 215–30.
19. Langmuir, *History, Religion, and Antisemitism*, 288.
20. In Jacob R. Marcus, ed., *The Jew in the Medieval World: A Source Book: 1315–1791* (New York, 1978), 121–6, esp. 125.
21. From Marvin Perry *et al.*, eds., *Sources of the Western Tradition* (Boston, 1987), 1:257.
22. Langmuir, *History, Religion, and Antisemitism*, 299.
23. Ruben, *Corpus Christi*, 113.
24. Cited in Brian Tierney, ed., *The Middle Ages*, vol. 1, *Sources of Medieval History*, 5th ed. (New York, 1992), 260.

25. Bernard Hamilton, *The Medieval Inquisition* (London, 1981), 25.

26. Langmuir, *History, Religion, and Antisemitism*, 263.

27. Walter L. Wakefield and Austin P. Evans, eds., *Heresies of the High Middle Ages* (New York, 1969, 1991), 217–19.

28. Hamilton, *The Medieval Inquisition*, 38–9.

29. See Emmanuel Le Roy Ladurie, *Montaillou: The Promised Land of Error*, trans. Barbara Bray (New York, 1979).

30. Malcolm Lambert, *The Cathars* (Oxford, 1998), 315.

31. Gabriel Audisio, *The Waldensian Dissent: Persecution and Survival c1170–c1570*, trans. Claire Davison (Cambridge, 1999), 73.

32. As cited by Cohn, *Europe's Inner Demons*, 22.

33. Gavin Langmuir, *Toward a Definition of Antisemitism* (Berkeley, 1990), chap. 12.

34. Willam Monter, "Witchcraft," in Hans J. Hillerbrand, ed., *Oxford Encyclopedia of the Reformation* (New York & Oxford, 1996), IV: 276–82, here 276–7. Hereafter *OER*.

35. Robert E. Lerner, *The Heresy of the Free Spirit in the Later Middle Ages* (Berkeley, 1972), 136–7.

36. Ibid., 18–19, 63–5.

37. Ginzburg, *Ecstasies*, 68; and Malcolm Barber, "Lepers, Jews and Moslems: The Plot to Overthrow Christendom in 1321," *History* 66 (1981), 1–17.

38. Langmuir, *History, Religion, and Antisemitism*, 303.

39. John Edwards, "Why the Spanish Inquisition?'" in *Christianity and Judaism*, ed. Diana Wood (Oxford, 1992), 221–36, here 230.

40. As cited by Edwards, "Why the Spanish Inquisition?," 230–1.

41. Cecil Roth, *The Spanish Inquisition* (New York and London, 1964), 52–3.

42. Eugen Weber, *Apocalypses: Prophecies, Cults and Millennial Beliefs through the Ages* (Toronto, 1999), 58.

43. Julio Caro Baroja, "Witchcraft and Catholic Theology," in *Early Modern European Witchcraft: Centres and Peripheries*, eds. Bengt Ankarloo and Gustav Henningsen (Oxford, 1990), 19–43, here 26.

44. As cited in Alan C. Kors and Edward Peters, eds., *Witchcraft in Europe, 1100–1700: A Documentary History* (Philadelphia, 1972), 79.

45. Baroja, "Witchcraft and Catholic Theology," 27.

46. Kors and Peters, *Witchcraft*, 80–1.

47. Ibid., 82.

48. Veenstra, *Magic and Divination*, 48–50.

49. Ibid., 77–8.

50. Richard Kieckhefer, *European Witch Trials: Their Foundations in Popular and Learned Culture, 1300–1500* (London, 1976), esp. 108–74.

51. Cohn, *Europe's Inner Demons*, 198–203.

52. Wolfgang Behringer, *Shaman of Oberstdorf: Chonrad Stoeckhlin and the Phantoms of the Night*, trans. H. C. Erik Midelfort (Charlottesville, 1998), 130–1.

53. Arno Borst, "The Origins of the Witch-Craze in the Alps," in Arno Borst, *Medieval Worlds: Barbarians, Heretics, and Artists in the Middle Ages*, trans. Eric Hansen (Chicago, 1991), 101–22.

54. Borst, *Medieval Worlds*, 121, summarizing František Graus, *Das Spätmittelalter als Krisenzeit* (1969).

55. Richard Kieckhefer, "Avenging the Blood of Children: Anxiety Over Child Victims and the Origins of the European Witch Trials," in *The Devil, Heresy and Witchcraft in the Middle Ages: Essays in Honor of Jeffrey B. Russell*, ed. Alberto Ferreiro (Leiden, 1998), 91–110.

56. Kieckhefer, *European Witch Trials*, 119.

57. Ibid., 10–26.

58. Wolfgang Behringer, *Witchcraft Persecutions in Bavaria: Popular Magic, Religious Zealotry and the Reason of State in Early Modern Europe*, trans. J. C. Grayson and David Lederer (Cambridge, 1997), 70.

59. Kieckhefer, *European Witch Trials*, 122–3.

60. Franco Mormando, *The Preacher's Demons: Bernardino of Siena and the Social Underworld of Early Renaissance Italy* (Chicago, 1999), 88.

61. Ginzburg, *Ecstasies*, 297–300.

62. Mormando, *The Preacher's Demons*, 52.

63. Ibid., 53–4.

64. As cited by Kieckhefer, "Avenging the Blood," 95.

65. Mormando, *The Preacher's Demons*, 81.

66. Kieckhefer, "Avenging the Blood," 102.

67. Behringer, *Shaman of Oberstdorf*, 131.

68. See, for example, Andreas Blauert, ed., *Ketzer, Zauberer, Hexen: Die Anfänge der europäischen Hexenverfolgungen* (Frankfurt am Main, 1990).

69. Martine Ostorero, *Folâtrer avec les démons* (Lausanne, 1995).

70. Cohn, *Europe's Inner Demons*, 230.

71. Ibid., 231.

72. Fredericq, *Corpus*, 3:93–109.

73. This inquiry seems to have resulted in the sorcery trial on October 27, 1460 in Lille of Caterine Patée. Ibid., 3:112–13.

74. Joseph Klaits, *Servants of Satan: The Age of the Witch Hunts* (Bloomington, 1985), 42.

75. Kieckhefer, *European Witch Trials*, 133–40.

76. Eric Wilson, "The Text and Context of the Malleus Maleficarum (1487)," Ph.D. Diss. (Cambridge University, 1991), 71–6.

77. Jürgen Petersohn, "Konziliaristen und Hexen: Ein unbekannter Brief des Inquisitors Heinrich Institoris an Papst Sixtus IV aus dem Jahre 1484," *Deutsches Archiv für Erforschung des Mittelalters* 44 (1988), 120–60.

78. Eric Wilson, "Institoris at Innsbruck: Heinrich Institoris, the *Summis Desiderantes* and the Brixen Witch-Trial of 1485," in *Popular Religion in Germany and Central Europe, 1400–1800*, eds. Bob Scribner and Trevor Johnson (Houndmills, Eng., 1996), 87–100, esp. 100.

79. Ibid., 86–7.

80. Ibid., 89–90.

81. Walter E. Stephens, "Witches Who Steal Penises: Impotence and Illusion in *Malleus maleficarum*," *Journal of Medieval and Early Modern Studies* 28 (1998), 495–529; also his *Demon Lovers: Witchcraft, Sex, and Belief* (Chicago, 2002).

82. Wilson, "Institoris at Innsbruck," 96.

83. Ulric Molitor, *Des Sorcières et des Devineresses*. Reproduit en fac-simile d'après L'Édition Latine de Cologne 1489 et Traduit pour la Première fois en France. Bibliothèque Magique des XV e et XVI e Siècles I (Paris, 1926), 81.

84. Fredericq, *Corpus*, 2:273–7.
85. Ibid., 3:141–3.
86. Ibid., 1:458–9.
87. Ibid., 2:278.
88. Ibid., 2:288–9.
89. Ibid., 2:291.
90. Ibid., 2:279.
91. Ibid., 2:280–92, here 290–1.
92. Ibid., 3:158.
93. Ibid., 1:483–6.
94. Therese Decker and Martin W. Walsh, eds., *Mariken van Nieumeghen: A Bilingual Edition* (Columbia, SC, 1994).
95. Dyan Elliot, *Fallen Bodies: Pollution, Sexuality, & Demonology in the Middle Ages* (Philadelphia, 1999).
96. Richard Marius, *Luther: The Christian between God and Death* (Cambridge, MA, 1999), 41–2.

The Reformation and the End of the World

1. Wilson, "The Text and Context," 105–7.
2. Erasmus, "A Journey for Religion's Sake," in *Scheming Papists and Lutheran Fools: Five Reformation Satires*, ed. Erika Rummel (New York, 1993), 88–117, esp. 99–100 and 116.
3. In *The Erasmus Reader*, ed. Erika Rummel (Toronto, 1990), 144.
4. Marius, *Luther*, 44.
5. Heiko A. Oberman, *Luther: Man between God and the Devil*, trans. Eileen Walliser-Schwarzbart (New Haven, 1989), 102.
6. Ibid., 104.
7. As cited in Ibid.; originally from Luther's "Table Talk" (*Tischreden*), informal comments recorded by Luther's students and dinner companions.
8. Ibid., 102–3.
9. Robin Barnes, "Apocalypticism," *OER* I: 63–7, here 65.
10. Piero Camporesi, *Bread of Dreams: Food and Fantasy in Early Modern Europe*, trans. David Gentilcore (Oxford, 1989).
11. Claus-Peter Clasen, *Anabaptism: A Social History, 1525–1618* (Ithaca, 1972), 180.
12. Werner O. Packull, "The Image of the 'Common Man' in the Early Pamphlets," *Historical Reflections*, 12 (1985), 253–77.
13. James M. Stayer, *The German Peasants' War and Anabaptist Community of Goods* (Kingston and Montreal, 1991), 7.
14. Peter Blickle, *The Revolution of 1525* (Baltimore, 1981).
15. Thomas Müntzer, "Sermon Before the Princes," in George H. Williams and Angel M. Mergal, eds., *Spiritual and Anabaptist Writers* (Philadelphia, 1957), 47–70.
16. Hans-Jürgen Goertz, "Thomas Müntzer: Revolutionary in a Mystical Spirit," in *Profiles of Radical Reformers*, eds. Hans-Jürgen Goertz and Walter Klaassen (Kitchener and Scottdale, 1982), 29–44, here 39–40.

17. Tom Scott and Robert W. Scribner, eds., *The German Peasants' War. A History in Documents* (Atlantic Highlands, NJ, 1991), 158.
18. James M. Stayer, "Anabaptists," *OER*, I: 31–2.
19. Ibid., 34.
20. Cited by Stayer, *The German Peasants' War*, 63–4.
21. Stayer, *The German Peasants' War*; C. Arnold Snyder, *Anabaptist History and Theology: An Introduction* (Kitchener, Ontario, 1995).
22. Scott and Scribner, *The German Peasants' War*, 328–30.
23. Barnes, "Apocalypticism," 65.
24. See Gary K. Waite, *David Joris and Dutch Anabaptism, 1524–1543* (Waterloo, 1990).
25. See Gary K. Waite, "'Man is a Devil to Himself': David Joris and the Rise of a Sceptical Tradition towards the Devil in the Early Modern Netherlands, 1540–1600," *Nederlands Archief voor Kerkgeschiedenis/Dutch Review of Church History*, 75/1(1995), 1–30.
26. From John Dillenberger, ed., *Martin Luther: Selections from his writings* (New York, 1961), 349.
27. Scott and Scribner, *The German Peasants' War*, 225.
28. Ibid., 226.
29. Fredericq, *Corpus*, IV: 137–8.
30. Natalie Zemon Davis, "Women on Top," in her *Society and Culture in Early Modern France* (Stanford, 1975), 124–51.
31. Merry E. Wiesner, "Nuns, Wives, and Mothers: Women and the Reformation in Germany," in *Women in Reformation and Counter-Reformation Europe*, ed. Sherrin Marshall (Bloomington, 1989), 8–28, esp. 10.
32. "Dit zijn de mirakelen die Luther doet," in Herman Pleij, ed., *'T is al vrouwenwerk. Refreinen van Anna Bijns* (Amsterdam, 1987), 49.
33. Merry E. Wiesner-Hanks, "Women," *OER* IV: 290–8, esp. 295.
34. Wiesner, "Nuns, Wives, and Mothers," 15.
35. Gary K. Waite, "Between the devil and the inquisitor: anabaptists, diabolical conspiracies and magical beliefs in the sixteenth-century Netherlands," in *Radical Reformation Studies: Essays presented to James M. Stayer*, eds. Werner O. Packull and Geoffrey L. Dipple (Aldershot, 1999), 120–40.
36. Ibid., 132.
37. Sigrun Haude, *In the Shadow of 'Savage Wolves': Anabaptist Münster and the German Reformation during the 1530s* (Leiden, 2000), 14.
38. Sigrun Haude, "Anabaptist Women – Radical Women?," in *Infinite Boundaries: Order, Disorder, and Reorder in Early Modern German Culture*, ed. Max Reinhart (Kirksville, MO, 1998), 313–28.
39. Haude, *In the Shadow*, 112.
40. *Newe zeytung von den Wydertaufferen zu Münster* (Nurnberg, 1535) fol. Biiir.
41. Haude, *In the Shadow*, 20.
42. Waite, "Between the Devil and the Inquisitor," 130–1.
43. Albert F. Mellink, ed., *Documenta Anabaptistica Neerlandica*, II: *Amsterdam (1536–1578)* (Leiden, 1980), 263.
44. D. Jonathan Grieser, "Seducers of the simple folk: The polemical war against anabaptism (1525–1540)," Th.D. diss. (Harvard University, 1993), 24; Sigrun Haude, *In the Shadow*.

45. Irvin B. Horst, *The Radical Brethren: Anabaptism and the English Reformation to 1558* (Nieuwkoop, 1972), 77.

46. James Contreras and Gustav Henningsen, "Forty-four Thousand Cases of the Spanish Inquisition (1540–1700): Analysis of a Historical Data Bank," in Gustav Henningsen and John Tedeschi, eds., *The Inquisition in Early Modern Europe: Studies on Sources and Methods* (Dekalb, IL, 1986), 100–24.

47. Mark U. Edwards, *Luther's Last Battles: Politics and Polemics, 1531–46* (Ithaca, 1983).

48. However, see also F. E. Beemon, "The Myth of the Spanish Inquisition and the Preconditions of the Dutch Revolt," *Archiv für Reformationsgeschichte* 85 (1994), 246–64.

Heresy, Doubt, and Demonizing the "Other"

1. Brian P. Levack, "The Decline and End of Witchcraft Prosecutions," in *Witchcraft and Magic in Europe: The Eighteenth and Nineteenth Centuries*, eds. Marijke Gijswijt-Hofstra, Brian P. Levack, and Roy Porter, vol. 5, The Athlone History of Witchcraft and Magic in Europe, eds. Bengt Ankarloo and Stuart Clark (London, 1999), 1–94, here 41.

2. The terminology of religiosity and official religion is from Langmuir, *History, Religion, and Antisemitism*.

3. Gerald Strauss, *Luther's House of Learning: Indoctrination of the Young in the German Reformation* (Baltimore, 1978).

4. See esp. Alfred F. Soman, "The Parlement of Paris and the Great Witch Hunt (1565–1640)," *Sixteenth Century Journal* 9 (1978), 31–44.

5. *Die catalogen oft inuentarisen vanden quaden verboden boucken, ende van andere goede, diemen den iongen scholieren leeren mach: na aduys der Uniuersiteyt van Loeuen* (Louvain, 1550), bir.

6. Samme Zijlstra, *Nicolaas Meyndertsz van Blesdijk. Een bijdrage tot de geschiedenis van het Davidjorisme* (Assen, 1983), 110–14.

7. Christopher W. Marsh, *The Family of Love in English Society, 1550–1630* (Cambridge, 1994).

8. Benjamin J. Kaplan, *Calvinists and Libertines: Confession and Community in Utrecht, 1578–1620* (Oxford, 1995).

9. Dirck Volckertsz Coornhert, *Wercken* (Amsterdam, 1630/31), vol. 1, 89r.

10. Andrew C. Fix, *Prophecy and Reason. The Dutch Collegiants in the Early Enlightenment* (Princeton, 1991).

11. Jonathan Pearl, *The Crime of Crimes: Demonology and Politics in France, 1560–1620* (Waterloo, 1998), 30–1.

12. Midelfort, *Witch Hunting in Southwestern Germany*, 27.

13. Perez Zagorin, *Ways of Lying: Dissimulation, Persecution, and Conformity in Early Modern Europe* (Cambridge, MA, 1990).

14. Willem Frijhoff, "Het Gelders Antichrist-tractaat (1524) en zijn auteur," *Archief voor de Geschiedenis van de Katholieke Kerk in Nederland*, 28 (1986), 192–217, esp. 206–7. See also Clark, *Thinking with Demons*, 333.

15. Barnes, "Apocalypticism," *OER* I: 63–7, here 66; and Andrew Cunningham and Ole Peter Grell, *The Four Horsemen of the Apocalypse: Religion, War, Famine and Death in Reformation Europe* (Cambridge, 2000), 9.

16. Stuart Clark, "Protestant Demonology: Sin, Superstition, and Society (c.1520–c.1630)," in Ankarloo and Henningsen, *Early Modern European Witchcraft*, 45–81, here 47–8.

17. Ottavia Niccoli, *Prophecy and People in Renaissance Italy* (Princeton, 1990).

18. A point made by R. Po-chia Hsia, "Jews," *OER* 2: 339–45, here 340.

19. R. Po-Chia Hsia, *The Myth of Ritual Murder. Jews and Magic in Reformation Germany* (New Haven, 1988), 125–31, esp. 131.

20. As cited in Ibid., 132.

21. Ibid., 136–62.

22. *Corte ende waerachtighe beschrijuinge van eenen Jode/Ghenaemt: ASVERVS Die by de Kruysinghe Christi gheweest is/ . . .* (Sleswicht, 1601).

23. Hsia, "Jews," 343.

24. Bernard Lewis, *Cultures in Conflict: Christians, Muslims, and Jews in the Age of Discovery* (New York and Oxford, 1995).

25. Cervantes, *The Devil in the New World*, 6.

26. Ibid., 8.

27. Ibid., 16.

28. *Wunderbarliche vnd erschröckliche geschichte/so durch donner vnd blitz zu Mechelen in Brabant . . . geschehen* (n.p., n.d. [1546]).

29. *Newe zeittung/ der man furmals nicht viel gehöret/ die sich begeben haben in Nidderland/ zu Mecheln* (n.p., n.d. [1546]).

30. See also Sabine Holtz, "Der Fürst dieser Welt: Die Bedrohung der Lebenswelt aus lutherisch-orthodoxer Perspektive," *Zeitschrift für Kirchengeschichte*, 107 (1996), 29–49, esp. 29.

31. *Den val der Roomscher Kercken/mer al hare afgoderie* (n.p., 1556).

32. Carleton Cunningham, "The Devil and the Religious Controversies of Sixteenth-Century France," *Essays in History* 35 (1993), 34–47, here 37.

33. Craig M. Koslofsky, *The Reformation of the Dead: Death and Ritual in Early Modern Germany, 1450–1700* (Basingstoke, 2000).

34. *Een Colloquie oft tsamensprekinghe van twee personagien/ waer af die eene Pasquillus/ ende de andere Marphorius genaemt is* (n.p., n.d. [1565]), Aiiv and Biv v.

35. *Een schoone Vraeghe van eenen Bwr hoe dat hy eenen Pape geuraecht heeft/van weghen sommigher Articulen* (n.p., 1565), Aiiij v.

36. The above quotations are from Stuart Clark, *Thinking with Demons*, 140.

37. Robert W. Scribner, "The Reformation, Popular Magic, and the 'Disenchantment of the World'," *Journal of Interdisciplinary History*, 23 (1993), 475–94, here 486.

38. Pearl, *The Crime of Crimes*, 32.

39. These citations are from Ibid., 66–8.

40. Denis Richet, "Sociocultural Aspects of Religious Conflicts in Paris during the Second Half of the Sixteenth Century," in *Ritual, Religion, and the Sacred: Selections from the Annales, Economies, Sociétés, Civilisations* vol. 7, eds. Robert Forster and Orest Ranum, trans. Elborg Forster and Patricia M. Ranum (Baltimore and London, 1982), 182–221, here 194; also Natalie Zemon Davis, "The Rites of Violence," in *Society and Culture in Early Modern France*, 152–85, esp. 179.

41. As cited by Pearl, *The Crime of Crimes*, 71.
42. Willem Verlinde, *Een Claer betooch vanden oorspronck der Lutherie, Van die menichvuldicheyt der Secten* (Brugge, 1567), 262–3.
43. Verlinde, *Oprecht Tryakel Teghen t'venijn alder dolinghen onser tijdts* (Antwerpen, 1567), 121r.
44. Stuart Clark, "Inversion, Misrule and the Meaning of Witchcraft," *Past and present* 87(May 1980), 98–127, esp. 99, 127.
45. Werner O. Packull, *Hutterite Beginnings: Communitarian Experiments during the Reformation* (Baltimore, 1995), 173.
46. Kevin C. Robbins, "Magical Emasculation, Popular Anticlericalism, and the Limits of the Reformation in Western France circa 1590," *Journal of Social History* 31 (1997), 61–83.
47. As cited by Midelfort, *Witch Hunting in Southwestern Germany*, 59.
48. Packull, *Hutterite Beginnings*, 194.
49. Christoffen Erhard, *Gründliche kurtz verfaste Historia. Von Münsterischen Widertauffern: vnd wie die Hutterischen Brüder* (München, 1588).
50. Johann Carion, *Een Chronijcke van al tghene datter gheschiet is vant beghinsel des weerelts totten iare M.CCCCC.ende xliii.* (Antwerpen, 1543), 62v.
51. Grieser, "Seducers of the Simple Folk", 24; Haude, *In the Shadow of 'Savage Wolves'*.
52. *Histoire memorable de la persecution et saccagement du peuple de Merindol et Cabrieres* (1555), as translated by Maxwell-Stuart, *The Occult in Early Modern Europe*, 169.
53. David W. Sabean, *Power in the Blood. Popular Culture & Village Discourse in Early Modern Germany* (Cambridge, 1984), 58.
54. Justus Menius, *Von dem Geist der Widerteuffer* (n.p., 1544), 4v.
55. Adam Crato, *Rettung Des Christlichen Tauffbuchleins Heern D. Martini Lutheri.* (n.p., 1591), 3, 8 and 10. For this controversy, see Bodo Nischan, "The Exorcism Controversy and Baptism in the Late Reformation," *The Sixteenth Century Journal*, 18 (1987), 31–51.
56. Scribner, "The Reformation, Popular Magic," 487.
57. (Sigmund Feyerabend) *Theatrvm Diabolorum* (Franckfurt am Main, 1569), introduction.
58. H. C. Erik Midelfort, "The Devil and the German People: Reflections on the Popularity of Demon Possession in Sixteenth-Century Germany," in *Religion and Culture in the Renaissance and Reformation*, ed. Steven Ozment (Kirksville, MO, 1989), 99–119, here 111 and 115.
59. Behringer, *Witchcraft Persecutions in Bavaria*, 112–13.
60. Lorna Jane Abray, *The People's Reformation: Magistrates, Clergy, and Commons in Strasbourg 1500–1598* (Oxford, 1985), 170–4.
61. Linda C. Hults, "Baldung and the Witches of Freiburg: The Evidence of Images," *Journal of Interdisciplinary History* 18 (1987), 249–76.
62. John D. Derksen, "Strasbourg's Religious Radicals from 1525 to 1570: A Social History," Ph.D. diss., Univ. of Manitoba, 1993, 289–96; Marc Lienhard, Stephen F. Nelson, and Hans Georg Rott, eds., *Quellen zur Geschichte der Täufer*, vol. 16, *Elsass IV, Stadt Straßburg 1543–1552* (Gutersloh, 1988), Beilage, 537.

63. Lienhard, Nelson and Rott, *Stadt Straßburg*, 119–21.
64. "Witchcraft in Geneva, 1537–1662," *Journal of Modern History* 43 (1971), 179–204, esp.189; reprinted in E. William Monter, *Enforcing Morality in Early Modern Europe* (London, 1987).
65. Monter, "Witchcraft in Geneva," 190–1.
66. Sigrid Brauner, *Fearless Wives and Frightened Shrews: The Construction of the Witch in Early Modern Germany*, ed. Robert H. Brown (Amherst, 1995).
67. Haude, "Anabaptist Women – Radical Women?," 313–28.

The Reformation, Magic, and Witchcraft, 1520–1600

1. Michael H. Keefer, "Agrippa's Dilemma: Hermetic 'Rebirth' and the Ambivalences of *De Vanitate* and *De Occulta Philosophia*," *Renaissance Quarterly* 41 (1988), 614–53.
2. Frances A. Yates, *The Occult Philosophy in the Elizabethan Age* (London, 1979), 44–5.
3. Cornelius Agrippa, *De Occulta Philosophia*, book 1, chapter 2, as translated in Maxwell-Stuart, *The Occult in Early Modern Europe*, 116.
4. This discussion and citations are from Wayne Shumaker, *The Occult Sciences in the Renaissance: A Study in Intellectual Patterns* (Berkeley, 1972), 136–8.
5. Charles G. Nauert, Jr., "Agrippa, Heinrich Cornelius," *OER* I: 12–13, here 12.
6. George Mora, gen. ed., *Witches, Devils, and Doctors in the Renaissance: Johann Weyer, 'De praestigiis daemonum'* (Binghamton, NY, 1991), xxx.
7. As cited by Richard H. Popkin, *The History of Scepticism from Erasmus to Spinoza*, 2nd ed. (Berkeley, 1979), 24.
8. Paola Zambelli, "Magic and Radical Reformation in Agrippa of Nettesheim," *Journal of the Warburg and Courtauld Institutes* 39 (1976), 69–103.
9. Henry Cornelius Agrippa, *Of the Vanitie and Vncertaintie of Artes and Sciences*, ed. Catherine M. Dunn (Northridge, CA, 1974), 129–30. See also Levack, *The Witch-Hunt*, 55–6.
10. James R. Keller, "The Science of Salvation: Spiritual Alchemy in Donne's Final Sermon," *Sixteenth Century Journal*, 23 (1992), 486–93, esp. 487.
11. Allison P. Coudert, *The Impact of the Kabbalah in the Seventeenth Century: The Life and Thought of Francis Mercury van Helmont (1614–1698)* (Leiden, 1999), 144–5.
12. Ibid., 227.
13. Andrew Weeks, *Paracelsus: Speculative Theory and the Crisis of the Early Reformation* (Albany, 1997), 31.
14. Cunningham and Ole Peter Grell, *The Four Horsemen of the Apocalypse*, 87.
15. Cited in Behringer, *Witchcraft Persecutions in Bavaria*, 116.
16. Clark, "Protestant Demonology," 71–2.
17. Midelfort, *Witch Hunting in Southwestern Germany*, 37–8.
18. Mora, *Witches, Devils, and Doctors*, xxxi.
19. Clark, *Thinking with Demons*, 205.
20. Mora, *Witches, Devils, and Doctors*, 285.
21. Ibid., 294–5.

22. Both citations are from H. C. Erik Midelfort, the first from "Johann Weyer in medizinischer, theologischer und rechtsgeschichtlicher Hinsicht," in *Vom Unfug des Hexen-Processes: Gegner der Hexenverfolgungen von Johann Weyer bis Friedrich Spee*, eds. Hartmut Lehmann and Otto Ulbricht (Wiesbaden, 1991), 53–64, esp. 59; the second from "Johann Weyer and the Transformation of the Insanity Defense," in *The German People and the Reformation*, ed. R. Po-Chia Hsia (Ithaca and London, 1988), 234–61, esp. 238.

23. Mora, *Witches, Devils, and Doctors*, 529–35.

24. Ibid., 324.

25. Clark, *Thinking with Demons*, 202–3.

26. Johann Weyer, *De praestigiis daemonvm* (n.p., 1567), Av v.

27. See Gary K. Waite, "The Radical Reformation and the Medical Profession: The Spiritualist David Joris and the Brothers Weyer (Wier)," in *Radikalität und Dissent im 16. Jahrhundert/Radicalism and Dissent in the Sixteenth Century*, eds. Hans-Jürgen Goertz and James M. Stayer (Berlin, 2002), 167–85; and Hans de Waardt, "Johan Wiers *De Praestigiis*: Mythes en Motivatie," in Jan Jacob Cobben, ed. *Duivelse Bezetenheid: Beschreven door dokter Johannes Wier, 1515–1588* (Rotterdam, 2002), 17–74.

28. Bodin, *On the Demon-Mania of Witches*, 37.

29. Ibid., 38. For Adeline, see also Cohn, *Europe's Inner Demons*, 230.

30. Bodin, *On the Demon-Mania of Witches*, 38, 44.

31. Ibid., 146.

32. Ibid., 147.

33. Ibid., 148–9.

34. Mora, *Witches, Devils, and Doctors*, 583–4.

35. Fredericq, *Corpus*, 5:213–17.

36. Monter, "Witchcraft," *OER* IV, 277–8.

37. Bob Scribner, "Witchcraft and Judgement in Reformation Germany," *History Today* (April, 1990), 12–19, here 12. The following example comes also from Scribner.

38. Hans de Waardt, *Toverij en samenleving. Holland 1500–1800* (Den Haag, 1991), 52.

39. These cases are all from De Waardt, *Toverij en samenleving*, 52–63.

40. Referring to a particularly puzzling case from the seventeenth century, Erik Midelfort asks why this case was not treated as witchcraft. He replies, "But also perhaps because ordinary people were having trouble keeping the supposedly clear categories of witchcraft and possession clearly separate." H. C. Erik Midelfort, *A History of Madness in Sixteenth-Century Germany* (Stanford, 1999), 77.

41. Bodin, *On the Demon-Mania of Witches*, 109.

42. See Carleton Cunningham, "The Devil and the Religious Controversies of Sixteenth-Century France," *Essays in History*, 35 (1993), 34–47; and Pearl, *Crime of Crimes*, 43–5.

43. Pearl, *Crime of Crimes*, 44.

44. D. P. Walker, *Unclean Spirits: Possession and Exorcism in France and England in the Late Sixteenth and Early Seventeenth Centuries* (Philadelphia, 1981), 27.

45. Pearl, *Crime of Crimes*, 44.

46. See Irena Backus, ed., *Guillaume Postel et Jean Boulaese: De summopere (1566) et Le Miracle de Laon (1566)* (Geneva, 1995).

47. De Waardt, *Toverij en samenleving*, 67.
48. J. ter Gouw, *Geschiedenis van Amsterdam* (Amsterdam, 1878–1893), vol. 5 (1886), 412.
49. *Newe zeittung. In welcher Kürtzlich, ordentlich vnd warhafftighlich, nach aller vmstendigkeit erzelet wird, was sich in der berhümbten Kauffstadt Antorff zwischen den 18. vnd 28. Augusti dieses 1566* (n.p., 1566).
50. G. Brandt, *Historie der Reformatie, en andre kerkelyke geschiedenissen in en ontrent de Nederlanden* (Amsterdam, 1671), vol. I: 356–7.
51. De Waardt, *Toverij en samenleving*, 70–4; A. Querido, *Storm in het weeshuis: De beroering onder de Amsterdamse burgerwezen in 1566* (Amsterdam, 1958).
52. Waite, "Between the Devil and the Inquisitor," 139.
53. Levack, *The Witch-Hunt*, 120.
54. E. William Monter, "Heresy Executions in Reformation Europe, 1520–1565," in *Tolerance and Intolerance in the European Reformation*, eds. Ole Peter Grell and Bob Scribner (Cambridge, 1996), 48–64, esp. 49–50.
55. Willem de Blécourt/Hans de Waardt, "Das Vordringen der Zaubereiverfolgungen in die Niederlande Rhein, Maas und Schelde entlang," in Andreas Blauert, ed., *Ketzer, Zauberer, Hexen. Die Anfänge der europäischen Hexenverfolgungen* (Frankfurt a.M., 1990), 182–216.
56. I am currently preparing a more detailed study on this subject tentatively entitled "Anabaptists, the Devil, and Witchcraft in The Netherlands and Germany, 1535–1600."
57. Carlo Ginzburg, *Night Battles: Witchcraft & Agrarian Cults in the Sixteenth & Seventeenth Centuries*, trans. John and Anne Tedeschi (New York and Middlesex, 1983).
58. Julio Caro Baroja, *The World of the Witches*, trans. O. N. V Glendinning (Chicago, 1964), 148.
59. John Tedeschi, "Inquisitorial Law and the Witch," in Ankarloo and Henningsen, *Early Modern European Witchcraft*, 84–118, here 85; Ruth Martin, *Witchcraft and the Inquisition in Venice, 1550–1650* (Oxford, 1989), 6.
60. Martin, *Witchcraft*, 15.
61. Johan Weyer, foreword, *De praestigiis daemonvm*. Aivr–Av v.

Religious Conflict and the Rise of Witch-Hunting 1562–1630

1. Martino del Rio, *Disquisitiones Magicae*, in Maxwell-Stuart, *The Occult in Early Modern Europe*, 165.
2. *Demonolatry by Nicolas Remy, Privy Councillor to The Most Serene Duke of Lorraine, and Public Advocate to his Duchy, in 3 Books . . .* trans. E. A. Ashwin, ed. Montague Summers (London, 1930), v.
3. Sharpe, *Instruments of Darkness*, 141.
4. Behringer, *Witchcraft Persecutions in Bavaria*, 116–17.
5. Briggs, "Many Reasons Why", 49–63, esp. 55.
6. Levack, *The Witch-Hunt*, 21–4.
7. Monter, "Heresy executions in Reformation Europe."
8. Weber, *Apocalypses*, 70.

9. In Wolfgang Behringer, ed., *Hexen und Hexenprozesse in Deutschland* (München, 1988), 136–7.

10. Midelfort, *Witch Hunting in Southwestern Germany*, 88–90.

11. Details of this will be provided in my unpublished "Anabaptists, the Devil, and Witchcraft in The Netherlands and Germany." For other areas, see Achim R. Baumgarten, *Hexenwahn und Hexenverfolgung im Naheraum: Ein Beitrag zur Sozial- und Kulturgeschichte* (Frankfurt am Main, 1987), 87.

12. *Dionysius Dreytweins Esslingische Chronik (1548–1564)*, ed. Adolf Diehl (Tübingen, 1901), 246.

13. Wolfgang Behringer, "Witchcraft Studies in Austria, Germany and Switzerland," in Barry, Hester, and Roberts, *Witchcraft in Early Modern Europe*, 64–95, here 75.

14. Behringer, "Witchcraft Studies," 87–8.

15. P. G. Maxwell-Stuart, *Witchcraft in Europe and the New World, 1400–1800* (Basingstoke, 2001), 56–7.

16. W. Rummel, *Bauern, Herren und Hexen: Studien zur Sozialgeschichte sponheimischer und kurttrierscher Hexenprozesse, 1574–1664* (Göttingen, 1991).

17. Midelfort, *Witch Hunting in Southwestern Germany*, 138; Levack, *The Witch-Hunt*, 116–17.

18. Midelfort, *Witch Hunting in Southwestern Germany*, 101.

19. Both citations are from Midelfort, *Witch Hunting in Southwestern Germany*, 104 and 108 resp.

20. As cited in Ibid., 109.

21. Ibid., 112.

22. For Junius' letter, see E. William Monter, ed., *European Witchcraft* (New York, 1969), 81–7.

23. Clark, *Thinking with Demons*, 140.

24. Behringer, *Witchcraft Persecutions in Bavaria*, 83.

25. Gerhard Schormann, *Der Krieg gegen die Hexen: Das Ausrottungsprogramm des Kurfursten von Koln* (Gottingen, 1991).

26. Gisela Wilbertz, Gerd Schwerhoff and Jürgen Schleffer, eds., *Hexenverfolgung und Regionalgeschichte: Die Grafshaft Lippe im Vergleich* (Bielefeld, 1994), esp. Christine Meier, "Die Anfänge der Hexenprozesse in Lemgo," 83–106, here 90–3.

27. Levack, *The Witch-Hunt*, 22–3.

28. E. William Monter, *Witchcraft in France and Switzerland: The Borderlands during the Reformation* (Ithaca, 1976), 42–66, and *Enforcing Morality in Early Modern Europe* (London, 1987), chap. X "Witchcraft in Geneva, 1537–1662," 179–204 esp. 186–7.

29. Monter, *Witchcraft in France*, 196.

30. Ibid., 116–18.

31. Henry Boguet, *An Examen of Witches Drawn from various trials of many of this sect in the district of Saint Oyan de Joux . . .* trans. E. Allen Ashwin, ed. Montague Summers (1929, facsimile ed. New York, 1971), 4.

32. Ibid., 14.

33. Ibid., 10.

34. Monter, *Witchcraft in France*, 72.

35. Sophie Houdard, *Les sciences du diable: Quartre discours sur la sorcellerie, Xve-XVIIe siecle* (Paris, 1992), 159.

36. Boguet, *Examen of Witches*, xxxi–xxxix.

37. J. Monballyu, *Van hekserij beschuldigd: Heksenprocessen in Vlaanderen tijdens de 16de en 17de eeuw* (Kortrijk-Heule, 1996); and his website at: www.kulak.ac.be

38. Dries Vanysacker, "Het aandeel van de zuidelijke Nederlanden in de europese heksenvervolging," *Trajecta* 9 (2000), 329–49.

39. Alfons K. L. Thijs, *Van Geuzenstad tot katholiek bolwerk: Maatschappelijke betekenis van de kerk in contrareformatorisch Antwerpen* (Turnhout, 1990), 127–36.

40. Midelfort, *A History of Madness*, 77.

41. Remy, *Demonolatry*, ix.

42. Ibid., 188.

43. Macfarlane, *Witchcraft in Tudor and Stuart England*.

44. James Sharpe, introduction, ibid., xxi.

45. Francis Coxe, *A short treatise declaringe the detestable wickednesse of magicall sciences, as Necromancie, Coniurations of spirites, Curiouse Astrologie and suche lyke* (n.p., 1561).

46. *The Examination of John Walsh, before Maister Thomas Williams, ... touchyng Wytchcrafte and Sorcerye, in the presence of diuers gentlemen and others* (London, 1566).

47. Sharpe, *Instruments of Darkness*, 29–30.

48. Keith Thomas, *Religion and the Decline of Magic* (New York, 1971), 462.

49. Deborah Willis, *Malevolent Nurture: Witch-hunting and Maternal Power in Early Modern England* (Ithaca and London, 1995).

50. Malcolm Gaskill, "Witchcraft in Early Modern Kent: Stereotypes and the Background to Accusations," in Barry, Hester, and Roberts, *Witchcraft in Early Modern Europe*, 257–87, here 262.

51. Sharpe, *Instruments of Darkness*, 48–9.

52. Macfarlane, *Witchcraft in Tudor and Stuart England*, 186–8. See most recently Scott McGinnis, "'Subtiltie' Exposed: Pastoral Perspectives on Witch Belief in the Thought of George Gifford," *Sixteenth Century Journal* 33 (2002), 665–686.

53. George Gifford, *Sermons vpon the Whole Booke of the Revelation* (London, 1596), 163.

54. See Max Weber, *The Protestant Ethic and the Spirit of Capitalism* (New York, 1958).

55. Sharpe, *Instruments of Darkness*, 201.

56. As cited by Willis, *Malevolent Nurture*, 118–19.

57. As cited by Sharpe, *Instruments of Darkness*, 89.

58. Richard Godbeer, *The Devil's Dominion: Magic and Religion in Early New England* (Cambridge, 1992), 120–1.

59. As cited by Sharpe, *Instruments of Darkness*, 93.

60. Ibid., 238.

61. D. P. Walker, *Unclean Spirits*, 43–9.

62. Samuel Harsnett, *A Declaration of egregious Popish Impostures, ... vnder the pretence of casting out deuils* (London, 1603).

63. I. D., *The most wonderfull and true storie, of a certaine witch named Alse Gooderige of Stapen hill ...* (London, 1597).

64. As cited by Walker, *Unclean Spirits*, 55.

65. *A Godly and comfortable treatise, Very necessary for all such as are ouer-laden with the burden of their sinnes, & do seeke comfort in christ ...* (London, 1585), C5v.

66. *Triall of Maist. Dorrell, Or A Collection of Defences against Allegations not yet suffered to receiue convenient answere* (n.p., 1599), 3–8.

67. Sharpe, *Instruments of Darkness*, 98.

68. Christopher Haigh, "Success and Failure in the English Reformation," *Past and Present* 173 (November, 2001), 28–49.

69. *A Detection of damnable driftes, practized by three Witches arraigned at Chelmisforde in Essex, . . . whiche were executed in Aprill. 1579* (London, 1579).

70. *A rehearsall both straung and true, of hainous and horrible actes committed by Elizabeth Stile, Alias Rockingham, Mother Dutten, Mother Deuell, Mother Margaret, . . .* (London, 1579).

71. *The Apprehension and confession of three notorious Witches. . . . executed at Chelmes-forde, . . . the 5 day of Iulye, last past, 1589* (London, 1589).

72. Thomas Cooper, *The Mystery of Witchcraft* (London, 1617), A4v–A5r.

73. Christina Larner, *Enemies of God: The Witch-hunt in Scotland* (Baltimore, 1981), 53–8.

74. As cited in Ibid., 68.

75. *Newes from Scotland. Declaring the damnable life of Doctor Fian a notable Sorcerer, who was burned at Edenbrough in Ianuarie last* (London, 1591).

76. P. G. Maxwell-Stuart, "Witchcraft and the Kirk in Aberdeenshire, 1596–97," *Northern Scotland*, 18 (1998), 1–14.

77. Larner, *Enemies of God*, 74–5; see also Brian P. Levack, ed., *Articles on Witchcraft, Magic and Demonology*, vol. 7, *Witchcraft in Scotland* (New York and London, 1992), introduction.

78. Levack, *The Witch-Hunt*, 116, 203–4.

79. Joan Hoff and Marian Yeates, *The Cooper's Wife is Missing: The Trials of Bridget Cleary* (New York, 2000).

Religious Pluralism and the End of the Witch-Hunts

1. Clark, *Thinking with Demons*, 545.

2. From a survey of Paul Valkema Blouw, *Typographia Batava, 1541–1600*, 2 vols. (Nieuwkoop, 1998).

3. Hans de Waardt, *Toverij en samenleving*, 337.

4. Hans de Waardt, "Rechtssicherheit nach Zusammenbruch der zentralen Gewalt. Rechtspflege, Obrigkeit, Toleranz und wirtschaftliche Verhältnisse in Holland," in *Das Ende der Hexenverfolgung*, eds. Sönke Lorenz and Dieter R. Bauer (Stuttgart, 1995), 129–52.

5. Willem de Blécourt, "On the Continuation of Witchcraft," in Barry, Hester, and Roberts, *Witchcraft in Early Modern Europe*, 335–52.

6. De Waardt, *Toverij en samenleving*, 161; also Marcel Gielis, "The Netherlandic Theologians' Views of Witchcraft and the Devil's Pact," in *Witchcraft in the Netherlands from the Fourteenth to the Twentieth Century*, eds. Marijke Gijswijt Hofstra amd Willem Frijhoff (Rotterdam, 1991), 37–52.

7. Kaplan, *Calvinists and Libertines*; the case described here is detailed in his "Possessed by the Devil? A Very Public Dispute in Utrecht," *Renaissance Quarterly* 49 (1996), 738–59.

8. As cited by Kaplan, "Possessed by the Devil?", 743.

9. Ibid., 747–8.

10. Herman Herberts, *Een corte ende grondige verclaringe van den Antichrist* (Vianen, n.d. [c.1584]).

11. Hiël [Hendrik Jansen Barrefelt], *Het Boeck Der Ghetuygenissen vanden verborghen Acker-schat ...* (n.p., n.d. [Antwerp, c.1580]), 94.

12. Dirck Volckertsz Coornhert, *Wercken* (Amsterdam, 1630/31), vol. 1, 89r and 232v. See also Mirjam G. K. van Veen, "Spiritualism in the Netherlands: From David Joris to Dirck Volckertsz Coornhert," *Sixteenth Century Journal* 33 (2002), 129–50.

13. Marijke Gijswijt-Hofstra, "Doperse geluiden over magie en toverij: Twisck, Deutel, Palingh en Vale Dale," in *Oecumennisme: Opstellen aangeboden aan Henk B. Kossen ter gelegenheid van zijn afscheid als kerkelijk hoogleraar*, ed. A. Lambo (Amsterdam, 1989), 69–83, here 75–6. Deutel's work is *Een kort tractaetje tegen de toovery, als mede een verklaringe van verscheyden plaetsen der H. Scrifture* (Hoorn, 1670).

14. Abraham Palingh, *'tAfgerukt Mom-aansight der Tooverye: Daar in Het bedrogh der gewaande Toverye, naakt ontdekt, ...* (Amsterdam, 1659).

15. Fix, *Prophecy and Reason,* and "Angels, Devils, and Evil Spirits in Seventeenth-Century Thought: Balthasar Bekker and the Collegiants," *Journal of the History of Ideas* 50 (1989), 527–47.

16. G. J. Stronks, "De betekenis van *De betoverde weereld* van Balthasar Bekker," in *Nederland betoverd: Toverij en Hekserij van de veertiende tot in de twintigste eeuw,* eds. Marijke Gijswijt-Hofstra and Willem Frijhoff (Amsterdam, 1987), 207–11.

17. Popkin, *The History of Scepticism,* 229–47.

18. Coudert, *The Impact of the Kabbalah.*

19. My thanks to Dr. Stephen Snobelen, of the University of King's College, Halifax, for providing a copy of his "Lust, Pride and Ambition: Isaac Newton and the Devil," forthcoming in *Newton 2000: Newtonian Studies in the New Millennium,* ed. James E. Force and Sarah Hutton, c. 2003. See also Margaret J. Osler, ed., *Rethinking the Scientific Revolution* (Cambridge, 2000).

20. Ginzburg, *Night Battles.*

21. Stephen Haliczer, ed., *Inquisition and Society in Early Modern Europe* (London, 1987), 1–3.

22. John Tedeschi and William Monter, "Toward a Statistical Profile of the Italian Inquisitions, Sixteenth to Eighteenth Centuries," reprinted in John Tedeschi, *The Prosecution of Heresy: Collected Studies on the Inquisition in Early Modern Italy* (Binghamton, NY, 1991), 89–126.

23. Francesco Maria Guazzo, *Compendium Maleficarum,* ed. Montague Summers, trans. E. A. Ashwin (New York, 1988; 1929 ed.), iv.

24. Ibid., 111.

25. Ibid., 33–4.

26. Ibid., 16.

27. Ibid., 39.

28. As cited by John Tedeschi, "The Roman Inquisition and Witchcraft: An Early Seventeenth-Century 'Instruction' on Correct Trial Procedure," in Tedeschi, *The Prosecution of Heresy,* 205–27, here, 206.

29. Gustav Henningsen, *The Witches' Advocate: Basque Witchcraft and the Spanish Inquisition* (Reno, Nevada, 1980), 23.

30. Stephen Haliczer, "The First Holocaust: The Inquisition and the Converted Jews of Spain and Portugal," in Haliczer, *Inquisition and Society*, 7–18, here 10.
31. Ibid., 11–16.
32. Henningsen, *Witches' Advocate*, 24.
33. Ibid., 129–30.
34. Ibid., 193–4.
35. Ibid., 304–5.
36. John Tedeschi, "Inquisitorial Law and the Witch," in Ankarloo and Henningsen, *Early Modern European Witchcraft*, 84–118.
37. See Maxwell-Stuart, *Witchcraft in Europe*, 78–9.
38. Levack, *The Witch-Hunt*, 208–9.
39. Per Sörlin, *'Wicked Arts': Witchcraft & Magic Trials in Southern Sweden, 1635–1754* (Leiden, 1999), 29.
40. Levack, *The Witch-Hunt*, 212–13.
41. Juhan Kahk, "Estonia II: The Crusade against Idolatry," in Ankarloo and Henningsen, *Early Modern European Witchcraft*, 273–84, here 283; see also Maria Madar, "Estonia I: Werewolves and Poisoners," in Ibid., 257–72.
42. Levack, *The Witch-Hunt*, 214–18; here 217.
43. Karen Lambrecht, *Hexenverfolgung und Zaubereiprozesse in den schlesischen Territorien* (Cologne, 1995).
44. Paul Barber, *Vampires, Burial, and Death: Folklore and Reality* (New Haven, 1988).
45. Lambrecht, *Hexenverfolgung*, 350–401.
46. Gábor Klaniczay, "Hungary: The Accusations and the Universe of Popular Magic," in Ankarloo and Henningsen, *Early Modern European Witchcraft*, 219–56.
47. As cited by Walker, *Unclean Spirits*, 29.
48. Anita M. Walker and Edmund H. Dickerman, "'A Woman under the Influence': A Case of Alleged Possession in Sixteenth-Century France," *Sixteenth Century Journal*, 22 (1991), 535–54.
49. Klaits, *Servants of Satan*, 104–5.
50. Ibid., 113–15.
51. Sebastien Michaëlis, *The admirable historie . . .* trans. W. B. (London, 1613), 260.
52. Clark, *Thinking with Demons*, 432.
53. Robert Rapley, *A Case of Witchcraft: The Trial of Urbain Grandier* (Montreal and Kingston, 1998).
54. Midelfort, *Witch Hunting in Southwestern Germany*, 112.
55. Behringer, *Witchcraft Persecutions in Bavaria*, 212.
56. Ibid., 215.
57. Ibid., 246.
58. Owen Davies, "Urbanization and the Decline of Witchcraft: An Examination of London," *Journal of Social History*, (1997), 597–617.
59. Reginald Scot, *Discoverie of Witchcraft (London 1584)* (rep. Amsterdam and New York, 1971), 507–11; also 539–41.
60. Thomas, *Religion and the Decline of Magic*, 475.
61. David Wootton, "Reginald Scot /Abraham Fleming /The Family of Love," in *Languages of Witchcraft: Narrative, Ideology and Meaning in Early Modern Culture*, ed. Stuart Clark (Houndmills, UK, 2001), 119–38.

62. Robert Filmer, *An Advertisement to the Jury-men of England, Touching Witches. Together with a Difference Between An English and Hebrew Witch* (London, 1653), 6.

63. These arguments are drawn largely from Sharpe, *Instruments of Darkness*, 213–33.

64. Ibid., 236–50.

65. Jerome Friedman, *The Battle of the Frogs and Fairford's Flies: Miracles and the Pulp Press during the English Revolution* (New York, 1993).

66. Peter Elmer, "'Saints or Sorcerers': Quakerism, Demonology and the Decline of Witchcraft in Seventeenth-century England," in Barry, Hester, and Roberts, *Witchcraft in Early Modern Europe*, 145–79; Sharpe, *Instruments of Darkness*, 251–75.

67. Sharpe, *Instruments of Darkness*, 271.

68. Ian Bostridge, "Witchcraft Repealed," in Barry, Hester, and Roberts, *Witchcraft in Early Modern Europe*, 309–34.

69. Snobelen, "Lust, Pride and Ambition."

70. As cited by Gábor Klaniczay, "Decline of Witches and Rise of Vampires in 18th Century Habsburg Monarchy," *Ethnologia Europaea: Journal of European Ethnology* 17 (1987), 165–80, here 167. See also his *The Uses of Supernatural Power: The Transformation of Popular Religion in Medieval and Early-Modern Europe* (Princeton, 1990).

Conclusion

1. Aldous Huxley's *The Devils of Loudon* (New York, 1952), implicitly condemned the McCarthy hearings by revealing how the persecutors of Urbain Grandier had manipulated evidence and public opinion in ways that Huxley's contemporaries would have easily recognized. See Rapley, *A Case of Witchcraft*, 219.

2. Sönke Lorenz, Dieter R. Bauer, Wolfgang Behringer, and Jürgen Michael Schmidt, eds., *Himmlers Hexenkartothek: Das Interesse des Nationalsozialismus an der Hexenverfolgung* (Bielefeld, 2000), viii.

3. Isak Niehaus, with Eliazaar Mohlala and Kally Shokane, *Witchcraft, Power and Politics: Exploring the Occult in the South African Lowveld* (London, 2001).

ANNOTATED BIBLIOGRAPHY

The subject matter of this book is a vast one that encompasses several major historical fields. This bibliography will therefore point the reader to only a selection of the more accessible recent literature from which to pursue more detailed reading; more specialized literature and primary sources are cited in the Notes section. Only a handful of the extensive non-English language works is included here. Most of the contemporary pamphlets cited in the text come from two sources: IDC Microform collection of pamphlets published in the Netherlands: W. P. C. Knuttel, ed., *Catalogus van de pamfletten-verzameling berustende in de Koninklijke Bibliotheek*, 9 vols. (Utrecht, 1978); and Early English Books Online, accessed at the University of Cambridge. On the web there are some valuable sites, and a lot that tend toward myth making and the expression of uninformed opinion. A very helpful site is The Witchcraft Bibliography Project at www.hist.unt.edu/witch.htm

The Devil, Heresy, and Magic in the Later Middle Ages

For the medieval cosmos, see the concise description by Peter Burke, *The Italian Renaissance: Culture and Society in Italy* (Cambridge, 1986). Burke's *Popular Culture in Early Modern Europe* (New York, 1978) is still an authority on the subject of popular and elite cultures, while a good introduction to popular medicine is John Henry, "Doctors and Healers: Popular Culture and the Medical Profession," in *Science, Culture and Popular Belief in Renaissance Europe*, eds. Stephen Pumfrey, Paolo L. Rossi, and Maurice Slawinski (Manchester, 1991), 191–221. Although ostensibly narrowly focused, Caroline Walker Bynum's *Holy Feast and Holy Fast: The Religious Significance of Food to Medieval Women* (Berkeley, 1987) provides a revealing glimpse into how medieval folk conceived of the intersections of the material and immaterial worlds. For clerical conceptions of female sexuality and how this was demonized through the late Middle Ages, see Dyan Elliot, *Fallen Bodies: Pollution, Sexuality, & Demonology in the Middle Ages* (Philadelphia, 1999). Johan Huizinga's classic study of belief and culture in the late Middle Ages has been recently retranslated as *The Autumn of the Middle Ages*, trans. Rodney J. Payton and Ulrich Mammitzsch (Chicago, 1996). John Bossy's "Moral Arithmetic: Seven Sins into Ten Commandments," in Edmund Leites, ed., *Conscience and Casuistry in Early Modern Europe* (Cambridge, 1988), has proved a widely influential interpretation of the transformation of attitudes toward sin and guilt.

On specific aspects of the medieval/early-modern cosmos, see Miri Rubin, *Corpus Christi: The Eucharist in Late Medieval Culture* (Cambridge, 1991); Philippe Ariès, *The Hour of our Death*, trans. Helen Weaver (New York, 1981); Nancy Caciola, "Wraiths, Revenants and Ritual in Medieval Culture," *Past and Present*, 152(1996), 3–45; and the several works of Piero Camporesi, esp. *The Fear of Hell: Images of Damnation and Salvation in Early Modern Europe*, trans. Lucinda Byatt (Oxford, 1990), and *Bread of Dreams: Food and Fantasy in Early Modern Europe*, trans. David Gentilcore (Oxford, 1989). Illuminating discussions of medieval popular religion are found in Aron Gurevich, *Medieval Popular Culture: Problems of Belief and Perception*, trans. János M. Bak and Paul A. Hollingsworth (Cambridge, 1988). For saints, see Peter Brown, *The Cult of the Saints: Its Rise and Function in Latin Christianity* (Chicago, 1981), and Renate Blumenfeld-Kosinski and Timea Szell, eds., *Images of Sainthood in Medieval Europe* (Ithaca, 1991). On Purgatory, see Jacques Le Goff, *The Birth of Purgatory*, trans. Arthur Goldhammer (Chicago, 1984). Although controversial, the works of Lionel Rothkrug raise important questions about the nature of popular religion and the cult of saints; most recently "German Holiness and Western Sanctity in Medieval and Modern History," *Historical Reflections* 15(1988), 161–249; but see also Steven D. Sargent, "A Critique of Lionel Rothkrug's List of Bavarian Pilgrimage Shrines," *Archiv für Reformationsgeschichte*, 78(1987), 351–8.

The importance of the Devil to the medieval understanding of the cosmos is not always appreciated, but see esp. Elaine Pagels, *The Origin of Satan* (New York, 1995); and Jeffrey Burton Russell, *Lucifer: The Devil in the Middle Ages* (Ithaca and London, 1984). For magic in the early Middle Ages, see Bengt Ankarloo and Stuart Clark, eds., *Witchcraft and Magic in Europe: Ancient Greece and Rome*, The Athlone History of Witchcraft and Magic in Europe (London, 1999); and Valerie I. J. Flint, *The Rise of Magic in Early Medieval Europe* (Princeton, 1991). For medieval magic in general, see Richard Kieckhefer, *Magic in the Middle Ages* (Cambridge, 1989), and his response to Flint, "The Specific Rationality of Medieval Magic," *American Historical Review* 99(1994), 813–36. Kieckhefer has also provided a comparison of medieval saints and witches in "The Holy and the Unholy: Sainthood, Witchcraft, Magic in Late Medieval Europe," *Journal of Medieval and Renaissance Studies* 24(1994), 355–85. Elizabeth M. Butler's highly readable 1949 study, *Ritual Magic*, has been recently reissued as part of the "Magic in History" series (University Park, PA, 1998). In this series is also an excellent collection of essays, Claire Fanger, ed., *Conjuring Spirits: Texts and Traditions of Medieval Ritual Magic* (1998). See also Alberto Ferreiro, ed., *The Devil, Heresy & Witchcraft in the Middle Ages. Essays in Honor of Jeffrey B. Russell* (Leiden, 1998), and Charles Burnett's more specialist *Magic and Divination in the Middle Ages: Texts and Techniques in the Islamic and Christian Worlds* (Hampshire, UK, 1996). P. G. Maxwell-Stuart's *The Occult in Early Modern Europe: A Documentary History* (Basingstoke, 1999) provides an illuminating collection of translated primary sources, while Richard Kieckhefer has published a fascinating description and critical edition of a necromancer's manual in *Forbidden Rites: A Necromancer's Manual of the Fifteenth Century* (University Park, PA, 1997).

A helpful overview of Renaissance magic is Wayne Shumaker, *The Occult Sciences in the Renaissance: A Study in Intellectual Patterns* (Berkeley, 1972). See also Anthony Grafton, *Cardano's Cosmos: The Worlds and Works of a Renaissance Astrologer* (Cambridge, MA, 1999), while the classic is still Frances A. Yates, *The Occult Philosophy in the Elizabethan Age* (London, 1979).

For medieval antisemitism, see especially Gavin Langmuir's *History, Religion, and Antisemitism* (Berkeley, 1990) and *Toward a Definition of Antisemitism* (Berkeley, 1990). On the stranger elements of Christian belief about Jews, see Joshua Trachtenburg, *The Devil and the Jews: The Medieval Conception of the Jew and its Relation to Modern Antisemitism* (New York, 1966). For the role of preachers in stirring up antisemitic sentiment, see Jeremy Cohen, *The Friars and the Jews: The Evolution of Medieval Anti-Judaism* (Ithaca, 1982). On the 1321 leper/Jew conspiracy, see Carlo Ginzburg, *Ecstasies: Deciphering the Witches' Sabbath* (New York, 1991), 33–86. For the perception of Jews in an apocalyptical framework, see Andrew Colin Gow, *The Red Jews: Antisemitism in an Apocalyptic Age, 1200–1600* (Leiden, 1995). The best study of ritual murder charges is R. Po-Chia Hsia, *The Myth of Ritual Murder. Jews and Magic in Reformation Germany* (New Haven, 1988), along with his account of one episode, *Trent 1475: Stories of a Ritual Murder Trial* (New Haven, 1992). On the Christian use of the Cabala, see most recently Allison P. Coudert, *The Impact of the Kabbalah in the Seventeenth Century: The Life and Thought of Francis Mercury van Helmont (1614–1698)* (Leiden, 1999).

Good surveys of the medieval Inquisition are Bernard Hamilton, *The Medieval Inquisition* (London, 1981), and Edward Peters, *Inquisition* (Berkeley, 1989). There is a vast literature on the Spanish Inquisition; for a highly readable account, see Henry Kamen's *The Spanish Inquisition: An Historical Revision* (London, 1997); also E. William Monter, *Frontiers of Heresy: The Spanish Inquisition from the Basque Lands to Sicily* (Cambridge, 1990). For a concise summary of the history of the pure blood laws, see Jerome Friedman, "Jewish Conversion, the Spanish Pure Blood Laws and Reformation: A Revisionist View of Racial and Religious Antisemitism," *Sixteenth Century Journal* 18(1987), 1–30. Bernard Lewis' *Cultures in Conflict: Christians, Muslims, and Jews in the Age of Discovery* (New York and Oxford, 1995) provides an accessible discussion of the interaction of the three religious cultures around 1492.

For the perceived threat of heretics, see R. I. Moore, *The Formation of a Persecuting Society: Power and Deviance in Western Europe, 950–1250* (Oxford, 1987), and Jeffrey Richards, *Sex, Dissidence and Damnation: Minority Groups in the Middle Ages* (London, 1991). An excellent introduction to the Waldensians is Gabriel Audisio, *The Waldensian Dissent: Persecution and Survival c1170–c1570*, trans. Claire Davison (Cambridge, 1999); while Malcolm Barber, *The Cathars: Dualist Heretics in Languedoc in the High Middle Ages* (Harlow, UK, 2000), and Malcolm Lambert, *The Cathars* (Oxford, 1998) are good places to start for the Cathars. On the Free Spirits, see Robert E. Lerner, *The Heresy of the Free Spirit in the Later Middle Ages* (Berkeley, 1972). An excellent collection of primary sources is Walter L. Wakefield and Austin P. Evans, eds., *Heresies of the High Middle Ages* (New York, 1969, 1991).

Although its argument that sects of Devil-worshipers existed as forms of popular protest against the church is debatable, Jeffrey B. Russell's *Witchcraft in the Middle Ages* (Ithaca, 1972) still contains much useful information on medieval witchcraft. An influential interpretation which sees the witch stereotype arising primarily out of elite, clerical culture is Norman Cohn, *Europe's Inner Demons* (London, 1975). The best, detailed account of medieval trials is still Richard Kieckhefer, *European Witch Trials: Their Foundations in Popular and Learned Culture, 1300–1500* (London, 1976); while J. R. Veenstra's *Magic and Divination at the Courts of Burgundy and France. Text and Context of Laurens Pignon's* "Contre les Devineurs" *(1411)* (Leiden, 1998) uncovers a great deal about magic and witchcraft in French courts; for early French trials, see also Martine Ostorero, *"Folâtrer avec les démons". Sabbat et chasse aux sorciers à Vevey (1448)* (Lausanne, 1995). Franco Mormando's *The Preacher's Demons: Bernardino of Siena and the Social Underworld of Early Renaissance Italy* (Chicago, 1999) is excellent on the role of preachers such as St. Bernardino of Siena in inciting anti-witch sentiment. Other important studies of medieval witch trials are: Edward Peters, *The Magician, the Witch, and the Law* (Philadelphia, 1978); Arno Borst, *Medieval Worlds: Barbarians, Heretics, and Artists in the Middle Ages*, trans. Eric Hansen (Chicago, 1991); and Andreas Blauert, *Frühe Hexenverfolgungen: Ketzer-, Zauberei- und Hexenprozesse des 15. Jahrhunderts* (Hamburg, 1989).

On Krämer, witchcraft and Conciliarism, see Eric Wilson, "Institoris at Innsbruck: Heinrich Institoris, the *Summis Desiderantes* and the Brixen Witch-Trial of 1485," in Bob Scribner and Trevor Johnson, eds., *Popular Religion in Germany and Central Europe, 1400–1800* (Basingstoke, 1996), 87–100, and his dissertation, "The Text and Context of the *Malleus Maleficarum* (1487)," Ph.D. Diss. (Cambridge University, 1991); the specialist study is Jürgen Petersohn, "Konziliaristen und Hexen: Ein unbekannter Brief des Inquisitors Heinrich Institoris an Papst Sixtus IV. aus dem Jahre 1484," *Deutsches Archiv für Erforschung des Mittelalters* 44(1988), 120–60. For Krämer and doubt, see Walter E. Stephens, "Witches Who Steal Penises: Impotence and Illusion in *Malleus Maleficarum*," *Journal of Medieval and Early Modern Studies* 28(1998), 495–529, and his *Demon Lovers: Witchcraft, Sex, and Belief* (Chicago, 2002). The major collection of primary sources relating to the medieval witch-hunts is Joseph Hansen, ed., *Quellen und Untersuchungen zur Geschichte des Hexenwahns und der Hexenverfolgung im Mittelalter* (Bonn, 1901). A number of important sources have been translated in Alan C. Kors and Edward Peters, eds., *Witchcraft in Europe, 1100–1700: A Documentary History* (Philadelphia, 1972).

The Reformation and the End of the World

The Reformation is a massive field with an impressive number of scholarly conferences and journals devoted to it and to its many subfields, particularly *The Sixteenth Century Journal* and the *Archiv für Reformationsgeschichte/Archive for Reformation History*, which publishes a yearly literature review. The four-volume *Oxford Encyclopedia of the Reformation*, ed. Hans J. Hillerbrand (New York and Oxford, 1996), presents excellent summaries of research on virtually every topic relating to the Reformation. Also helpful is Thomas A. Brady, Jr., Heiko A. Oberman, and James D. Tracy, eds., *Handbook of European History 1400–1600: Late Middle Ages, Renaissance and Reformation*, 2 vols. (Leiden, 1995).

Two excellent recent surveys of the subject are Carter Lindberg, *The European Reformations* (Oxford, 1996) and Euan Cameron, *The European Reformation* (Oxford, 1991), although neither devotes much attention to the question of magic and witchcraft. For early-modern Europe, see most recently Euan Cameron, ed., *Early Modern Europe: An Oxford History* (Oxford, 2001). Christopher R. Friedrichs, *The Early Modern City, 1450–1750* (London, 1995) provides an evocatively written description of urban life in the era.

On the importance of anticlericalism in the Reformation, see Peter A. Dykema and Heiko A. Oberman, eds., *Anticlericalism in Late Medieval and Early Modern Europe* (Leiden, 1993), and Kevin C. Robbins, "Magical Emasculation, Popular Anticlericalism, and the Limits of the Reformation in Western France circa 1590," *Journal of Social History* 31(1997), 61–83. On the Reformation and the end of the world, refer to Andrew Cunningham and Ole Peter Grell, *The Four Horsemen of the Apocalypse: Religion, War, Famine and Death in Reformation Europe* (Cambridge, 2000); Bernard McGinn, *Antichrist: Two Thousand Years of the Human Fascination with Evil* (New York, 1994); Walter Klaassen, *Living at the End of the Ages: Apocalyptic Expectation in the Radical Reformation* (Lanham, 1992); Ottavia Niccoli, *Prophecy and People in Renaissance Italy* (Princeton, 1990); and Robin Barnes, *Prophecy and Gnosis: Apocalypticism in the Wake of the Lutheran Reformation* (Stanford, 1988). For apocalyptical thought and witchcraft, see esp. Stuart Clark's magnificent *Thinking with Demons: The Idea of Witchcraft in Early Modern Europe* (Oxford, 1997), 321–74, a massively important work on many fronts.

Two recent biographies of Luther highlight the Reformer's battle against death – Richard Marius, *Martin Luther: The Christian between God and Death* (Cambridge, MA, 1999) – and the Devil – Heiko A Oberman, *Luther: Man Between God and the Devil*, trans. Eileen Walliser-Schwarzbart (New Haven, 1989). For the "mature" Luther and his more noxious views, see Mark U. Edwards, *Luther's Last Battles: Politics and Polemics, 1531–46* (Ithaca, 1983).

On images and iconoclasm, see Lee Palmer Wandel, *Voracious Idols and Violent Hands: Iconoclasm in Reformation Zurich, Strasbourg, and Basel* (New York, 1995); Bryan D. Mangrum and Giuseppe Scavizzi, eds., *A Reformation Debate: Karlstadt, Emser, and Eck on Sacred Images. Three Treatises in Translation* (Toronto, 1991); and Carlos M. N. Eire, *War against the Idols: The Reformation of Worship from Erasmus to Calvin* (Cambridge, 1986). On the Reformation and the "people", a good start is Lorna Jane Abray, *The People's Reformation: Magistrates, Clergy, and Commons in Strasbourg 1500–1598* (Oxford, 1985). The literature on the Peasants' War of 1525 is massive; for the relationship between it and the Reformation, see James M. Stayer, *The German Peasants' War and Anabaptist Community of Goods* (Montreal and Kingston, 1991). An excellent collection of sources has been collected by Tom Scott and Bob Scribner, eds., *The German Peasants' War: A History in Documents* (New Jersey, 1991), who also provide a concise summary of its history. The most important influential interpretation has been Peter Blickle, *The Revolution of 1525: The German Peasants' War from a New Perspective*, trans. Thomas A. Brady, Jr. and H. C. Erik Midelfort (Baltimore, 1981).

For a clear and fairly comprehensive survey of Anabaptism, refer to C. Arnold Snyder, *Anabaptist History and Theology: An Introduction* (Kitchener, 1995); while George H. Williams, *The Radical Reformation*, 2nd English ed. (Kirksville, 1992) is encyclopedic in its scope. For Anabaptist women, see C. Arnold Snyder and

Linda A. Huebert Hecht, eds., *Profiles of Anabaptist Women: Sixteenth-Century Reforming Pioneers* (Waterloo, 1996); and Sigrun Haude, "Anabaptist Women – Radical Women?" in Max Reinhart, ed., *Infinite Boundaries: Order, Disorder, and Reorder in Early Modern German Culture* (Kirksville, 1998), 313–28. The best work on Melchior Hoffman is Klaus Deppermann, *Melchior Hoffman: Social Unrest and Apocalyptic Visions in the Age of Reformation*, trans. Malcolm Wren, ed. Benjamin Drewery (Edinburgh, 1987). Werner O. Packull's *Hutterite Beginnings: Communitarian Experiments during the Reformation* (Baltimore, 1995) is the best place to start for the communitarian Anabaptists.

   Good introductions to the Catholic Reformation are found in John Bossy, *Christianity in the West, 1400–1700* (Oxford, 1985); John W. O'Malley, *Catholicism in Early Modern History: A Guide to Research* (St. Louis, 1988); and Jean Delumeau, *Catholicism between Luther and Voltaire: A New View of the Counter-Reformation* (London, 1977); while Craig Harline provides an excellent survey of recent research in "Official Religion – Popular Religion in Recent Historiography of the Catholic Reformation," *Archiv für Reformationsgeschichte* 81(1990), 239–62. For the Reformations in particular national contexts, see Andrew Pettegree, ed., *The Early Reformation in Europe* (Cambridge, 1992). For the Reformation in France and its persecution, see William Monter, *Judging the French Reformation: Heresy Trials by Sixteenth-Century Parlements* (Cambridge, MA, 1999).

Heresy, Doubt, and Demonizing the "Other"

The effects of the polemical battles of the Reformation era have provoked considerable debate; an excellent beginning point for the French conflicts are Jonathan Pearl, *The Crime of Crimes: Demonology and Politics in France, 1560–1620* (Waterloo, 1998); Carleton Cunningham, "The Devil and the Religious Controversies of Sixteenth-Century France," *Essays in History* 35(1993), 34–47; and of course Natalie Zemon Davis, "The Rites of Violence," in her *Society and Culture in Early Modern France* (Stanford, 1975), 152–85. Bodo Nischan, "The Exorcism Controversy and Baptism in the Late Reformation," *The Sixteenth Century Journal*, 18(1987), 31–51, details the polemical debate over exorcism in northern Germany, while H. C. Erik Midelfort, "The Devil and the German People: Reflections on the Popularity of Demon Possession in Sixteenth-Century Germany," in *Religion and Culture in the Renaissance and Reformation*, ed. Steven Ozment (Kirksville, MO, 1989), 99–119, explores its potential impact in the rise of demon possession cases.

   On diabolical conspiracies as applied to Anabaptists, see Sigrun Haude, *In the Shadow of "Savage Wolves": Anabaptist Münster and the German Reformation during the 1530s* (Leiden, 2000); Gary K. Waite, "Between the Devil and the Inquisitor: Anabaptists, Diabolical Conspiracies and Magical Beliefs in the Sixteenth-Century Netherlands," in *Radical Reformation Studies: Essays presented to James M. Stayer*, eds., Werner O. Packull and Geoffrey L. Dipple, St. Andrews Studies in Reformation History (Aldershot, 1999), 120–40; also Gary K. Waite, "Talking Animals, Preserved Corpses and Venusberg: The Sixteenth-Century Worldview and Popular Conceptions of the Spiritualist David Joris (1501–1556)," *Social History*, 20 (1995), 137–56. For Guillaume Postel, see William J. Bouwsma, *Concordia Mundi: The Career and Thought of Guillaume Postel (1510–1581)* (Cambridge, MA, 1957);

on the Family of Love in the Netherlands, see Alastair Hamilton, *The Family of Love* (Greenwood, SC, 1981); while for the English Familists refer to Peter Lake, *The Boxmaker's Revenge* (Stanford, 2001) and Christopher W. Marsh, *The Family of Love in English Society, 1550–1630* (Cambridge, 1994).

For Protestant polemics against Anabaptism in general, see John S. Oyer, *Lutheran Reformers Against Anabaptists: Luther, Melanchthon and Menius and the Anabaptists of Central Germany* (The Hague, 1964); for Calvin, see Willem Balke, *Calvin and the Anabaptist Radicals* (Grand Rapids, 1981). On the question of religious tolerance, see Ole Peter Grell and Bob Scribner, eds., *Tolerance and Intolerance in the European Reformation* (Cambridge, 1996), esp. the chapter by E. William Monter, "Heresy Executions in Reformation Europe, 1520–1565," 48–64. On the polemical battle around miracles and saints, see Philip M. Soergel, *Wondrous in his Saints: Counter-Reformation Propaganda in Bavaria* (Berkeley, 1993). On the Genevan Calvinists and the Devil, see "Witchcraft in Geneva, 1537–1662," *Journal of Modern History* 43(1971), 179–204, reprinted in E. William Monter, *Enforcing Morality in Early Modern Europe* (London, 1987).

The Reformation, Magic, and Witchcraft, 1520–1600

For the classic discussion of religion and magic, see Keith Thomas, *Religion and the Decline of Magic* (New York, 1971). See also the sources in Maxwell-Stuart, *The Occult in Early Modern Europe*. On the crisis of Renaissance thought in the second half of the sixteenth century, see William J. Bouwsma, *The Waning of the Renaissance, ca. 1550–1640* (New Haven, 2000).

On the Reformation and the efforts to transform popular culture, see Gerald Strauss, *Luther's House of Learning: Indoctrination of the Young in the German Reformation* (Baltimore, 1978); David W. Sabean, *Power in the Blood. Popular Culture & Village Discourse in Early Modern Germany* (Cambridge, 1984); and Robert W. (Bob) Scribner, *Popular Culture and Popular Movements in Reformation Germany* (London, 1987). See also Scribner and Johnson, *Popular Religion in Germany*; and C. Scott Dixon, *The Reformation and Rural Society: The Parishes of Brandenburg-Ansbach-Kulmbach, 1528–1603* (Cambridge, 1996). The various works of Natalie Zemon Davis on the beliefs and culture of early-modern Europe continue to inspire new approaches to the field: *Fiction in the Archives: Pardon Tales and their Tellers in Sixteenth-Century France* (Stanford, 1987), *The Return of Martin Guerre* (Cambridge, MA, 1983), and the stimulating essays in *Culture and Society in Early Modern France*. "Microhistory", or using a close examination of a single case to comment on popular culture has proved helpful, at least to a limited extent. See the pioneering effort of Carlo Ginzburg, *The Cheese and the Worms*, trans. John and Anne Tedeschi (Middlesex, 1982). On the Reformation's impact on the concept of death and accompanying ritual practices, see Craig M. Koslofsky, *The Reformation of the Dead: Death and Ritual in Early Modern Germany, 1450–1700* (Basingstoke, 2000); and Susan C. Karant-Nunn, *The Reformation of Ritual: An Interpretation of Early Modern Germany* (London, 1997). On images and popular culture, see Keith Moxey, *Peasants, Warriors and Wives: Popular Imagery in the Reformation* (Chicago, 1989); and Robert W. Scribner, *For the Sake of Simple Folk: Popular Propaganda for the German Reformation* (Cambridge, 1981).

For Protestants and magic, see especially Clark, *Thinking with Demons*, 489–508, and "Protestant Demonology: Sin, Superstition, and Society (*c.* 1520–1630)," in *Early Modern European Witchcraft: Centres and Peripheries*, eds. Bengt Ankarloo and Gustav Henningsen (Oxford, 1990), 45–81; Darren Oldridge, "Protestant Conceptions of the Devil in Early Stuart England," *History Today* 85(2000), 236–46; Moshe Sluhovsky, "Calvinist Miracles and the Concept of the Miraculous in Sixteenth-Century Huguenot Thought," *Renaissance and Reformation* 19/2(1995), 5–25; and J. L. Teall, "Witchcraft and Calvinism in Elizabethan England: Divine Power and Human Agency," *Journal of the History of Ideas* 23(1962), 21–36. While focused primarily on the English colonies, Richard Godbeer's *The Devil's Dominion: Magic and Religion in Early New England* (Cambridge, 1992) is insightful on Protestant notions of magic and the Devil in general. On the intersection of apocalyptical and demonological beliefs, see Clark, *Thinking with Demons*, 315–434. The best work on Luther and witchcraft is Joerg Haustein, *Martin Luthers Stellung zum Zauber- und Hexenwesen* (Stuttgart, 1990).

For Agrippa, see Charles G. Nauert's *Agrippa and the Crisis of Renaissance Thought* (Urbana, 1965); also Frank L. Borchardt, "The *Magus* as a Renaissance Man," *The Sixteenth Century Journal*, 21(1990), 56–76; and Michael H. Keefer, "Agrippa's Dilemma, Hermetic 'Rebirth' and the Ambivalences of *De vanitate* and *De occulta philosophia*," *Renaissance Quarterly*, 41(1988), 614–53.

Johann Weyer's book has been translated and edited in George Mora, gen. ed., *Witches, Devils, and Doctors in the Renaissance: Johann Weyer* "De praestigiis daemonum" (Binghamton, NY, 1991); while Jean Bodin's rebuttal has appeared as Randy A. Scott and Jonathan L. Pearl, eds., *Jean Bodin, On the Demon-Mania of Witches* (Toronto, 1995). Further on Weyer, see H. C. Erik Midelfort, *A History of Madness in Sixteenth-Century Germany* (Stanford, 1999), esp. 182–227; Gerhild Scholz Williams, *Defining Dominion. The Discourses of Magic and Witchcraft in Early Modern France and Germany* (Ann Arbor, 1995); Hartmut Lehmann and Otto Ulbricht, eds., *Vom Unfug des Hexen-Processes: Gegner der Hexenverfolgungen von Johann Weyer bis Friedrich Spee* (Wiesbaden, 1991); and Clark, *Thinking with Demons*. Hans de Waardt has debunked several myths about the life and ideas of Weyer in "Johan Wiers *De Praestigiis*: Mythes et Motivatie," in Jan Jacob Cobben, ed., *Duivelse Bezetenheid: Beschreven door dokter Johannes Wier, 1515–1588* (Rotterdam, 2002), 17–74.

On the Devil in the New World, see especially Fernando Cervantes, *The Devil in the New World. The Impact of Diabolism in New Spain* (New Haven, 1994); Mary Elizabeth Perry and Anne J. Cruz, eds., *Cultural Encounters: The Impact of the Inquisition in Spain and the New World* (Berkeley, 1991).

For the Nicole Aubrey possession, see Cunningham, "The Devil and the Religious Controversies," and Pearl, *Crime of Crimes*, 43–5. For contemporary pamphlets about the case, see Irena Backus, ed., *Guillaume Postel et Jean Boulaese:* De summopere*(1566) et* Le Miracle de Laon *(1566)* (Geneva, 1995), and *Le Miracle de Laon: Le Deraisonnable, Le Raisonable, L'Apocalyptique et le Politique Dans Les Récits du Miracle de Laon (1566–1578)* (Paris, 1994).

For Protestant visionaries, see Jürgen Beyer, "A Lübeck Prophet in Local and Lutheran Context", in Scribner and Johnson, *Popular Religion*, 166–82; and Willem Frijhoff, *Wegen van Evert Willemsz. Een Hollands weeskind op zoek naar zichzelf 1607–1647* (Nijmegen, 1995).

On the early witch trials in the Spanish Inquisition, see Julio Caro Baroja, *The World of the Witches*, trans. O. N. V Glendinning (Chicago, 1964); and Stephen Haliczer, ed., *Inquisition and Society in Early Modern Europe* (London and Sydney, 1987).

On the Reformation and antisemitism, see Hsia, *Ritual Murder*, as well as Heiko A. Oberman, *The Roots of anti-Semitism in the age of Renaissance and Reformation*, trans. James I. Porter (Philadelphia, 1984); Maria R. Boes, "Jews in the Criminal-Justice System of Early Modern Germany," *Journal of Interdisciplinary History* 30(1999), 407–35; and David B. Ruderman, *Kabbalah, Magic, and Science: The Cultural Universe of a Sixteenth-Century Jewish Physician* (Cambridge, MA, 1988).

On popular magical and medical traditions in early-modern Europe, see Marijke Gijswijt-Hofstra, Hilary Marland, and Hans de Waardt, eds., *Illness and Healing Alternatives in Western Europe* (London, 1997); and Willem de Blécourt, "Witch Doctors, Soothsayers and Priests: On Cunning Folk in European Historiography and Tradition," *Social History* 19(1994), 285–303, which notes the ongoing importance of soothsayers for their clients. On Paracelsus and the Reformation, see esp. Andrew Weeks, *Paracelsus: Speculative Theory and the Crisis of the Early Reformation* (New York, 1997). For later Paracelsianism and alchemy, see Allen G. Debus and Michael T. Walton, eds., *Reading the Book of Nature: The Other Side of the Scientific Revolution* (Kirksville, MO, 1998); and Coudert, *The Impact of the Kabbalah*.

Religious Conflict and the Rise of Witch-Hunting, 1562–1630

The subject of the witch-hunts has had a shorter period of scholarly attention compared to the Reformation, yet in the last four decades its scholars have produced an overwhelming number of studies and an equally daunting range of interpretations. Helpful surveys in English are led by Brian P. Levack's very fine *The Witch-Hunt in Early Modern Europe*, 2nd ed. (London and New York, 1995), which concentrates on the judicial process, especially how the beliefs and practices of the local judiciary were a major determinant in the severity of witch-hunting in a particular region; it also contains an excellent chapter on the subject of the effects of the Reformation upon witch-hunting. Robert W. Thurston's, *Witch, Wicce, Mother Goose* (Harlow, England, 2001) discusses the transformation of medieval conspiratorial fears into the persecution mania of the sixteenth century, but dispenses with the Reformation in a single paragraph. P. G. Maxwell-Stuart's concise *Witchcraft in Europe and the New World, 1400–1800* (Basingstoke, 2001) is an excellent starting point. An influential interpretation that debunks many myths surrounding the witch-hunts and which points out its rather mundane aspects is Robin Briggs' *Witches and Neighbors* (New York, 1996). Anne Llewellyn Barstow's *Witchcraze: A New History of the European Witch Hunts* (New York, 1994) reasserts the case for the primacy of misogyny in the selection of victims, but see Briggs' caveats. Several older surveys remain important on specific aspects of the witch-hunts: Joseph Klaits, *Servants of Satan: The Age of the Witch Hunts* (Bloomington, 1985) is good on demonic possession in France and the sexual dimension of witch trials; G. R. Quaife, *Godly Zeal and Furious Rage: The Witch in Early Modern Europe* (London, 1987) is still a useful survey; Geoffrey Scarre, *Witchcraft and Magic in 16th and 17th Century Europe* (Houndmills, 1987) is extremely concise.

The recent anthropological interpretation of H. Sidky's *Witchcraft, Lycanthropy, Drugs, and Disease: An Anthropological Study of the European Witch-Hunts* (New York, 1997) suffers from a tendency to make caricatures of the perspectives of important historians, such as Keith Thomas. A less polemical anthropological effort is Andrew Sanders, *A Deed without a Name: The Witch in Society and History* (Oxford, 1995), which uses the early-modern hunts to condemn modern "witch-finders" who seek to persecute minority groups. Stuart Clark's *Thinking with Demons* intricately reveals the belief structure of the educational elites who sought to comprehend the function of demons and magic in the natural world and to suppress superstition or demonic practices. A scholarly encyclopedia of witchcraft is in the works: *ABC-CLIO Encyclopedia of Witchcraft: The Western Tradition*, ed. Richard Golden (Santa Barbara).

Along with these monographs, there are also several excellent collections of essays that have moved scholarship ahead by leaps and bounds: Kathryn A. Edwards, ed., *Werewolves, Witches, and Wandering Spirits: Traditional Belief and Folklore in Early Modern Europe* (Kirtsville, MO, 2002). Stuart Clark, ed., *Languages of Witchcraft: Narrative, Ideology and Meaning in Early Modern Culture* (Houndmills, 2001); Jonathan Barry, Marianne Hester, and Gareth Roberts, eds., *Witchcraft in Early Modern Europe: Studies in Culture and Belief* (Cambridge, 1996); Bengt Ankarloo and Gustav Henningsen, eds., *Early Modern European Witchcraft: Centres and Peripheries* (Oxford, 1990); and now the multi-volume series edited by Bengt Ankarloo and Stuart Clark for the series Athlone History of Witchcraft and Magic in Europe. Brian Levack has also edited two series of volumes collecting important essays on the subject, many of them difficult to find elsewhere, the first a twelve-volume set entitled *Articles on Witchcraft, Magic and Demonology: A Twelve Volume Anthology of Scholarly Articles* (New York, 1992), and now a six-volume collection, *Witchcraft, Magic, and Demonology* (New York, 2001).

On the role of children in the witch-hunts, see Lyndal Roper, "'Evil Imaginings and Fantasies': Child-Witches and the End of the Witch Craze," *Past and Present* 167 (2000), 107–39, which presents a psychological interpretation of the phenomenon; and Robert S. Walinski-Kiehl, "The Devil's Children: Child Witch Trials in Early Modern Germany," *Continuity and Change* 11(1996), 171–89, which relates trials of children to moral crusades imposing social and moral discipline. On confessional conflict and witch-hunting, see also his "'Godly States', Confessional Conflict and Witch-hunting in Early Modern Germany," *Mentalities* 5(1988), 13–24. On a more macabre theme, see Charles Zika, "Cannibalism and Witchcraft in Early Modern Europe: Reading the Visual Images," *History Workshop Journal* 44(1997), 77–105. Edward Bever has offered an intriguing psychological perspective on how magical curses may have "worked" in "Witchcraft Fears and Psychosocial Factors in Disease," *Journal of Interdisciplinary History* 30(2000), 573–90.

Studies of witch-hunting in specific regions multiply daily. A good survey of the German research is provided by Wolfgang Behringer, "Witchcraft Studies in Austria, Germany and Switzerland," in Barry, Hester, and Roberts, *Witchcraft in Early Modern Europe*, 64–95, and, of course his important analysis of Bavarian trials, *Witchcraft Persecutions in Bavaria: Popular Magic, Religious Zealotry and the Reason of State in Early Modern Europe*, trans. J. C. Grayson and David Lederer (Cambridge, 1997), a nice companion piece to H. C. Erik Midelfort's essential *Witch Hunting in Southwestern Germany, 1562–1684: The Social and Intellectual Foundations* (Stanford,

1972). Behringer's study of a single soothsayer, *Shaman of Obersdorf: Chonrad Stoeckhlin and the Phantoms of the Night*, trans. H. C. Erik Midelfort (Charlottesville, 1998), is another very successful microhistory that reveals much about the early-modern mentality. Important essays on the subject are provided by Robert W. Scribner's "The Reformation, Popular Magic and the 'Disenchantment of the World,'" *Journal of Interdisciplinary History* 23(1992–3), 475–94, and "Witchcraft and Judgement in Reformation Germany," *History Today*, 40(1990), 12–19. The standard German survey is Gerhard Schormann, *Hexenprozesse in Deutschland* (Göttingen, 1981). Other good discussions of religion and witchcraft in Germany are offered by Alison Rowlands, "Witchcraft and Popular Religion in Early Modern Rothenburg ob der Tauber," in Scribner and Johnson, *Popular Religion*, 101–18; and Edmund Kern, "Confessional Identity and Magic in the Late Sixteenth Century: Jakob Bithner and Witchcraft in Styria," *Sixteenth Century Journal* 25(1994), 323–40. Behringer has edited a valuable collection of sources from Germany in *Hexen und Hexenprozesse in Deutschland* (München, 1988). Although there is no English work on the subject, Harald Schwillus's *Kleriker im Hexenprozeß. Geistliche als Opfer der Hexenprozesse des 16. und 17. Jahrhunderts in Deutschland* (Würzburg, 1992), shows that a large number of clergy were themselves accused of witchcraft in Germany.

For the witch-hunts in France, see the brief summary in Robin Briggs, *Early Modern France, 1560–1715*, 2nd ed. (Oxford, 1998), 192–6, as well as his *Communities of Belief: Cultural and Social Tension in Early Modern France* (Oxford, 1989) and *Witches and Neighbors*. Refer also to E. William Monter, *Witchcraft in France and Switzerland: The Borderlands during the Reformation* (Ithaca, 1976). For religious conflict and witchcraft in France, see Cunningham, "The Devil and the Religious Controversies," and Pearl, *The Crime of Crimes*. On demon possession cases, see also D. P. Walker, *Unclean Spirits: Possession and Exorcism in France and England in the Late Sixteenth and Early Seventeenth Centuries* (Philadelphia, 1981). Anita M. Walker and Edmund H. Dickerman sympathetically interpret the story of individual French "witches" or demoniacs in several essays: "Magdeleine des Aymards: Demonism or Child Abuse in Early Modern France?" *The Psychohistory Review* 24(1996), 239–63; "The Haunted Girl: Possession, Witchcraft and Healing in Sixteenth Century Louviers," *Proceedings of the Annual Meeting of the Western Society for French History* 23 (1996), 207–18; and "'A Woman under the Influence': A Case of Alleged Possession in Sixteenth-Century France," *Sixteenth Century Journal*, 22(1991), 535–54. See also Charlotte Wells, "Leeches on the Body Politic: Xenophobia and Witchcraft in Early Modern French Political Thought," *French Historical Studies*, 22(1999), 351–77.

The most comprehensive recent survey of English witch trials is James Sharpe, *Instruments of Darkness: Witchcraft in England 1560–1750* (London, 1996), and now a more concise summary, *Witchcraft in Early Modern England* (Harlow, 2001). Sharpe has also produced his own gripping microhistory of a particular case in *The Bewitching of Anne Gunter: A Horrible and True Story of Deception, Witchcraft, Murder, and the King of England* (New York, 2000). Alan Macfarlane's *Witchcraft in Tudor and Stuart England: A Regional and Comparative Study*, 2nd ed. with introduction by James Sharpe (London, 1999) is still required reading. A very useful collection of primary sources is found in Barbara Rosen, ed., *Witchcraft in England, 1558–1618* (Amherst, 1991, 1969).

On English women and witch trials, see Diane Purkiss, *The Witch in History: Early Modern and Twentieth-Century Representations* (London, 1996); and Deborah Willis, *Malevolent Nurture: Witch-hunting and Maternal Power in Early Modern England* (Ithaca, 1995). On the witch-trial pamphlets and their "closeness to events," see esp. Marion Gibson, *Reading Witchcraft: Stories of Early English Witches* (London and New York, 1999). For Scotland, Christina Larner's *Enemies of God: The Witch-hunt in Scotland* (Baltimore, 1981), and *Witchcraft and Religion: The Politics of Popular Belief*, ed. Alan Macfarlane (Oxford, 1984) are still the standard, although refer also to Julian Goodare, "Women and the Witch-Hunt in Scotland," *Social History* 23(1998), 288–308; P. G. Maxwell-Stuart, "Witchcraft and the Kirk in Aberdeenshire, 1596–97," *Northern Scotland*, 18(1998), 1–14; Lawrence Normand and Gareth Roberts, eds., *Witchcraft in Early Modern Scotland: James VI's Demonology and the North Berwick Witches* (Exeter, 2000); and P. G. Maxwell-Stuart, *Satan's Conspiracy: Magic and Witchcraft in Sixteenth-Century Scotland* (East Lothian, 2001). For Ireland's distinctiveness in this regard, see Joan Hoff and Marian Yeates, *The Cooper's Wife is Missing: The Trials of Bridget Cleary* (New York, 2000).

For the southern Low Countries, see Dries Vanysacker, "Het aandeel van de zuidelijke Nederlanden in de europese heksenvervolging," *Trajecta* 9 (2000), 329–49, which also highlights the very strong contrast between the southern and northern provinces. See also his study of witchcraft in the Flemish city of Bruges, *Hekserij in Brugge: De magische leefwereld van een stadsbevolking, 16de-17de eeuw* (Brugge, [1988]). Also good on the legal dimensions is J. Monballyu, *Van hekserij beschuldigd: Heksenprocessen in Vlaanderen tijdens de 16de en 17de eeuw* (Kortrijk-Heule, 1996). There is little in English, but see Robert Muchembled, "Witchcraft, Popular Culture, and Christianity in the Sixteenth Century with Emphasis upon Flanders and Artois," in *Ritual, Religion, and the Sacred: Selections from the Annales, Economies, Sociétés, Civilizations* vol. 7, eds. Robert Forster and Orest Ranum, trans. Elborg Forster and Patricia M. Ranum (Baltimore, 1982), 213–36. Influential studies of three regions are provided in M.-S. Dupont-Bouchat, W. Frijhoff and R. Muchembled, *Prophètes et sorciers dan les Pays-Bas, XVIe-XVIIIe siècles* (Paris, 1978).

For the northern provinces, see Marijke Gijswijt-Hofstra, "The European Witchcraft Debate and the Dutch Variant," *Social History* 15(1990) 181–94; Marijke Gijswijt-Hofstra and Willem Frijhoff, eds., *Witchcraft in the Netherlands from the Fourteenth to the Twentieth Century* (Rotterdam 1991); and Hans de Waardt, *Toverij en samenleving. Holland 1500–1800* (Den Haag 1991), which contains a concise summary in English.

On the gender of witch suspects, a topic barely touched upon in this study, there is a vast and growing literature. Apart from the surveys of witch-hunting cited above, see also Sigrid Brauner, *Fearless Wives and Frightened Shrews: The Construction of the Witch in Early Modern Germany* (Amherst, 1995); Jean R. Brink, Allison P. Coudert, and Maryanne C. Horowitz, eds., *The Politics of Gender in Early Modern Europe* (Kirksville,1989); Lyndal Roper, *Oedipus and the Devil: Witchcraft, Sexuality and Religion in Early Modern Europe* (Routledge, 1994); Willis, *Malevolent Nurture*; Diane Purkiss, *The Witch in History: Early Modern and Twentieth-Century Representations* (London, 1996); Elspeth Whitney, "The Witch 'She'/The Historian 'He': Gender and the Historiography of the European Witch-Hunts," *Journal of Women's History* 7(1995), 77–101; Robin Briggs, "Women as Victims? Witches, Judges and the Community," *French History* 5 (1991), 438–50; and Stuart

Clark, "The 'Gendering' of Witchcraft in French Demonology: Misogyny or Polarity?" *French History* 5(1991), 426–37. David Harley has essentially demolished the myth that the witch-hunts were an attack on midwives in "Historians as Demonologists: The Myth of the Midwife-Witch," *Social History of Medicine* 3(1990), 1–26; see also Jane P. Davidson, "The Myth of the Persecuted Female Healer," *Journal of the Rocky Mountain Medieval and Renaissance Association* 14(1993), 115–29; and Malcolm Gaskill, "The Devil in the Shape of a Man: Witchcraft, Conflict and Belief in Jacobean England," *Institute of Historical Research*, 71(1998), 142–71. On the images of witches see most recently Margaret A. Sullivan, "The Witches of Dürer and Hans Baldung Grien," *Renaissance Quarterly* 53 (2000), 333–41.

Religious Pluralism and the End of the Witch-Hunts

On the subject of skepticism, see Richard H. Popkin, *The History of Skepticism from Erasmus to Spinoza*, 2nd ed. (Berkeley, 1979); D. P. Walker, *The Decline of Hell: Seventeenth-Century Discussions of Eternal Torment* (Chicago, 1964); and Perez Zagorin, *Ways of Lying: Dissimulation, Persecution, and Conformity in Early Modern Europe* (Cambridge, MA, 1990). For the Netherlands, see Andrew C. Fix, *Prophecy and Reason. The Dutch Collegiants in the Early Enlightenment* (Princeton, 1991) and "Angels, Devils, and Evil Spirits in Seventeenth-Century Thought: Balthasar Bekker and the Collegiants," *Journal of the History of Ideas* 50(1989), 527–47. On spiritualism and skepticism, see Samme Zijlstra, "Anabaptists, Spiritualists and the Reformed Church in East Frisia," *Mennonite Quarterly Review*, 75 (2001), 57–73; Gary K. Waite, "From David Joris to Balthasar Bekker?: The Radical Reformation and Scepticism towards the Devil in the Early Modern Netherlands (1540–1700)," *Fides et Historia* 28 (1996), 5–26; and the several works of Benjamin J. Kaplan, especially *Calvinists and Libertines: Confession and Community in Utrecht, 1578–1620* (Oxford, 1995), "Remnants of the Papal Yoke: Apathy and Opposition in the Dutch Reformation," *Sixteenth Century Journal* 25(1994), 653–69, and "Confessionalism and Popular Piety in the Netherlands," *Fides et Historia* 27(1995), 44–58.

An excellent survey of witchcraft in the later period is Bengt Ankarloo and Stuart Clark, eds., *Witchcraft and Magic in Europe: The Eighteenth and Nineteenth Centuries* (Philadelphia, 1999). See also Sönke Lorenz and Dieter R. Bauer, eds. *Das Ende der Hexenverfolgung* (Stuttgart, 1995).

For the ending of witch-hunting in England, see especially Ian Bostridge, *Witchcraft and Its Transformations c. 1650–1750* (Oxford, 1997), and his "Witchcraft Repealed, " in Barry, Hester, and Roberts, *Witchcraft in Early Modern Europe*, 257–87; also Owen Davies, *Witchcraft, Magic and Culture, 1736–1951* (Manchester, 1999), as well as his "Methodism, the Clergy, and the Popular Belief in Witchcraft and Magic," *History Today* 82(April 1997), 252–65, and "Urbanization and the Decline of Witchcraft: An Examination of London," *Journal of Social History* (1997), 597–617. For the religious polemics, see Peter Elmer, "'Saints or Sorcerers': Quakerism, Demonology and the Decline of Witchcraft in Seventeenth-Century England," in Barry, Hester, and Roberts, *Witchcraft in Early Modern Europe*, 145–79; T.L. Underwood, *Primitivism, Radicalism and the Lamb's War: The Baptist–Quaker*

Conflict in Seventeenth-Century England (New York, 1997); and Jerome Friedman, *The Battle of the Frogs and Fairford's Flies: Miracles and the Pulp Press during the English Revolution* (New York, 1993).

Good introductions to the Mediterranean Inquisitions and witchcraft are, for Italy, John Tedeschi, *The Prosecution of Heresy: Collected Studies on the Inquisition in Early Modern Italy* (Binghamton, 1991); John Tedeschi, "Inquisitorial Law and the Witch," in Ankarloo and Henningsen, *Early Modern European Witchcraft*, 84–118; Ruth Martin, *Witchcraft and the Inquisition in Venice, 1550–1650* (Oxford, 1989); and Carlo Ginzburg, *Night Battles: Witchcraft & Agrarian Cults in the Sixteenth & Seventeenth Centuries*, trans. John and Anne Tedeschi (New York, 1983).

For Spain, the best is still Gustav Henningsen, *The Witches' Advocate: Basque Witchcraft & the Spanish Inquisition* (Reno, Nevada, 1980). See also Kamen, *The Spanish Inquisition*; Perry and Cruz, *Cultural Encounters*; Haliczer, *Inquisition and Society*; Gustav Henningsen and John Tedeschi, *The Inquisition in Early Modern Europe. Studies on Sources and Methods* (Dekalb, IL, 1986); and Baroja, *The World of the Witches*.

Alfred Soman has revealed profound judicial skepticism with respect to witch trials on the part of the jurists of the Parlement of Paris in *Sorcellerie et justice criminelle (16–18e siècles)* (Guildford, 1992) and "The Parlement of Paris and the Great Witch Hunt (1565–1640)," *Sixteenth Century Journal* 9(1978), 31–44. On French demoniacs and exorcisms, see Walker, *Unclean Spirits*; Robert Rapley, *A Case of Witchcraft: The Trial of Urbain Grandier* (Montreal and Kingston, 1998); and Moshe Sluhovsky, "A Divine Apparition or Demonic Possession? Female Agency and Church Authority in Demonic Possession in Sixteenth-Century France," *Sixteenth Century Journal*, 27(1996), 1039–55. On demonic possession in a Reformed context, see also Benjamin J. Kaplan, "Possessed by the Devil? A Very Public Dispute in Utrecht," *Renaissance Quarterly* 49(1996), 738–59.

Good English language introductions to witch-hunting in Scandinavia are: Per Sörlin, *"Wicked Arts": Witchcraft & Magic Trials in Southern Sweden, 1635–1754* (Leiden, 1999); and Bengt Ankarloo, "Sweden: The Mass Burnings (1668–1676)," in Ankarloo and Henningsen, *Early Modern European Witchcraft*, 285–319.

For Eastern Europe, begin with the intriguing studies by Eva Pocs, *Between the Living and the Dead: A Perspective on Witches and Seers in the Early Modern Age* (London, 1999); and Gabor Klaniczay, *The Uses of Supernatural Power: The Transformation of Popular Religion in Medieval and Early-Modern Europe* (Princeton, 1990). On the vampire epidemic, see also Paul Barber, *Vampires, Burial, and Death: Folklore and Reality* (New Haven, 1988).

On skeptics of witchcraft, see Hartmut Lehmann and Otto Ulbricht, eds., *Vom Unfug des Hexen-Processes. Gegner der Hexen verfolgungen von Johann Weyer bis Friedrich Spee* (Wiesbaden, 1992).

INDEX